SO LONG A SAGA

SO LONG A SAGA

Four Centuries of Badaga Social History

PAUL HOCKINGS

MANOHAR
2013

First published 2013

ISBN 978-93-5098-018-7

Published by
Ajay Kumar Jain *for*
Manohar Publishers & Distributors
4753/23 Ansari Road, Daryaganj,
New Delhi 110 002

Printed at
Salasat Imaging Systems
Delhi 110 035

Men that undertake only one district are much more likely to advance natural knowledge than those who grasp at more than they can possibly be acquainted with; every kingdom, every province should have its own monographer.

GILBERT WHITE
The Natural History of Selborne (1789)

A research site, when only one is chosen, can hardly be said to be typical except in terms of the criteria employed. This is a continuing problem of anthropology and can be justified both on the grounds that it is better to know one place well than all places superficially and also that many interrelations found in one centre probably hold more generally even in contrasting areas.

JOHN C. CALDWELL, P.H. REDDY, & PAT CALDWELL
The causes of demographic change: Experimental research in South India. (1988)

Contents

MAPS

DIAGRAMS

TABLES

PLATES

the memorial ceremony (*manevale*) in Kaḍana:ḍu, March 1905. (Photo courtesy of Mission 21)

Plate 13 *Left*: Women with offerings at a funeral. *Right*: Men's dancing dress, only seen now at a few funerals.

Plate 14 *Left*: Terraced fields growing potatoes and eucalyptus trees below Orana:yi, 1963. *Right*: Widower with a ceremonial knife at his wife's funeral; Hulla:ḍa, 1963.

Plate 15 *Top*: A band of Kota musicians. *Bottom*: Chetti merchants resting their bullocks on the way up the Coonoor Ghat road. (Both photos *ca* 1900, courtesy of Mission 21)

Plate 16 *Top*: Two locally influential Europeans: Mr John Sullivan (1788-1855), and (right) Br. J. Friedrich Metz (1819-85; ink and watercolour sketch, at 24; courtesy of Mission 21). *Bottom*: A Kuṟumba man, *ca* 1900 (from Thurston and Rangachari 1909, IV: opp. 157); and (*right*) an old Adigari lady, wearing her personal *linga*.

Acknowledgements

A much shorter version of this book came out over thirty years ago under another title, *Ancient Hindu Refugees: Badaga Social History 1550-1975*. This revised and much-expanded edition is still perhaps not an orthodox history of a people, given that much of the material is not methodically derived from manuscripts or any other written sources. From the start, a wider variety of sources had to be utilized: manuscripts, yes, but only half-a-dozen of them; also some eight or nine dissertations, perhaps 150 books and 120 articles in books or journals. But beyond all these, I had to resort to archaeological inference and place-name analysis, and most importantly to the standard sources of almost any anthropological field-worker, his own observations of the culture and the countryside, combined with the information that my local contacts provided me with. Chapters 14-17 in particular relate largely to the half-century of my personal acquaintance with the Badaga people. During that time I have seen many schoolboys and schoolgirls become middle-aged parents, and have come to miss the many older friends and informants who have passed away during the time I have been acquainted with the Badagas. At the same time I have been able to witness some fundamental changes in their culture as a newly emerging, urbanizing middle class has managed to make its mark on Nilgiri commerce, education, administration, law, and the plantation industry – and indeed, far beyond these hills. In describing these developments I usually refrain from mentioning the names of particular persons who have become outstanding in these various fields, although I am sure that most Badaga readers of this Revised Edition will be able to supply such names.

During this recent period three people have made detailed studies of the Badaga culture, and their main contributions will be briefly referred to here. Aside from my own studies of various aspects of that culture (see the References), Frank Heidemann has made a detailed analysis of the politico-economic relations in Kotagiri *taluk*, and in the process he has also made the first study of the immigrant Sri Lankan Tamilian labourers in that area. In addition to this important contribution, Christiane Pilot-Raichoor has made the first thorough study of the Badaga language, showing beyond all doubt, I think, that it now deserves the status of a distinct South Dravidian language rather than being viewed, as previously, as a dialect of Kannaḍa.

A work of this size calls forth the assistance of numerous friends and colleagues. First and foremost I have to thank over 700 Badagas who have been interviewed. The late M.N. Thesingh, an Adigari, and K. Lakshmanan, a Gauḍa, were my constant companions and guides during the four years (spread through 1962-63, 1969-70, 1972, 1976-77, and later on, in 1990 and 1994) that I have spent with the Badagas. The Rev. Philip K. Mulley, a Christian Badaga, also provided unending help over the years, and is still an invaluable source of Nilgiri data. It is a pleasure to record my gratitude to all of them, with their friends and families, for their unswerving assistance.

Many colleagues have given advice and encouragement, notably Murray B. Emeneau, David G. Mandelbaum, Wilbur Schramm, and Anthony R. Walker. Robert W. Gage was of great assistance on statistical procedures, and Nina M. Richardson did some of the initial research for Chapters 12-13. K. Lakshmanan, Alice Streckeisen, Elizabeth C. Traugott and Reiner Protsch all helped me with a welter of translation. Br. R. Bächtold, Paul Jenkins, and Guy Thomas, Archivists of the Basel Mission, and the many nameless librarians at the University of California, Berkeley, the Connemara Library in Madras (Chennai), la Bibliothèque nationale de France, the British Museum, the Government Epigraphist's Office, the University of Illinois libraries, the Collector's Office in Ootacamund, the Bodleian, the University of Chicago's Regenstein Library, the National Museum of Ethnology, in Osaka, and the University of Wisconsin Library, have all exerted themselves over the years in the hunt for obscure but relevant publications.

This research has been supported by several funding agencies, among them the American Institute of Indian Studies (I was their very first beneficiary, in 1962), the University of Illinois, at Chicago, the Social Science Research Council, the Ford Foundation, the Council for Scientific and Industrial Research, and the former Institute for Communication Research at Stanford University. To each and all, my thanks for the sinews of war.

Lastly I would like to emphasise my gratitude to Professors Frank M. Heidemann, William A. Noble, and Christiane Pilot-Raichoor for their perennial support on Badaga matters; and also to Dr. Amelia Reyes and the late Mary F. Hockings, long ago, for their patient typing, editing, re-typing and re-editing of the earlier version of this volume (Hockings 1980a); also thanks must go especially to Raymond L. Brod and William A. Noble for preparing most diagrams and maps. My thanks too to Bryan Alexander, Dr P.J. Vasantham, Wing-Cmdr. B. Jayaprakash, and Mission 21 for several of the photographs. At a crucial moment, N. Sekaran presented me with a new computer and met my production expenses too. And let us not forget our publishers, Manohar Publishers and Distributors, whose editing and workmanship have always been meticulous and very helpful.

PAUL HOCKINGS

Silicon Valley, California
2013

Abbreviations

ac.	acre (1 ac. = 0.4 ha.)
Anon.	Anonymous
Assoc.	Association
BEMS	Basel Evangelical Missionary Society
Br.	Brother (Pastor)
ca	circa, about
Capt.	Captain
CE	dates in the Common Era (AD, *Anno Domini*)
cf.	compare
ch.	chapter
cm.	centimetre (1 cm . = 0.39 in.)
Cmdr.	Commander
C.M.S.	Church Missionary Society
contd.	continued
DAT	dative case
diag.	diagram
Dist.	District
Dr.	Doctor
E	east
ed.	editor, edited
edn.	edition
est.	estimate
et al.	et aliis, and others
fig.	figure
Fr.	(Catholic) Father
GEN	genitive case
ha.	hectares (1 ha. = 2.47 ac.)
I.	Island
ibid.	in the same publication
idem	in the same place
kg.	kilogram (= 2.2 lbs.)
km.	kilometre (0.62 mile)
lit.	literally
Lt.	Lieutenant

m.	metre (1 m. = 3.28 feet)
Maj.	Major
M.C.S.	Madras Civil Service
mHz	megaHertz
Miss.	Missionary
M.L.A.	Member of the Legis- ative Assembly
M.L.C.	Member of the Legislative Council
mm.	millimetre (= 0.04 in.)
M.P.	Member of Parliament (or Lok Sabha)
Msgr	Monsignor
Mt.	Mountain
n.	note
N	north
opp.	opposite
pl.	plural
Pl., Pls.	plate(s)
pp.	pages
pt.	part
R.	River
Re., Rs.	Rupee(s)
ref.	reference
Rev.	Reverend
S	south
S.C.	Scheduled Castes
ser.	series
sp., spp.	species
sq.	square
St.	Saint
trans.	translation, translator
USA	United States of America
vol.	volume
vv.	verses
W	west

Introduction

THE NEW LAND

Documentation of the Badaga culture spans a period from 1812 to the present: exactly two centuries of changing conditions that were described briefly by several dozen Western observers, though not trained anthropologists or historians. It was only in 1997 that Frank Heidemann (1997, 2006) provided a long anthropological analysis of their society, to complement my own studies from fieldwork done intermittently during 1962-94. The Badagas of modern days are also observers, often very astute ones, of their own changing culture; but even the best-informed among the elders know little about the way of life followed by their ancestors before the twentieth century, and almost nothing has been written by them about their history.

In this work I have tried to present data that will answer certain questions about change in a small South Indian community, drawing on three sources: namely what modern Badagas believe and can tell us about their society, what the numerous outside observers have written, and what I myself saw and heard while visiting and sometimes living among the Badagas during the past fifty years. It must be stressed that these sources are distinct and will not always yield precisely the same conclusions; in part therefore the answers to my questions may depend on the source of the evidence.[1]

The theory of structural-functional anthropology is ill-equipped to explain sociocultural change. Bronislaw Malinowski stated (1926: 132) that functional theory 'aims at the explanation of anthropological facts at all levels of development by the part which they play within the integral system of culture, by the manner in which they are related to each other within the system, and by the manner in which this system is related to the physical surroundings'. But what if an anthropological 'fact', such as the historic conversion of some members of the community to Christianity, does not appear to play any part in the integral system of the culture and bears no clear relationship to those other 'facts' that are integral to that culture? How did the regional millenarian movement of the 1860s, for instance, contribute to the integration of their culture? – The Badagas got the idea that a god was coming to them to consume the German missionary and perform the miracles of Jesus Christ. He did not deliver on his promises, the sick were not cured, and many went back home extremely dejected. Yet, important though it seemed to Badagas at the time, this cult movement neither perceptibly integrated their society nor as it happened disintegrated it; nor did it persist for very long. What then was its function, and how could we explain the movement in structural-functional terms? In fact many such aspects of cultural change during the period we are to examine cannot really be adequately explained by reference to universal hypotheses about the workings of society. Instead we must attempt to show how the local problems of the Badagas have given rise to local changes, local compromises, explanations and solutions, all of which have been worked out by the Badagas using their own terms of reference, to suit their special, local needs. Natural changes have no doubt been induced by outsiders, rather than introduced; the Badagas themselves were responsible for modifications in their way of life and the environment since the very first contact with aliens in 1603.

The modern anthropologist no longer searches for objective 'facts' but works to demonstrate social relationships; and is not primarily concerned about origins, as was once true. Only when we have determined the nature of cultural change among Badagas and have given some explanations of it will we be ready to make any comparisons with the way other societies have operated and changed; and not in this book. We should not try to explain the particular case of this community by introducing some extraneous model of society, be it structural-functional or evolutionary, and expecting it to fit the Badaga data so as to explain them fully. Thus the present study is a contribution to the already well-known ethnography and history of one small Indian region, not an essay in comparative sociology.

The Badagas are fully aware of how they differ from other communities in this region. Thus only people of their community have Badagu as their mother-tongue; only Badaga men and women used to wear the distinctive dress and carried a characteristic mark on the forehead; only Badagas live in their recognized villages, which bear distinctively Badaga place-names; and only Badagas can marry Badaga women and thus belong throughout their lives in a widespread network of kin. As the community is a grouping where potential membership is the same as actual membership, no problem has previously arisen over who is a Badaga and who is not.

The coherence of Badaga society was already a *fait accompli* by 1820, and we know of no important villages founded much after that date. Evidence for this lies with one William Keys, an official who in 1812 had already recorded 41 principal and 119 subordinate Badaga hamlets. Even though most of these were just one row of four to six houses, it is clear that the 41 principal villages were actually the heads of the communes (of which there are now 40 on the plateau, the abandoned Tudu:ru included; Keys 1812: xlviii).[2] In effect, the Badaga colonization of the Nilgiris and the consolidation of various refugee groups into a unity were events that had already occurred before Keys' visit, in what we might academically call prehistory. From the Badagas' point of view, however, the advent of a few foreign writers did not nudge their community from the darkness of prehistory into the gloomy light of historicity. Until now no Badaga has published a detailed history of the community: are they therefore still prehistoric? Certainly not; the question is an inappropriate and patronising one. So what I am presenting in this study comes from that approach in modern anthropology known as ethnohistory.

Be that as it may, the Badaga past is of great importance to them, and is still broadly recalled in an oral history of legends that are taken for fact, and in most cases probably are elaborated from actual events of long ago. Badaga legends are quite consistent from one part of the district to another and are sufficiently precise about the more insignificant details to convince me that, like the Maori genealogists of old, Badagas have long maintained a fairly accurate interest in their past and in teaching the young about it (especially now when some of those young people are growing up in places well beyond the Nilgiris). Some of these unwritten legends take the form of epic ballads that are sung throughout the night while waiting for a sick person to die and in other situations where time is to be passed. This should not deceive us into considering the legends mere entertainment: it is true that they are enthralling to listeners, but legends are also crucial to their convictions about how the social system should operate. It is these highly credible tales about who settled which village, and much else, that explain to all the 135,000 or so Badagas their regulations governing village exogamy and other aspects of the relationship between a kinship system, a social hierarchy and a pattern of settlement.

Instead of relegating Badaga legend to the 'folklore' pigeon-hole in the hope that a content analysis will later be made of it, I will examine briefly what the tales and legends do and do not cover in Badaga prehistory. Most of them recount supposed events, often mysterious, often tragic, events in the lives of personages who lived on the Nilgiri Hills. Stories of love and magic belong to this group. A second group consists of political tales, legends of chieftains and East India Company officials who came to the hills for conquest, plunder, or even just sport. A third group are the legends of Badaga colonization. These three groups deal with varying aspects of their origins. The tales of personal exploits, some amorous and others adventurous in nature, are told to explain the beginning of particular lineages or villages. The political tales explain the origin of communes and the emergence of various village officials. The accounts of who settled which place, and where they came from, now explain the complex pattern of clan exogamy within the community. And a fourth group of legends embrace all sorts of events and arrangements that resulted from Badagas' contact with the Toda, Kota and Kuṟumba tribes indigenous to the area. These legends validate the whole system of economic interdependence which held these groups rigidly together for so long and has resulted in a minimum division of labour *within* the Badaga community itself (see Chapters 7-9).

Here, then, are the quasi-historical events Badagas have chosen to remember. Yet the one great event of their past not so clearly recalled now is the actual flight from Mysore, either because different refugees experienced it in quite different ways and at different times, or perhaps too because people wished to put that event behind them. They are explicit that their ancestors did not all come to the Nilgiris at the same moment, and yet one hears many nowadays claim they had been refugees fleeing from Tipu Sultan – some time in the 1790s. So vague are people about their distant ancestors' actual flight that the main legend I heard on the subject is obviously coloured by a nineteenth-century borrowing from the *Book of Exodus*. It tells how the ancestral Badagas, being hotly pursued by Moslem soldiers, reached the Moyar River, the northern limit of the district, at which point the waters opened up and enabled them to pass. As one might guess, the pursuers were all drowned when the river closed up again behind the Badagas.

While it is likely that the latest arrivals were people indeed fleeing from Tipu's forces and from the economic effects of the four Anglo-Mysore Wars, the great bulk of them had been refugees from earlier scourges or were even purposely brought to settle the hills in some cases, the main influx arriving over the period 1565-1617.

For the early days of their settlement we (surprisingly) have the independent manuscript record of Jacome Fenicio (*ca* 1558-1632), an Italian priest who visited the Nilgiris in 1603 and met both Badagas and Todas there. When we couple this fact with the linguistic evidence that Badagas speak a language closely related to Kannaḍa, it becomes most likely that the first major wave of refugees arrived as the Moslem hordes were destroying the great Hindu empire of Vijayanagara in Karnataka following the historic battle of Talikōta in 1565. There is no doubt that this was the direction from which the Badagas came. Aside from the linguistic evidence, their very name means 'northerner', and the adherence of some to the Lingayat faith is equally telling, for that sect is almost confined to Karnataka state.

The 468 villages and hamlets in which they have lived were nearly all in existence when the British first settled on these hills a mere twenty years after Tipu's death – and there is no need to apologize for my use of the word 'refugees' for, as Badagas have constantly been telling curious visitors since the 1820s, their ancestors indeed fled from the home villages in a small rural area of southern Mysore when pursued by Moslem soldiers, one of the groups leaving in such haste that they had left a baby behind: such unfortunate people were nothing other than 'events-alienated' refugees. Buchanan, a contemporary observer of that part of Mysore, noted that, following Lord Cornwallis's invasion of the area in 1792 (that same Cornwallis who had so disgraced himself at Yorktown in 1781), '. . . the people had been forced by Tippu Sultan to leave the open country and retire to the forests where they lived in huts and procured provisions as best they could. A large proportion of them had perished of hunger, and the country was only sparsely populated even in 1800 . . .' (Dutt 1908: 210). Without doubt some among these forest dwellers made their way up into the Nilgiris where they found a scattering of their compatriots already settled. By the start of the nineteenth century the Badagas were consolidated as a distinct Nilgiri society and their work of colonization completed. It was around 1820 that the first British settlers arrived, and since that time the Badagas have become a highly successful agricultural community that now views itself as indigenous to the Nilgiri Hills and forms a part of a larger multi-ethnic society there: today they are 18 per cent of the district's total.

Nor are Badaga legends more informative about the period *before* they had left the state of Mysore (now Karnataka). The names of a few ancestral villages there are still recalled, as too are the lineages descended from them; but little else. The Ha:ruva clan are reputed (chiefly by themselves) to have been Brahmins; the Oḍeya phratry bears the same name as one high-ranking Lingayat subcaste in Mysore. But beyond these sparse indicators and the general impression one forms that the refugee peasants were illiterate and not at all urbanized, we can really say nothing much about 'Badaga' social organization before their migration from that core area. Perhaps that is the way they would have it, for there is nothing very relevant to their present organization in a pattern of hierarchically organized, multicaste villages – which is what recent Mysore society has been and presumably was in medieval times too.

Once settled on the Nilgiri Hills the immigrants encountered challenges there that were quite new to them. Life in Mysore during the medieval Vijayanagara Empire, and after its collapse, had undoubtedly been far from calm; indeed many during those troubled years were impelled to desert their native villages because of social unrest in the area. Yet the regulation of their lives had until this exodus been certain: the demands of the religious calendar, of their caste regulations, of the annual agricultural cycle, of client and patron, and of the ruling families were well-known and omnipresent. One could only escape from that society, if need be, by embracing nature in the guise of an ascetic, and very few did that.

In the Nilgiris the separation of society and nature was perhaps more severe, a stark contrast that would not brook the ambivalence of ascetics wandering beyond the pale of society into the uncertain embrace of nature. Here asceticism was unknown and nature anything but warm: she flaunted a dismal climate in which men and women could easily die from exposure and cold when cut off from their fellows. Unlike anywhere else in southern India, winter frost does form here at night. The jungles surrounding every hamlet were infested with all the dangerous animals known to Mysore, but here they were more proximate, seemingly more numerous and minatory. Whatever medicinal value the vegetation had was something yet to be discovered by a few therapists (Hockings 1980b: 182-208). The small community of Badagas here collaborated comfortably with the neighbours, the Todas and Kotas, and probably took concubines if needed from other local tribes. But around this plural society in a buffer zone they all drew a rigid boundary: everything beyond it was the terrifying realm of the wild. It contained not only the obvious terrors – the wild buffaloes, tigers, panthers, elephants, hyenas, gaur (or bison), sloth bears, wolves, and crocodiles – but the even more frightening and mysterious Kuṟumba sorcerers, who might within an instant become any one of these animals, with dire results.

This sharp division between nature and society was expressed in a variety of ways. Clearest perhaps was the ethical prescription that while it is evil for a Badaga to kill people he does good in the eyes of the community *and of God* if he kills Kuṟumbas or tigers, 'since these are both murderers' (as the matter was once explained to me). The Badagas have always been what would popularly be viewed as a most superstitious people: they would suspect a sorcerer's malice behind every noise in the jungle, every unexplained malady, every strange event at night (see below, pp. 161-63); and they could glean a multitude of tidings, both good and bad, from the everyday behaviour of snakes, crows, jackals, cattle and dozens of other creatures and conditions that surround them (Hockings 1988: 229-35; 2012: 663-65). A further indication of the gulf between nature and society here is perhaps that in their pre-British law the severest Badaga punishment short of hanging was that of ostracism – expulsion from the village; and this was reserved for the enormity of incest.[3]

For an Indian peasant society the Badagas have several unusual features, fit to provide enough exotica for any undergraduate anthropology course. This fact has not been fully appreciated by the many dozens of ethnologists who over the years came to the Nilgiris and attached themselves with passion either to the colourful Todas or the shy jungle tribes (Walker 1997: *passim*; Hockings 2012: 29-36); for although Badaga people may outwardly appear to be a much more 'typical' Indian farming community, they do not have true subcastes or multicaste villages: they may practice both hypergamy *and* hypogamy, even across the vegetarian boundary; several forms of polygamy are or at least were acceptable; they used to maintain a sort of young men's house until the twentieth century; marriage is permitted across generation levels to the point where a man might theoretically marry a woman, her daughter *and* her mother together, so long as he was not the father of any of them; and villages used to hold a huge memorial ceremony every thirty years or so once all members of a particular generation had died out (Hockings 1991: 61-64; 2012: 14-18). If we only add to these social features the frequent ghost exorcisms, annual firewalking, and even the occasional massacre in the distant past, then the anthropologist has much to explain.

On the other side of the coin, contemporary Badagas have much to learn about their ancestry. All cultures, their own included, will change through time, and the less relevant details of the distant past tend to become forgotten by later generations. In general,

> There is in our days a rapid erosion of traditions. Traditional societies little by little cease to function; the storytellers no longer have any reason for existing; the old people die off; and the young either do not know the tradition or mix it up with scholarly ideas and pretended rationalizations. Nowadays the people to whom enquiries could be directed are no more than a small minority. (Deschamps & Poirier 1968: 1442, trans.)

This book, then, is one small step towards preserving a set of oral traditions that reach back over more than four centuries in a corner of southern India.

THE TERRAIN

The Nilgiri Hills, also known (like a dozen other regions) as the Blue Mountains, are a massif some 1500 sq. km. in area, and form a buffer zone in southern India situated at the juncture of the three linguistic and cultural areas of Karnataka, Malabar and Tamilnad (Noble & Hockings, in Hockings 2012: 646-48). During the British period (1799-1947) this formed an administrative unit of the Madras Presidency. Today the Nilgiris are one small district of Tamil Nadu state, where it adjoins Kerala and Karnataka, altogether covering 2,543 sq. km. This is the homeland of the Badaga, Toda, Kota and various Kuṟumba and Iṟula communities; but nowadays numerous other peoples also live there and greatly outnumber these indigenous groups; thus Badagas today (2013) form little more than 18 per cent of the district's population.

The plateau is generally in the elevation range of 2,000-2,500 m., and one peak, Doḍḍabeṭṭa, among the highest in peninsular India, reaches 2,633 m. (Hockings 2012: 270-71). In contrast to this, the warmer western quarter of the district averages around 1,000 m. in elevation and forms a major part of the Wainad Plateau (Fletcher, in Hockings 2012: 969-78). The major indigenous communities in the Wainad area are quite different: they are Paṇiyas, Jēnu Kuṟumbas, and Chettis, although there are also a few Badagas (Wainad Gauḍas) and Kotas.

The escarpment of the Nilgiri Plateau falls away steeply on all sides, on the eastern edge actually dropping some 2,000 m. over a distance of about 3 km. These slopes are covered in dense subtropical jungle that harbours tigers, leopards, buffalo, gaur, elephants, snakes and malarial mosquitoes, and the formerly dangerous hunting tribes that are still feared by some for their sorcery. Until the advent of the British early in the nineteenth century the three communities living on the summit of these hills – the Badagas, Kotas and Todas – were therefore extremely isolated; and there were no roads.

The undulating, unevenly wooded downland of the entire plateau has considerable variation in rainfall. The Nilgiris receive from 1500 to 4000 mm. of rain annually, depending on topographical aspect. Western parts of the plateau rely mainly upon the southwest monsoon in July and August; the eastern parts derive much of their rain from the northeastern monsoon in Oct.-Dec. The average mean daily temperature in the centre of the plateau is about 15° C, while down in the Wainad the climate is much hotter and also wetter.

For the mildly invigorating qualities of its climate the plateau is therefore scarcely rivalled anywhere in the Asian tropics, and from 1819 onwards British residents began to take full advantage of this healthful region as a convenient alternative to making the sea trip to Mauritius or Cape of Good Hope. Ootacamund and Simla were in fact the first two hill stations to be established anywhere in South Asia by the British, in 1821 and 1822 respectively (Hockings 2012: 415-16). Soon the new towns of Coonoor, Kotagiri and Ootacamund (the district headquarters), and then later the military cantonment at Wellington, took shape and expanded too. More recently the small town of Gudalur (Gu:ḍalu:ru) has grown up in the Wainad, at the foot of the western escarpment of the Nilgiris. Today Ootacamund, Coonoor, Kotagiri and Gudalur are the headquarters of the four administrative divisions or *taluks* into which the district was divided over the past century; but there are now six of these altogether, since Kunda and Pandalur were recently sliced off from the others.

THE NILGIRI POPULATION

When European people began to settle on the plateau they brought with them a broad variety of Tamilian, Mysorean, Malabari or other dependents, including a few Eurasians, as servants, clerks and workers. It was through this contact, as explored by gossip, published memoirs and the local press, that people of southern India began to learn about the strange men, scarcely Hindus, who already inhabited these hills. Immigrants too began to seek labouring jobs on the tea and coffee plantations from the 1850s; and as they took up this new occupation they brought the indigenous Nilgiri tribes into closer contact with many traditions and practices of popular South Indian Hinduism. Today the plantations are the main source of the district's income, and still employ thousands of migrant labourers from elsewhere in South India or Sri Lanka (then Ceylon). In 1991 there were some 370,000 recent immigrants living in the Nilgiris, thus over half of the total population of 704,827 at that time (see Appendix 1). But even in Ouchterlony's report of 1847 (1848/58) we read that less than half the district population, including Badagas, was indigenous – the effect of only a quarter-century of development then.

These newer immigrants belong to a wide range of castes. Normally, while maintaining occupational roles in Nilgiri society, they also attempt to continue the behaviour that distinguishes their own castes and try to keep up social ties with relatives back in their diverse places of origin. Many now retire to those places. From the point of view of the indigenous Nilgiri communities, however, their caste distinctions are of little importance; immigrants are classified under seven broad headings: Tamilians, Kanarese, Andhras, Malayalis, Christians, Moslems and, in former days, Europeans (*dore*, lit. 'king'). The local inhabitants are quite aware that there are caste-like divisions within these categories but are unconcerned with them; and as the immigrants are classed according to mother-tongue or religious creed, they are not even organized by Nilgiri residents into a simple caste hierarchy. It is true that Andhras, for example, are felt to have an inferior status; but this is because they are usually day-labourers for Nilgiri farmers. Their low status, like that of any other labourers, comes from their poverty and poor education rather than from caste affiliations. The British held high status, despite being beef-and-brandy consumers, since they held the power. There *is* a status hierarchy in the Nilgiris, but it has economic and educational determinants that do not parallel the traditional ritual determinants of caste ranking elsewhere in India (Hockings 2012: 840-48).

Except among Todas, Kotas and Europeans, the rate of population growth in the Nilgiris district has been quite high over the past two centuries. During the decade 1991-2001 it was about 7.69 per cent, attributable to some immigration as well as to the increase of births over deaths; but this was actually a very big drop from the 27.57 per cent increase noted during 1971-81, a jump that had resulted in part from the in-migration of Tamilian refugees from Sri Lanka. During 2001-11, however, the growth in the whole district was only 3.50 per cent. These demographic data, along with a high rate of literacy and the fact that plantations have made this into one of the wealthier districts in southern India (despite its being only two per cent of the state's area), indicate that the Nilgiris are by no means typical of rural India in economic matters. Indeed they tend towards the upper extreme when one looks at volume of immigration, natural wealth, and – most important – rural literacy, female literacy, education, and knowledge of the outside world.

NOTES

1. I have not adopted the once-common but chauvinistic approach of seeking out the Aryan, Dravidian or autochthonous elements in Badaga culture – in my view, a sterile exercise, and moreover an outdated one. They do speak a Dravidian language, but that is all that need be said on the matter.
2. Most of the communes (*u:ru*) today, even several ones that only consist of one or two hamlets (*haṭṭi*), are marked by the presence of *one* ceremonial arch or other stone structure (*akka bakka*, Pl. 6). This only exists where there exists a Hiriyade:va temple; Heidemann 2006: 2; Hockings 2012: 208, fig. 45); see p. 68. Only one current commune, Pedduva, has two *akka bakkas*, one in Pedduva hamlet and another in Naduhaṭṭi. Quite possibly there were two communes here in Keys' time (*ca* 1812). Thus his figure of 41 'villages' would conform with ours.
3. An ostracized person would not go to live in the jungle, but would look for some distant hamlet where he might be accepted; see below, pp. 195, 212-13.

CHAPTER 1

Into the Mountains, into the Forest

THE MYSORE CONNECTION

There is no doubt that before they settled in the Nilgiris the homeland of the Badagas was in villages of the southern Mysore Plain. Their own legends as well as those of the Kotas are quite explicit on this point; and, most interestingly, some of the clans have even been able to identify places in Mysore whence their ancestors had come. Indeed, the most northerly village they now inhabit is still just inside Karnataka state.

The very name, *Baḍaga,* is obviously prime evidence of their origin to the north of the Nilgiris – for the Kannaḍa word *baḍaga* means 'northerner'. It does also have the meaning 'servant'. If we postulate that the name derives somehow from Kannaḍa *baḍaka* instead (though phonetics certainly suggests otherwise), then we have the additional meanings 'lean, thin, feeble man' or 'a man who beats and bangs' (Kittel 1894: 1068-73). In this way there are hypothetically four etymologies for the name; but the last two meanings verge on the scurrilous, however, are not supported by linguistics, and would hardly be used by any immigrants in self-identification. One would expect such epithets to be applied to immigrants only by some other group, perhaps the Todas had they known Kannaḍa; yet Todas call them *ma·v*. But were any of the Badagas ever servants?

There are two very small phratries living on the northern edge of the plateau near Si:gu:ru. These are the Kumba:ras ('potters') and the Be:ḍas ('hunters'), the latter from Nāgataḷḷi, and both groups report that they came initially to this locality while in the service of the chieftain of Ummattūr (a *pāḷayakkāraṉ* or warlord who was then ruling Tiṉaikaṇāmbai-nāḍu in the southern Mysore district; cf. Rea 1910: 115; Pope 1879: 346-47, note). Their traditional occupations, as the two names indicate, were quite lowly, so the title of 'servant' might have been applied to both these tiny groups; but that would not explain at all how the entire, much larger immigrant community came to be called *Baḍaga* (and moreover, *-k-* is a distinct phoneme from *-g-* in Kannaḍa, so we are talking about two different words). In this context it is important to note that most of the immigrants had anyway arrived before these 'servants', the Be:ḍas and Kumba:ras, who only reached the hills in the later seventeenth century; yet we find that in 1603 the Italian, Fr. Fenicio, was already calling the community *Badega* in his report, and mentioning the relationship established with the Todas.[1]

We are thus left with the presumption (confirmed by all informants) that Badagas are so called because of their northern origin.[2] The case of the Be:ḍas and Kumba:ras, two phratries with the same material culture, language and social organization as other Badagas and a demonstrable tie with Karnataka, merely bears out the long-standing connection with that State.

The fact that a sizeable minority of the community (well over 10,000, though not enumerated by the *Census of India*) is Lingayat further underlines the tie with Mysore, for this religious sect finds nearly all of its followers within Karnataka state, virtually none living in Tamil Nadu apart from these few in the Nilgiri region. Some Lingayat Badagas are even able to relate how their ancestors left two now-deserted villages in Mysore, and that they were by then already converts to Lingayatism (or Virashaivism), a small Hindu Saivite sect.[3]

DATING THE MIGRATION

Legends are always inaccurate or silent over dates, if only because they pass orally from generation to generation without any modification of reference to times past – and they very rarely carry any calendrical reference point, such as the English '1066' or the French '1789'. There are, however, various other kinds of evidence that also shed some light on the dating of this crucial southward migration.

Published Estimates

Several writers familiar with Badaga culture have recorded estimates of the dating of this event (Table 1), based in part on accounts that they heard. Serious attention should be paid, I feel, to the earlier publications, as they commonly relied directly on the verbal information of eighteenth–nineteenth century Badagas. It will be seen that most of these authorities place the migration in the sixteenth century (the average actually comes out around 1560!), and several mention the break-up of the Vijayanagara Empire (which covered roughly modern Karnataka) in 1565: with all the social unrest there, it was certainly an apt period that prompted refugees to begin departing.

Table 1: Estimates of the Badagas' Arrival Date

Author	*Publication date*	*Estimate*
John Sullivan	1819 (p. liv)	'about 300 years ago'
Benjamin Ward	1821 (lxx)	'about four centuries ago'
Thomas Baber	1830 (315)	'about three centuries ago'
Henry Harkness	1832 (105-06)	'about six generations ago, during the anarchy which succeeded upon the downfall of the Vijayanagara empire,' i.e. 1565
Medical Board Office	1844 (20)	'about 200 years ago'
Harry Congreve	1847 (122)	'six generations ago'
John Ouchterlony	1848 (81)	'3 or 4 centuries ago'
Georg Bühler	1849 (110)	'more than 400 years ago'
Richard Burton	1851 (1991:334)	'in the days of Hyder or Tippoo'
John Dulles	1855 (458-59)	'six generations since'
W. Ross King	1870 (20)	'not much more than two hundred years ago' . . . 'six or seven generations'
George U. Pope	1879 (346, note)	'Many fled . . . in 1613'
Harriet G.M. Murray-Aynsley	1883 (143)	'about three hundred years ago, after the breaking-up of the Vijayanagar kingdom'
William Stokes	1883b (288)	'about 322 years ago'
Edward Balfour	1884 (I, 224)	'about the 15th century'
Harold Stuart	1893 (243)	'about three centuries ago'
Hanna Rhiem	1900 (498 trans.)	'about three hundred years ago'
Thomas F. MacNamara	1912 (149)	'the fall of the kingdom of Vijianagar'
Feodor Jagor	1914 (47, trans.)	'not later than 1250'
Edmond Périé	1933 (97, trans.)	'some 350 years . . . when the Vijayanagar Empire collapsed'
Kamil Zvelebil	1955 (2001:145)	'several centuries ago (maybe half a millennium ago)'
E.R.C. Davidar	1997 (185)	'in the seventeenth century'
Frank Heidemann	1997 (59, trans.)	'after the fall of the Vijianagara Empire'

There has, however, been a contrary idea held by a few twentieth-century Badagas that their ancestors had come at a much earlier date than most of the above-cited European inquirers have suggested. Thus the antiquarian M.K. Belli Gowder dismisses the oft-mentioned ravages of Tipu Sultan in the late eighteenth century as a cause of the migration (as most people would), and instead suggests that the Moslem invasion responsible was that of Malik Kafur, the Sultan Ala-ud-din's favourite slave, who laid waste the Hoysaḷa kingdom in 1315.[4] Kariabettan, another modern Badaga writer who was M.K. Belli Gowder's younger neighbour and doubtless had read his personal manuscripts, offers an eleventh century dating, but presents no further evidence and thus cannot be relied upon too much (he may indeed have been thinking about a well-known Kannaḍa inscription that mentions *Todas*, dated to 1116); but Jagor was a meticulous and very observant, if brief, German visitor.[5] It may be noted that the most recent *Gazetteer of the Nilgiris* (Gopalakṛishnan 1995: 196) cites an archaeologist, K.S. Ramachandran, to the effect that the early Badagas 'had turned the dolmens into sacred places, not looking [at] them as temples but actual gods. . . . Hence, the conclusion that the builders of the dolmens were the ancestors of the Badagas has little doubt.' Though perhaps the dolmens referred to are the well-known ones in Me:lu:ru (Pl. 3), Śo:lu:ru and one or two other villages, for the most part dolmens were uncut stone circles and monoliths on the hilltops that have been dated to the Iron Age, and marked burial sites, usually at a considerable distance from any Badaga home (Hockings 1976; and Zagarell, in Hockings 2012: 583-87). Ramachandran's is by no means a valid argument, for the current religious use of any structure quite often differs substantially from what its original builders had intended; and moreover I can cite the case of a 'draw-well cairn' (Breeks' term) with cinerary burial on the summit of Pykara Hill that I mapped in 1963 (Hockings 1976): at the time it showed no signs whatever of any Hindu worship, least of all a shrine structure. Yet a mere decade later a small stone shrine had been built against one side of the circle, and when I revisited it there was clear evidence of recent *pūja* there; by whom, I have no idea. Another example: a small plaster bust of Chopin, the sort that used to sit on one's piano, and was no doubt thrown out by some Europeans after chipping, was on a plinth on Parson's Valley road in 1963; later (1990) there was a shrine with a new image at that spot.

Linguistic Evidence

For a thousand years or more there were three major literary languages in this part of southern India: Tamil spoken to the southeast of the Nilgiris, Kannaḍa (or Canarese) to the north, and Malayalam, an offshoot of Tamil, to the west. Without any shadow of doubt Badaga is much closer in grammar and vocabulary to Kannaḍa than it is to either Tamil or Malayalam. Dravidian scholars have long noted the similarity of Badaga to medieval Kannaḍa: in particular, the two forms of *r* in Badaga phonology reportedly 'had dropped out of use [i.e. in Kannaḍa literature] prior to the time of the grammarian Kési-rája, who lived in the thirteenth century'.[6] M.B. Emeneau, however (personal comment, Dec. 1999), discounting this argument, said that for lack of early Badaga inscriptions or other documents nothing can be said about their language until the mid-nineteenth century, when Muzzy commented on it that 'Their language differs considerably from the commonly spoken Canarese' (Muzzy 1844: 358) – though this would *not* imply that it was therefore somehow closer to Tamil or Malayalam. Modern linguistic research suggests quite a close similarity with A:lu Kuṟumba, another Nilgiri language.

Calendrical Evidence

The Badaga calendar was different from the Tamilian and Kanarese ones, though they all divide the year into twelve zodiacal or solar months, and share some of the same names for months. The Badaga month called *A:ḍi*, for example, falls two months before the Tamilians' *Āḍi* (Cancer). There is no evidence or even a recollection that the Badagas ever inserted an intercalary month every ten years, as is done elsewhere in India, and indeed they had no central authority to demand such an intercalation; but something else has been happening to change their calendar. In 1918 Richards (1920: 24) recorded the sequence of Badaga months, and identified *A:ḍi*, for example, as May-June. Some 23 years later the Badaga antiquarian M.K. Belli Gowder equated *A:ḍi* with June (Belli Gowder 1923-41: 109). Some 23 years later yet I recorded *A:ḍi* as equivalent to June-July.

What has been happening, then? I conclude that the early Badagas were recognizing a 366-day year, with the result that every 23 years their calendar became further advanced against the Gregorian one by about 17 days, because a year is really much closer to 365 days. Hence in the 46 years between 1918 and 1964 we have seen their calendar advance by 35 days, or just over one month (as was recorded by Richards and myself). Today, however, these people normally follow printed calendars and almanacs.

This observation leads to a quite illuminating result for our present purposes. As was just shown, Badaga *A:ḍi* in 1918 was two months ahead of Tamil *Āḍi*. If, as was suggested, the Badagas had consistently been reckoning 366 days to each year, this was 18 hours 11 minutes (or 0.7576 of a day) in excess of the correct solar figure. This means that their *A:ḍi* would *last* have been *synchronous* with the Dravidian *Āḍi* (July, in Winslow 1862: 64) approximately 402 years prior to 1918, i.e. just half-a-century before the fall of Vijayanagar. This is not to suggest that the Badagas had become separated from their Kanarese brethren at quite such an early date; but rather that this was their reference point, the *terminus post quem* at which the earliest Badaga refugees had learnt the Kanarese calendar when they had still been children. The first old men to set foot on the hills, presumably late in the sixteenth century, had thus referred back to that time in their memories once they began counting the passage of months on the Nilgiris and teaching their calendar to the youngsters.

Exactly the same kind of argument can be based on the fact that in 1918 Badaga *A:vaṇi* and *Peraṭṭa:di* were also two months ahead of the eponymous Tamil months. A problem arises, however, with the months *Tai* and *A:ṇi*, also occurring in both languages, because the Badaga *Tai* and *A:ṇi* are *three* months ahead of their Tamil eponym. Perhaps at some time in the nineteenth century, after some education and almanacs had come into the district, an attempt was made to add an intercalary month, namely *Hemma:ti*, and with these confusing results. *Hemma:ti* derives from a Sanskrit word (for 'cold weather') which does not seem to occur in other Dravidian calendars at all. In the sequence of months, this has been positioned immediately after Badaga *Tai*. (For more on the Badaga conceptualization of time, see Hockings 1989a: 215-18; 2012: 173-75.)

Archaeological Considerations

Here a small digression on mining and archaeology is pertinent, although it takes us away from the Badagas. Finds of Roman coinage in burials on the Wainad and even once on the Nilgiri Plateau, and in numerous hordes on the Coimbatore Plain, suggest that traders with Rome, or more likely Alexandria, were actively exploiting the gold mines of this area. We find no mention of gold from this region, however, in the *Periplus of the Erythræan Sea* (of about 70 CE), which is otherwise rich in details about Indian products two millennia ago. That there was indeed a native population in the Nilgiris and Wainad in the first millennium CE is indicated by the many cinerary burials of this period on the hilltops; several contained Roman coins, while one has a radiocarbon date of about 1100 CE. There is also a reference in the Tamil classic *Silappaḍikāram* to the Chēra king Senguttuvan attending a dance performance 'at Nilagiri' with his army (*Silappaḍikāram: Vañjikanḍam, Kalkot Kaḍai*, xxvi, *vv*. 85, 105, 120; cf. Breeks 1873; Grigg 1880; Das 1957; Naik 1966; Hockings 1976; Noble 1976, 1989; Zagarell 1994, 1995).

Gold workings in the Nilgiri Wainad undoubtedly date back over many centuries:

> There are miles of country where almost every stone has been turned over, hillsides entirely sluiced away, mountain slopes simply honey-combed with shafts, remains of old aqueducts, adits, and bunds. . . . The existing caste of gold workers are the Korumbars, but they confine themselves entirely to alluvial washings. When questioned they tell you of a tradition . . . of hill-men called Vehdahs, . . . by whose hands all these wonderful quarryings were carried out. (Sewell 1882: 224)

The cinerary burials and Wainad gold mines are not connected with Badaga history, it seems, aside from a possibility that chieftains of Ummattūr fortified Nellia:ḷa before coming to the Nilgiri Plateau because they were engaged in gold-mining thereabouts.

More relevant perhaps are accounts of old workings on the Nilgiris proper, around Ootacamund and Nanjena:ḍu – the very name *Nanjena:ḍu* means 'gashed tract of land'. Midway between these two places, on One Cairn Hill, and close to where a Roman *aureus* was found long ago, there was apparently a medieval (Hoysaḷa?) town of gold miners whose mines were protected by a now-disappeared mud fortress. Traces of their town stretch for nearly a kilometre, and the adjoining valley, behind 'Bishopsdown', was known to the Todas as *poṉ fïṭ* (gold mountain).[8] Badaga traditions do not mention this town and its mining activities at all, and there is no basis for supposing Badagas might have initially occupied the hills as prospectors – or even mine-slaves. There is no Badaga name for this ancient mining town, and no Badaga or Toda legends referring to it in any way, so one has to conclude the town at One Cairn Hill no longer existed by the time the first Badagas arrived. In more recent times there has been no gold mining in the district, except in the Wainad during the feverish speculation of 1879-82 (Francis 1908: 16-19; Hockings 2012: 391-95; for other references, see Hockings 1975: 49-50; 1996: 221-31; 2012: 173, 634). If such old quarries (some of which might even be from the Roman period) have any relevance at all to Badaga history, it can only be because the chieftains of Ummattūr may have first turned their attention towards the Nilgiris in search of the gold that it was rumoured could be found there. But they found Badaga tribute instead, and demanded it.

Since the first edition of this book appeared (under a different title) in 1980, Allen Zagarell has conducted an extensive archaeological survey of the Moyar Valley and the adjacent northern slopes of the Nilgiris. This area was in ancient times an important passage for trade and military movements between the Mysore Plain and the Coimbatore Plain, via the Gajaḷaṭṭi Pass. Zagarell was able to identify innumerable burial sites and quite a few former settlements in this area. He even cites a Tamil place-name here that would have been *Yavaṉa Tāvaḷam*, 'village of the foreigners [or Europeans?] in a fertile place' (Zagarell, however, has 'storage depot of the foreigners'; 1995: 94; cf. Winslow 1862: 575). According to an Iṟula man, 'during Vijayanagar times, the area contained 99 villages and towns' (Zagarell 1994: 190; cf. Hayavadana Rao 1908: 93). Surface finds show that the population used to be quite dense in that era, and one should not forget that only 2 miles west of Śāmarājnagar town, and within easy walking distance of the Moyar Ditch, are the extensive ruins of an ancient city traditionally known as Manipūr (Hayavadana Rao 1930: 653). These dense settlements were evidently supported in medieval times by intensive irrigation agriculture.

> A large stela from Maditorai, near Thengumarahada, tells of giving the entire region from Anekatti to Kadu-devan-paliyam (i.e. the entire stretch of the Moyar Ditch), probably Kalampaliyam, to a Lingayat priest for irrigation cultivation. This corresponds to evidence for irrigation cultivation found in the eastern ditch area, as well as field walls in the midst of jungle. . . . The same text mentions not only a Moyar sime (i.e. the Moyar administrative district), but also a Nilgiri sime ['administrative division']. (Zagarell 1994: 188)

This was 'in the Vijayanagar period'. Similar epigraphic evidence supports Zagarell's contention that the Moyar Valley area was thickly populated and was integrated fully within the Vijayanagara polity (1316-1565):

> The inscriptions note the collection of taxes by or through state functionaries. Land was apportioned to important dignitaries for their control and sustenance. Indeed, the entire lower region of the Nilgiris is reported to have been under irrigation cultivation under the direction of Lingayat priests, a system common in the state-organized sector of India. Cultivators from the outside were being imported into the area. There was a degree of hierarchy of administrators, including influential village/regional headmen. Temples were established and then funded by the ceding of taxes of particular villages. . . . Thus, this region was certainly under state authority just shortly before Finicio's report . . . (of 1603; Zagarell 1995: 93).

Even earlier periods of state administrative influence in this area are adduced by Zagarell. After referring to local rock paintings 'of the first millennium B.C.' (Zagarell 1994: 187; 1995: 93; Zagarell, in Hockings 2012: 796-98), he makes the important observation that:

> By the seventh to ninth centuries CE, the high levels of skill usually representative of state organization are found in the statuary in the Moyar Ditch. Particularly, a Pallava-style reproduction of Vishnu is connected with a temple structure. By the end of the ninth, and through the tenth and eleventh centuries, state-inspired inscriptions can be found scattered in the Moyar Ditch. One of these, an inscription and stela dating to the eleventh or twelfth century, mentions merchants in the Moyar valley, suggesting trade moving through this area. Another inscription, untranslated, thought to be tenth century in date . . . , attached to a hero-stone near Kalada Mirda, . . . denotes the death of a warrior hero amid a series of dolmens and other structures. . . . There are other major sites connected with fallen figures dating to the eleventh through the thirteenth centuries. (Zagarell 1994: 187-88)

In roughly the same medieval period, as was mentioned, there existed the large but unexcavated town that lay on One Cairn Hill, in woodland just to the south of Ootacamund. But despite the tangible evidence of this Nilgiri town, of many hilltop megalithic burials like that which once existed on the summit of One Cairn Hill, and of recent evidence for very substantial medieval occupation, military fortifications and agriculture in the Moyar Valley, we do not have any precise evidence of the ethnic Badagas having been a part of all this. In a loose sense perhaps, and to the extent that settlers in this hill region most probably came from the north during the Hoysaḷa and Vijayanagara periods, they might indeed have been designated *baḍagas*, i.e. 'northerners'. Zagarell identifies them as Okkaligas and Lingayats (1994: 191), two large social categories of southern Mysore. Present-day Badagas do sometimes assert that there were Badagas on the hills by the eleventh century, as we mentioned: in a rough manuscript the local folklorist M.K. Belli Gowder (1938-41: 5-8) dated their arrival (somewhat uncertainly) to 'seven hundred years back', or 'from 1300 to 1600', while his near-neighbour N. Kariabettan (1958b: 2, trans.) suggested 'in the 11th century'. Neither gave any corroborating evidence, however; and there are certain considerations which suggest that those early 'northerners' were not people ancestral to the Badaga community of the past four centuries, and indeed that Belli Gowder's suggested dates were quite wrong.

In the first place, very significantly, the plateau town just referred to is *not* recalled in any Badaga legend; 'nothing is known of [its] history' (Price 1908: 221); even its site seems to have gone unrecognised until discovered by British coffee planters, and I found no name for it in the Badaga language or their ballads. Secondly, as we will see, the paramount chief living at Tu:ne:ri, and the nineteen generations of his predecessors there, would only situate the founding father Hucci Gowder at about 1600 (if we allow *ca* 20 years per generation), not in the eleventh century. (Tu:ne:ri appears to have been their first settlement.) Thirdly, there is the consideration that legends of the main aboriginal groups do not accord much antiquity to the Badaga settlers, indeed do not really present them as players on the Nilgiri legendary scene in the way that the other tribes were.

In short, there is no particular reason to believe that the medieval Moyar or plateau populations were ancestral to the Badaga community, when Badaga legend itself locates their original homeland in a series of contiguous named villages close to Mysore city. Early on, Fenicio referred to only *three* Badaga villages and no town in 1603. So, although it can be granted, with Zagarell, that 'the upper hills had extensive, long term relationships with surrounding state and complex societies' (1997: 34), something an archaeological survey would readily support, there was most likely a hiatus in this longstanding relationship which saw the end of the 'Nilgiri city' near Ootacamund, the decline and total ending here of Vijayanagara state power, and then the arrival of a few new settlers – namely, the early Badaga families – at the end of the sixteenth century. Even Fr. Fenicio's party on their brief visit, arriving from the southwest in 1603, was an augury of things to come, a new kind of relationship with the outside world.

Other Historical Evidence

While archaeology is thus of no great assistance, kinship does provide a rough guide to the antiquity of the Badaga community. As was just mentioned, the Gauḍa headman of Tu:ne:ri, paramount chief of the Badagas, can name nineteen generations of forefathers. His was quite possibly the first village founded on the plateau (Francis 1908: 364), and as eighteen of the successive headmen were resident there the antiquity of Tu:ne:ri must go back to the start of the seventeenth century, if we allow twenty years per generation (which is reasonable for a peasant society).[9]

A further point: funeral ritual is always conservative, and that of immigrants always follows practices from the 'old country': Italian-American graves closely resemble those in the cemeteries of Italy, while in India the 'English' cemeteries in places like St. Stephen's, Ootacamund, are indeed quite recognizably English in their style and aura. In the case of Badaga funerals there has definitely been an evolution over the past two or more centuries (Hockings 2001), but one feature found in the nineteenth-century accounts is quite interesting to us because of its conservatism. When a person is dying his relatives should put a small gold coin smeared with butter into his mouth for him to swallow. (If he dies without it, then it is put in the mouth anyway.) The coin was essential (though rarely given nowadays) because it was considered to be the fee for the guardian of a bridge that the departed soul must cross (Gover 1871: 66). Originally, we are told, and until a century ago, the gold coin was a *haṇa*, or *Canteroy fanam* (Yule & Burnell 1903: 157-58). It dated from the reign of Kaṇṭhirava Narsa Rāja, who ruled Mysore during 1639–59 (Belli Gowder 1923-41: 7; Hockings and Pilot-Raichoor 1992: 125). By that time, we may presume, the first generation of Badaga settlers on the Nilgiris were beginning to die off, and the elders who formulated the funerary protocol for them instituted the continuing ritual use of this particular mintage of coin. Coins from other South

Indian polities might well have been used, even East India Company ones; but the tradition was only for this particular Mysorean *haṇa*.

It has been argued that the respect shown to Badagas by both Todas and Kotas, as in their customary salutations, indicates that the Badagas had entered the Nilgiris while the Mysore kings were still in the ascendancy and maintaining some territorial claims over the Nilgiris (Grigg 1880: 218; see below, 31); and indeed, though these Badagas did not in any way represent the monarch, the earliest of them may well have arrived before about 1617. The small Be:ḍa phratry, who came rather more recently as huntsmen and tax collectors in the retinue of a chieftain of Ummattūr, 'still call the Mysore chiefs . . . their Kartas or lords' (Grigg 1880: 268-69, quoting Metz 1864). This suggests another *terminus post quem* for the advent of these people. The chieftains of Ummattūr ceased to be independent in 1519, and from then on they were indeed under the sway of, first, the ruler of Vijayanagara and then the Rāja of Mysore, becoming his tributary chieftains (polegars, *pāḷayakkāraṉ*); both they and these Rājas continued to rule until the twentieth century (Arokiaswami 1956: 161-62; Nayak 1978: 38-39).

None of this confirms the widespread tale of flight from Moslem oppressors, which depicts some Badagas as initially coming to the Nilgiri tribes with caps in hand: 'Because of the trouble that the Mohammedan made for us . . . we have come, making ourselves to escape. This country is yours. . . . We are helpless. You must help us.' Such is the Kota version of their plea. In response a council of Todas, Kotas and Kuṟumbas allowed the Badagas to settle, provided they paid the now-customary tribute to these tribes (Harkness 1832: 106-07; Natesa Sastri 1892: 735-54; Rhiem 1900: 498; Emeneau 1946: 257; see below, 149-50).

Another persuasive line of argument is that all Hindu Badagas are Shaivites (including those who are Lingayats), whereas in southern Mysore there is now a large minority of Vaishnavites. That sect had its inception there with the conversion of the Mysore kings to Sri-Vaishnavism in 1617, after which widespread disturbances occurred between Vaishnavites and Shaivites; it suggests that some Badagas were already in the Nilgiris by that date and so not affected in the way that lowland communities were by this new orthodoxy (Grigg 1880: 218; Macleane 1893: 64; Hayavadana Rao 1930, vol. 2, pt. 3: 2241, 2368; Wilks 1930, vol. 1: 52). That some few were indeed in these hills in 1603 was confirmed, of course, by Fenicio's account, which is the only document we have from that era.[10]

Clearly there had been several waves of immigrants brought here sometimes by famine conditions, sometimes by Moslem or even Vaishnavite attempts at forcible conversion, sometimes, as we shall suggest, by a Mysorean policy to colonize the hills. The Kotas are explicit that once a few Badagas had arrived more came over the succeeding years (Belli Gowder 1938-41: 3; Emeneau 1946: 259). Ouchterlony even implies (1848/58: 278) that some may have come as late as early in the nineteenth century.[11] Among the earliest places settled were several claiming their ancestors had fled from Tāyūr, Saragūr, or the Haḍināḍ Twenty Thousand country. 'Many fled with the Rajah of Oomatoor in 1613, when he was driven from his city by Râj Wadaiyâr [of Mysore] . . .' (Pope 1879: 346-47, note). And such people had every reason to flee from southern Mysore in the years 1610-17, given the level of instability in the local towns:

> In April 1610, Rāja Woḍeyar acquired Siriyūr [the southernmost outpost, a fortress on the Nilgiri slopes 16.5 km north of Ootacamund] from Nanjuṇḍa-Arasu of Piriyāpaṭṭaṇa. In July 1612, he took Saragūr from Śrīkaṇṭha Woḍeyar. Early in 1614, Rāja Woḍeyar apparently found in Nanjarāja Woḍeyar of Haḍinaḍ Twenty Thousand country a serious competitor for the sovereignty of the Seringapatam province. At the head of a large army, . . . Nanjarāja began the offensive against Rāja Woḍeyar by walking away with the latter's horse . . . Rāja Woḍeyar decided upon hostilities and laid siege to Tāyūr. . . . A fierce fight ensued, in which Nanjarāja was, with considerable loss, slain, and his camp plundered.
>
> In December 1614, Rāja Woḍeyar acquired Hura, and in February 1615, Haradanahaḷḷi. . . . In February 1615, he also acquired, and exacted tribute from, Talakāḍ . . . , Hullahaḷḷi . . . , Kaḷale . . . , Heggaḍdēvankōṭe . . . , Maḷalavāḍi . . . , Biḷikere . . . , Kottāgāla and Ammachavāḍi. In March, Mūgūr . . . , and in November, Kikkēri and Hosahoḷalu . . . were taken. In March 1617, Māvattūr was acquired . . .
>
> By about the middle of 1617, Rāja Woḍeyar had effectively established his sway over a greater portion of the present district of Mysore. He was evidently at the height of his power . . .
>
> The kingdom of Mysore, in 1617, extended from Seringapatam in the north to Ummattūr and Terakaṇāmbi in the south . . . . (Abridged from Hayavadana Rao 1943: 65-67; quoted in Hockings 2012: 420)

Not all Badagas migrated within a generation or two, however, and while some may well have been fleeing from Moslem invaders after 1565, and others from this military turmoil of the early seventeenth century, still other bands came later and for other reasons. It is very likely that the upheavals associated with the late eighteenth-century Anglo-Mysore Wars forced yet more villagers to decamp to the safety of these hills and join Badagas already there (Ouchterlony 1848/58: 278). The early British explorers Ward (1821) and Harkness (1832) both recorded that these people had settled over many years, and Ward added that some had been 'invited' there by the chieftains of Ummattūr, under whose suzerainty the Nilgiris had rested for a period. This story suggests that some Badagas, refugees from famine rather than Islam, had settled in the hills as part of a pacification programme aimed at increasing the revenue that came from there.[12] But others, it is popularly supposed, fled from Moslem rulers who wanted to marry or, worse, seduce good-looking Hindu girls. In search of a refuge from that looming threat their families travelled in some cases for over 100 km. On reaching the Nilgiri Hills the women were given facial tattoos and dressed in white cloths (as they still sometimes are) to resemble Kota or Iṟula tribal women, while men adopted the embroidered Toda shawl for greater warmth (Pls. 4, 16), something one would never have seen in Mysore. In effect, a conscious and lasting attempt was being made to resemble in appearance the hill tribes and to adopt a tribal model of social organization that might promote a peaceful adaptation, while perhaps frustrating the worst intentions of these Moslem soldiers.[13]

The early pattern of occupancy was one of scattered homesteads in widely scattered parts of the plateau. The clusters of small wood-and-clay huts[14] developed into lineage centres and so into hamlets, usually maintaining strict exogamy. Upon marriage a bride moved to her husband's settlement. Elopement or marriage by capture were by no means unknown occurrences, to which Toda men sometimes lent their support. Until the advent of a local *Pax Britannica* in the early nineteenth century, the houses were built around three sides of a plaza, with its open side facing downhill for defensive purposes (Bacon 1840: 206). In modern times only De:na:ḍu on the eastern edge has preserved something of that plan; the other hill villages, of which there are 434 more, are laid out as several parallel lines of houses running along a hillside. Traditionally the senior brother among the patrilineal descendants of the founder has been the village headman (Diag. 8, p. 103). As is true of headmen across peasant

India, his functions were to dispense justice, perform certain ritual activities, manage the social order, control access to land, and in pre-British times collect tribute. Neighbouring villages (*haṭṭi*), although often of different lineages and even of different phratries, grouped themselves together for protective purposes under the headmanship of one prominent village into what I have called communes (*u:r/u:ru*).[15] Thus Ke:ti, for example, is the leading village in Ke:ti commune (Pl. 1), which embraces 24 other contiguous villages, nearly all belonging to one maximal lineage (*kuḍumbu*). The village headman, a Gauḍa from Ke:ti, is also the headman of the commune. The division of Poranga:ḍ, for another example, into communes and village settlements is illustrated in Map 4.

To summarize our conclusions briefly, migration from Mysore[16] probably had begun by the mid-sixteenth century, and then became more intensive during the anarchy that followed the battle of Talikōta (1565) and the collapse of the Vijayanagara Empire. The question of when the immigration ceased depends on several items of historical evidence: Fr. Fenicio saw some Badagas at Me:lkunda in 1603; undoubtedly the Oḍeyas, Kumba:ras and Be:ḍas came late in that same century; and scarcely any new villages have been formed since British people arrived in 1819.[17] The answer thus lies between these two dates, and I conclude that before 1819 the Badagas had created a closed community in this place, as Keys (1812) implies. The absence of any Vaishnavites among them favours an earlier dating for the termination of their migrations.[18] What led to their ultimate synœcism as a single multi-clan community, we can only guess but it reflects the need to maintain kin relationships in an alien environment.

In the following chapter we will examine how these clusters of villages and waves of immigrants became organized into the phratries by the development of reciprocal marriage regulations.

NOTES

1. See Ward 1821: lxx. *Baḍaga* is pronounced with stress on the first syllable and a retroflexed *ḍ*.
2. They do not intermarry with other Badagas but find their spouses either within their own phratry or from castes also called Kumba:ras and Be:ḍas in southern Mysore.
3. The first European to write of any Badagas was St. Francis Xavier,

who in 1542-44 described them unflatteringly as a 'horde of plundering ruffians', 'bloodthirsty horsemen', and 'savage brigands'; cf. Coleridge 1872, vol. 1: 218, 234-35. But these people are said to have been royal tax gatherers in Travancore, where they bore the name Badagas or Vadhougers simply in reference to their northern origin. They greatly oppressed St. Francis' converts among the Travancore fisherfolk, we are told; Coleridge 1872, vol. 1: *passim*, and Thurston & Rangachari 1909, vol. 7: 266. Elsewhere they are stated to have come from Vijayanagara; Maffei 1589, vol. 1 (pt. 4): 431; Bertrand 1848: 2; Coleridge 1872, vol. 1: 219, n. 12. It seems unlikely that these people had any connection whatever with the Nilgiri Badagas though, especially as some authorities considered them to have been Telugu speakers; Bertrand 1848: 2, n. 1; Grigg 1880: 219; Natesa Sastri 1892: 830-31.

4. India now has perhaps six million Lingayats. Except for the districts of Kolhapur (in Maharashtra), Hyderabad (Andhra Pradesh), Coimbatore and the Nilgiris, they are found solely within Karnataka state.
5. Belli Gowder was a Badaga antiquarian *manqué*; in his unpublished notes (kept by his descendants in Accaṇakal) he, perhaps mistakenly, took this date for 1212; Belli Gowder 1938-41: 5.
6. Of course, since Jagor's posthumous book was edited from his notes by the Indologist Albert Grünwedel, there is a possibility that this date is *his* estimate. Another casual visitor in the later nineteenth century, Madame Blavatsky, in her quite preposterous account, first says '600', then '700' and finally 'about a thousand years ago'! (She got her information from Gen. Henry R. Morgan, a forester, Theosophist and local resident, with whom she was staying.) Some modern Badagas have cited such early dates, but always without any corroboration or context. Clearly, some of the more casual authors mentioned in Table 1, like Madame Blavatsky, were repeating comments they had heard at the Ooty Club rather than investigating the question.
7. Francis 1908: 129; his claim that Badaga has *beṭṭa* for modern Kannaḍa *beṭṭu* ('hill') is inexact.
8. Congreve 1847: 96-98; Grigg 1880: 243; Sewell 1882: 226; Price 1908: 221. (Price introduces a word of caution by suggesting the *aureus* dug up in Ootacamund could well have been in a much later burial; 1908: 144.) There is a grant of 1120 CE stating that Vishṇuvardhana, the first Hoysaḷa king, 'turned the Nila mountain into a city'; Hayavadana Rao 1908: 92. (He is the first of numerous Hoysaḷa and Vijayanagara kings to bear the honorary title *Nīlagiri-sādhāra*, 'subduer of the Nilgiris', which occurs in 15 other inscriptions between 1255 and the sixteenth century.) The Toda name for this area south of Ootacamund is *poṉ ṫïṭ* – 'gold mountain', and gold was formerly obtained from quartz here; *South of India Observer* 1880: 6; Francis 1908: 357.

9. Belli Gowder 1923-41: 24-26; and 1938-41: 5-6; Hockings 2012: 660-61. It was the grandfather of Tu:ne:ri's founder who migrated with his followers from Mysore, at about the time the Vijayanagara Empire collapsed. But at least some part of the Tu:ne:ri population derived from Maḍitore, and there are still ritual connections between the two villages. I have heard, however, that the headman of Śo:lu:ru had some kind of 'jurisdictional mandate' (perhaps the 'kutchery' referred to below, p. 66, n. 7) even prior to the establishment of Tu:ne:ri; so that possibly there were a few Badaga settlers on the hills even before 1600. In the later twentieth century the Badagas were only practising adult marriage, and the generation length was then 26 years (Hockings 1999: 144-45); but earlier, when girls married at around puberty and there were no schools, it could have been no more than 20 years.
10. He reports three 'villages', although there may have been more at the time, especially if the word *u:r* (commune) had been inaccurately translated as 'village' or if other settlers later considered Badagas were not then treated as such, or indeed were simply not known of in that part of the plateau. An inscription on a dolmen at Me:lu:ru relating to a tiger and a grant bears the Sāka date 1518 (i.e. 1596 CE; cf. also Pl. 3), but since it is in Tamil it may have nothing to do with the Badagas, whose literati (if any) would presumably have written in Kannaḍa; Breeks 1873: 102-03; Grigg 1880: 240. But Hayavadana Rao (1908: 100) disagrees with this view, believing the dolmen to have been erected more recently by two Gauṇḍans.
11. The possibility of a quite recent arrival of some Badagas was implied in Ouchterlony's report: 'They admit that before the days of the East India Company [i.e. before 1799] they used to pay one-sixth of their produce to the todars, but that was when their number was small; and *when more of their tribe came from the north country* to join them, and when they began to imbibe notions of independence from the Europeans, they reduced their tribute . . .' (Ouchterlony 1848/58: 278; italics added). We may recall too Sir Richard Burton's 1851 comment that they 'immigrated from the plains in the days of Hyder or Tippoo' (1851 [1991]: 334); evidently not a modern notion.
12. Ward 1821: lxx-lxxi; Harkness 1832: 109. Certain Badaga villages still claim to have been founded by an official from the Ummattūr chiefdom; see Chapter 2.
13. Benbow 1930: 1-3; Karl 1945: 1. A reference to the Mysorean practice of wearing a *sāri* is to be found in the funeral symbolism, wherein a female corpse is offered a piece of coloured cloth (*e:baṇṇa*; Hockings 2001: 11-12). Legend maintains that when the seven brothers of Maduve clan were fleeing from Mysore they left behind a baby slung from the rafters in a *sāri*. In token of their grief the women never more used *sāris* or cradles after settling in the Nilgiris, it is said.

14. The village of Bandime, near Wellington, for example, consisted solely of 'five huts, four cattle sheds, one buffalo enclosure and two stone idols' in 1850; Sutton 2009: 36.
15. This usage accords with the definition in recent editions of Webster's *Dictionary*, e.g. 1967: 460. At present there are 38 communes on the plateau: 15 in Poranga:ḍ, 10 in Me:kuna:ḍ (and one abandoned), 8 in Todana:ḍ, and 5 in Kunda. See below, p. 208.
16. There have been a few modern Badaga theorists who claim for the community an overseas origin as Jews or a northern origin as Buddhists from Bengal, Assam or Nepal; these ideas are based on totally flimsy parallels in culture or vocabulary and have no historic basis. Even so, they have acquired a little currency in recent years.
17. Many Badagas now believe it was the excesses of Tipu Sultan's regime that prompted the migration; but the better informed admit that this would not allow sufficient time depth to encompass the history and consolidation of the community. Dabbakambe, founded near Kotagiri around 1930, is the only case of a very new Badaga village.
18. Rhiem (1900: 499-500) claims one unidentified village as Vaishṇavite. This was perhaps Pannamaḍe hamlet, adjoining Hulikal, which has a temple to Rangana:ta; cf. Jagor 1876: 202. There have actually been several villages which, over the past century, have built Vaishṇavite temples, including Iḍukore, Ka:ṭe:ri, Muttina:ḍ, Nundua, and Tanga:ḍu.

CHAPTER 2

Origins of the Badaga Phratries

We shall now review legends of how the various clans and phratries became established on the hills, to clarify the history of their intermittent migration. The recently formed Christian phratry will not be considered at this point, however, as it is mainly relevant to my discussion of modern cultural change.[1] The Badaga Christians, whether Protestant or Catholic, are today distributed among 14 intermarrying clans that trace their descent from six of the Hindu phratries.

The social categories in what follows are treated roughly in order of social superiority. That hierarchy is not accepted, however, by Ha:ruvas and their supporters. As Ha:ruvas come from the Bra:ma sept they have in the past century laid claim to an origin as Brahmins, and hence see themselves as superior to Oḍeyas and all other Badagas. At the other extremity they consider the Kumba:ras and Be:ḍas to rank below Toreyas, since the traditional occupations of the former groups – potters and huntsmen – could well place them below Toreya servants in the caste ideology of the Indian plains, where such craftsmen have commonly been treated as Untouchables. The great majority of Badagas, in contrast, place Oḍeyas at the top and Toreyas at the bottom of their social hierarchy.

OḌEYAS

The highest-ranking Badaga Lingayats are generally acknowledged to have been among the later groups to arrive. The contention that they were already Lingayat at that time (Macleane 1893: 64) hardly provides a clue to the date of their migration, for their sect was established back in the mid-twelfth century (a date that constitutes a *terminus post quem*). Within sixty years of the death of the founder Basava (ca 1106–68 CE) this egalitarian Hindu faith had spread across the Kannaḍa-speaking region. It became the state religion when

King Vijāya Woḍeyar ascended the Vijayanagara throne in 1399, and remained so until 1610. However a distant descendant of his, Rāja Woḍeyar (who ruled from 1578 to 1617), drove the eponymous Oḍeya chieftain Uḍaiya Rāya of Ummattūr up into the Nilgiris and captured his realm in 1613. The Badaga Oḍeyas now claim to have come up with this man and to be descended through him from the royal house of Mysore (Pope 1879: 346-47, note; Grigg 1880: 218-20, 225; Natesa Sastri 1892: 754-55; Rice 1897, vol. 2: 296, 364; Hayavadana Rao 1930, vol. 5: 862; Hockings 2012: 541-46). Some came from the Lingayat monastery at Angala and first settled at a subsequently abandoned village called Ukkupa:ḷe near Ćinna Kunnu:r, on the northern edge of the Nilgiri Plateau. Traditionally these were the Oḍeyas of Maduve clan, who had previously been Jangama priests. When other Oḍeyas arrived from Tagaḍūr they formed a separate clan called Ko:ve:ru, as they were of that sept. Yet other Oḍeyas came to the Nilgiris from a monastery at Saragūr, and since that had been a village in the former Hindu kingdom of Kongu this particular clan of Oḍeyas have ever since been nicknamed Kongaru ('Kongu people') by other Badagas. That the Oḍeyas had diverse origins is implied by the fact that they belong to seven septs (*kolas*), which is a rather a large number (see below, pp. 108-10); only the much larger Gauḍa section springs from nearly as many. Later on, when Tipu's troops had seized the Nilgiri fortress of Male Ko:ṭe, an Ummattūr outpost, the Oḍeyas who were dependent on its chiefs were reportedly left destitute, yet they remained on the hills.[2]

The relative recency of this Oḍeya migration derives some support from Badaga dialectology. As mentioned, there are perhaps six dialects of the language, three of these seemingly distinctive by reason of geography: speakers living in the Kundena:ḍ, Hasanu:ru and Wainad areas used to be quite isolated from the main part of the community, a situation that would have encouraged the growth of separate dialects in the course of several centuries. The differentiation of Oḍeya and of Kumba:ra–Be:ḍa from Standard Baḍagu cannot, however, be explained in geographic terms, for the Oḍeyas, Kumba:ras and Be:ḍas live in or beside villages where Standard Baḍagu is spoken. Only if we postulate that these three groups came speaking a more modern form of Kannaḍa than the earlier immigrants who spoke a medieval caste-dialect can we account for this disparity.[3] Their own legend fully bears out this hypothesis: as we

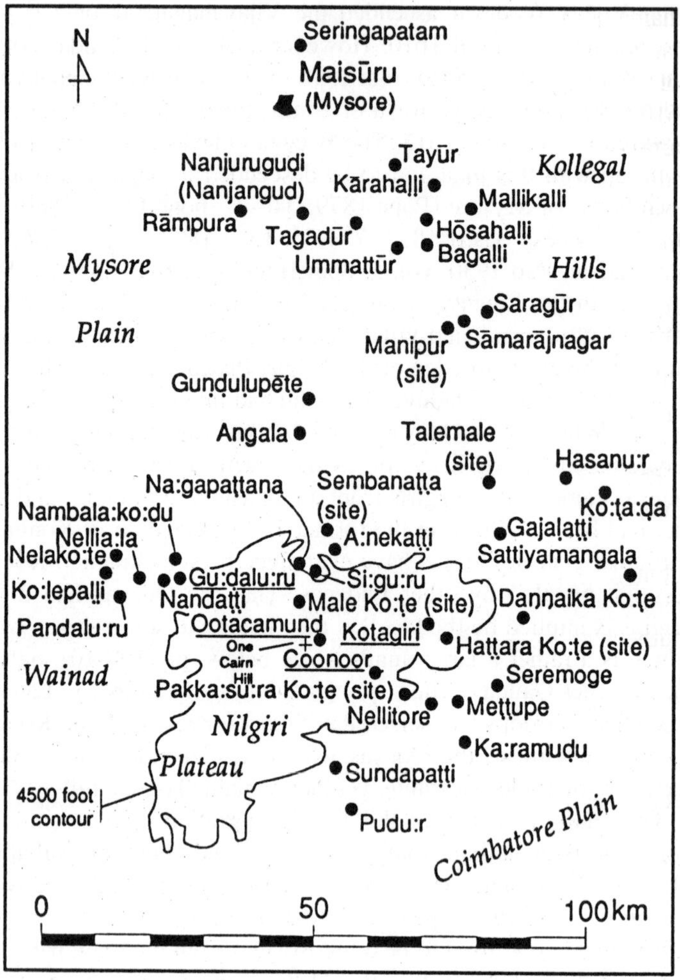

Map 1: Sketch map to illustrate the migrations of the Badagas

have mentioned, they claim to have all come to the hills together in the service of an Ummattūr chieftain when the Gauḍas had already arrived, the Oḍeyas as Lingayat priests, the Kumba:ras as palace servants, the Be:ḍas as huntsmen and tribute collectors. Not only do the Oḍeyas claim to be descended from the royal house, however (Metz 1864: 48-49; Grigg 1880: 220; Natesa Sastri 1892: 754-55); the Kumba:ras also maintain they 'belonged to' the ruling family of

Chāmarāj Woḍeyar, though this was most probably a servile rather than a kin relationship, particularly as this phratry was Shaivite (but not Lingayat), while the royal family has been Vaishnavite since 1610. The fact that the Oḍeyas speak a dialect distinct from Kumba:ra–Be:ḍa reflects former class distinctions. As in many parts of India, the orthodox vegetarian high-status Oḍe:yaru priests seemed to speak differently from the low-status, meat-eating servants of the chieftain, for the two groups did not intermarry or mix socially.

KONGARU

Although this name is applied to many Oḍeyas and is also an epithet for a stupid fellow, *Kongaru* literally means 'people from the plains', i.e. from the nearby medieval kingdom of Kongu.

There are several villages of Badagas called Kongaru; this is the name of a high-ranking clan too, aside from other usages of the word. Reputedly the Kongaru of Ha:laṭṭi were descended from concubines in the service of the chieftain of Male Ko:ṭe. Other Kongaru were Lingayats who, like the Adigaris, had come from Saragūr in southern Mysore. Their traditional occupation, up to 1900, was said to have been that of temple custodians and priests (Rhiem 1900: 499-500). They are considered as the descendants of an Oḍeya man and a Gauḍa woman. Again we come upon a tale of some Kongaru having fallen away from their principles and denied *lingas* (Pl. 16) because one of their youths ate meat to please a low-caste girl whom he loved (Metz 1864: 49-50; Grigg 1880: 221; Tignous 1911: 117; Hockings 2012: 544).

HA:RUVAS

This clan's name is the Kannaḍa word for 'Brahmin'.[4] Now a distinct clan, Ha:ruvas press the claim to Brahmin origin although local legend does not fully support this. Instead it is generally believed that the Ha:ruvas were a group of priests (of a sept called Bra:ma) who accompanied some Gauḍas, though not the earliest group, when they entered the hills.[5] They came from Hōsahaḷḷi-Girubeṭṭa (or else perhaps Hacciṇi Nāgapaṭṭana), and since they brought no women with them were unable to maintain the endogamy that is so fundamental for all Brahmins.[6] For a while they intermarried with the Gauḍas of

Kasturi clan – itself said to have been descended from fallen-away Brahmins – and in later years Ha:ruvas also married Kongaru, Adigaris and Kaṇakkas. Up till the eighteenth century the shortage of marriageable women, which had prompted some fraternal polyandry and perhaps occasional misalliances with Kuṟumba or Iṟula women, was somewhat aggravated by the infrequent practice of *sati* (suttee) among Ha:ruva, Gauḍa, even Toreya widows. This custom came to an end, probably under Moslem influence, before the British had reached the hills, and all Badaga widows have been able to remarry freely ever since, while polyandry has long since disappeared in the community.[7]

Although Ha:ruvas may marry Gauḍas there is a legend that the two groups were originally 'brothers' and thus agnates. When these people first came to the hills, so the tale goes, they were wandering through a forest in search of food. At last they found some flesh and many ate it; those who abstained became Ha:ruvas, priests to the rest (Belli Gowder 1923-41: 45; Benbow 1930: 9, 11). Another legend on the same theme relates that the founders of Me:lu:r Hosaṭṭi, the first Ha:ruva village, were brothers named Uliajjan and Guruajja. The elder of them once decided to eat flesh, but when Guruajja found out he went off to found the villages of Tanga:ḍu and Ha:lakore; their descendants went on to found other hamlets. Uliajjan became an outcast whose descendants have been absorbed into various Gauḍa villages (Jogi Gowder, no date: 1-2). The sequence of founding of the Ha:ruva villages is shown in Diag. 1.

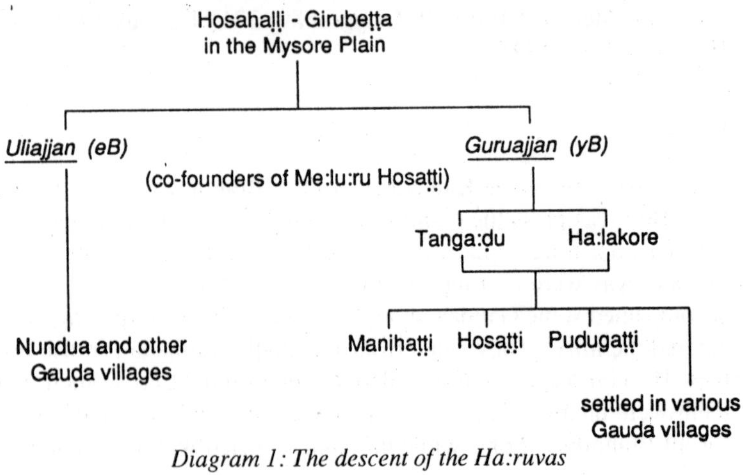

Diagram 1: The descent of the Ha:ruvas

ADIGARIS

This clan recall that their Virashaiva ancestors, quite distinct from the Oḍeyas, came in a large group from Mallikaḷḷi via Saragūr (in southern Mysore) and settled at Nellitore, a place sacred to them on the edge of the Coimbatore Plain, directly below Pakka:su:ra Ko:ṭe. It was here that the Virashaiva saint Kariabeṭṭa Ra:ya had earlier drowned himself. Until recently the ruins of their houses were visible; the pool where he drowned still exists (Zagarell 1994: 193-94). After half-a-century there the community was nearly exterminated by malaria, but six surviving men moved up onto the plateau. They stayed for a while at Tudu:ru and Taḍasumorahaṭṭi, then founded the first five of the 16 villages that Adigaris still inhabit (Francis 1908: 316). The sequence of their foundation is shown in Diagram 2. The founder of Adigaraṭṭi was then made a magistrate (*adigari*) by a power, presumably at Ummattūr, who was nominally ruling over the Nilgiris. The Oḍeya families already living there could not believe that the Adigaris were truly Lingayats (perhaps because they were themselves of a more conservative Virashaiva sect), and therefore refused marriage with them. It was this exclusiveness which drove the Adigaris, Kaṇakkas and Kaggusis into marrying non-Lingayats, though more usually Adigaris marry Kaṇakkas.

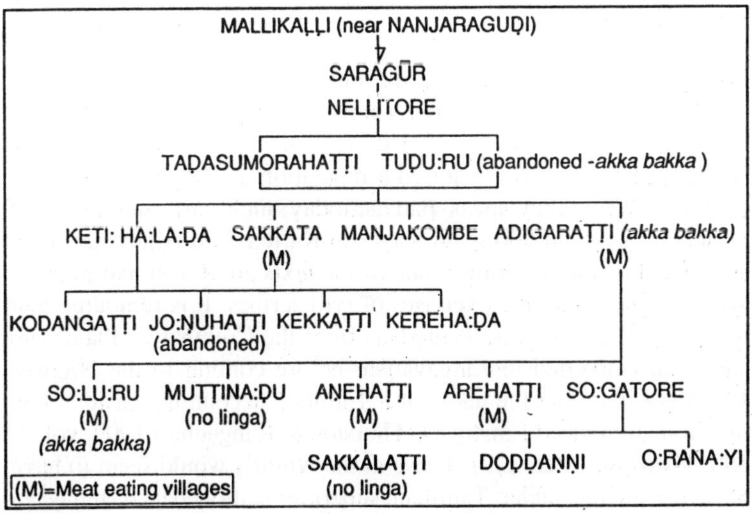

Diagram 2: The Descent of the Adigaris

Certain of the villages (marked by *M* in this Diagram) are now non-vegetarian. There are legendary explanations for this phenomenon. Just as in the story of the founding of Me:lu:r Hosaṭṭi, it is said that Sanga, the founder and headman of Adigaraṭṭi, was starving and hence began to shoot birds and eat them.[8] His younger brother Linga was so incensed by this that he went away and founded another village, So:gatore. In Adigaraṭṭi and several other villages the founding Adigaris were obliged to marry local Gauḍa women who retained their own customs, among them the eating of meat. The descendants of one man who married a Solaga tribeswoman at Śo:lu:ru became Gauḍas too. In Sakkata the Adigari was obliged to marry a Toreya woman, who also could not become a vegetarian.[9] Their offspring married Gauḍas and followed Gauḍa customs, it is said; but their recent descendants in that village are Toreyas.

Since that time a separate clan of meat-eating Adigaris has been in existence, people who are not permitted to wear the *linga* (Pl. 16) and who only intermarry with Gauḍas. To all intents and purposes their four villages are now considered to be Gauḍa. More recently two other villages, Muṭṭina:ḍu and Sakkaḷaṭṭi, have stopped wearing the *linga* yet retained vegetarianism, and they are still considered to be Adigaris for marriage purposes.

KAṆAKKAS

Prior to 1819 Kaṇakkas were the only literate people in the hills. They were brought there more recently than all other Badagas by the commander of Haṭṭara Ko:ṭe (Uḍura:ya Ko:ṭe) to keep the village accounts; but they also acquired a reputation as local therapists and exorcists. While they speak Badaga today, their early writings, still preserved on about 500 palm leaves in Ka:ṭe:ri and Ajju:r, are in an antiquated script of Tamil. Some of the texts are devotional in character, but many are the exercises of tyro scribes. It is rumoured that in origin Kaṇakkas were Gauṇḍans from the Coimbatore Plain who had been converted to Lingayatism before coming to the Nilgiris. *Kaṇakkaṉ* is in fact the name of a Tamilian accounting caste, a few of whom are indeed Lingayats (Thurston & Rangachari 1909, vol. 3: 150; Winslow 1862: 229). These in the Nilgiris would seem to have been for awhile under Tamilian superiors stationed at Daṇṇayaka Ko:ṭe or nearby Koḷḷantore.[10]

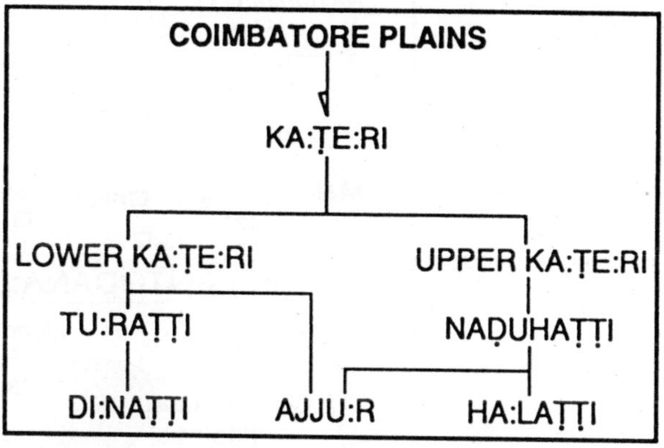

Diagram 3: The descent of the Kaṇakkas

The first Kaṇakka village to be founded was Ka:ṭe:ri, towards the centre of the plateau. The man who started it was Jambulingayya, a secretary of the chieftain Bijjaṇarasu. He had two wives whose descendants occupied upper and lower Ka:ṭe:ri respectively; and later generations from each of these neighbourhoods founded other Kaṇakka villages, as indicated in Diag. 3.

Both the Kaṇakkas and the Adigaris began to intermarry and with Ha:ruvas too soon after settling in the hills; their numbers must have been so few. Adigaris also married Gauḍa women, while Kaṇakkas intermarried with Kaggusis and Kongaru. These latter steps were forced on the Lingayat clans by a shortage of girls in their own community at that time; properly they should only have married other Lingayats.

KAGGUSIS

These people originated in Tagaḍūr, from whose Mysorean monastery they left as a band of refugee Jangamas or monks; one clan of Oḍeyas had an identical origin. They first settled at the village of Kaggusi, and there left off wearing *lingas* because of the necessity to marry with local Gauḍa women and the pollution of their *lingas* (Pl. 16) that would follow as a consequence. Later they spread out to establish or occupy another six villages; but then, on the occasion of a severe drought, some retreated from Kaggusi to the eastern lowlands and founded a village near Hasanu:ru, where they still live (Hockings 2012: 546).

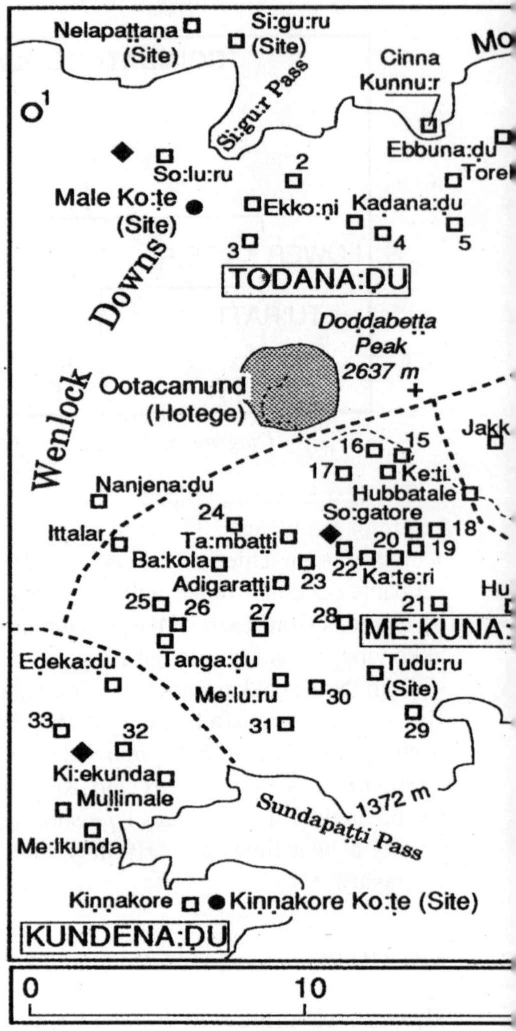

Map 2: The Nilgiri

KEY: A few ancient *fortresses* are marked as (Site).[11] K. Kota villages.[12] Selected villages (in alphabetical order): 16, Accanakal; 6, Ajju:r; 10, Be:rage:ṇi; Bikkaṭṭi; 13, Dabbakambe; 27, De:vaso:le (bazaar); 8, Dimbaṭṭi; 14, Eḍapiḷḷu; 26. Ha:lakore; 4, Ha:laṭṭi; 7, Honnatale; 15, Hulla:ḍa; 2, Hullaṭṭi; 3, Kallaṭṭi; 9, Kappaṭṭi; 17, Kereha:ḍa; 28, Ko:ḍe:ru; 29, Kolekombe (bazar); 25, Maṇihaṭṭi; 31, Manjakombe; 32, Mañju:ru; 30, Me:lu:ru

Plateau

Hosaṭṭi; 23, Muṭṭina:ḍu; 18, Ne:rikambe; 24, Nundua; 1, Ö·nṭöw (a Toda temple). 22, O:rana:yi; 19, Sakkaḷaṭṭi; 21, Se:la:se (bazaar); 12, So:lu:r-maṭṭa (bazaar); 11, Tumbimale; 5, Tu:ne:ri; 20, Tu:raṭṭi. Villages that head COMMUNES are marked on the map by name, as also are the modern TOWNS (stippled). The four traditional divisions (*na:ḍu*) are indicated in BLOCK letters.

GAUḌAS

Not only are there ten times as many Gauḍas as members of any other phratry, their legendary history is very much more complex than any other. So too is their social structure, for the Gauḍas have belonged to six exogamous septs (*kolas*, see below, pp. 108-10).

It is remarkable that, aside from the Lingayats, who mainly originated in Saragūr and Angala, most of the Badaga community came from a cluster of villages in a small area of about 20 by 30 km., which lies just to the east of the Mysore temple centre of Nanjangud (Hockings 2012: 417-21).

Three facts are relevant to a dating of the Gauḍa arrival on the Nilgiris. They themselves claim to have arrived in the Nilgiris ahead of any other group, and Lingayats and Ha:ruvas confirm that their ancestors found Gauḍas there when they first arrived. Secondly, the paramount chief, a Gauḍa living at Tu:ne:ri, can number 19 generations of ancestors, which would put their arrival back to about the year 1600. Thirdly, we may recall that Fr. Fenicio saw Badagas at the village of Melcuntaõ in 1603, and mentioned their relations with Todas. Assuming this was just a Portuguese spelling for the Gauḍa village of Me:lkunda, lying at the head of the Sundapaṭṭi Pass in Kundena:ḍ – and no other village offers a closer identification than this (cf. Walker 1998: 106) – we deduce that at least some segment of the Gauḍa population had immigrated a century or so before the Kumba:ra, Be:ḍa and various Lingayat groupings did.

This accords with a Badaga tradition that the very first group of migrants were three brothers of the Kasturi sept or clan, led by Bijjana Ra:ju (or Bijjaṇarasu), who came from Kārahaḷḷi and settled in the Ke:ti Valley, Kundena:ḍ and Ćinna Kunnu:r.[11] Later the eastern half of the plateau was settled, we are told, by seven brothers, their sister Elingi with her husband, a cousin. Later yet other Gauḍas including descendants of five of these brothers went off to Todana:ḍ and Me:kuna:ḍ divisions (Diag. 4; Hockings 2012: 815-16).

It is not impossible that the Kasturi Gauḍas had the same Virashaiva origins as the Adigaris or Oḍeyas. Some hold the belief that they were at first vegetarians and Lingayats. As so often happened in those legendary times a Kasturi tasted meat, for which his daughter made him give up his *linga* to her husband, a Lingayat Adigari. Thereafter the Kasturis intermarried mainly with other Gauḍas.[12] A comparable story maintains that some Gauḍas of Neḍuguve are descended from 'Kongaru', i.e. Oḍeyas of Selandi clan, after some fell away from their phratry's principles, and they were denied wearing personal *lingas* when one of their youths ate meat to please a Gauḍa girl whom he loved.[13]

Kasturi (musk), we may note, is also the name of a sept among the Kanarese Okkaligas (Thurston and Rangachari 1909, vol. 1: 75, and 3: 256; see below, p. 109). This too reflects the Gauḍas' origin, (and many Badagas at the 1891 census enumeration actually gave their caste as 'Okkaliga').[14] Today few Badagas agree to a connection with the Okkaliga community, perhaps because there are thousands of poor Okkaligas on the Nilgiri Plateau today, recent immigrants working there as labourers and with whom Badagas do not associate except as employers or landlords. A more likely explanation, however, is that enumerators in 1891 overlooked the fact that *okkaliga* merely means 'permanent resident' in Baḍagu and is not necessarily considered a clan or caste designation amongst them. Nonetheless there are informants in the Nilgiris and Hasanu:ru who agree to an origin among the Okkaligas of Mysore; and both communities share the same quite distinctive personal names (Hockings 2012: 629-30).

There is an ancient settlement of Okkaligas in the Coimbatore Plain, for example at the village of Nellitore from which the Adigaris and the 'seven brothers' ascended the Nilgiri slopes. The legend of how they got to Nellitore is worth recounting.

> . . . Tippu Sultan wanted to marry an Okkaliga bride. The Okkaligas consented to it at first due to fear of the fanatic king, but subsequently decided to run away. So they dressed up a dog like a bride, left it in the house and then ran away towards the south by the night. They were, it seems, chased by the Muslim troops but luckily there were floods in the river as soon as the Okkaligas crossed it. The Muslim troops finding it not possible to cross the river returned to Mysore and the Okkaligas peacefully settled in the forest marginal areas. (Nambiar & Bharathi 1965: 3)

What is remarkable is that precisely the same legend, admittedly embellished with details from the *Book of Exodus* (xiv, *vv*. 21-30), has been offered by Badagas from both the Nilgiris and Hasanu:ru to flesh out the tale of their flight from Mysore:

> About three hundred years ago one of the Moslem kings desired one of their daughters, and when she refused marriage he threatened to burn and plunder their villages. But the pride of the people was greater than their fear. To find one of their daughters in the harem of a Moslem dog [*sic*] was

something that could not be tolerated . . . ; and so, incited by their priests, they decided to escape . . . . With women, children, livestock, and all their cherished possessions, they swiftly escaped to the bank of a river which divided the wild tribes of the Nilgiris from the province of the sultan . . . a part of the army was hastily sent after the fleeing people, who were by that time near the banks of the Mayar [Moyar], which formed the boundary. But how could they cross over? Strange to say, . . . the river parted and the followers reached the bank on the other side, while the disciples of the Prophet were suddenly swallowed up by the closing waters. (Rhiem 1900: 498, trans.)

As Nellitore is at the foot of the Nilgiri escarpment one is again led to suppose that some Badaga Gauḍas derived from this Okkaliga caste. The probability is indeed high, for most of the Gauḍas admit that they came from farming communities in the plains of southern Mysore, where Okkaligas are today the dominant farming castes.

Another important Gauḍa clan is called Maduve (marriage) (also the name of a sept; see Diag. 4, and Thurston & Rangachari 1909, vol. 4: 292). As was mentioned, it was founded by a family of seven brothers led by one Acciṇi, who fled from Talemale with a sister, Elingi, who was in danger of being ravished by a Moslem chieftain there (Belli Gowder 1923-41: 1; 'Miles' 1951: 69; Hockings 2012: 815-16). 'Each of these brothers is said to have built a house for himself and his family in different parts of the hills, and new villages were constructed by their descendants; so that the Badagas of this class are now scattered over all the tract . . .' (except Todana:ḍ; Metz 1864: 56-57). The sister's husband founded Jakkana:ri village, which thereafter had close affinal relations with the Maduve clan. Two of her brothers, Acciṇi and the blind Kuruḍu, founded numerous villages in Poranga:ḍ (Porangana:ḍu) division, while the other five brothers went off to other divisions. As these people had been subject to the tributary chieftain of Haṭṭara Ko:ṭe the clan was sometimes called Haṭṭara (from *haṭṭaru*, 'retinue'; Metz 1864: 56-57). That chieftain also had a palace north of the Nilgiris, at Talemale, and in the nineteenth century people of that area still interdined with these particular Badaga Gauḍas (Metz 1864: 47-48; today the palace is in ruins; Nicholson 1898: 426).

Nineteenth-century writing on Badagas mentions numerous other 'castes' and 'sects', but they are in reality clans or lineages within the Gauḍa phratry, and others are septs; for example, the Du:ma, Kuṇaja, Ma:ri, Ma:ṇikka and Beḷḷi (Metz 1864: 57-60; Shortt and Ouch-

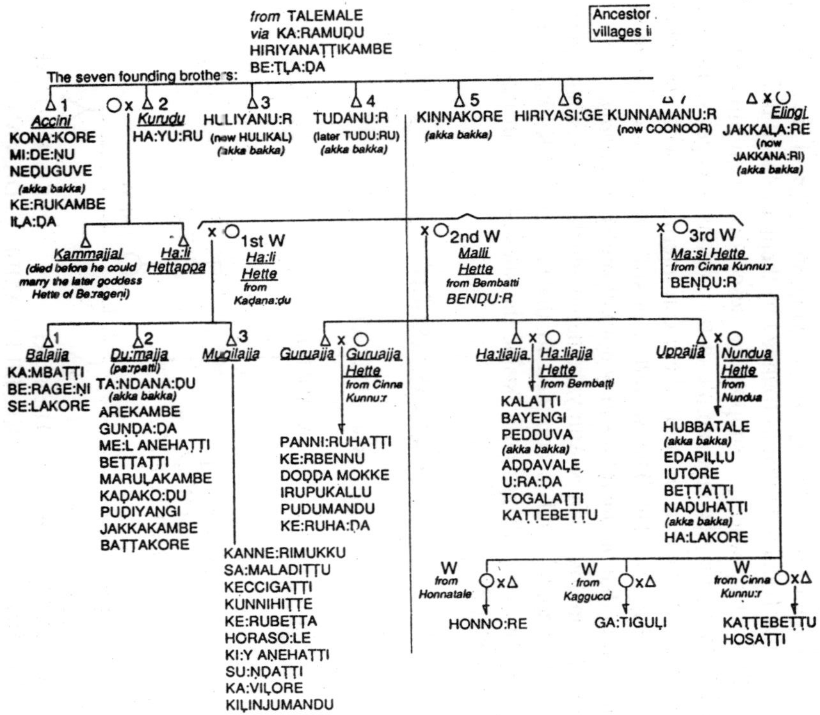

Diagram 4: The Descent of the Maduve Clan of Gauḍas

terlony 1868: 58-59; Grigg 1880: 221-22; Macleane 1893: 64; Thurston & Rangachari 1909, vol. 1: 75; on septs see below, pp. 108-10).

The total number of named lineages among the Gauḍas, such as Du:ma and Kuṇaja, must approach a hundred; some have legends of origin, too, as do their clans. Ma:ri clan, for instance, to which the paramount chief belongs, migrated from villages near the great temple of Nanjangud (Nañjaraguḍi) carrying an image of the goddess Ma:ri;[15] the Todana:ḍ villages founded by them are listed in Diag. 5. The Beḷḷi clan, who are supposedly descended from silversmiths (*beḷḷi*, silver), may be an example of the various lineages started by itinerant tradesmen: commonly these can intermarry with any other Gauḍa lineage or clan. The Selandi sept still preserves a vestige of totemism in that the members may not kill spiders (*selandi*).

One anomalous clan is Anniya, a name which signifies 'strangers, different people', and is confined to the Gauḍas of Ku:kallu and Nanjena:ḍu, two villages built beside the sites of ancient mud-forts (see Chapter 3).

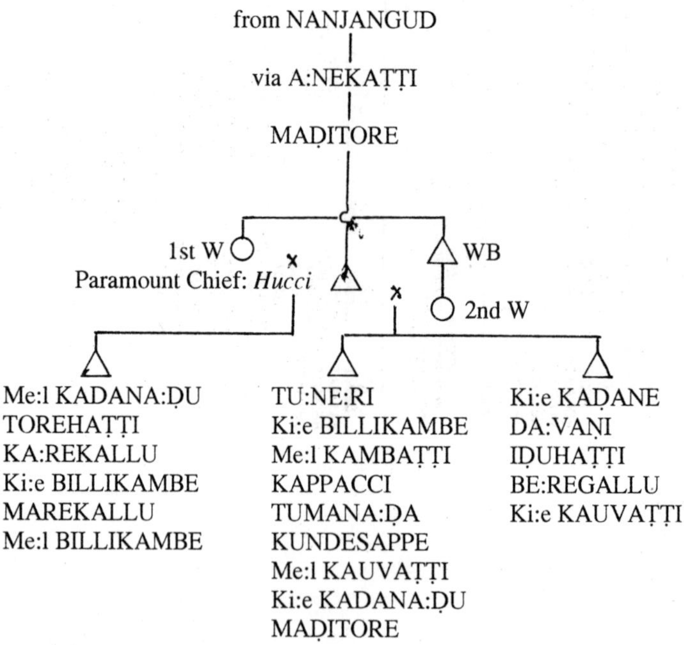

Diagram 5: The villages of Ma:ri clan of the Gauḍas

On the fringes of the plateau one can find quite atypical marriage arrangements. In the southernmost village of Kiṇṇakore, the Gauḍas have, for example, a lineage intermarrying with Gauḍas of the other Kundena:ḍ villages and also with Gauḍas and Kanarese Okkaligas living at the foot of the hills in Aṭṭapa:ḍi and Pudu:r.[16] In twelve villages around Hasanu:ru, 40 km. northeast of the plateau, there live about a thousand Badagas forming three phratries. They usually find it more convenient now to intermarry among their neighbours (observing clan and sept exogamy) than make the long journey to the Nilgiris in search of spouses (who would often be unwilling to settle in such a remote area anyway; Hockings 2012: 135-36, and below).

WAINAD GAUḌAS

The small community of Wainad Gauḍas (totalling 951 in 1970, and perhaps 1,500 today) is descended from Badaga Gauḍas (Hockings 2012: 980-81). Apart from their own assertion of this and their continuing intermarriage with Gauḍas of Todana:ḍ certain aspects of the material culture underline the connection: similar traditional nose, ear, finger and ankle ornaments have been worn by both communities; they have the same typically Badaga cuisine (Hockings et al., in Hockings 2012: 237-40; and their dialects are very similar. Furthermore, it is recognized that the people of Nandaṭṭi (in the Wainad), for instance, are agnates to the villagers of Nundua and Ta:mbaṭṭi (in the Nilgiris), and that thc Nandaṭṭi Gauḍas had settled at Gu:ḍalu:ru in the Wainad prior to founding Nandaṭṭi sixteen generations ago.[17] Once every few years a party of Wainad Gauḍas attends the chariot-dragging festival in Nundua as a mark of their relationship. Śo:lu:ru (in Todana:ḍ) has a similar link with each of the twenty-one Wainad villages.

The migration down into the Wainad occurred probably in the eighteenth century: it was occasioned by a shortage of land around some Nilgiri villages, and by the acute poverty of farmland in the Kundena:ḍ area. The Mantadan Chettis (not considered Badagas; Hockings 2012: 559-60) amongst whom the Wainad Gauḍas settled, came originally from the same Kongu country which had been the homeland of many Gauḍas. Unlike Gauḍas, however, these Chettis settled directly in the Wainad during medieval times, without pausing first on the Nilgiri Plateau. So close is the association between

Mantadan Chettis and the Todana:ḍ Badagas that these two communities also used to exchange visits on the occasion of some festivals and funerals. Certain Chettis living in the Muḍumalai Park of the Wainad (now in the Nilgiri Biosphere Reserve) are called Huliya:ḷa Gauḍas; they went there from the nearby Badaga village of Hullaṭṭi, on the Nilgiris, but now intermarry only with Mantadan Chettis. The Wainad Gauḍas otherwise do not marry with these Chettis although they did so in earlier centuries. The two communities interdine and attend each other's ceremonies.

BADAGAS OF HASANU:RU

Some 7 km. east of Hasanu:ru in the Biligiri Rangan Hills are eleven Badaga villages; a twelfth lies in Karnataka, 13 km. to the north of that town. These villages are in jungle clearings at an elevation of a thousand metres, and were established there at least two centuries ago by Badagas who were forced out of the northern part of the Nilgiris by a famine.[18] The Hasanu:ru Gauḍas are explicit that they had been Gangadikāra Gauḍas in Mysore; and they retain precisely the same stories about their flight as are still recounted in the Nilgiris (see above, particularly n. 12; Thurston & Rangachari 1909, vol. 1: 75, and 3: 256; Nambiar & Bharathi 1965, 3; Hockings 2012: 135-36).

TOREYAS

No legend of a separate origin has been collected from the Toreyas, and no historical connection can be traced between them and the Kanarese Toreas or Bestas, though the latter 'are numerous in the southern parts of Mysore . . . [and] are also found in the adjacent districts of Coimbatore and Salem' (Nanjundayya & Ananthakrishna Iyer 1931, vol. 4: 637). The Badaga Toreyas occasionally arrange marriages with this caste; but since the dialects of the two differ the practice is most uncommon. Those Toreas found in the plains are said to have once been fishermen and palanquin-bearers and more recently cultivators, contractors, petty tradesmen and police constables (Thurston & Rangachari 1909, vol. 7: 176). Although it is quite possible that certain Toreyas of this caste went to the Nilgiris, at first in the useful role of palanquin-bearers, and their villages are mostly concentrated on the easternmost part of the hills near the slopes leading up from the Coimbatore Plain, their occupations in the Nilgiris have been cultivators, messengers for the commune headmen and til lthe mid-nineteenth-century weavers; and they had reportedly been menials and watchmen for ancestral Badagas even in Mysore (Harkness 1832: 112; Metz 1864: 59-60). A common origin for some Nilgiri and lowland Toreyas is possible, as both belong to the Na:ga and Beḷḷi septs, among several others (as do the Ālu Kuṟumbas, another local non-Badaga community).

Those of the Nilgiris claim their origin within the Gauḍa phratry and explain their status as being the descendants of sons deputed to do certain chores. The Gauḍas and Ha:ruvas still indeed call them 'sons', an ambiguous term that may either refer to their servile status or suggest they sprang from the unsanctioned unions of Gauḍas (possibly with non-Gauḍa women). One astute nineteenth-century observer said of them: '. . . they are prohibited from intermarrying with the other or high-caste Badagas, as long as they are sons to them . . .' [19]

NOTES

1. See below, pp. 211-46 ; also Diag. 10. There was said to be a Christian community – but most probably not of Badagas – near Avuḷance (Avalanche) in the Kundena:ḍ division in medieval times: Fr. Fenicio came in search of it, and the Todas have a legend about it; cf. Fenicio 1603 [1906]: 719-20; Metz 1864: 44; Hayavadana Rao 1908: 106; Walker 1998: 95-96; Walker, in Hockings 2012: 314-21.
2. Metz 1864: 53. The correct Kannaḍa name for Seringapatam is Sri Raṅga Paṭṭana, whose temple is there. The town is situated on an island about 5 km. long in the Kaveri R. On septs, see below, pp. 108-10; for more details on the Oḍeya migration, see Hockings 2012: 541-44.
3. The Adigaris and Kaṇakkas have a dialect hardly varying from Standard Baḍagu because of their ready intermarriage and frequent social intercourse with Gauḍas, Ha:ruvas and Kaggusis; the Oḍeyas, Be:ḍas, and Kumba:ras are essentially endogamous groupings, and thus culturally a little more apart from the rest.
4. Kittel 1894: 1650; Burrow & Emeneau 1984: no. 4091b. Walhouse's alternative suggestion (1878: 127; cf. Thurston & Rangachari 1909, vol. 1: 73) that the name means 'jumper', and refers to their method of firewalking, is unconvincing. Men of most phratries walk ceremonially across fire, individuals walking or jumping as they choose.

5. Natesa Sastri 1892: 754; Francis 1908: 131; Thurston and Rangachari 1909, vol. 1: 73; Jogi Gowder, no date: 1; Hockings 2012: 406-07; it is a Brahmin sept in Mysore.
6. Metz 1864: 56; Macleane 1893: 64. The same was true of Kaggusis; see above, pp. 37, 123.
7. Harkness 1832: 106-07, note; King 1870: 6, 20-21; Noble 1976: 115-16. One of the Badaga legends about the ancestress Hette is that she committed *sati*; Hockings 1989a: 223-28; Heidemann 2006: 169-212. For vestiges of Badaga polyandry, see Natesa Sastri 1892: 754, 832, and Stuart 1893: 243. Todas and Kuṟumbas practised polyandry until very recent years; Thurston 1906: 108-13.
8. Metz 1864: 50-51; Belli Gowder 1923-41: 28; Hockings 2012: 2, 544-45). Adigaraṭṭi derives from *adigari* (powerful man) and *haṭṭi* (village). A variant of this legend has the early Adigaris following a chieftain who was named Kariabeṭṭa Ra:ya and who, just like Moses, was fated to lead them to the promised land without setting foot on it himself. After passing through Hasanu:ru to Nellitore and staying there for a time, they went on to Aṭṭapa:ḍi, at the foot of the southeast slopes, and some settled there. Their Lingayat descendants still inhabit that village but are now Gauḍas. The chieftain led the remainder on to found another village called Ne:ribennu, in Kundena:ḍ; it no longer exists. After the chieftain had died there some of the settlers went on to Nedika:ḍu, near Adigaraṭṭi, and soon founded the latter village. Descendants of the chieftain's family and retinue thus came to be called 'powerful men' because of their association with him, in recognition of which the *janmis* gave them the duty of village magistrates.
9. The pollution of having eaten meat can be removed from men alone.
10. Metz 1864: 50-54; Grigg 1880: 221; Thurston & Rangachari 1909, vol. 1: 73. The correct name for the outpost usually called Danayakan Kotte or Daṇṇayaka Ko:ṭe (Pl. 2) is Da:na Na:yaka Ko:ṭe, 'the fort of the commander Dāna'; Nicholson 1898: 425-26. It was established in 1318 by Māḍappa Dandanāyaka, who then was ruling over the Nilgiris and Wainad; Rea 1910: 111; Belli Gowder 1923-41: 100; Zagarell 1994: 194. The site is first shown on European maps, as Demicotta or Denaikencotta, in 1778 and 1792 (Gole 1984: 50a). On the site of Koḷḷantore, see pp. 36, 59 and 65.
11. Belli Gowder 1923-41: 29-30; Karl 1945: 2; the eldest, a cripple, had settled at Cinna Kunnu:r. Among the very early villages in Todana:ḍ were Kaḍana:ḍu, settled from Kārahaḷḷi (near Tagaḍūr); Tu:ḍegu:r Ekko:ṇi, from Kavaspāḍi (or Agasvadi) or else Tāyūr; Ćinna Kunnu:r, from Kongahaḷḷi (near Ummattūr); Ebbuna:ḍu, from Urigaddige or Hōsahaḷḷi; Ku:kallu, from Guṇḍulupēṭe; Honnatale, from Honnahaḷḷi; and So:lu:ru, from Sūlūr. The earliest Me:kuna:ḍ villages were Me:lu:ru, settled from Urigaddige or Beḷḷāḍi; Tudu:ru, settled by the fourth

of seven brothers from Poranga:ḍ and later deserted; Ta:mbaṭṭi, also settled from Poranga:ḍ; Ki:yu:ru and Nundua, settled from Urigaddige (the latter said to have been brass-smiths there; Metz 1867: 97); Hulikal, from Honnahaḷḷi; and Ke:ti, from Kongahaḷḷi. The earliest Kundena:ḍ villages were also settled from Kongahaḷḷi. Apart from Honnatale, Ki:yu:ru and Nundua, each of the above Badaga villages became the head of a commune as other hamlets grew up around it; and each is marked as head of a commune by having a ceremonial stone structure called *akka bakka*. This very interesting structure might sound from the name as though it was intended as a monument to the founders of the Vijayanagara Empire in 1336. That dynasty was founded by several sons of Sangama I, of whom the most important were Harihara I and Bukka-Rāya I, 'commonly spoken of in tradition as Hakka and Bukka . . .' (Hayavadana Rao 1930, vol. 2, pt. 3: 1415). Such a symbolic assertion that these early Badaga villages somehow viewed themselves as a part of the Vijayanagara Empire would, if sustainable, be evidence of a date for their establishment well before 1565. But in fact *bakka* cannot be considered as linguistically equivalent to Bukka in Kannaḍa, and the term *akka bakka* really just means today 'a place where grain used to be collected as tribute' (*hakku bakku*) or perhaps just 'a place set apart [ritually]' (Hockings & Pilot-Raichoor 1992: 4). There are now 30 such structures; Heidemann 2006: 2; Hockings 2012: 108, fig. 45; and see p. 68 and Pl. 6.

12. Some call the Kasturis Gangalūru; Metz 1864: 58-59, quite possibly a variant of Gangaḍikara, the name of a large section of Okkaligas.
13. Metz 1864: 49-50; Grigg 1880: 221; Tignous 1911: 117. A variant account is that he thought he had eaten meat, although the item was really a wild vegetable in the curry.
14. Thurston & Rangachari 1909, vol. 1: 74. It may he significant that in the same census certain Okkaligas in Mysore gave their subcaste as *Badagar*; Rice 1897, vol. 1: 229. And Belli Gowder 1923-41: 80 derives only the Kasturi clan from Gangaḍikaras, but Gauḍas of Hasanu:ru claim the same origin.
15. Metz 1864: 47-48, 57-58; he gave the villages as Tayūr and Tagaḍūr. Tayūr had a well-built mud-fortress on a river bank. By 1801 it was in ruins and the countryside showed signs of having been much more cultivated in previous times; Buchanan 1807: 150-51.
16. Fenicio possibly passed through Pudu:r in 1603, causing the Badagas to flee from the jungle; cf. Fenicio 1603 [1906]: 729-30; Walker, in Hockings 2012: 314-21.
17. Baber 1830: 314; for an instance of intermarriage between Nandaṭṭi and So:lu:ru, see Emeneau 1971: 611.
18. This account of their migration has been confirmed by villagers in that area.

19. Natesa Sastri 1892: 755; Thurston & Rangachari 1909, vol. 1: 73. A comparable usage is found in southern Karnataka; Epstein 1962: 181.

CHAPTER 3

The Hill Forts

BE:ḌAS, KUMBA:RAS AND HILL FORTS

For two other small phratries, the Be:ḍas and Kumba:ras, their origins can best be explored in the context of the hill fortresses where they lived. While the history of these forts in themselves is not central to Badaga social history – indeed they were not built either by or for the Badagas, so far as we know – the fortification network forms such a prominent feature of pre-modern relations with powers in the plains that some discussion of the fortresses is appropriate in this place (Hockings 2012: 339-45).

These forts were scattered outposts of Ummattūr, a small town in southern Mysore (with a fortified hilltop at nearby Bāgaḷḷi) which was tributary to the kings of Vijayanagara during the fifteenth and sixteenth centuries, and to the kings of Mysore in the seventeenth and early eighteenth centuries.

> In 1610 one of these, king Rája Wodeyar (Udaiyar) of Mysore, drove out of Seringapatam the Vijayanagar general; and two years later he was granted that place and the Ummattúr country near it by the then nominal king of Vijayanagar. . . . Thenceforth the kings of Mysore became rulers of the Wynaad and titular possessors of the Nilgiri hills, and the latter were apparently under the immediate rule of dependents of theirs called the Udaiyars or Rájas of Ummattur. . . . (Hayavadana Rao 1908: 93; see too Rice 1897, vol. 1: 357, 364; Rea 1910: 115; Hayavadana Rao 1930, vol. 5: 861-62)

As a result of this political situation the plateau became involved in a long military struggle mainly for control of the tribute collection from the Badaga farmers. That tribute was then levied mostly in the form of grain, something that Todas did not produce and which a few hundred Kotas had scarcely any of. This struggle, sometimes between Moslems and Hindus, prompted the construction or capture of certain fortresses, mainly to guard the passes around the foot of

Map 3: Medieval Fortifications in the Nilgiri Area

and leading up into the Nilgiris, but incidentally to terrorize the tiny Badaga population as well. The great majority of these forts are on or below the northern slopes of the Nilgiri massif, from Sultan's Battery in the west to Sattiyamangaḷa town in the east, with relatively few fortresses on other sides (Map 3). The extraordinary visibility, even as far as Seringapatam in those days, allowed commanders of the hill garrisons to detect obvious military manoeuvres in the plains and sometimes guided them to cross the plateau and cut the enemy troops off as they came round the foot of its escarpments.

As an example of such movements a Kota folklorist has described how Haidar Ali attacked the 'king of Madurai', Virapāndya Dēvan, in Daṇṇayaka Ko:ṭe in 1759, but was forced to retreat. The 'king' then sent an army into the Nilgiris to suppress Haidar's hill forts there and this resulted in a battle at the Badaga commune of Tudu:ru (1760) in which Virapāndya lost three thousand troops and Haidar emerged victorious to capture Daṇṇayaka Ko:ṭe for himself, while the beaten troops fled to Salem district.[1] (Tudu:ru was subsequently deserted, the remnants of its ravaged 36-village population settling in the nearby village of Ko:ḍe:ru; Hockings & Pilot-Raichoor 1992: 295-96, 836; Hockings 2012: 960.)

It was during the sixteenth or seventeenth century that a pair of important Nilgiri fortresses were erected, Male Ko:ṭe on the northern rim of the plateau and Haṭṭara Ko:ṭe on the east side (reputedly founded in 1578). A third fort, Pakka:su:ra Ko:ṭe (or Gaganasukki), had been built somewhat earlier on the Hulikal Drug mountain summit to the southeast (Harkness 1832: 104, 107, 124; Hockings 2012: 343-44, 431; see below, pp. 59-61). These forts were strategic outposts of Daṇṇayaka Ko:ṭe, and had commanding views across the plains for miles (Price 1908: 2). Tradition has it that one Ummattūr chieftain established altogether nine fortified settlements in the area, and the ruins of the others may still to be seen below the slopes – for example, at Ma:vaṇṇaḷḷa (cf. Table 2 and Map 3). Also he caused 350 Badaga 'families' to migrate into the hills, probably scattering them in every village (the number is suspiciously close to the '338 idols' that Metz recorded, as well as the total number of plateau villages today; Metz 1864: 61; Belli Gowder 1923-41: 104, also 1938-41: 8). It is therefore interesting to note that the only Badagas belonging to Anniya clan (meaning 'strangers, different people') are the Gauḍas of Ku:kallu and Nanjena:ḍu, both of them very near sites of former mud-forts. If those imported families only contained four members each, this would have accounted for a half of the Badaga population enumerated at the very first census in 1812. The Kotas still recall how Umat Arč (the Lord of Ummattūr) and Udr Arč (the Lord Uḍaiya Rāya) came to Ke:ti 'to collect the revenue money and built houses and lived there with wife and children' (Emeneau 1946: 259). In Badaga tradition too Bijjaṇarasu, son of an Ummattūr chieftain, possibly founded Ke:ti and there collected an annual tribute of 500 gold coins from all of Me:kuna:ḍ. Another of these chieftains was so incensed when the unfortunate paramount chief Toṇḍa (thief, robber) did not pay the tribute within a week that, according to legend, 'the Rajah took his head and put it at the front door and the body was put at the back door and the arms and feet were bound on poles near the way' (Metz 1864: 110). The efforts of the headman of Ba:kola, in contrast, in collecting a record amount of tribute for the chieftains were rewarded with the gift of a silver ring (still held in his family) and the title of *pa:rpatti*, in Karnataka a revenue officer.[2] That *pa:rpatti* (since 1897, a disputed role; Pl. 9) is the divisional headman for Me:kuna:ḍ.

Most likely it was the chieftains or commanders of the three main hill forts who, during the seventeenth century, divided the plateau up into three areas of influence (*na:ḍu*) for tribute-gathering purposes: thus Male Ko:ṭe commanded Todana:ḍ, Haṭṭara Ko:ṭe Poranga:ḍ, and Pakka:su:ra Ko:ṭe Me:kuna:ḍ. '. . . In consequence of disputes between the Burghers [Badagas] and Kothers [Kotas] regarding their respective boundaries, a general settlement of their lands took place under the auspices of the three chiefs, when the lines of demarcation were definitively fixed; and . . . ever since, up to the present time, no disputes about them have ever been known to occur.'[3] The fourth small division, Kundena:ḍ, was not even recognized to be one until after 1830, and moreover was so poor until the twentieth century that it would have yielded scant tribute, being too remote from Ummattūr, having little cultivation and a proverbial poverty that often obliged Kundena:ḍ people to subsist on bamboo shoots, or even sell their children into servitude elsewhere on the plateau.[4]

The Lingayat chieftains at both Male Ko:ṭe and Haṭṭara Ko:ṭe invited Mysore Lingayats in particular to settle in the hills (Harkness 1832: 107, 109-10; Congreve 1847:122; Belli Gowder 1938-41: 12). This was the origin of the Oḍeyas who continued to function as the

Lingayat priests, the Adigaris who were magistrates, and the Kaṇakkas, accountants and therapists (as their names indicate). Around the same time (the mid-seventeenth century) Be:ḍas were brought to the hills from Hullangu:ru, just to the north, as hunters or tax gatherers.[5] Though heartily disliked, they settled permanently outside the walls of Male Ko:ṭe and probably near Haṭṭara Ko:ṭe too. Kumba:ras also came up in the palace retinue and settled near the fortresses. Some, however, who came from Beḷḷāḍi in Mysore, intermarried only with the Gauḍas and settled at Me:lu:ru. The Gauḍas of Accanakal, near Ke:ti, claim to be descended from the Lingayats of Ummattūr.

MALE KO:ṬE

Male Ko:ṭe (mountain fort)[6] was also known as Hussainabad under Tipu Sultan's regime. The fort, made of mud faced with stone, encircled by a ditch, was reputedly built some three to four centuries ago by two brothers, Sadasiva Rāja and Bhujanga Rāja (otherwise Bijjaṇarasu or Bujalingarasu). These men came from Ummattūr in the service of its chieftain who was, they say, the father of the latter, and they acted as *janmis* or tribute collectors for the Nilgiri area.

A variant tradition, useful for its detail, claims that Lord Bujalinga was himself the chieftain of Ummattūr. This was evidently not a local misconception; for the ever-reliable Hayavadana Rao has identified this man in a number of historical documents of Mysore, even going so far as to provide us with a definite date:

> . . . the attention of Chikkadēvarāja Woḍeyar in 1676 was directed towards the consolidation of the southern conquests of his predecessor [Dēvarāja Woḍeyar] . . . Again, in February [1677] Toda-nāḍu . . . in the south was acquired from Bhujangaiya, son of the Woḍeyar of Ummattūr. (Abridged from Hayavadana Rao 1943, vol. 1: 280-81)

It is asserted that this Bujjalingarasu (*arasu* = *ayya*, 'lord') had a son or brother named Bijjaṇarasu, and a son named Rudrarasu. He also had a Kaṇakka secretary, by the name of Sivalingayya, whose younger brother Jambulingayya acted as a secretary to Bijjaṇarasu. Bujjalinga (in the mid-seventeenth century[7]) wanted to incorporate the Nilgiris into his territory. He went there with a large retinue, and on the plains just to the north of the Si:gu:ru slopes he built a Lingayat monastery, the ruins of which are still to be observed at Śembanaṭṭa Math (or monastery, originally called Jambunath). From there the chieftain moved to Nelapaṭṭaṇa, a few kilometres away, and there he built a fort which is still partially standing. Later he ascended the slopes and established a camp at Ko:ṭaṭṭi (fort hamlet) near Śo:lu:ru, and later still he built Male Ko:ṭe nearby.

After conquering the Nilgiris this Ummattūr chieftain was paid an annual tribute of 900 gold coins (but whence?) by the headman of Śo:lu:ru. Once in control Lord Bujjalinga took seven men on a trip to examine Mu:kurti Peak, a prominent Nilgiri landmark.[8] On the way there one of these Badagas, who was conversant with omens or astrology, announced that the time was inauspicious, but Bujjalinga carried on with this excursion. Meanwhile the watchman at Male Ko:ṭe[9] sent word to Bujjalinga's elder brother who immediately came and captured the fort. Bujjalinga then had to move to Nellia:ḷa in the Wainad, for he was afraid to return to Male Ko:ṭe. Later his 'secretary' went back to the hills and built a house in the Kaṇakka village of Ajju:r (where some ancient inscribed palm leaves are now kept; Belli Gowder 1923-41: 29-30), while the chieftain apparently regained control of the fortress from his brother. It is recalled that once while staying at Male Ko:ṭe he was '. . . invited by the then Náyar chief of Nelliálam to help him against his brother, who had turned him out. Bhujanga [Bujjalinga] did so with success; so much so that he took Nelliálam for his own and drove out the whole of the Náyar family.' [10] No wonder the brothers had found it advisable to erect sturdy mud-fortresses wherever they went!

Their family thus became the chieftains of Nellia:ḷa, overlords of a considerable territory, as well as tax gatherers for the Nilgiris in the late seventeenth century. They were popularly called *arasu* (or Lord; Richards 1932: 173). For their own convenience, we have seen, the brothers brought with them some Kanarese Be:ḍas and Kumba:ras to be servants, and Oḍeyas to act as their family priests. Gauḍas in the commune of Tu:ḍegu:r (which surrounds Male Ko:ṭe) claim to have come from ten villages immediately north of the Moyar River, also in the retinue of these chieftains. They also maintained a small garrison, originally under Uḍaiya Ra:ya (or perhaps Rudrayya), a Kanarese Lingayat who was responsible for the actual construction of Male Ko:ṭe and the more easterly fort known as Uḍura:ya Ko:ṭe. This man was evidently an astute strategist; he was probably identical with Bujjalinga's son Rudrarasu, or otherwise an experienced military commander. In his old age he is said to have retired to Nellia:ḷa, to build yet another fortress there.

The tax collectors of Nellia:ḷa continued in office at Male Ko:ṭe without serious interruption, until a century later either Tipu Sultan or his father drove them back to Nellia:ḷa, mutilated some Vishṇu images there and took over their Nilgiri fortress (Francis 1908: 371). With the fleeing chieftain of the day there went some Badagas, who became Wainad Gauḍas, and a small party of Todas too who settled near Nellia:ḷa and indeed remained there until about 1925 (Harkness 1832: 166-67, note).

It is certain that Male Ko:ṭe and the other hill-forts were occupied by Haidar Ali's troops, too, though probably never visited by him.

> He . . . appears to have seized upon two of the three forts which commanded the passes . . . viz. Hoolicul Droog and Mullaycotta [i.e. Male Ko:ṭe], and having deepened their ditches, heightened their walls, and otherwise strengthened them, he put strong garrisons into them, which both controlled the Hill tribes, and observed and harassed the kingdoms below them. (Ouchterlony 1848: 82)

Some years back several large lead ingots were found in a field near Male Ko:ṭe, material his soldiers would have used to cast the needed musket balls of varying bores. Furthermore,

> He undoubtedly collected revenue on the plateau . . . his officers used to despoil whole villages of all their grain and force the ryots [peasants] to carry their own plundered property down to Dannáyakankóttai . . . which he had re-named Sharifábád and where he kept a strong force and a big magazine.[11]

A worthier aspect of his revenue administration was arguably that he 'had abolished the ancient system of division of produce and had introduced a fixed money assessment on the cultivated lands of each village' (Grigg 1880: 312). Evidently there were three Badaga settlements designated for collecting revenue from the three divisions of the plateau: Ajju:r for Todana:ḍ, Ke:ti for Me:kuna:ḍ, and Kacceriha:ḍa for Poranga:ḍ (‹ *kacceri* + *ha:ḍa* 'revenue office + flat ground', which is now called Kalla:ḍa).

The last occupant of Male Ko:ṭe was Syyud Budan, a captain (*killidar*) in charge of sixty or seventy infantrymen from Tipu's army. The fort was then named Hussainabad. It had two watchposts nearby, built by Tipu's men and armed with two small cannon, where the soldiers kept watch for forces coming from the direction of Nellia:ḷa. Every two months the garrison was relieved from Daṇṇayaka Ko:ṭe, in the Coimbatore Plain.[12] But after its quiet surrender to the Madras Regiment of the East India Company in 1791 (Phythian-Adams 1958: 87) that fort too was deserted, and today it stands in ruins. But meanwhile, what about the Nellia:ḷa chieftain who was attacked by Tipu's forces?

The then chief, another Sadásiva Rája Urs, is said to have submitted to them and helped them in an attack upon Nambalakód [a neighbouring territory in the Wainad]. When Tipu's men withdrew, the chief of Nambalakód fell upon Nelliálam in revenge, and the then Arasu [chieftain] was so hard pressed that he hurriedly despatched his pregnant wife and her handmaidens into the surrounding jungle and then, to avoid capture, committed suicide in front of the gate of his fort, which was afterwards plundered by the men of Nambalakód. Such is the family tradition.[13]

But the chieftain's family lost even more than honour, leader and headquarters, for the right to collect tribute in Todana:ḍ passed after Tipu's defeat from them to the victorious family of Nambala:ko:ḍu, 8 km. away from Nellia:ḷa. Although by 1830 the Nilgiris were under the Collector of Coimbatore this headman still had the right to collect taxes within Todana:ḍ, which he referred to as *nangana:ḍ* (our country; Baber 1830: 314-15). Early in the nineteenth century he used to obtain some Rs. 6,000 annually from Todana:ḍ.[14]

It is remarkable that for two centuries after the eclipse of the Nellia:ḷa chieftains with the dramatic suicide just described, the Badagas of Todana:ḍ still maintained a close relationship with this tragic family. Until about 1950 they would visit Nellia:ḷa to resolve some difficult disputes as well as to pay their respects to the Ra:ni during major family ceremonies (Richards 1932: 173). This family is still Lingayat and Kannaḍa-speaking and until seventy years ago continued to intermarry with the Lords of Ummattūr.[15]

UḌURA:YA KO:ṬE

Uḍura:ya Ko:ṭe, or Haṭṭara Ko:ṭe, and nowadays called Ko:ṭeha:ḍa (fort terrace), was described in 1847 as being

situated on a small table-land and sequestered by hills clothed with jungle. The position is strong, being nearly environed with a morass and stream running along the channel of a deep fissure in the ground. The remains of the fort indicate it was originally constructed of earth in some places, and in other parts of uncemented stones. In shape it is an oblong, the longer side measuring one hundred paces, the shorter fifty-three, and consisting of a double line of works one within the other, the space between the two occupying twenty-five paces in breadth. The remains of two square towers are visible adjoining the outer line, one seated on the west face and the other on the south; the gateway probably ran under the former.

Within the walls I found some remains of stone buildings, consisting of large blocks and flags unwrought, and two upon which the marks of the chisel were apparent. . . . Fragments of ornamented pottery were dispersed around. (Congreve 1847: 121; cf. Breeks 1873: 106; Sewell 1882, vol. 1: 228; Francis 1908: 333-34; Belli Gowder 1923-41: 105-06; Hockings 2012: 342-43)

This fortress lay 4 km. southeast of Kotagiri, on a terrace in Burnside Estate where no traces of these buildings and few of the moats can now be found (half-a-century ago, I looked). A Badaga tradition suggests that Uḍaiya Ra:ya, a Shaivite chieftain, also built the fort on the plains at Koḷḷantore, located on the Bava:ni River near Seremoge (Sirumugai) in the far west of Coimbatore district (Congreve 1847: 122; Francis 1908: 333-34; Thurston & Rangachari 1909, vol. 1: 72). After conquering all of the Poranga:ḍ villages (Map 4), he won from them an annual tribute of 700 gold coins. This revenue from Poranga:ḍ passed through these two forts to Ummattūr, while only the Todana:ḍ tribute was collected at Male Ko:ṭe. Haṭṭara Ko:ṭe was captured by Haidar Ali in the late eighteenth century and was also occupied by a Moslem garrison under his despotic son Tipu. At that time it bore the name Syyudabad; the hundred soldiers there under a captain (*killidar*) named Ali Khan were responsible to a commander at Daṇṇayaka Ko:ṭe, on the plains below (Harkness 1832: 126; Macleane 1893: 1023). Here, as at Male Ko:ṭe, the garrison was 'to keep the mountaineers in check and also to assist the Sultan's servants in collecting the yearly revenue' (Ward 1821: lxv).

HULIKAL DRUG

The third ancient fortress of note is today the most visible and by far the best known, since it still has impressive stone and mud walls. This is Pakka:su:ra Ko:ṭe (or Gaganasukki Ko:ṭe), commonly called Drug Fortress because it was built on the Hulikal Drug mountain summit 6 km. to the south-east of Coonoor (Harkness 1832: 104, 107, 124; Francis 1908: 328-30; Hockings 2012: 431). It too was an important outpost of Daṇṇayaka Ko:ṭe, having commanding views across the plain (Price 1908: 2). Sir Richard Burton (famed equally as explorer and eroticist) left his impression of the view:

> The rock upon which we tread falls with an almost perpendicular drop of four thousand feet into the plains. From this eyrie we descry the houses of Coimbatore, the windings of the Bhawany [Bava:ni R.], and the straight lines of road stretching like ribbons over the glaring yellow surface of the low land. A bluish mist clothes the distant hills of Malabar, dimly seen upon the horizon in front. Behind, on the far side of the mighty chasm, the white bungalows of Coonoor glitter through the green trees, or disappear behind the veil of fleecy vapour which floats along the sunny mountain tops. (Burton 1851 [1991]: 268)

Not only have much of the stone walls survived, but an impressive elephant track cut all the way up from the plains may be found leading to the fort. This fort occupies the whole of the crest, being about 500 m. long and 100-200 m. in breadth. Its location is almost impregnable:

> The old fort stands on a precipitous site, three sides of which fall almost sheer down to the Coonoor ravine on the one hand and the Coimbatore plain on the other, while the fourth is connected with the rest of the range only by a narrow neck the last part of which will not admit more than one man at a time. The great natural strength of the position has been ingeniously increased by the manner in which the defences have been built close along the edge of the precipices and strengthened by projections wherever the possibility of an escalade existed, and a high wall fitted with embrasures and loopholes has been erected to face the entrance from the narrow neck. (Francis 1908: 328)

It is a medieval structure, and in fact probably older than the other two mud-fortresses just discussed, but was used to control Me:kuna:ḍ in the same way that they were used to extract tribute from the other two ancient divisions of the plateau (Ouchterlony 1848: 81; Francis 1908: 329). According to tradition, it was refurbished by Haidar Ali in the mid-eighteenth century.

Pakka:su:ra, a mythical chief of Hulikal Drug, is depicted by the Badagas as a demon whom the villagers on the plains had to feed daily with a virgin and a cartful of rice, complete with driver. 'These were supplied till they had given up the three hundred virgins, when they could give no more and the giant in his anger destroyed the village' (Sandford 1894: 470; cf. Congreve 1847: 142; Francis 1908: 329). He would, they said, contemptuously kick the cart over the precipice after each meal; but in the end he was to be slain by the hero Bhima. This tall story is actually a parochialized version of a tale in the *Māhābhārata* (I, 160), as Sandford makes clear:

> Besides the daily tribute already mentioned, once a year a human being, a male buffalo and a he-goat had to be sent as an offering to the giant. One day when the time came for this sacrifice, the victim, when leading the buffalo and the goat towards the mountain was met by the Pandyan king's brother, named Bhima, who stopped the man and asked where he was going. The man told Bhima his mission, who replied that he was tired of his life and he would become the sacrifice in his stead. Bhima went on and met the giant and fought with him and overcame him. He then slaughtered the goat and the buffalo and feasted and returned to the village and told the people what he had done, but they, fearing that the giant was not really dead, but would in time return and punish them all the more severely, deserted the country and never returned. (Sandford 1894: 470-71)

Pakka:su:ra Ko:ṭe was more or less ruined by the end of the eighteenth century, though some houses remained and it was still used by Tipu Sultan during his campaigns because of its strategic position. Those final campaigns were memorialized in a fine Victorian novel by Col. P. Meadows Taylor called *Tippoo Sultaun: A Tale of the Mysore War* (1840; four of its chapters are set in this fortress). Nearby there were two small supporting forts, namely Ka:re Ko:ṭe (or Kare Ko:ṭe), about 6 km. SSE of Coonoor, and Ki:e Ko:ṭe (lower fortress), 4.5 km. SSE of Coonoor. Pakka:su:ra Ko:ṭe itself was also called Me:l Ko:ṭe, 'upper fortress'. There was one Badaga hamlet close by, named Ko:ṭaṭṭi/Ko:ṭehaṭṭi (or fortress hamlet), but its exact location is uncertain because it was lost to tea plantation in the later nineteenth century.

THE FORTIFICATION SYSTEM

The three forts discussed above were only a small if crucial part of a regional fortification system that embraced over three dozen fortresses, some of stone and other minor ones of reinforced mud, and all of them now in ruins. (Further details are given on each in Table 2, Hockings & Pilot-Raichoor 1992, and Hockings 2012: 339-45. All are shown on Map 3, and a few are marked as well on Map 2 by the letter *F*.) It is important to note that only ten of these fortified sites are on the summit of the hills, while 30 others are either located on the surrounding slopes or are on the plains nearby. In fact, Map 3 shows clearly that by far the heaviest concentration of the fortresses is around the strategic northern and northeastern escarpments of the massif, with few forts guarding the southern flanks or on the plateau itself (these latter indicated in Table 2 with underlining). Most of those situated on the plateau commanded, visually and thus militarily, the old passes up into the Nilgiris, viz: Male Ko:ṭe overlooked the Sigur Ghat; Pakka:su:ra Ko:ṭe overlooked the Coonoor Pass (the Kallar R.); Kiṇṇakore controlled the Mannar Ghat; Uḍuraya Ko:ṭe overlooked a valley which led up to the Kotagiri area; Ko:ṭe Beṭṭu overlooked the Sispara Ghat; Ku:kallu overlooked a path up the escarpment from the Moyar River near the Gajaḷaṭṭi Pass. The local names of all forty fortifications are given in Table 2.

Table 2: Ancient Fortifications in the Nilgiri Area

Northern Defenses

1. Allira:ni Ko:ṭe, a ruined fort mentioned in Kota and Kuṟumba legends, lying in the Moyar Ditch *ca* 22 km. NE of Kotagiri, near the Gajaḷaṭṭi Pass and the ruined site of Yavaṉa Tāvaḷam (Zagarell 1995: 94).
2. Attitore, *ca* 15 km. NNW of Ootacamund, located on the banks of the Attitore haḷḷa, with a fort (with ruins of an extensive village; after its destruction the inhabitants moved to Hosu:r, 'new village').
3. De:vara:yapaṭṭaṇa, a one-time fortification below the Nilgiri escarpment, 1 km. N of Ma:siniguḍi bazaar, 19 km. NNW of Ootacamund ('Round about the present village of Masiniguḍi are numerous ruined villages, sculptured cromlechs and a much defaced inscribed slab. The place appears to have got its name of Dēvarayapura from King Krishna Dēva Raya, whose minister granted it, in his name, to Madhava Nayak of Kotesime' – Hayavadana Rao 1930: 314-15; Dēva Raya, however, was a title of all the Vijayanagara kings).
4. E:ru:r/Ye:ru:r, a former fortress below the Nilgiri escarpment, 16.5 km. NE of Ootacamund.
5. Ha:la Ko:ṭe, a ruined fort with watchtower on the lower slopes of the Nilgiris, *ca* 12 km. NNW of Kotagiri.
6. Haralaṭṭi/Haralaṭṭi Ko:ṭe, site of a ruined fortress below the Nilgiri escarpment, 18 km. NNW of Ootacamund.
7. Ka:ramale, a one-time fortress 10.5 km. N of Ootacamund, at the foot of

Table 2 (contd.)

the Si:gur Ghat.

8. Koraḷava:ḍi, a former fortress below the Nilgiri slopes, 13 km. N of Ootacamund.
9. Ku:kal/Ku:kallu, a hamlet 6 km. NW of Kotagiri; it is possibly not to be identified with a fort so named in an inscription of King Vishṇuvardhana, the first Hoysaḷa king, dated to 1141; however, there is *another* site marked 'Kukal' on some one-inch survey maps which is 7 km. NE of this village and strategically balanced right on the edge of the plateau overlooking the Moyar Ditch; yet since the words *ku: kallu* mean 'sounding stones' this might just refer to another megalithic burial site in the area (Hayavadana Rao 1910: 308-09).
10. Ma:daraṭṭi, a former fortress located below the northern slopes of the Nilgiris, 18.5 km. NNW of Ootacamund.
11. Male Ko:te, a ruined stone and earthen fortress 7 km. NNW of Ootacamund, built by Bujjalingarasu and used by the forces of Tipu Sultan (see above, pp. 55-58).
12. Male:pura, a ruined fortress below the Nilgiri escarpment, 14 km. N of Ootacamund.
13. Muttikere, a former fortress below the northern Nilgiri slopes, 16 km. NNW of Ootacamund, on the W bank of the Si:gu:ru River.
14. Nelapaṭṭaṇa, a ruined fort at the foot of the escarpment 14.5 km. NNW of Ootacamund.
15. Osahaḷḷi/Hosahaḷḷi/Hosu:r, a former fortress and hamlet at the foot of the Sigur Ghat, 13.5 km. N of Ootacamund (marked on an 1871 map as Athamsahib village, a reference perhaps to its founder or chief man; according to legend, this village and the surrounding land were given to a Muslim cavalry captain, possibly that same man, in the sixteenth century).
16. Śembanaṭṭa, a ruined fort and former monastery below the Nilgiri escarpment, 16.5 km. N of Ootacamund.
17. Siriyu:r/Siru:r, a former fortification below the northern Nilgiri slopes, 16.5 km. NE of Ootacamund.
18. Sokkanaḷḷi/Sokkanahaḷḷi, a ruined fort with temple below the Nilgiri escarpment, 12.5 km. N of Ootacamund.
19. Śo:lapa:ḷaya, a former fortress below the Nilgiri escarpment, 17.5 km. NNE of Ootacamund.
20. Talemale, in the Biligiri Ranga Hills, 40 km. NE of Ootacamund; it has a ruined fortress 'made out of bamboo bushes' which was militarily strategic in Hoysaḷa times; inscriptions are dated 1117 and 1162 CE.
21. Toṭḷuhangu/To:ṭalinga, a ruined fortress below the Nilgiri escarpment, 15.5 km. NNW of Ootacamund; (‹ *to:ṭa* + *linga*, 'field + emblem of Śiva', a possible ref. to polished stone axeheads that are occasionally to

Table 2 (contd.)

be found in fields here, and are taken for *lingas*).

22. Ummattūr (with a fortified hilltop at nearby Bagaḷḷi, a former *polegar*'s or tributary chieftain's headquarters in Karnataka, 44 km. N of Kotagiri and 37 km. NE of Guṇḍulupēṭe.

Western Defenses

23. Ko:te Bettu (fortress mountain) is a hill reaching 2,380 m., 26.5 km. SW of Ootacamund, overlooking the Sispara Ghat leading into Kerala; its name indicates there was once some fortification there.
24. Nambala:ko:ḍu, a village in the Wainad, *ca* 8 km. NW of Gu:ḍalu:ru; ‹ *Nambolu + a: + ko:ḍu*, '[a name] + that + peak', referring to a ruined fortress at the site that had been occupied by Uḍaiya Ra:ya after he was driven out of the Nilgiri Hills early in the seventeenth century by Ummattūr Arasu and took on the title Nambolu or Me:l Na:ḍu Arasu, 'Lord of the Upper Country'.
25. Nelako:ṭe, 14 km. WNW of Gudalur, beside Nellia:ḷa village, has two ruined brick fortresses associated with Tipu Sultan and Kerala Rāma Varma, the Pazhassy Rāja or 'Pychy rebel' (Hayavadana Rao, in Hockings 2012: 748-50).

Eastern Defenses

26. Daṇṇayaka Ko:ṭe, a former mud and stone fortress, bazaar and *taluk* headquarters on the Bhavani R., where Badagas used to pay their land taxes until 1830; 48 km. N of Coimbatore and 23 km. E of Kotagiri, on the Coimbatore Plain. (The fort was the headquarters of a *faujdar* or military governor and magistrate during the late eighteenth century, last saw military action during the Third Mysore War, passed to the East India Company in 1799, was in ruins by 1860, and was submerged under the Bhavani Dam in 1955, but it is still visible in dry years; Pl. 2. Its founder, it has been suggested, was Perumāḷa-Dēva Daṇṇāyaka, a general under Narasimha III, *ca* 1300 CE).
27. Gaganasukki Ko:te (also called Pakka:su:ra Ko:ṭe, Me:l Ko:ṭe or Hulikal Duruga), a headland of 1,918 m. elevation, 6 km. ESE of Coonoor (fortified with stone walls in the middle ages; in ruins, but was used by Tipu Sultan; see above, pp. 59-61).
28. Halevi:ra Ko:ṭe/Halevi:raso:mi Ko:ṭe, a ruined fortress on the lower Nilgiri slopes *ca* 19.5 km. NE of Kotagiri.
29. Kaḷḷampa:ḷaya, a Mele Nāḍu Iṟula hamlet, site of a Śiva temple and ruined fortress, 17.5 km. ENE of Kotagiri; ‹ Tamil *kaḷḷaṉ* + *pāḷaiyam*, ? 'robber + camp' (cf. Winslow 1862: 766)

Table 2 (contd.)

30. Ka:re Ko:te/Kare Ko:te, a ruined fortress *ca* 6 km. SSE of Coonoor.
31. Ki:e Ko:te, a former fort 4.5 km. SSE of Coonoor, quite near Gagana-sukki Ko:ṭe.
32. Koḷḷantore, a ruined fortress 21 km. E of Kotagiri on the Bhavani R., supposedly built by Uḍura:ya.
33. Meṭṭupe (in Tamil, Meṭṭuppāḷaiyam), on the Bhavani R., now a large market town, but only 614 inhabitants in 1891; while no fort is known, the name is eloquent (Ka. *miṭṭe* + *pāḷaiya*, 'foot-hill + army camp'); see Hockings 2012: 592; Winslow 1862: 766.
35. Sattiyamangaḷa, an ancient Tamilian town, stone fortress and market centre on the Bhavani R., 54 km. ENE of Coonoor.
36. Seremoge (in Tamil, Sirumugai), a small town beside the Bhavani R., 23.5 km. E of Coonoor; anciently the site of a chieftain's fort.
37. Udura:ya Ko:te, a fortress 4 km. SE of Kotagiri (see above, pp. 58-59).

South-central Defenses

38. Kinnakore, the southernmost Badaga hamlet, 21 km S of Ootacamund, with a ruined earthen fort.
39. Nanjena:du, a Badaga hamlet 9 km. SW of Ootacamund; traces were found nearby of an ancient gold-working town, and of a mud-fort, where some coins of Asaf Jah Nizam-ul-Mulk, Viceroy of the Deccan in 1722-48, have been found; (Hockings 2012: 634).
40. One Cairn Hill, unnamed site of a medieval town of gold-miners 3 km. S of Ootacamund, protected by a now-disappeared mud-fortress.

NOTES

1. Ranganātan 1960: 4. This story is not accurate in its details, for in 1760 the Governor of Madurai was an English creature, one Yusuf Khan; perhaps Ranganātan was referring to a skirmish with a tributary chieftain (a polegar or *pāḷayakkāran*; Winslow 1862: 766).
2. Buchanan 1807, 136. This and some other rings still in the possession of several of the headmen (though not the paramount chief) were given by Chikkadēvarāja (1672-1704), who supposedly took Kaḍana:ḍu from Ummattūr in 1676; Belli Gowder 1923-41: 100; Wilks 1930, vol. 2: 225; Emeneau 1971: 102; Zagarell 1994: 197-98.
3. Ouchterlony 1848, 81; see below, p. 170. For 'the three kings or chiefs of the mountains,' see Harkness 1832: 120. An inscription at Rāmpura, west of Nanjaraguḍi (in Karnataka), dated to 1504 CE, describes one Govaṇṇa Woḍeyar, a native of that place, as a 'champion over the three

kings, protector of the Nilagiri'; Rice 1894, vol. 3: 100, 191, n. 47. Emeneau 1971: 1 records 'three kingdoms' in Toda thinking. (For such small territories the word 'chieftancy' might be more appropriate.)

4. The exceptional nature of Kundena:ḍ is underlined by the common Badaga phrase, 'All the four divisions, including Kunda.' The relative recency of its settlement is also indicated by the fact that it lies to the west of Me:kuna:ḍ, which itself means 'western division'. Keys 1812: xlviii; Macpherson 1820: lviii; Ward 1821: lxi. Keys erroneously calls Toda-na:ḍ 'Kothanaud'; but there was no such name.
5. Previously they had come there from Nāgataḷḷi, in Mysore state; Belli Gowder 1923-41: 30.
6. A ruined stone and earthen fortress 7 km. NNW of Ootacamund (Jervis 1834: 15; Macleane 1893: 246; Francis 1908: 350; Thurston & Rangachari 1909, vol. 1: 70; Hockings 2012: 341-42).
7. The dating of these two brothers through a legend is problematic. A Badaga antiquarian (Belli Gowder 1926) published an account based, he said, on palm leaves in old Canarese script that were kept in a local temple (at Ajju:r) and accompanied by a translation done by German missionaries (perhaps Br. J.M. Bühler). M.K. Belli Gowder described Bujjalinga as a 'descendant of the Hoysala kings', and proceeded to assign the date of 1277 in one manuscript and 1297 in another for the time 'when the first batch of Badagas came to the hills under the chief Bujalinga Raju'. That such a precise date in the Gregorian calendar was arrived at solely from the palm leaves is in itself utterly unlikely, especially when Belli Gowder admits that he was not allowed to see the palm-leaves (1923-41: 29-30); nor for that matter was I. But evidently this whole argument for such an early date is based on a misreading of published historical texts: it was not in 1277 but in 1677 that 'Todanāḍu . . . in the south was acquired from Bhujangaiya, son of the Woḍeyar of Ummattūr' (Hayavadana Rao 1943: 281). Unaware of this huge four-century discrepancy, Belli Gowder then elaborates: '. . . there was confusion and famine in Mysore and Bujalinga Raju migrated to the Nilgiris with a few cultivators of the tribe Okalijas from the countries surrounding Gundelpet [Guṇḍulupēṭe]. He established his kutchery [treasury] in Todanaad' (at Ajju:r, he says elsewhere). Later, Belli Gowder continues, 'the Badagas remained secluded on the Nilgiris, and copied the manners, customs, and dress of the Todas. Wodeya chiefs appointed monigars [headmen] and collected revenue, and even at these times regular coins appear to have been in currency . . . The Todas recognized the Badagas as conquerors, and the Badagas adopted the customs of the Todas, but retaining the religion of Siva'.
8. Their names are still recalled, and they came from the Badaga villages of Tu:ḍegu:r, Kaḍana:ḍu, Ha:laṭṭi, Ebbuna:ḍu and Ku:kallu. Mu:kurti is a celebrated landmark in the western Nilgiris, a peak reputedly formed

when the mythical Rāma cut off the nose of Rāvana's sister and dropped it at this place; Jagor 1876: 202; Hockings 2012: 602-03.

9. Murudan, the son of a loose Badaga woman.
10. Francis 1908: 371; thus also Belli Gowder 1923-41: 101. The conquered chieftain was Vaṇdur Kovilagam.
11. Francis 1908: 330 (he errs in identifying Pakka:su:ra Ko:ṭe as Tipu's Syyudabad); Ouchterlony 1848: 82.
12. Harkness 1832: 59; see Pl. 2. One of these watchposts was actually a small natural mesa that is surrounded by sheer cliffs, so that access could be controlled by just two or three armed men, as at Hulikal Drug. It stands above and to the west of the Sigur Ghat road.
13. Francis (1908: 371): 'other accounts state that the family fled from Mysore State as late as the time of Tipu and settled in Nellialam under the permission of' the Pychy rebel . . .'.
14. Poranga:ḍ and Me:kuna:ḍ at that time were paying a similar sum to two other *janmis*; one the Padignacar Kolgum (i.e. Padinnara Kovilagam), a chief of the Samuri (Zamorin) family, the other Pandalūr Nāyar, of south Malabar; Baber 1830: 314-15; cf. Fenicio 1603 [1906]: 729. The East India Company continued for some time with the practice of tax farming: 'From the year 1799 to 1819 . . . revenue was collected from them for the company by a nạtive renter' (Burton 1851 [1991]: 270). Much earlier, in Vijayanagara times, 'not only do the inscriptions suggest the collection of taxes from the upper-level plateau communities, but local stories also describe such collections'; Zagarell 1995: 93.
15. Francis 1908: 350, 370; Kariabettan 1958a: 14. About seventy years ago the family of the Ummattūr Lords in their ancestral home at Bagaḷḷi (5 km. from Ummattūr) sold all remaining lands and left the area. Bauramma, last Queen of Nellia:ḷa, was born about the year of the Indian Mutiny; she died at the age of 94, whereupon Rāja Shankar Rayal sold what remained of the reạlm and retired to Mysore. The recent rulers are indicated in the Diagram below, numbered in order of their succession.

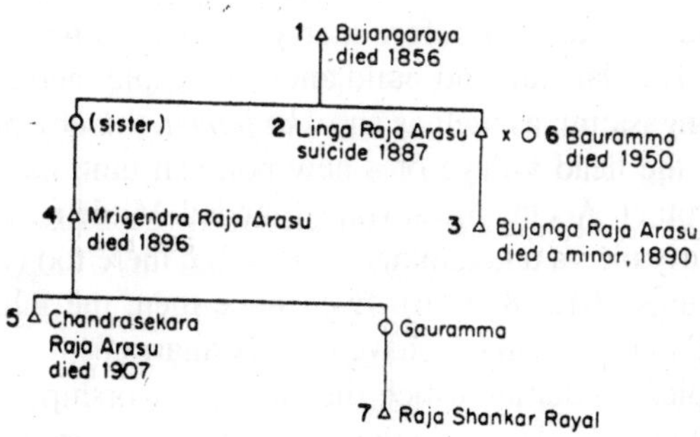

CHAPTER 4

The Cultural Ecology of Settlements

POPULATION AND THE GODS

The Badagas thus came to the Nilgiri Plateau as refugees from just to the north, around four centuries ago, and then settled on land that in part they cleared from virgin tropical montane forest and that was in part granted them by a council of men from the indigenous Toda, Kota and perhaps Kuṟumba tribes, people who had been living in a thin scattering of hamlets on these hills for already at the very least a millennium. Sketchy versions of the migration legend tell how the heroic founders of lineages and tiny Badaga settlements wandered around, establishing one hamlet or another, and then another, no doubt as slow population growth began to place too much pressure on the closest land and better prospects for shifting cultivation were heard of further away.

It is important to recall that these people not only founded new hamlets but also built the first Hindu temples in each, hence instituting the cult of their particular deity (the *iṣṭade:vade*). Thus the blind Kuruḍu founded Ha:yu:ru and built a temple there to the Saivite god Maha:lingasa:mi. He died before marrying, but his relatives moved on to found Ta:ndana:ḍu and build another temple there, also to the god Maha:lingasa:mi, as well as an *akka bakka*, thereby proclaiming the place as the head village of a new political unit, the commune. Kuruḍu's brother Acciṇi meanwhile founded Mi:de:ṇu and built a temple to Hiriyade:va and another *akka bakka* there too (Heidemann 2006; Hockings 2012: 815-16). Ever since then, the inhabitants of these three Poranga:ḍ villages have not intermarried.

The complex of deities which the Badagas worship is typical of Hindu societies. One deity – in their view, Siva – is pre-eminent, but is worshipped in a number of forms or aspects. Some aspects of the god are considered to be his family members, and of these his wife Pa:rvati is the most widely worshipped one, throughout India; but the Badaga complex includes other sorts of deity who do not fit into this celestial kinship pattern. Hence the occurrence of numerous purely local deities and spirits, which occasioned the missionary Metz to observe that there were 'no less than 338 idols on the hills' (1864: 61). Large as that number is, it may not have been much of an exaggeration on his part, if one takes into consideration each village shrine in his day, as he was mainly counting such highly localized deities, many of them only worshipped at one place – if indeed they had a shrine at all.

Badagas are commonly aware that a deity known by a special name at a particular place may be a variant of the supreme god Siva. Thus there is a god with the extraordinary name of Kakkayya (literally 'vomit Lord'), who is worshipped at three places; in actuality an aspect of Siva, who according to certain legends swallowed poison that he later threw up. No doubt in other cases there may be nothing more solid than a vague assertion to link a particular god or goddess somehow with the family of Siva. This is a likely scenario in the cases of minor personages who are the ancestral spirits of particular clans. Thus Anganade:svara (the *-i:svara* is a name of Siva) is a god worshipped by one Oḍeya clan and some Adigaris. Angama:sti is a goddess worshipped only by certain Oḍeyas. Some minor gods have a particular and fairly restricted function to perform: thus Maleya Ma:ḍappa (or Halevi:raso:mi; Davidar 1997: 186), for example, is a deity who protects cattle. Like him, Malle:svara is an aspect of Siva to whom Badagas pray that their cattle will not succumb to disease. And Mallima: is yet another aspect of Siva, who can protect people from attack by wild elephants, a serious threat in this area.

Some of the deities are essentially nature spirits. Of these Ganga (or I:rama:sti), the water goddess, is of crucial importance in such an agricultural society; she is also equated with Siva's consort, Pa:rvati (who, in turn, is often equated with the Badagas' own ancestress, Hette). Some nature spirits are now scarcely remembered unless a reference to them is preserved in some place-name or prayer. There exists, for example, a hill in the Wainad named Ammanmuḍi Beṭṭa ('headland-of-the-goddess mountain'; Hockings and Pilot-Raichoor 1992: 25), which has an ancient shrine on its summit devoted to some lineage ancestress (perhaps not Badaga). It seems the worship of mountain peaks was in general an ancient practice in this part of South India, and still occurs among the foraging tribe of Hill Pandarams some 175 km. SSE of the Nilgiris (Morris 1992: 100).

The Badagas can hence be seen, at least in the first two centuries of their occupation here, as frontiersmen who depended on the protection of local deities, whilst their population and settlements were slowly expanding with the years. We may presume that much of the highland culture of the early Badagas (exclusive of most religious practices) was less an adaptation of lowland traditions that they had brought with them than a borrowing of useful traits from the material cultures of the Kotas and Todas. In 1603 there were, we presume, scarcely two or three hundred Badagas inhabiting three villages (cf. Fenicio 1603 [1906]: 723). Two centuries later, according to the first British census in 1812, they numbered 2,207 people. But at this time, to judge by that same sketchy census (which possibly excluded children), Badagas had already – prior to when any early European settlers arrived – become the numerically dominant community on the plateau: the Todas then numbered only 179, and the Kotas 130 (see Appendix 2); the various Kuṟumbas and Iṟulas, altogether eleven tribes living on the lower Nilgiri slopes, were not counted at all then, although they were undoubtedly present. Furthermore, during this same period of two centuries the Badaga settlement pattern had become such a dispersed one that their hamlets increased in number from three to over 430, with newer hamlets often hiving off from older ones as more arable land was needed by their growing populations. The diverse character of the resultant settlement pattern, with just over 150 hamlets in Poranga:ḍ alone, is illustrated in Map 4. This expansion was in part the effect of fertile land still being available and in part the result of an effective indigenous therapeutic system used in what was basically a healthy environment.

A NEW SYSTEM OF THERAPY

By the time of the earliest, and quite peaceful, British visits two centuries ago (Hockings 2012: 422), the Badagas had clearly succeeded in adapting to their social and geographic environment: they were there to stay. We may presume that natural selection helped the population build up a genetic resistance to whatever montane illnesses had not previously affected the people when they had been living on

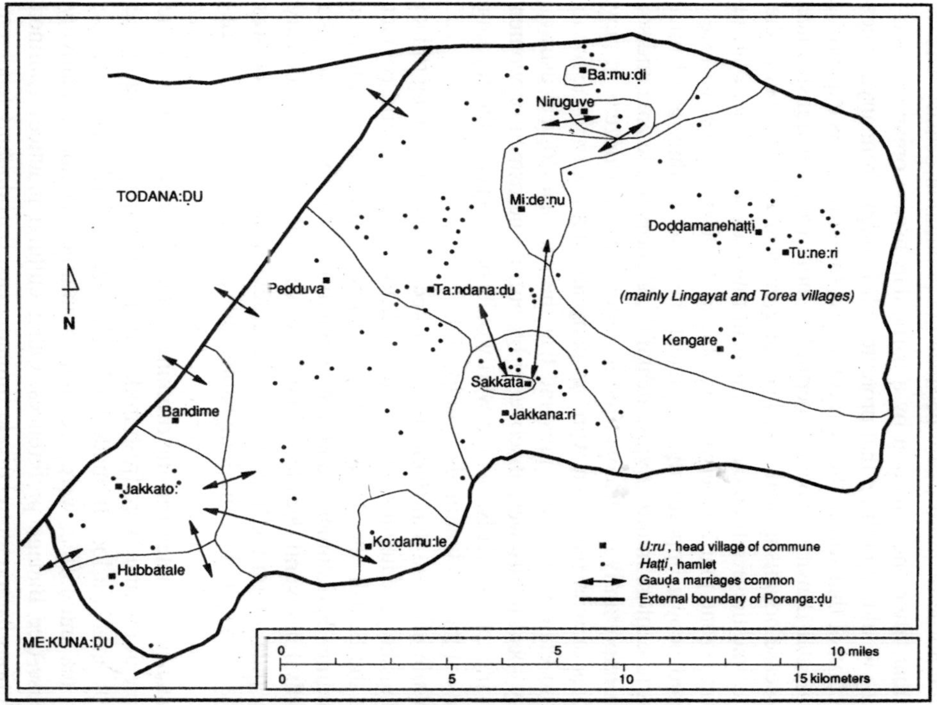

Map 4: The current settlement pattern in Poranga:ó

the Mysore plains. Some lowland disease organisms or vectors were no longer able to survive at the new elevation, either because it was too high and cold for them or because the hosts among the scattered, tiny population died off without these organisms getting transferred to new hosts; or more likely because the population density was so low that, after one infection by a particular disease organism, antibodies would be built up that protected all Badagas from any further infection of that sort in the near future. As the settlements expanded, the greater density of people permitted more frequent transference of disease organisms and so called for greater health care; but at the same time these settlements, located in much of the Nilgiri Plateau within a zone that lay between 1,200 and 2,200 m. above sea level, offered people opportunities to select the more healthy residential sites, to explore micro-environmental differences in the area and so, most importantly, to discover the medicinal uses for dozens of new species of wild plant that were in many instances only to be found on the Plateau. We may presume that the pharmacological uses of many local plants were discovered by buffalo herdsmen or women working as goatherds, people who would be observing the feeding habits of their sick animals closely all day.

While it is true that Badagas do not keep goats today, they did so during the seventeenth century and later too. After peaceful contact with the British, the Badagas achieved a new equilibrium with their changing environment, and the population was able to increase rapidly for several decades while there was still a very low density of population on the hills. Why? One relevant factor, I suspect, was that a change in their drinking habits followed the arrival of the British (from 1819 onward), and that this was associated with greater resistance to bacteria in the drinking water. The main drinks of the people at the time were fresh milk and stream water. And yet by the 1840s arrack, a locally made liquor (Hockings 2012: 82-83), along with tea and coffee, were becoming common and indeed relatively disease-free Badaga preferences. Other cultural practices confined infectious bacteria to relatively limited areas. Buffalo dung tended to accumulate in one or two stone kraals built just outside the villages (Pl. 11). At the same time, indiscriminate spitting was not much tolerated, and spittoons (*ecca kiṇḍi*) were therefore in common use: an old proverb stressed that 'You must see [the proper] people and ask [questions]; find [the proper] place and spit' (Hockings 1988: 435, no. 889). With the prevalence of such an attitude, the spread of various viruses and of the *Mycobacterium tuberculosis* was greatly curtailed. The regular everyday washing of the body and shaving of pubic hair also contributed to good health, by restricting the incidence of bodily fungi and lice-borne diseases.

The ecological significance of these various beliefs and practices is that as the Nilgiri population increased during the nineteenth century and some village streams began to be polluted by the new population pressure and its waste products, the Badagas managed to avoid some contamination by a switch, as mentioned, from drinking water and fresh milk to tea, coffee and sometimes alcohol, all of which would be relatively free of bacterial organisms. A new balance with their environment that this change brought about was certainly one factor in the remarkable increase in the Badaga population since the advent of the British administration (Appendix 2).

At the same time that this change in drinking habits was occurring their eating habits were undergoing an equally radical transformation. In part this was due to the several dozen types of fruit, grain and vegetable introduced from Europe by British settlers and adopted by most Badagas. The variety of their diet was greatly improved.

VILLAGE NAMES AS ECOLOGICAL INDICATORS

A study of the Badaga hamlet names yields an insightful picture of the early settlements formed during the two centuries that preceded the first British report (Keys 1812).

Perhaps a somewhat lyrical description of the Nilgiri Plateau from a century ago, in the heyday of British rule, may at this point aid the reader's understanding of the data that are to follow:

> The plateau is a true tableland, its average height being very uniform. But there is not a square mile of level ground in the whole of it, its surface being broken by endless undulations which in places swell into considerable and distinct ranges. It rises most abruptly from the plains below it; and on the west, above the Ouchterlony Valley and southwards, its sides are often sheer, bare walls, hundreds of feet in height and too steep even for trees to obtain a footing on them. Elsewhere dense forest covers almost the whole of its slopes. . . . It is first of all divided east and west into two fairly equal but dissimilar parts by a range of heights running north and south of which Dodabetta ('big mountain') is the tallest. . . . East and south of the Dodabetta range . . . the plateau . . . is extensively cultivated by the immigrant tribe known as the Badagas. This does not improve its appearance;

the great forests have mostly been felled and their place taken by the poorest low scrub or by fields of miserable cereals surrounding the squat red-tiled houses of numerous hamlets; the country is deeply scoured by every shower of rain until the infertile red and yellow sub-soil clays are laid bare; and, owing to the Badagas' former custom of shifting their cultivation from year to year to new patches of land, grass has been prevented from getting any firm hold on the denuded hill-sides. Only on the slopes of the plateau (which are too steep for cultivation) and in a few isolated Government reserves, does the forest flourish in its virgin beauty.

West of Dodabetta, however, the Badagas are more rare; hardly a field or a village (except the little clusters of huts belonging to the pastoral Tóḍas) is to be seen; and the country consists of a sea of rounded green hills, rising now and again into more prominent heights and ranges, which are covered with short grass . . . These rounded hills are divided each from each by streams or bogs, and nestling in their wrinkles are beautiful little woods [sholas], . . . the edges of which have been so sharply defined by years of grazing and (perhaps) grass fires that they look almost like artificial plantations. . . . (Slightly abridged from Francis 1908: 3-5)

A few of the village names defy any interpretation, either by me or by the best informants, probably because they have altered too much to be recognizable now as Baḍagu substantives. But leaving these ones aside we still have, in the list of toponyms which follows (Table 3), a corpus of 527 meaningful toponyms for a community of 468 hamlets, some of them no longer occupied. (See Appendix 3; names of fortresses have been left out of this count, as they were not primarily Badaga settlements and sometimes predated the arrival of the Badagas, as did their names.) Some descriptive toponyms are repeated in several locations, for obvious reasons (e.g. Naḍuhaṭṭi, 'middle hamlet', or Hosaṭṭi, 'new hamlet'); numbers given after some explanations below indicate cases where such a toponym is found more than once in the Nilgiris. Thus the number of these etymologies exceeds the number of hamlets, past and present, because of the duplications in names, because of rare cases where a village has had two names, and because some names appear twice in this list simply because of my classification of their constituent morphemes. We can now examine (Table 3) the likely meanings of toponyms, given here in a phonemic transcription of Baḍagu, a Dravidian language, using Roman alphabetization (colons indicate long vowels). All the names are listed with more detail in Hockings and Pilot-Raichoor (1995), with exact locations, as indeed are the names of most hills, streams, and even many settlements of the neighbouring tribes.

Table 3: Badaga village names

1. *Names from a Topographic Feature, or the Sky*

Aḍḍavaḷe < *aḍḍave* + *hoḷe*, 'crooked + stream' (2 cases)[1]
A:ka:su < Skt. *ākāśa*, 'clear space, sky, ether'
Aṇehaṭṭi < *aṇe* + *haṭṭi*, 'ridge + hamlet' (4)
Aṇikore < *aṇi* + *kore*, 'forked location + place'
Aravanga:ḍu < *are* + *(v)e:ṇu* + *ka:ḍu*, 'flat rock + edge + forest'
Arebeṭṭu < *are* + *beṭṭu*, 'flat rock + mountain'
A:regacci < *a:re* + *gacci*, 'ridge + bees' nest'
Arehaṭṭi < *are* + *haṭṭi*, 'flat rock + hamlet' (6)
Arekaḍavu < *are* + *kaḍavu*, 'rock + passage' (2)
Arekambe < *are* + *kambe*, 'flat rock + ridge'
Arekaṇḍi < *are* + *kaṇḍi*, 'flat rock + boundary'
Arekore < *are* + *kore*, 'rock + place'
Aruve:ṇu < *aruve* + *e:ṇu*, 'ravine + edge' (2)
Asugenetore < *asuvene* + *tore*, 'medicinal plant + riverbank'
Aṭṭapa:ḍi < Ka. *aṭṭa* + *paḍi*, 'raised place + settlement'
Attiha:ḍa < *atti* + *ha:ḍa*, 'fig tree + flat ground'
Attitore < *atti* + *tore*, 'fig tree + riverbank'
Attitorekaḍavu < *atti* + *tore* + *kaḍavu*, 'fig tree + riverbank + ford'
Aṭṭubailu < *aṭṭu* +*bailu*, 'steep place + entrance'
Avuḷance < *avuḷi* + *ance*, 'twin + landmark', ref. to the pair of neighbouring peaks, Guḍika:ḍu Beṭṭa and Naria:ḍu Beṭṭa
Ba:ko:re < *ba:ku* + *o:re*, 'pleasant-looking + slope'
Ba:muḍi (?) < *bambe* + *muḍi*, 'sp. of grass + headland'
Ba:muḍigu:ḍu < *bambe* + *muḍi* + *gu:ḍu*, 'sp. of grass + headland + habitation'
Bandime < *bandu* + *mi:*, 'tight set + topland'
Bebbe:ṇu < *bebbu* + *e:ṇu*, 'lonely + crest'
Beḷḷigere < *beḷḷi* + *gere*, 'silvery + escarpment'
Beḷḷikal < *beḷḷi* + *kal*, 'whitish + stone', i.e. a silvery haze on the slopes
Be:rage:ṇi < *be:ru* + *ge:ṇi*, 'knotted roots + waterhole'
Beṭṭaṭṭi < *beṭṭa* + *haṭṭi*, 'mountain + hamlet' (3)
Billikambe < *billi* + *kambe*, 'Nilgiri rhododendron + ridge' (2)
Billimale < *billi* + *male*, 'rhododendron + hill'
Bittolakaṇḍi < *bittu* + *hola* + *kaṇḍi*, 'seed + field + dale', i.e. a field that will not require much effort
Ćinna Kunnu:r < *cinna* + *kunnu* + *u:r*, 'small + escarpment + head village'
Dabbakambe < *dabbe* + *kambe*, 'darbha grass + ridge'
De:gili/De:hili < I̱rula *de:* + *egili*, 'threshold, ingress, access + ridge'
Dimbaṭṭi < *dimbu* + *haṭṭi*, 'soft place + hamlet', a reference to its pillow-like location

Table 3 (contd.)

Diṭṭuhaṭṭi ‹ *diṭṭu* + *haṭṭi*, 'knoll + hamlet'
Doḍḍaṇṇi ‹ *doḍḍa* + *haṇṇi*, 'big + swamp', ref. to the Pa:la:ḍa valley below
Doḍḍu:rkambe ‹ *doḍḍa* + *u:ru* + *kambe*, 'big + head village + ridge'
Ebbuna:ḍu ‹ *ebbu* + *na:ḍu*, 'rising + tract', ref. to its location on a hillock
E:cala:ḍa ‹ *e:calu* + *ha:ḍa*, 'wild date + valley'
Eḍapiḷḷu ‹ *eḍe* + *piḷḷu*, 'middle + narrow access', i.e. on the road midway between Iutore and Banḍuso:le
Eḷemiccaguḷi ‹ *eḷe* + *miccu* + *guḷi*, 'gouge + lightning + pit'
Ellekaṇḍi ‹ *elle* + *kanḍi*, 'boundary + basin-like location'
Erekaṇḍi ‹ *ere* + *kanḍi*, 'cliff + basin-like location'
Etelarekaṇḍi ‹ *etelare* + *kaṇḍi*, '*Pimpinella* sp. + small tableland'
Ga:ikaṇḍi ‹ *ga:i* + *kaṇḍi*, 'wind + basin-like location'
Goḍalaṭṭi ‹ *goḍalu* + *haṭṭi*, 'dale + hamlet'
Go:ṇuhaṭṭi ‹ *go:ṇu* + *haṭṭi*, 'crooked edge + hamlet'
Guṇḍa:ḍa ‹ *guṇḍu* + *ha:ḍa*, 'boulder + flat place'
Guṇḍaṭṭi ‹ *guṇḍu* + *haṭṭi*, 'round rock + hamlet'
Ha:ḍaṭṭi ‹ *ha:ḍu* + *haṭṭi*, 'valley + hamlet'
Ha:la:ḍa ‹ *ha:lu* + *ha:ḍa*, 'milk + flat place' (2)
Haḷḷa:ḍi ‹ *haḷḷa* + *aḍi*, 'stream + below'
Hattare ‹ *hattu* + *are*, 'small group + rocks'
Ha:vare ‹ ha:vu + *are*, 'snake + slab'
Himbara Hosaṭṭi ‹ *himbara* + *hosa* + *haṭṭi*, 'backyard + new + hamlet'
Himbarakaṇḍi ‹ *himbara* + *kaṇḍi*, 'backyard + ridge'
Honnatale ‹ *honna* + *tale*, 'golden brown + headland'
Honnemuḍi ‹ *honne* + *muḍi*, 'St. John's wort + headland'
Hubbatale ‹ *hubbe* + *tale*, 'hill forest indigo + headland'
Huguo:ru/Huguo:re ‹ *hugu* + *o:ru/o:re*, 'ingress + grazing place'
Hulla:ḍa ‹ *hullu* + *ha:ḍa*, 'grass + level ground'
Hullolakaṇḍi ‹ *hullu* + *hola* + *kaṇḍi*, 'grass + field + basin-like location'
Humbarakaṇḍi ‹ *hu:* + *mara* + *kaṇḍi*, 'flower + tree + ridge'
Huṭṭu:r Beḷḷa:ḍa ‹ *huṭṭu* + *u:ru* + *beḷḷe* + *ha:ḍa*, 'beautiful + village + white + flat ground'
Iḍuhaṭṭi ‹ *iḍu* + *haṭṭi*, 'nook + hamlet'
Iḍukore ‹ *iḍi* + *kore*, 'dell + patch of ground'
Iḷa:ḍa ‹ *iḷu* + *a:ḍa*, 'seven + valleys', ref. to seven streams that flow there
Iutore ‹ *iu* + *tore*, 'seven + springs'
Jakkakambe ‹ *jakkaḷu* + *kambe*, 'Nilgiri barberry + ridge'
Jakkaḷo:re ‹ *jakkaḷu* + *o:re*, 'Nilgiri barberry + slope'
Jakkana:ri ‹ *jakkaḷu* + *(n)a:re*, 'Nilgiri barberry + rocky hilltop'
Jakkata ‹ *sakke* + *tale*, 'jackfruit + headland'
Jakkatakambe ‹ *jakkaḷu* + *tale* + *kambe*, 'Nilgiri barberry + headland +

Table 3 (contd.)

ridge'
Kaḍako:ḍu < *kaḍe* + *ko:ḍu*, 'end point + limit'
Kaḍekambaṭṭi < *kaḍe* + *kambu* + *haṭṭi*, 'last + pole + hamlet', i.e. the final point of Ta:ndana:ḍu commune
Kakkoḍḍe < *kakku* + *oḍḍe*, 'distant + sloping land'
Kalna:yi < *kal* + *na:yi*, 'stone + neck of land'
Kambu:r < *kambe* + *u:r*, 'ridge + head village'
Ka:rakore < *ka:ra* + *kore*, 'hot + place'
Ka:rekallu < *ka:re* + *kallu*, 'clouds + stone'
Kariamale < *karia* + *male*, 'black + hill'
Karimorahaṭṭi < *kari* + *mora* + *haṭṭi*, 'charcoal + trees + hamlet', or possibly < *kare* + *maravu* + *haṭṭi*, 'contour + concealed + hamlet', a reference to its hidden position near the Nilgiri escarpment
Ka:ṭe:ri < Kota *ka·ṭ* + *e·r*, 'scene + river'
Kaṭṭebeṭṭu < *kaṭṭe* + *beṭṭu*, 'bald + mountain'
Kavaraṭṭi < *kavare* + *haṭṭi*, 'fork-like location + hamlet'
Ka:vitore < *ka:ve* + *tore*, 'drainage + dale'
Kembu:tuke:ru < *kembu:tu* + *ke:ru*, 'southern crow-pheasant + pond'
Kendore < *ken* + *tore*, 'reddish + dale'
Kengal < *kengu* + *kal*, 'reddish + stone'
Kengamuḍi < *kengu* + *muḍi*, 'reddish + headland'
Kengare < *kengu* + *are*, 'reddish+slab', or *ken* + *kare*, 'reddish + ridge'
Kenguṇḍu/Kenguṇḍe < *kengu* + *kuṇḍe*, 'red + dell'
Kera:ḍakambe < *kere* + *ha:ḍa* + *kambe*, 'pond + flat place + ridge'
Ke:rbennu < *ke:ru* + *bennu*, 'pond + curving slope'
Ke:rbeṭṭa < *ke:ru* + *beṭṭa*, 'pond + mountain'
Kereha:ḍa < *kere* + *ha:ḍa*, 'pond + level ground', i.e. a small pond used to form in a depression there after rains
Kerepa:ḍu < *kere* + *pa:ḍu*, 'pond + settlement'
Ke:rkambe < *ke:ru* + *kambe*, 'pond + ridge'
Ke:rkaṇḍi < *ke:ru* + *kaṇḍi*, 'pond + small tableland'
Kesala:ḍa < *kesaru* + *ha:ḍa*, 'marsh + flat land'
Ke:titore < *Ke:ti* + *tore*, '[a name] + dale'
Kiṇṇakore < *kiṇṇalu* + *kore*, 'saucer + patch of ground'
Kodamuḍi < *kodavu* + *muḍi*, 'weed + headland'
Kokkutale < *kokku* + *tale*, 'crooked + headland'
Koṇagaṭṭi < *koṇa* + *kaṭṭu*, 'extremity + edge'
Koṭṭunaṭṭi < *koṭṭu* + *(n)haṭṭi*, 'crest + hamlet'
Ku:katore < *ku:* + *kal* + *tore*, 'sounding + stones + dale'
Kunnakambe < *kunna* + *kambe*, 'little + ridge'
Kunnu:r < *kunnu* + *o:re*, 'escarpment + slope', a ref. to its position on the

Table 3 (contd.)

edge of the plateau

Kunnu:raṭṭi ‹ *kunnu* + *o:re* + *haṭṭi*, 'escarpment + slope + hamlet'

Kurutuguḷi ‹ *kurutu* + *gui*, 'clump of foliage + dell', or ‹ *gurutu* + *gui*, 'landmark + dell'

Maḍitore ‹ *maḍi* + *tore*, 'deep location + dale', a ref. to its position in the valley bottom

Malligo:re ‹ Skt. *mallikā* + Bad. *o:re*, 'jasmine + slope' (2)

Mandakaṇḍi ‹ *manda* + *kaṇḍi*, 'grassy slope + tableland'

Ma:niha:ḍa ‹ *ma:ni* + *ha:ḍa*, 'reeds + valley'

Manjakombe ‹ *manju* + *kambe*, 'cloud + ridge', i.e. located on the rim of the Nilgiri Plateau

Manjamale ‹ *manju* + *male*, 'cloudy + mountain'

Manjitala/Manjida ‹ *manji* + *tale*, 'fibre + headland' (2)

Manju:ru ‹ *manju* + *u:ruva*, 'cloud + drifting'

Ma:riammakaṇḍi ‹ *Ma:ri* + *amma* + *kaṇḍi*, '[Parvati] + goddess + dale'

Maruḷakambe ‹ *maruḷe* + *kambe*, 'forest mango + ridge'

Ma:sigaṇaṭṭi ‹ *ma:siga* + *haṇe* + *haṭṭi*, 'forest pepper + elevation + hamlet'

Ma:sikaṇḍi/Maccikaṇḍi ‹ Skt. *mahāśakti* + Bad. *kaṇḍi*, 'very mighty, Parvati + tableland'

Maṭṭakanḍi ‹ *maṭṭa* + *kaṇḍi*, 'extensive land + dale'

Me:lkunda ‹ *me:l* + *kunde*, 'upper + mountains'

Mi:de:ṇu ‹ *mi:de* + *e:ṇu*, 'ploughshare + ridge', since it was said to have been the first locality ever ploughed in Poranga:ḍu

Mi:ke:ru ‹ *mi:* + *ke:ru*, 'extreme + pond'

Morahoḍḍe ‹ *mora* + *(h)oḍḍe*, 'tree + bare slope'

Morakuṭṭi/Morakoṭṭuhaṭṭi ‹ *mora* + *kuṭṭi/koṭṭu*, 'black-bark tree + crest', a ref. to its location on a crest

Mo:rikallu ‹ *mo:ri* + *kallu*, 'rock-crossing+stone' or ‹ *mo:re* + *kallu*, 'face + stone'

Mo:ritore ‹ *mo:ri* + *tore*, 'culvert + flat place'

Mottakambe ‹ *motta* + *kambe*, ' Kur̲umba hamlet + ridge'

Muḍiakambe ‹ *muḍia* + *kambe*, 'last + ridge'

Mukkimale ‹ *mukki* + *male*, 'steep + mountain'

Mukkuhaṭṭi ‹ *mukku* + *haṭṭi*, 'nook + hamlet'

Muṭṭina:ḍu ‹ *muṭṭi* + *na:ḍu*, 'easy access + country' (2)

Naḍuvo:re ‹ *naḍu* + *(v)o:re*, 'middle + slope'

Naiyaṭṭi ‹ *na:yi* + *haṭṭi*, 'neck of land + hamlet'

Na:ragere ‹ *na:ra* + *gere*, 'sloping meadow + escarpment'

Neddilu ‹ *neddilu*, 'top of a ridge'

Ne:ribennu ‹ *ne:ri* + *bennu*, 'umbrella tree + shoulder', i.e. that tree sp. growing on an overhanging hill

Ne:rikambe ‹ *ne:ri* + *kambe*, 'umbrella tree + ridge' (2)

Table 3 (contd.)

Ni:raḷḷakambe < *ni:ru* + *haḷḷa* + *kambe*, 'water + stream + ridge'
Oḍḍe:ṇu < *oḍḍe* + *e:ṇu*, 'smooth slope + edge'
Oḍḍe:ru < *oḍḍe* + *e:ru*, 'sloping land + upward'
Oḍḍe:ruhaṭṭi < *oḍḍe* + *e:ru* + *haṭṭi*, 'sloping land + upward + hamlet'
Oḍḍupaṭṭare < *oḍḍu* + *paṭṭare*, 'top of hill + resting-place', i.e. a resting-place partway up a hill
O:rana:yi < *o:ra* + *na:yi*, 'sloping + neck of land' (Pl. 10, 14)
Pannave:ṇu < *pannave* + *e:ṇu*, 'buffer zone + ridge'
Panni:ruhaṭṭi/Panne:ruhaṭṭi < *panne* + *e:ri* + *haṭṭi*, 'extensive + upland + hamlet'
Pedduva < *pedda* + *hoḷe*, 'straight stream'
Pi:ṇaṭṭi < *pi:ṇa* + *haṭṭi*, 'prominence + hamlet' (2)
Po:ro:raṭṭi < *po:re* + *o:re* + *haṭṭi*, 'earth-cutting + slope + hamlet'
Puḍiyangi < *puḍi* + *hangu*, 'concealed + niche'
Pu:sekunnu:r < *pu:se* + *kunnu* + *u:r*, 'wild cat + escarpment + head village'
Se:la:ḍa < *se:le* + *ha:ḍa*, 'sebesten plum + flat place'
Se:lavare/Se:lo:re < *se:le* + *vare*, 'sebesten plum + slope'
Sibbikallukambe < *sibbi* + *kallu* + *kambe*, 'shell-[like] + stones + ridge'
Si:gaṭṭi < *si:gu* + *haṭṭi*, 'edge + hamlet'
So:leyaṭṭu < *so:le* + *aṭṭu*, 'wood + ravine'
Talemale < *tale* + *male*, 'headland + mountain'
Ta:ḷo:re < *ta:ḷu* + *o:re*, 'stoop down + slope'
Ta:maravare < *ta:mara* + *(v)are*, 'dark red + slab'
Ta:terebennu < *ta:tere* + *bennu*, 'bandicoot mud-holes + curved hillside'
Taṭṭene:ri < *taṭṭu*+ *ne:ri*, 'hillside + umbrella tree' (2)
Ti:ḍehaṭṭi < *ti:ḍe* + *haṭṭi*, 'mist + hamlet'
Ti:ḍere < *ti:ḍe* + *ere*, 'mist + scattered'
Toreyaṭṭi/Torehaṭṭi < tore + haṭṭi, 'dale + hamlet' (3)
Tudu:ru < *tudi* + *u:r*, 'toe-tip + head village', a ref. to its location at the very edge of the plateau
Tu:ha:ḍa < *tu:vu* + *ha:ḍa*, 'valley sides + flat place'
Tu:ne:ri < *tu:vu* + *ne:ri*, 'valley sides + mountain plum'
Tu:ne:ri < *to:* + *ne:ru*, 'kraal + headland' (2)
U:maraka:ṇḍi < *u:* + *mora* + *kaṇḍi*, 'blossom + tree + ridge'

2. *References to Land or Quality of the Soil*

Aṭṭumaṇṇu < *aṭṭu* + *maṇṇu*, 'deep + earth'
Baralaṭṭi < *baralu* + *haṭṭi*, 'dry + hamlet'
Ba:ramaṇṇu < *ba:ra* + *maṇṇu*, 'heavy + earth'
Baṭṭakore < *baṭṭa* + *kore*, 'chestnut-coloured + cultivated soil'
Be:ko:ḍu < *be:* + *ko:ḍu*, 'fertile + limit' (2)

Table 3 (contd.)

Beḷḷa:ḍa ‹ *beḷḷe* + *ha:ḍa*, 'white + flat ground' (2)
Bendaṭṭi ‹ *benda* + *haṭṭi*, 'burnt + hamlet', a ref. to former slash-and-burn cultivation (4)
Be:rage:ṇi ‹ *be:ru* + *ge:ṇi*, 'knotted roots + waterhole'
Be:raṭṭi ‹ *be:ru* + *haṭṭi*, 'roots + hamlet', i.e. a place with many roots in the soil
Bingicakallu/Bincikal ‹ *bingica* + *kal*, 'whitish + stone' (2)
Bittolakaṇḍi ‹ *bittu* + *hola* + *kaṇḍi*, 'seed + field + dale', i.e. a field which does not require much effort
Haṇemaṇṇu/Haṇeyamaṇṇu ‹ *haṇe* + *(ya)* + *maṇṇu*, 'wetland + GEN + earth'
Hanimaṇṇu ‹ *hani* + *maṇṇu*, 'wet + earth'
Hiṭṭegallu ‹ *hiṭṭe* + *kallu*, 'clods + stones'
Irupukallu ‹ *irupu* + *kallu*, 'sharp-edged + stone'
Jo:ṇuhaṭṭi ‹ *jo:ṇu* + *haṭṭi*, 'waterlogged land + hamlet'
Kalla:ḍa ‹ *kallu* + *ha:ḍa*, 'stone + flat ground'
Kallakore ‹ *kallu* + *kore*, 'stone + patch of ground'
Kallaṭṭi ‹ *kallu* + *haṭṭi*, 'stone + hamlet' (2)
Karukoḍḍe ‹ *karuku* + *oḍḍe*, 'black + sloping land'
Kekkaṭṭi ‹ *kekke* + *haṭṭi*, 'uncultivable soil + hamlet' (3)
Kempola ‹ *keppu* + *(h)ola*, 'reddish + field'
Ko:ṭa:ḍa/Ko:ṭeha:ḍa ‹ *ko:ṭe* + *ha:ḍa*, 'fortress + flat ground' (2)
Manepaṭṭu ‹ *mane* + *paṭṭu*, 'house + plot of land'
Maṇuhaṭṭi ‹ *maṇṇu* + *haṭṭi*, 'earth + hamlet' (3)
Marekallu (?) ‹ *mare* + *kallu*, 'break + stones'
Ma:vukallu ‹ *ma:vu* + *kallu*, 'clayish + stone'
Mokkaṭṭi ‹ *mokke* + *haṭṭi*, 'gravelly land + hamlet'
Muduhola ‹ *mudu* + *hola*, 'well-cultivated + field'
Nandaṭṭi ‹ *nanda* + *haṭṭi*, 'moist + hamlet', a ref. to its moist soil
Nanjena:ḍu ‹ *nanje* + *na:ḍu*, 'gashed + tract', ref. to the ancient iron or gold workings there
Nellihaṇe ‹ *nelli* + *haṇe*, 'emblic myrobalan + wetland'
Nundua ‹ *nundu* + *hola*, 'fertile + field', or *nundu* + *to:*, 'fertile + cattle pen'
Puṇaju:ru ‹ *puṇaji* + *u:ru*, 'dusty soil + head village'
Sibbikallukambe ‹ *sibbi* + *kallu* + *kambe*, 'shell-[like] + stones + ridge'
Tottamokke ‹ *tottu* + *mokke*, 'crude stone + rough ground'

3. *Nature of Vegetation and Jungle Produce*

Ajju:r ‹ *ajju* + *u:ru*, 'dry filaments + village'
Amba:le ‹ *amma* + *a:le*, 'goddess + jungle habitation'
Aravanga:ḍu ‹ *are* + *(v)e:ṇu* + *ka:ḍu*, 'flat rock + edge + forest'
Asugenetore ‹ *asuvene* + *tore*, 'medicinal plant + riverbank'

Table 3 (contd.)

Ba:kola < *ba:ku* + *hola*, 'scene + field'
Banahaṭṭi < *bana* + *haṭṭi*, 'forest garden + hamlet' (3)
Baralaṇe < *baralu* + *haṇe*, 'dried + grassland'
Be:kikare < *be:ki* + *kare*, 'jungle fire + boundary'
Bembaṇi/Bemmaṇi < *bebbu* + *haṇe*, 'lonely + meadow'
Bengaḷa:ḍa < *benki* + *ka:ḷu* + *ha:ḍa*, 'fire + forest + flat place'
Benga:ḷamaṭṭa/Benga:lu < *benki* + *ka:ḷu* + *maṭṭa*, 'fire+forest+flat ground'
Bu:dinaṭṭa < *bu:di* + *naṭṭa*, 'ash-mound+forest clearing'
Haṇemaṇṇu/Haṇeyamaṇṇu < *haṇe* + *(ya)* + *maṇṇu*, 'wetland + GEN + earth'
Hiriyasi:ge < *hiriya* + *si:ge*, 'large + thorny thicket'
Horaso:le < *hora* + *so:le*, 'outer + forest'
Hulla:ḍa < *hullu* + *ha:ḍa*, 'grass + level ground'
Hullangu:ru < *hullu* + *ga* + *u:ru*, 'grass + DAT + village' (2)
Hullattaṭṭi < *hullu* + *hattu* + *haṭṭi*, 'grass + growing up + hamlet'
Hullaṭṭi < *hullu* + *haṭṭi*, 'grass + hamlet'
Hullolakaṇḍi < *hullu* + *hola* + *kaṇḍi*, 'grass + field + basin-like location'
Humbarakaṇḍi < *hu:* + *mara* + *kaṇḍi*, 'flower + tree + ridge'
Ka:ḍaṭṭi < *ka:ḍu* + *haṭṭi*, 'forest + hamlet' (4)
Kaḍeso:le < *kaḍe* + *so:le*, 'last + forest'
Kaiga:ranaḍuhaṭṭi < Kur̲. *kayi* + *ke:r̲u* + Bad. *naḍu* + *haṭṭi*, 'hand + swamp + middle + hamlet'
Kambaṭṭi < *kambu* + *haṭṭi*, 'pole + hamlet', i.e. one with trees like poles (5)
Kambaṭṭikambe < *kambu* + *haṭṭi* + *kambe*, 'pole + hamlet + ridge', i.e. one with trees like poles
Ka:nabaḷḷi < *ka:na* + *baḷḷi*, 'jungle + fox hole'
Ka:repiḷḷu < *ka:re* + *piḷḷu*, 'thorny + path'
Kariamarahaṭṭi < *karia* + *mara* + *haṭṭi*, 'black + tree + hamlet'
Karikalbeḷ < *karigilu* + *be:*, 'scorched look + crops'
Karimora < *kari* + *mora*, 'charcoal + trees'
Ka:so:le < *ka:* + *so:le*, 'black + forest'
Ka:tarubana < *ka:taru* + *bana*, 'Kur̲umba sorcery + grove'
Kodamuḍi < *kodavu* + *muḍi*, 'weed + headland'
Koḍeka:ḍu < *koḍe* + *ka:ḍu*, 'umbrella + forest'
Ko:eka:ḷu (?) < *ke:i/ke:yi* + *ka:ḷu*, 'barking-deer + woodland'
Kundesappe < *kunde* + *sappe*, 'tight + clumps of tall grass'
Kurutuguḷi < *kurutu* + *gui*, 'clump of foliage + dell', or < *gurutu* + *gui*, 'landmark + dell'
Mandakaṇḍi < *manda* + *kaṇḍi*, 'grassy slope + tableland'
Mandaṭṭi/Mandaluhaṭṭi < *manda* + *haṭṭi*, 'grassy slope + camp' (3)
Ma:rakare (?) < *mohatra* + *kare*, 'tree + boundary', a ref. to the forest border
Oḍehaṭṭi < *oḍe* + *haṭṭi*, 'forest + hamlet'

Table 3 (contd.)

Oṭṭimara Hosaṭṭi ‹ *oṭṭi* + *mora* + *hosa* + *haṭṭi*, 'single + tree + new + hamlet'
Pandalu:ru ‹ *pandalu* + *u:ru*, 'canopy [of trees] + head village'
Se:leha:su ‹ *se:le* + *ha:su*, 'sebesten plum + canopy of trees'
Si:gemorahaṭṭi ‹ *si:ge* + *mora* + *haṭṭi*, 'bark + tree + hamlet'
Śo:la:ḍe ‹ *so:le* + *aḍe*, 'forest + closing in'
So:leyaṭṭu ‹ *so:le* + *aṭṭu*, 'wood + ravine'
So:lu:ru ‹ *so:le* + *u:ru*, 'forest + head village'
Tanga:ḍu ‹ *taṇ* + *ka:ḍu*, 'primordial + forest'
Ta:veka:ḍu ‹ *ta:ve* + *ka:ḍu*, 'fern + forest'
U:marakaṇḍi ‹ *u:* + *mora* + *kaṇḍi*, 'blossom + tree + ridge'
U:morahaṭṭi ‹ *u:* + *mora* + *haṭṭi*, 'blossom + tree + hamlet'

4. *Plant Species*

Attiha:ḍa ‹ *atti* + *ha:ḍa*, 'fig tree + flat ground'
Attikallu ‹ *atti* + *kallu*, 'fig tree + stone'
Attitore ‹ *atti* + *tore*, 'fig tree + riverbank'
Attitorekaḍavu ‹ *atti* + *tore* + *kaḍavu*, 'fig tree + riverbank + ford'
Avuṇḍeka:i ‹ *avuṇḍe* + *ka:i*, 'lamp oil plant + unripe fruit'
Baiga:ḍa ‹ *baige* + *ha:ḍa*, 'Indian willow + flat ground'
Ba:muḍi (?) ‹ *bambe* + *muḍi*, 'ginger grass + headland'
Ba:muḍigu:ḍu ‹ *bambe* + *muḍi* + *gu:ḍu*, 'ginger grass + headland + habitation'
Bannimora ‹ *banni* + *mora*, 'wattle + tree'
Bayengi ‹ *be:* + *hangu*, 'lentil + fenced field'
Beṇḍu:r ‹ *beṇḍe* + *u:ru*, 'okra + head village'
Be:vaṭṭi ‹ *be:vu* + *haṭṭi*, 'neem + hamlet'
Bikkaṭṭi ‹ *bikke* + *haṭṭi*, 'olive linden + hamlet' (5)
Bikkekaṇḍi ‹ *bikke* + *kaṇḍi*, 'olive linden + small tableland'
Bikkemarahaṭṭi/Bikkemorahaṭṭi ‹ *bikke* + *mora* + *haṭṭi*, 'olive linden + tree + hamlet' (2)
Bikko:lu ‹ *bikke* + *goḍalu*, 'olive linden + dale'
Billikambe ‹ *billi* + *kambe*, 'Nilgiri rhododendron + idge' (2)
Billimale ‹ *billi* + *male*, Nilgiri rhododendron + hill'
Cakkaḷaṭṭi/Sakkaḷaṭṭi ‹ *jakkaḷu* + *haṭṭi*, 'Nilgiri barberry + hamlet'
Dabbakambe ‹ *dabbe* + *kambe*, 'darbha grass + ridge'
E:cala:ḍa ‹ *e:calu* + *ha:ḍa*, 'wild date + valley'
Erigiha:ḍa ‹ *erigi* + *gui* + *ha:ḍa*, 'great millet + storage pit + lawn'
Etelarekaṇḍi ‹ *etelare* + *kaṇḍi*, '*Pimpinella* sp. + small tableland'
Ga:tigaṭṭi/Ga:tiguḷi/Ga:tige ‹ *ga:tige* + *haṭṭi*, 'sp. of bush + hamlet'
Haduveyu:ru/Havvu:ru ‹ *haduva* + *(y)u:ru*, 'Nilgiri elm + head village'
Halasaṇe ‹ *halasa* + *haṇe*, 'jackfruit + meadow'

Table 3 (contd.)

Hasalamorahaṭṭi ‹ *hasala* + *mora* + *haṭṭi*, 'jackfruit + tree + hamlet'
Honnaṭṭi ‹ *honne* + *haṭṭi*, 'St. John's wort + hamlet'
Honnemuḍi ‹ *honne* + *muḍi*, 'St. John's wort + headland'
Honno:re ‹ *honne* + *o:re*, 'St. John's wort + slope'
Hubbatale ‹ *hubbe* + *tale*, 'hill forest indigo + headland'
Imbimora Hosaṭṭi ‹ *imbi* + *mora* + *hosa* + *haṭṭi*, 'sweet lime + tree + new + hamlet'
Ittalar ‹ *etelare*, '*Pimpinella* sp.'
Jakkakambe ‹ *jakkaḷu* + *kambe*, 'Nilgiri barberry + ridge'
Jakkaḷoḍe ‹ *jakkaḷu* + *oḍe*, 'Nilgiri barberry + thicket'
Jakkaḷo:re ‹ *jakkaḷu* + *o:re*, 'Nilgiri barberry + slope'
Jakkana:ri ‹ *jakkaḷu* + *(n)a:re*, 'Nilgiri barberry + rocky hilltop'
Jakkata ‹ *sakke* + *tale*, 'jackfruit + headland'
Jakkatakambe ‹ *jakkaḷu* + *tale* + *kambe*, 'Nilgiri barberry + headland + ridge'
Kaḍugaṭṭi ‹ *kaḍugu* + *haṭṭi*, 'bird rape + hamlet'
Kalimora ‹ *ka:ḷe* + *mora*, 'black-bark + tree', sp. unknown
Kaṇḍibikke ‹ *kaṇḍi* + *bikke*, 'small tableland + olive linden'
Kanne:ri ‹ *kanne:raḷu*, 'mountain black plum' (2)
Kanne:rimukku ‹ *kanne:raḷu*+ *mukku*, 'mountain black plum + corner'
Kaṇuvaṭṭi ‹ *kaṇu(v)* + *haṭṭi*, 'edge of hill+hamlet' or ‹ *kanava* + *haṭṭi*, 'tree with phosphorescent bark + hamlet'
Kappaṭṭi ‹ *kappe* + *haṭṭi*, 'sp. of plant + hamlet'
Kattalebikke ‹ *kattale* + *bikke*, 'shady + Nilgiri mock-olive'
Ka:viḷo:re ‹ *ka:viḷu* + *o:re*, 'Bengal currant + slope'
Keccigaṭṭi ‹ *kecciga* + *haṭṭi*, 'Mysore thorn + hamlet' (2)
Kiḷinja:ḍa ‹ *kiḷinju* + *ha:ḍa*, 'pink cedar + valley'
Kiḷinjumandu ‹ *kiḷinju* + *mandu*, 'pink cedar + Toda hamlet'
Kiḷinjumorahaṭṭi ‹ *kiḷinju* + *mora* + *haṭṭi*, 'pink cedar + tree + hamlet'
Kodangaṭṭi ‹ *kodangu* + *haṭṭi*, 'patchouli + hamlet'
Ku:njo:le/Ku:nuso:le ‹ *ku:nu* + *so:le*, 'mushroom + wood'
Kuruṇekore ‹ *kuruṇe* + *kore*, 'rose-box tree + patch of ground'
Malligo:re ‹ Skt. *mallikā* + Bad. *o:re*, 'jasmine + slope' (2)
Mallikore ‹ Skt. *mallikā* + Bad. *kore*, 'jasmine + patch of ground'
Ma:niha:ḍa ‹ *ma:ni* + *ha:ḍa*, 'reeds + valley'
Maruḷakambe ‹ *maruḷe* + *kambe*, 'forest mango + ridge'
Ma:siganaṭṭi ‹ *ma:sikae* + *haṇe* + *haṭṭi*, 'forest pepper + elevation + hamlet'
Ma:sukoḷḷi ‹ *ma:su* + *koḷḷi*, 'chili + bush'
Ma:vuhaṭṭi ‹ *ma:vu* + *haṭṭi*, 'mango + hamlet'
Morakuṭṭi/Morakoṭṭuhaṭṭi ‹ *mora* + *kuṭṭi/koṭṭu* + *haṭṭi*, 'black-bark tree + crest + hamlet', in ref. to its location on a crest

Table 3 (contd.)

Muḷḷimale ‹ *muḷḷi* + *male*, 'bramble + mountain'
Nellihaṇe ‹ *nelli* + *haṇe*, 'emblic myrobalan + wetland'
Nellimandu ‹ *nelli* + *mandu*, 'emblic myrobalan + Toda hamlet'
Ne:ribennu ‹ *ne:ri* + *bennu*, 'umbrella tree + shoulder', i.e. that tree growing on an overhanging hill
Ne:rikambe ‹ *ne:ri* + *kambe*, 'umbrella tree + ridge' (2)
Ne:rimorahaṭṭi ‹ *ne:ri* + *mora* + *haṭṭi*, 'umbrella tree + tree + hamlet'
Ni:rbambehaṭṭi ‹ *ni:ru* + *bambe* + *haṭṭi*, 'water + ginger-grass + hamlet'
Oḍamaṇḍe (?) ‹ *oḍe* + *maṇḍe*, 'bamboo + head'
Perumpaḷḷi ‹ *perumbu* + *paḷḷi*, 'cane + hamlet'
Po:rti ‹ Toda *po•r* + *oty*, 'hollow in tree + fig tree'
Sakkato: ‹ *sakke* + *to:*, 'jackfruit + kraal'
Se:la:ḍa ‹ *se:le* + *ha:ḍa*, 'sebesten plum + flat place'
Se:lakore ‹ *se:le* + *kore*, 'sebesten plum + patch of ground'
Se:lavare/Se:lo:re ‹ *se:le* + *vare*, 'sebesten plum + slope'
Se:leha:su ‹ *se:le* + *ha:su*, 'sebesten plum + canopy of trees'
Se:lemorahaṭṭi ‹ *se:le* + *mora* + *haṭṭi*, 'sebesten plum + tree + hamlet'
Sippigehaṭṭi/Sippihaṭṭi ‹ *sippige* + *haṭṭi*, 'beard grass + hamlet'
Siribikke ‹ *siri* + *bikke*, 'auspicious + olive linden'
Soḍalivo:re ‹ *soḍali* + *(v)o:re*, 'spinous kino tree + slope'
So:gaṭṭi/So:gatore ‹ *so:ge* + *haṭṭi*, 'stink tree + hamlet'
Su:ṇḍaṭṭi ‹ *su:ṇḍe* + *haṭṭi*, 'Indian nightshade + hamlet' (4)
Taḍasumorahaṭṭi ‹ *taḍasu* + *mora* + *haṭṭi*, 'Indian linden + tree + hamlet', a ref. to how Kur̲umbas used to supply the Adigaris with this wood
Tambaṭṭi ‹ *tappe* + *haṭṭi*, 'ginger grass + hamlet'
Taṭṭene:ri ‹ *taṭṭu* + *ne:ri*, 'hillside + umbrella tree' (2)
Ta:veka:ḍu ‹ *ta:ve* + *ka:ḍu*, 'fern + forest'
Togalaṭṭi ‹ *togalu* + *haṭṭi*, 'jungle dhal + hamlet'
Tu:ḍale ‹ *tuḍe* + *tale*, 'hill mango + headland'
Tumbimale ‹ *tumbe* + *male*, 'Nilgiri nettle + mountain'
Tumbu:ru ‹ *tumbe* + *u:ru*, 'Nilgiri nettle + head village'
Tu:ne:ri ‹ *tu:vu* + *ne:ri*, 'valley sides + mountain plum'

5. *References to Local Animals and Hunting*

A:regacci ‹ *a:re* + *gacci*, 'ridge + bees' nest'
Di:naṭṭi ‹ *je:nu* + *haṭṭi*, 'honey + hamlet', i.e. one where much honey was to be found
Dumbimale ‹ *dumbi* + *male*, 'bee + mountain'
Happaṭṭi ‹ *happu* + *haṭṭi*, 'place where meat shared + hamlet'
Happuko:ḍu ‹ *happu* + *ko:ḍu*, 'place where meat is shared + limit'
Ha:vare ‹ *ha:vu* + *are*, 'snake + slab'

Table 3 (contd.)

Hulivare < *huli + (v)are*, 'tiger + hillside'
Huliyaṭṭi < *huli + (y)haṭṭi*, 'tiger + hamlet'
Kaḍana:ḍu < *kaḍe + na:ḍu*, 'stag + tract'
Ka:nabaḷḷi < *ka:na + baḷḷi*, 'jungle + fox hole'
Kappacci < *kappe + acci*, 'frog + division'
Kappatore < *kappe + tore*, 'frog + dale'
Kappaṭṭitore < *kappe + haṭṭi + tore*, 'frog + hamlet + dale'
Kembu:tuke:ru < *kembu:tu + ke:ru*, 'southern crow-pheasant + pond'
Ko:ḍakambe < *ko:ḍa + kambe*, 'bonnet macaque + ridge'
Ko:ḍamu:le < *ko:ḍa + mu:le*, 'bonnet macaque + corner'
Ko:eka:ḷu (?) < *ke:i/ke:yi + ka:ḷu*, 'barking-deer + woodland'
Koṇḍaṭṭi < *koṇḍa + haṭṭi*, 'black langur + hamlet'
Korangupaḍi < *korangu + paḍi*, 'macaque + settlement'
Kunnihaṭṭi < *kunni + haṭṭi*, 'bee + hamlet' (2)
Kunnihiṭṭe < *kunni + hiṭṭe*, 'bees + fallow land'
Kuriyamale < *kuri + ya + male*, 'wild goat + GEN + mountain'
Kurukutti < *kuri + kutti*, 'wild goat + herd'
Mullagu:r < *mullage + u:r*, 'hunting-spot + head village'
Naḷḷhaṭṭi (?) < *naḷḷi + haṭṭi*, 'field crab + hamlet'
Pu:sekunnu:r < *pu:se + kunnu + u:r*, 'wild cat + escarpment + head village'
So:reguṇḍu < *so:re + guṇḍu*, 'dove + big boulder'
Ta:terebennu < *ta:tere + bennu*, 'bandicoot mud-holes + curved hillside'

6. *References to Buffalo Herding*

Be:gamandu < *bi:ga + mandu*, 'kraal + Toda hamlet'
Be:lito: < *be:li + to:*, 'fence or hedge + kraal' – unusual, as the *to:* normally had stone walls
Bi:ganaṭṭi < *bi:ga + na + haṭṭi*, 'kraal + GEN + hamlet'
Danahaṭṭi < *dana + haṭṭi*, 'cattle + hamlet'
Da:vaṇi (?) < *da:vaṇe*, 'cattle market', and/or Kannaḍa *dāvaṇi*, 'assemblage'
Ekko:ṇi < *ekke + o:ṇi*, 'buffalo dung + track' (Pl. 3)
Ha:la:ḍa < *ha:lu + ha:ḍa*, 'milk + flat place' (2)
Ha:lakore < *ha:lu + kore*, 'milk+place', or < *ha:la + kore*, 'ploughman + place'
Ha:laṭṭaṇe < *ha:laṭṭuva + haṇe*, 'milk-pouring ritual + meadow' (2)
Ha:laṭṭi < *ha:lu + haṭṭi*, 'milk + hamlet' (3)
Ha:lu:ru < *ha:lu + u:ru*, 'milk + village'
Huguo:ru/Huguo:re < *hugu + o:ru/o:re*, 'ingress + grazing place'
Ka:yilaṭṭi < *ka:yi + (l)haṭṭi*, 'herding + hamlet'
Kenduva < *ken + to:*, 'reddish + kraal'
Moraṭṭuva (?) < *moraṭṭu + to:*, 'rough + kraal

Table 3 (contd.)

Muttarabi:ge ‹ *muttavar* + *bi:ga*, 'forefathers' + kraal'
Nundua ‹ *nundu* + *hola*, 'fertile+field', or *nundu* + *to:*, 'fertile + cattle pen'
O:ḍemandu ‹ *o:ḍe* + *mandu*, 'unripe bamboo + pen'
O:ṇikaṇḍi ‹ *o:ṇi* + *kanḍi*, 'cattle-track + small tableland'
Sakkato: ‹ *sakke* + *to:*, 'jackfruit + kraal'
Tu:ne:ri ‹ *to:* + *ne:ru*, 'kraal + headland' (2)
Tu:raṭṭi ‹ *tu:ru* + *haṭṭi*, 'cattle pen + hamlet'

7. *Names Showing Relation to Other Villages*

Angaḍihaṭṭi ‹ *a:ngai* + *aḍi* + *haṭṭi*, 'palm of hand + below + hamlet'
Baḍagahaṭṭi ‹ *Baḍaga* + *haṭṭi*, 'Badaga + hamlet'
Bembaṭṭi (?) ‹ *bebbu* + *haṭṭi*, 'lonely + hamlet'
Daḍahaṭṭi (?) ‹ *daḍḍa* + *haṭṭi*, 'fine + hamlet'
Doḍḍu:rkambe ‹ *doḍḍa* + *u:ru* + *kambe*, 'big + head village + ridge'
Doḍḍu:ru ‹ *doḍḍa* + *u:ru*, 'big + head village'
Eḍehaṭṭi ‹ *eḍe* + *haṭṭi*, 'middle + hamlet' (2)
Eḍeka:ḍu ‹ *eḍe* + *ka:ḍu*, 'middle + forest' (2)
Eḍeyu:ru ‹ *eḍe* + *(y)u:ru*, 'middle + head village'
Ha:yu:ru ‹ *ha:ya* + *u:ru*, 'deserted + head village' (3)
Horahaṭṭi ‹ *hora* + *haṭṭi*, 'outer + hamlet'
Hosaṭṭi ‹ *hosa* + *haṭṭi*, 'new + hamlet' (16)
Kaḍehaṭṭi ‹ *kaḍe* + *haṭṭi*, 'last + hamlet' (2)
Kauvaṭṭi ‹ *kauve* + *haṭṭi*, 'little + hamlet'
Koṇakore ‹ *koṇ* + *kore*, 'extremity + place'
Mainele ‹ *maiya* + *nele*, 'central + ocation' (2)
Me:laṭṭi ‹ *me:l* + *haṭṭi*, 'upper + hamlet' (3)
Me:lu:r/Me:lu:ru ‹ *me:l* + *u:ru*, 'upper + head village' (3)
Me:lu:r Hosaṭṭi ‹ *me:l* + *u:ru* + *hosa* + *haṭṭi*, 'upper + head village + new + hamlet'
Osahaḷḷi ‹ *osa* + *haḷḷi*, 'new + settlement'
Osake:ri ‹ *osa* + *ke:ri*, 'new + street'
Pudu:r ‹ Ma. *putu* +Bad. *u:r*, 'new + village'
Taleyaṭṭi/Talehaṭṭi ‹ *tale* + *haṭṭi*, 'upper + hamlet'
Ucca:le ‹ *uccu* + *a:le*, 'top + camp'
Ukkupa:ḷe ‹ *ukku* + *pa:ḷaya*, 'enter + small settlement, hamlet, camp'
U:rdiṭṭu ‹ *u:r* + *diṭṭu*, 'head village + hillock'
U:rhaṭṭi ‹ *u:r* + *haṭṭi*, 'head village + hamlet'
U:rumale ‹ *u:ru* + *male*, 'head village + hill'

Table 3 (contd.)

8. *References to a Cultural Feature*

Adigaraṭṭi ‹ *adigari* + *haṭṭi*, 'administration, control, authority + hamlet'
Amba:le ‹ *amma* + *a:le*, 'goddess + jungle habitation'
Arasukalluhaṭṭi ‹ *arasu* + *kallu* + *haṭṭi*, 'authority + stone + hamlet', a ref. to its ancient use as the meeting place for the commune of Kaḍana:ḍu, the stone being a place to sit
Aremaṇehaṭṭi ‹ *are* + *maṇe* + *haṭṭi*, 'slab+seat + hamlet'
Bakka:ḍa ‹ *bakka* + *ha:ḍa*, 'wooden pillar + flat ground'
Bayengi ‹ *be:* + *hangu*, 'lentil + fenced field'
Beḷaṭṭi ‹ *beḷu* + *haṭṭi*, 'prosperous + hamlet'
Beḷḷaṭṭi ‹ *beḷḷi* + *haṭṭi*, 'white + hamlet'
Bendaṭṭi ‹ *benda* + *haṭṭi*, 'burnt + hamlet', a ref. to former slash-and-burn cultivation (4)
Be:ragal/Be:ragalaṭṭi/Be:regallu ‹ Kuṟ. *báre* + *kállu*, 'lines + stone', a ref. to flat stones nearby covered in etchings and other incisions which in earlier times would have been 'read' by a Kuṟumba sorcerer in an effort to ward off buffalo diseases
Be:ṭḷa:ḍa ‹ *be:ṭḷu* + *ha:ḍa*, 'threshing-post + flat ground'
Bu:dinaṭa ‹ *bu:di* + *naṭṭa*, 'ash-mound + forest clearing'
De:vanatta ‹ *de:va* + *natta*, 'god + common place'
Diṇṇiyu:r ‹ *diṇṇe* + *(y)u:r*, 'shed + head village'
Doḍḍamanehaṭṭi ‹ *doḍḍa* + *mane* + *haṭṭi*, 'great + house + hamlet'
Ellekal ‹ *elle* + *kallu*, 'boundary + stones'
Ellekaṇḍi ‹ *elle* + *kaṇḍi*, 'boundary + basin-like location'
Ellena:yi ‹ *elle* + *na:yi*, 'boundary + neck of land', i.e. at the boundary between Me:kuna:ḍ and Poranga:ḍ
Eriguiha:ḍa ‹ *erige* + *gui* + *ha:ḍa*, 'great millet + storage pit + valley'
Ha:lakore ‹ *ha:lu* + *kore*, 'milk + place', or ‹ *ha:la* + *kore*, 'ploughman + place'
Ha:lappa ‹ *ha:la* + *appa*, 'ploughman + father'
Kacceriha:ḍa ‹ *kacceri* + *ha:ḍa*, 'revenue office + flat ground', so called because until the early nineteenth century revenue collectors from Daṇṇayaka Ko:ṭe had some sort of office here
Kaḍeguḍi ‹ *kaḍe* + *guḍi*, 'last + shrine'
Kagge:ri ‹ *kaggu* + *ke:ri*, 'deep + work-yard, street'
Kaligaṇaṭṭi ‹ *kaligaṇe* + *haṭṭi*, 'stone and wooden post + hamlet'
Ka:vaḍaṭṭi ‹ *ka:vaḍi* + *haṭṭi*, 'hobby-horse + hamlet'
Ki:ekunda ‹ *ki:e* + *kunde*, 'lower + Kundena:ḍ division'
Ko:ḍaṭṭi ‹ *ko:ḍu* + *haṭṭi*, 'border + hamlet'
Ko:ḍe:ru ‹ *ko:ḍu* + *e:ru*, 'boundary + ascent', i.e. a ref. to the boundary between Poranga:ḍ and Me:kuna:ḍ

Table 3 (contd.)

Ku:kal/Ku:kallu ‹ *ku:* + *kallu*, 'sounding + stones'
Ku:katore ‹ *ku:* + *kal* + *tore*, 'sounding + stones + dale'
Kuṇḍana:ḷi ‹ *kuṇḍu* + *na:ḷi*, 'log + slope', a ref. perhaps to rolling logs down into the nearby Kunda River
Ku:ṭuhaṭṭi ‹ *ku:ṭu* + *haṭṭi*, 'meeting + hamlet'
Mandaṇe ‹ *manda* + *haṇe*, 'council-place + level place'
Maṇikal ‹ *maṇi* + *kal*, 'bell + stone', a ref. to a stone that rang when struck
Manjitala/Manjida ‹ *manji* + *tale*, 'fibre + headland' (2)
Ma:riammakaṇḍi ‹ *Ma:ri* + *amma* + *kaṇḍi*, '[Parvati]+goddess+dale'
Ma:sikal ‹ *ma:sige* + *kal*, 'sculptured + stone', i.e. *sati*-stones in the vicinity
Mi:de:ṇu ‹ *mi:de* + *e:ṇu*, 'ploughshare + ridge', since it was said to be the first locality ever to be ploughed in Poranga:ḍ; it is near Kotagiri
Naḍuhaṭṭi ‹ *naḍu* + *haṭṭi*, 'middle + hamlet' (8)
Nanjena:ḍu ‹ *nanje* + *na:ḍu*, 'gashed + tract', ref. to the ancient iron or gold workings
Naṭṭakal ‹ *naṭṭa* + *kallu*, 'erected+stone', i.e. the site of a memorial or boundary stone
Naṭṭake:ri ‹ *naṭṭa* + *ke:ri*, 'affines + street'
Pannamaḍe (?) ‹ *panne* + *maḍe*, 'extensive + shrine'
Sa:maladiṭṭu ‹ *sa:malu* + *diṭṭu*, 'millet barn + boundary'
Si:gola ‹ *si:gu* + *hola*, 'margin + field', as it is on the boundary between Poranga:ḍ and Todana:ḍ
Ta:yimale ‹ *ta:yi* + *male*, 'goddess [Bava:ni] + mountain'
Ta:yu:r ‹ *ta:yi* + *u:r*, 'goddess [Bava:ni] + head village'
Ulupaṭṭi ‹ *ulupu* + *haṭṭi*, 'shack + hamlet'
Ukkiko:sipatti ‹ *ukki* + *ko:si* + *patti*, 'worm + cover + rope', ref. to a silken rope
Ummatapaḍige Me:lu:r ‹ *uma:ta* + *paḍi* + *me:l* + *u:r*, 'datura + measure + upper + head village'
Uyilaṭṭi ‹ *ugal* + *haṭṭi*, 'beyond a boundary + hamlet', as it is on the border between Todana:ḍ and Poranga:ḍ

9. *References to Badaga Men and Women or Clans*

Accanakal ‹ *ajja* + *na* + *kal*, 'ancestor + GEN + stone'
Ba:vaṭṭi (?) ‹ *ba:va* + *haṭṭi*, 'brothers-in-law + hamlet'
Jinjanahaṭṭi ‹ *Jinja* + *na* + *haṭṭi*, '[a name] + GEN + hamlet'
Ko:ka:la:ḍa ‹ *Ko:ka:l* + *ha:ḍa*, '[a name] + flat place'
Kunjano:re ‹ *Kunja* + *na* + *o:re*, '[a name] + GEN + slope'
Kuṭṭanaṭṭi ‹ *Kuṭṭa* + *na* + *haṭṭi*, '[a name] + GEN + hamlet'
Me:l Oḍeyaraṭṭi ‹ *me:l* + *oḍeya* + *haṭṭi*, 'upper + Oḍeya + hamlet'
Muḷḷihaṭṭi ‹ *muḷḷi* + *haṭṭi*, 'hag + hamlet'

Table 3 (contd.)

O:danaṭṭi ‹ *O:da* + *na* + *haṭṭi*, '[name of a founder] + GEN + hamlet'
Oḍeyaraṭṭi ‹ *oḍeya* + *haṭṭi*, 'Oḍeya + hamlet'
O:ranayi ‹ *O:ṛa* + *na* + *haḷi*, '[a name] + GEN + home farm'
Pudugaṭṭi ‹ P*uduga* + *haṭṭi*, '[Puduga's] + hamlet'
Ta:ndana:ḍu ‹ *ta:da* + *na:ḍu*, 'ancestor + tract'
Toreyaruhaṭṭi ‹ *Toreya* + *aru* + *haṭṭi*, 'Toreya + pl. + hamlet'
Tumana:ḍa ‹ *Du:ma* + *na* + *ha:ḍa*, '[a name] + GEN + flat ground'
Tumanaṭṭi ‹ *Du:ma* + *na* + *haṭṭi*, '[a name] + GEN + hamlet'

10. *References to Toda Men or Former Toda Sites*

Be:gamandu ‹ *bi:ga* + *mandu*, 'kraal+Toda hamlet'
Kammandu ‹ Toda *Kemeṉ* + Bad. *mandu*, '[name of extinct Toda clan] + Toda hamlet'
Ke:ḍuha:ḍa ‹ *ke:ḍu* + *ha:ḍa*, 'funeral+level ground', i.e. was a site for buffalo-sacrifice during Toda funerals in the nineteenth century
Kiḷinjumandu ‹ *kiḷinju* + *mandu*, 'pink cedar + Toda hamlet'
Nellimandu ‹ *nelli* + *mandu*, 'emblic myrobalan + Toda hamlet'
Pudumandu ‹ *pudu* + *mandu*, 'joint holding + Toda hamlet'

11. *Reference to a Kota Person or Feature*

Ke:ti ‹ Kota *ke•* *kaṭy*, '[place of] clinkers', a ref. perhaps to where Kota smelting once occurred
Ko:tibennu ‹ *ko:ti* + *bennu*, 'Kota woman + shoulder'

12. *References to Kuṟumbas and Former Kuṟumba or Iṟula Hamlets*

Bakka:raṭṭi ‹ *bakka* + *are* + *haṭṭi*, 'Kuṟumba shelter + slab + hamlet'
De:gili/De:hili ‹ Iṟula *de:* + *egili*, 'threshold, ingress, access + ridge'
De:na:ḍu ‹ *de:* + *na:ḍu*, 'Kuṟumba's cry + tract' (2)
De:na:ḍukombe ‹ *de:* + *na:ḍu* + *kombe*, 'Kuṟumba's cry + tract + Kuṟumba hamlet'
De:na:yi ‹ *de:* + *na:yi*, 'Kuṟumba's cry + neck of land'
De:pa:nu ‹ *de:* + *pa:nu*, 'Kuṟumba's cry + high ingress into a valley'
Ha:lakare/Ha:lake:ru ‹ Kuṟ. place-name
Hulikal/Hulikallu ‹ *Huliya* + *kal*, '[name of a Kuṟumba headman] + stone'
Ka:tarubana ‹ *ka:taru* + *bana*, ' Kuṟumba sorcery + grove'
Kolehaṭṭi ‹ *kole* + *haṭṭi*, 'magical killing + hamlet'
Kolekombe ‹ *kole* + *kombe*, 'magical killing + Kuṟumba hamlet' (3)
Koṇamotta ‹ *koṇa* + *motta*, 'extremity + Kuṟumba hamlet'
Mottakambe ‹ *motta* + *kambe*, 'Kuṟumba hamlet + ridge'

Table 3 (contd.)

13. *Fortifications*

Several Badaga hamlets were associated with former forts, viz:
Kiṇṇakore < *kiṇṇalu* + *kore*, 'saucer + patch of ground' (see p. 65, no. 38)
Ko:ṭa:ḍa/Ko:ṭeha:ḍa < *ko:ṭe* + *ha:ḍa*, 'fortress + flat ground' (2)
Ko:ṭaṭṭi/Ko:ṭehaṭṭi < *ko:ṭe* + *haṭṭi*, 'fortress + hamlet' (3)
Ku:kal/Ku:kallu < *ku:* + *kallu*, 'sounding + stones' (see p. 63, no. 9).

SELECTION OF AN ECOLOGICAL ZONE

A glance at this list of village names (Table 3; it is not exhaustive) emphasizes not only the significance of topography, vegetation and soil in naming and hence, we must presume, as factors in the choice of a new site, but also the *insignificance* of some other environmental features. No toponym, for example, refers to the extreme chilliness of this high elevation, even though the penetrating cold is a topic that regularly recurs in the conversation of recent immigrants from the lowlands.[2] No toponyms refer to wolves, leopards or sloth bears, although we know such animals inhabit the Nilgiris (wolves till quite recently). Only three refer to deities by name, although the Badagas do worship many of them. Very few toponyms mention Badaga settlers by name either; a marked contrast with other regions developed by Anglo-Saxon colonists (e.g. Miller 1969: 246). Most toponyms can be taken to reflect an economic or even an aesthetic interest in the montane environment as it was several centuries ago.

What is more remarkable than these omissions is that – unlike frontier-lands elsewhere – there seem to be no instances of any hamlet acquiring the *same* name as the Mysore village in which its settlers had originated. Instead of commemorating where they had come from with names similar to New London, New York, etc., this lack would accord with what we might expect of destitute and illiterate people wishing to break with their past and not even give clues as to where they had come from. Probably too a whole lifetime or more would pass before a cluster of homes was big enough to need a name. Yet, curiously enough, in several cases where legend does supply the name of the Mysorean village whence a particular lineage of settlers had come (but where epigraphy does not come to our aid), we find a euphonious similarity with the name given to their new

Nilgiri hamlet; e.g. Śo:lu:ru people ‹ Sūlūr. It is as though some refugees still wanted to be reminded of their old home but dared not be more explicit, for fear of attack from the new rulers of Mysore. If there be any truth to this hypothesis, it does provide an interesting instance of adaptive linguistic behaviour in the radically new environment. The following is a list of all Badaga hamlets for which local legend tells of a place of origin in Mysore; those that are marked with an asterisk are ones wherein the factor of euphony might have entered into the choice of a name.[3]

Kaggusi ‹ Hasanu:ru
Tu:ḍeguḷi ‹ Agasvadi
Ekko:ṇi ‹ Kavaspāḍi
Ćinna Kunnu:r ‹ Kongahaḷḷi
* Honnatale ‹ Honnahaḷḷi
* Śo:lu:ru ‹ Sūlūr
Ki:yu:ru ‹ Urigaddige
Nundua ‹ Urigaddige
Hosaṭṭi ‹ Honnahaḷḷi
Hulikal ‹ Honnahaḷḷi
Me:lu:ru ‹ Urigaddige or Beḷḷādi
Ke:ti ‹ Kongahaḷḷi
Tudu:r ‹ Accaḷḷi
* Jakkata ‹ Jakkaḷḷi
Kaḍana:ḍu ‹ Kakkadūr-Kārahaḷḷi
Ebbuna:ḍu ‹ Urigaddige or Hōsahaḷḷi
* Ku:kallu ‹ Guṇḍulupēṭe (*pe:ṭe* = market)

Two elements that commonly recur in the Badaga toponyms are *-u:ru*, 'head village', and *-haṭṭi*, 'hamlet'. Both now have specific meanings in the social organization that are not exactly paralleled in Mysore, the *-haṭṭi* (Kannaḍa *haḷḷi*) being a hamlet, a cluster of a few contiguous homes, and the *u:r* (*u:ru*) a commune or cluster of contiguous hamlets. There are, all told, 468 hamlets that were divided among 41 communes (though about 45 hamlets have been abandoned, and only 40 communes still function). Only four of these communes actually bear a toponym ending with *-u:ru*, however (these names being identical with the head hamlet in each commune; the former commune of Tudu:ru was a fifth). Yet we have found there are 16 toponyms ending in *-u:ru*. Clearly the political organization of Badaga hamlets into 41 communes (*u:ru*), and these into three (and rather more recently four) divisions, all under one paramount chief, is an organization that is in its formulation more recent than the assigning of names to hamlets. The Kannaḍa word *ūru*, 'village', might initially have been applied by the early settlers to the hamlets regardless of any status in a political or administrative hierarchy. The assigning of names to Badaga hamlets was in turn more recent than the actual founding of each hamlet by the builders of the first house. In the seventeenth and eighteenth centuries, when the total population was no more than one or two thousand people, and their density of settlement barely five people per sq. km., it might even have taken several generations before a hut or cluster of huts would have become sufficiently well-known to the neighbours living some kilometres away to merit the acquisition of a site-name. Since

> [t]he name of a village . . . depends for its existence upon the people in the *neighbouring* villages, not upon those who live in it: the latter are usually content in conversation to refer to it as "here" or "home" or "this village" as distinct from other places. It is the size of the area or population throughout which a place-name is accepted as an identificatory label that determines its persistence and permanence. (Wainwright 1962: 58, italics added)

As one might expect, not all of the early Badaga settlements *did* persist for very long: legend gives the names of several dozen that disappeared long ago. Best remembered is the commune of Tudu:ru (‹ *tudi* + *u:r*, 'toe-tip + head village' – as it was on the very edge of the plateau), which once consisted of 36 hamlets (Hockings 2012: 960).[4] 'Tradition says that the Badagas left these places and founded Athikarihatti [Adigaraṭṭi] and its hamlets instead, because the Kuṟumbas round about continually troubled them with their magic arts and indeed killed by sorcery several of their most prominent citizens' (Francis 1908: 316). A more sober reason for the abandonment, and one offered by modern informants, is that the population of all 36 hamlets was decimated by an epidemic disease some 150 or 200 years ago.[5] And scattered across the plateau were several other abandoned hamlets, including Neddilu, Mo:ritore, Eḍeyu:ru, along with several clustered together on land that was bought up by large tea plantations that lie near the southeastern edge of the plateau, around Hulikal, late in the nineteenth century.[6]

It appears that from the earliest phase of their settlement the Badagas were in frequent contact with Todas and Kuṟumbas, and took over a number of sites from both tribal groups. The unique instances of toponyms referring to Kotas and Iṟulas (?) suggest to us that these tribes, by contrast, were insignificant and not very numerous on the plateau. Even today the Kotas occupy only six villages there, and the Iṟulas fewer yet; they are mostly on the lower slopes.

The question naturally arises as to how the Mysore refugees were able to displace Toda and Kuṟumba homes. Local traditions offer only a partial answer. As we have seen, Kota folklore holds that when the first Badaga refugees reached the Nilgiris they met with a council from the three resident tribes: 'Because of the trouble that the Mohammedan made for us we have come, making ourselves to escape. This country is yours. We are helpless. You must help us' (Emeneau 1946: 257; cf. Ouchterlony 1848: 81). The Toda sites that they were given may well have been uninhabited religious centres and unoccupied hamlets that had previously belonged to Toda clans that had however now died out.[7] Kuṟumba sites had more probably been relinquished to Badagas only after the latter had engaged in violence towards the Kuṟumba sorcerers alleged to live in them. The burning of Kuṟumba hamlets was certainly an act of fearful Badagas

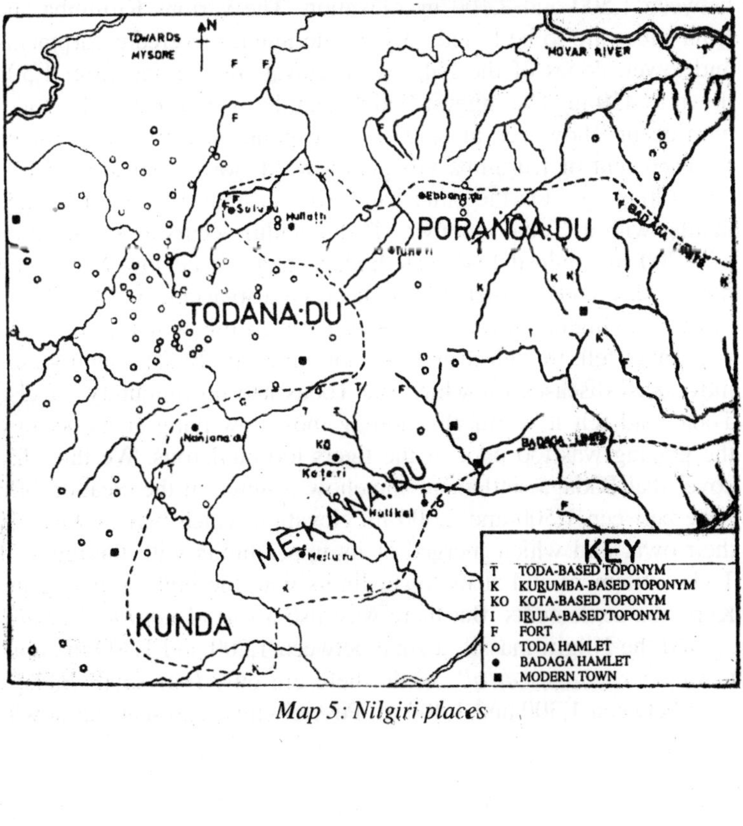

Map 5: Nilgiri places

that was repeated throughout the nineteenth century, for several instances of it have been recorded by the police and contemporary writers (Hockings 2012: 577; see below, pp. 232-34).

As an effect of the otherwise peaceful Badaga incursion, we can now identify some micro-environmental differences in the Badaga, Toda and Kuṟumba settlement patterns. The Todas now occupy the higher and more western plateau area commonly known as Wenlock Downs (Pl. 1), an undulating grassland (much of which has however recently been planted with bluegums, by the Forestry Department), interspersed with temperate sholas (copses) in the dales (Hockings 2012: 987-88). The elevation of their hamlets ranges from 1,400 to 2,000 m. The Badagas now occupy the eastern half of the Nilgiri Plateau, which is heavily cultivated by them, as well as by more recent settlers, and the settled parts of which range in elevation from 2,200 (Be:gamandu, Mainele and Di:naṭṭi hamlets) down to 1,300 m. In a sample of 373 Badaga villages that were clearly located on survey maps, it was noted that 343 (or 91 per cent) are to be found between 1,500 and 2,100 m. elevation. The various Kuṟumba and Iṟula tribes are to be found only on the jungle-covered escarpments and lower slopes of the Nilgiris, at elevations varying from 1,500 down to 450 m. The highest Badaga hamlet with a 'Kuṟumba' toponym occurs, however, at 1,800 m. and points silently to the forced displacement of Kuṟumba villagers towards lower and less healthy levels long ago. On the other hand, we find that the lowest Badaga hamlet with a 'Toda' toponym (Pudumandu) occurs at an elevation of 1,700 m.; indeed five such Badaga hamlets lie lower than any present-day Toda hamlet. This indicates a displacement of the Todas upwards to higher elevations. By what means this was accomplished we cannot tell, though it may be that either the Badaga immigrants introduced diseases for which the Todas had no immunity, or else Todas had felt it worth abandoning those low-lying areas because the grazing was too poor or the tigers too numerous. We thus discover that Badaga settlement somehow resulted in the creation of a zone between 1,500 and 2,000 m. elevation which was exclusively their own, and which merged at its upper limits with the areas of Toda settlement and at its lower limits with the highest among the Kuṟumba settlements. But there was also a sort of *cordon sanitaire* around the Nilgiri massif, a zone between 1,200 and 1,300 m., containing *no villages at all*, while there are only four small Badaga ones between 1,300 and 1,400 m. Possibly this represents an unwitting early protection against malaria and other health hazards found at the lower elevations (Hockings 1989d: 369; 2012: 554-55). The 1,400-m. line is the highest level at which the malaria-causing *Plasmodium* parasite can survive, since this is the highest elevation for its vector, the *Anopheles* mosquito (although up-draughts do sometimes blow mosquitoes up to higher altitudes, however).

The distribution of the Nilgiri ethnic groups, in relation to their physical environment, is summarised overleaf in Diagram 6.

What did early Badagas find attractive about this 1,500-2,000 m. zone in the Nilgiris? We can detect additional evidence for the kind of ecological niche in which they located themselves to begin with from the fact that 157 of the villages have some sort of floral component in their names. Of these 107 are named species belonging to a somewhat restricted ecological setting, and from these names it is thus possible to deduce what sorts of environment the original settlers chose.

The number of villages with plant species as referents:

forest locale	47
brush locale	12
grassland locale	18
swampland, riverbank locale	12
field, cultivar locale	5

Some further information about the floral characteristics of the Badaga zone can be gleaned from a different type of break-down, one based on 58 other Badaga toponyms referring to vegetational cover, which may be summarized thus.

Number of villages with, as referents:

forest (jungle)	15
isolated tree	8
grassland or meadow	9
(apparently) edge of forest or clearing	2
swampland and frogs	9
brush and weeds	6
riverbank	9

To this list might be added the 8 names referring to the presence of ponds and nine mentioning swidden cultivation.

We obviously cannot push the meaning of such figures very far, but they do suggest that (at least for floral toponyms where named

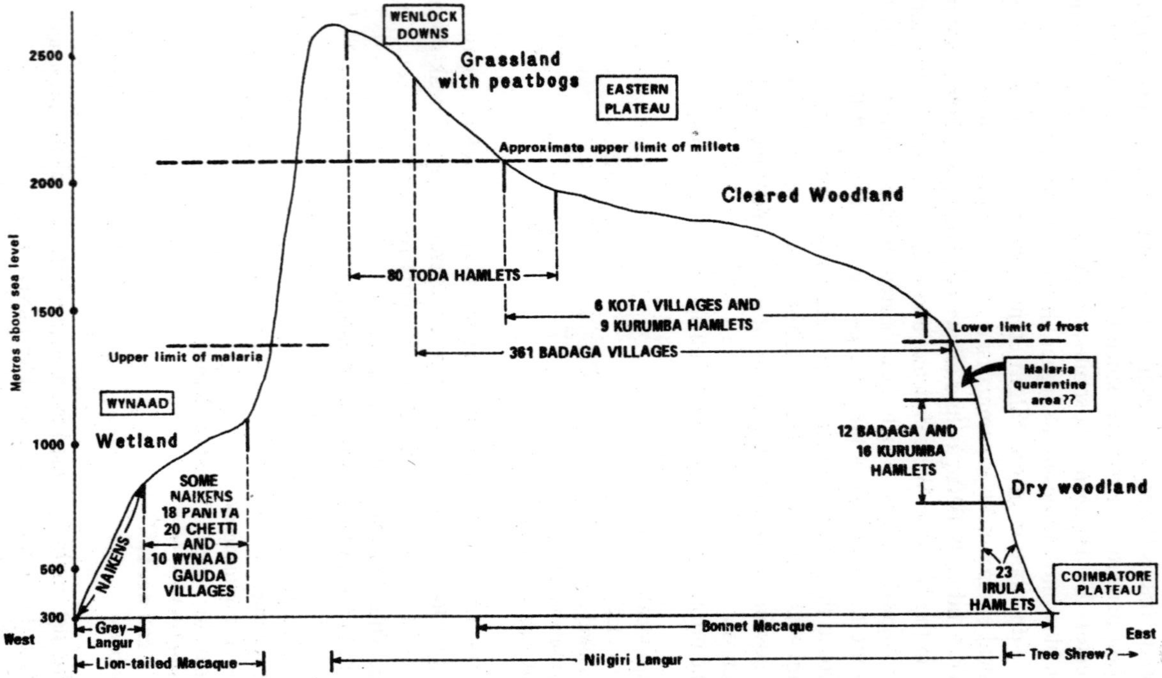

Diagram 6: East-West cross-section of the Nilgiri Hills

species are identifiable) more often than not the Badagas settled elsewhere than in the open but exposed grasslands favoured by the Todas for grazing. Beyond telling us what is fairly obvious – that marsh and swampland were always the least-favoured location for Badaga settlement, while riverbank locations are uncommon in the mountains – the latter breakdown does make it fairly clear that within their zone of occupation dense forests and clearings or the verges of woodland were commonly favoured spots over grassland or savannas for village sites, but that these latter were quite often chosen too, and doubtless among the cattle-herders. The extra work needed to make fields (or swiddens) by slash-and-burn techniques in the forest (referred to nine times) was more than compensated for by the much richer soil available there, at least for a few years, as compared with the lateritic grasslands and swamps where of course the Toda buffalo herds roamed. (Hamlets with names referring to rocks and stones, it is worth noting, are often located in areas that are or were forested: some large trees that stand alongside their temples may still bear witness to this. In eight toponyms, too, it seems a single tree is referred to; but this could be almost anywhere: perhaps on the edge of some woodland, an isolated tree in grassland or a few trees that were valued for their shade and thus remained as a village feature after many others had been cut down there.)

As for where to grow cultivars, Gamble and Fischer's admirable *Flora of Madras* (1915-36 [1956], used for the above numeration) lists the ranges in elevation for the following grains (among others), all of them quite important in the traditional Nilgiri economy:[8]

korali – Italian millet (*Setaria italica*) – 'widely cultivated'
sa:me – slender millet (*Panicum miliare*) – up to 2,150 m.
tene or *navane* – black Italian millet (*Sacciolepis indica*) – up to 2,000 m.
baragu – Kodo millet (*Paspalum scrobiculatum*) – up to 2,150 m.
ra:gi – finger or great millet (*Eleusine coracana*) – up to 1,500 m.

Metz's mid-nineteenth-cenury account of the major millets of the the area in his time adds a little to our understanding of the micro-environmental differences in their cultivation on the plateau, too:

> The most common grain is what the natives call Korrali, which . . . grows best in the colder districts Kundenad and Mekanad where the other finer grains do not grow.
>
> Sāmé . . . which is considered the best kind of the several small grains of the Hills. It grows in the warmer districts and must have better soil.

Tenney or Navoney . . . which also grows only in warm places . . .

Varagu . . . which grows only on the slopes of the Hills in feverish places and requires . . . a warmer climate, than the Hill plateau affords.

Ragy . . . grows also only in places where the cold Monsoon wind cannot come . . . (Abridged from Metz 1864: 152-53)

In general a careful observer, Br. Metz (Pl. 16) roamed the plateau daily for nearly a quarter of a century, visiting most villages and all the market places during 1849-74; he mentions here *baragu* and *ra:gi*, two species which were cultivated mainly by Kuṟumbas and Iṟulas on the lower slopes because of the greater warmth needed. Though grown occasionally in the lowest Badaga hamlets, neither was an important crop for them; the other three species were the main subsistence crops for Badagas, and they grew up to at least 2,000 m. Somewhat unexpectedly, among the village toponyms referring to particular plant species, there are only two places referring to millet – Togalaṭṭi (from *togalu*, 'jungle dhall', a wild millet-like grain, *Atylosia trinervia*), and Erigiha:ḍa (‹ *erigi+gui+ha:ḍa*, 'great millet + storage pit + lawn'; great millet is *Eleusine coracana*).

Deborah Sutton, who offers a detailed study of Badaga agriculture and land-holding in the nineteenth century, has shown how cultivation of the basic grains was fitted into the farming calendar:

The principal subsistence crops, korali (millet), sami (Italian Millet) and ragi, were grown through *bhurty* [swidden] cultivation. The Badagas cropped twice, cultivating mainly millets and legumes with a lesser amount of barley and wheat. Wheat was cultivated in the first crop along with barley in April and was kept largely for export and trade. The second crop. including opium poppy, was sown in October. Wheat was principally cultivated as a primitive form of cash crop, not for domestic consumption but to trade at distant markets. . . . The agricultural calendar ran from April to December, leaving January to March for house repairs and the collection of fuel. Wood was cut and left in the forest to be collected, along with other forest products, as necessary throughout the rest of the year. (Sutton 2009: 88-89)

But we should note that although the early Badagas were cultivators, they evidently thought of themselves as buffalo-herdsmen in the main; indeed their many epic ballads frequently refer to herding yet hardly ever mention their agriculture, even swidden cultivation, which was always widespread until the 1870s. The village toponyms include 27 references to herding, as well as a further 3 to hunting in the jungle, 9 to slash-and-burn cultivation, and 7 to honey-bees:

taken together, these are sure signs of people having had a mixed subsistence economy from the start.

We come to the conclusion that early Badagas displaced Kuṟumbas and perhaps some Todas as well in the zone which they made their own, one that was best suited to buffalo grazing and dry cultivation of their millets. (Rice, incidentally, would not grow here at all.) While the upper limits of the zone were apparently determined by the viability of these millets, the lower limits may have been determined not by horticultural requirements but by the elevation above which malarial parasites will not breed, about 1,400 m. (As was mentioned, the full development of the *Plasmodium* parasites in mosquito requires a minimum daily temperature of 60° F or 15.6° C, which is only maintained at the lower elevations that were relegated to the Kuṟumbas, Iṟulas and other groups.) By the mid-nineteenth century the linguist Hodgson found plateau sites 'where formerly Kurumba villages existed but where none are now found. It is well known that the Kurumbas were driven down from the healthful summit to the malarious slope of the hills . . .' (1856: 499-500).

Not only did the settlers displace residents from these other tribes: they also removed much of the forest cover and radically changed the Nilgiri ecology, in the view of many experts, well before the first British planters had arrived here in the 1860s. As the incidence of so many village names that refer to forest vegetation makes apparent,

> There can be little question that these tracts, which are now given up almost wholly to the plough or hoe, were once covered with dense jungle, except the more stony ridges and heights. This is evidenced by the numerous shóla trees, single or in groups of two or three, standing generally near a rock or stream, which have owed their escape from the general destruction to the superstitious fears of the people, who regard them as the homes of the unseen genii of the place. The frequent occurrence [barely four cases, in fact – P.H.] of the suffix *kád*, jungle or forest, in names of localities, where now hardly a tree is to be found, is additional proof . . . (Grigg 1880: 9).

This pronounced man-made ecological change has led to several studies exploring the likelihood that the more westerly grasslands now occupied by Todas were also originally heavily forested areas that had succumbed to annual fires started by these herdsmen (Noble 1967; Blasco 1971). While that question is of little relevance in the present study, it does emphasize the way in which ecological change may become so devastating as to alter the environment almost beyond recognition after a toponym has been assigned to some site there; so too with twentieth-century re-afforestation programmes.

NOTES

1. The + used in these lists merely links the morphemes in a word, and is not to be considered as a symbol of juncture. Numbers in parentheses indicate the number of times a toponym is repeated.
2. On cold winter nights frost can form.
3. Euphony is an important feature of Badaga speech and is a characteristic in hundreds of their proverbs; e.g.
   hattu jina sa:la / ondu jina su:la
   ten days debt, one day venereal disease:
   i.e. 'For ten days it will be a debt, but one day it will become a venereal sore' (Hockings 1988: proverb 803a)
4. Of these, Tudu:ru had an *akka bakka*. The full list of hamlet names is given in Appendix 3, in Hockings and Pilot-Raichoor (1992: 836, App. 3) and Hockings (2012: 110-13); but since these names are almost unknown to present-day Badagas we cannot be exact about their pronunciation or meaning.
5. Remnants of this population now live in nearby Ko:ḍe:ru and can still recall something of their history.
6. These latter were named Beṭṭaṭṭi, Ko:ṭaṭṭi, Kareko:ṭe (a fort), Banahaṭṭi, Ta:veka:ḍu, Bendaṭṭi and Pannamaḍe; Hockings & Pilot-Raichoor 1992: 837.
7. During the twentieth century there were several well-documented cases of Toda hamlets being abandoned, including one in the Wainad. Recently one clan died out.
8. It may be recalled that the Nilgiri Plateau rises to an elevation of 2,637 m. in Doḍḍabeṭṭa, 'Great Mountain'; Hockings 2012: 270-71.

CHAPTER 5

Social Groupings are Formed

The extensive oral history examined in Chapters 1-4 helps clarify distinctive features of each clan and phratry, even identifying some of their places of origin, the various routes they took into the hills, and the sequence in which they arrived.[1] These legends are more than fictional entertainment, for they are oral histories validating the continued occupancy of each village by the members of a particular clan. Many tales form a part of the extensive ballad repertoire.

Let us approach a question that is intended to clarify later chapters: once the migrants had left the Mysore caste system behind and settled in the Nilgiris, how was marriage regulated, and how was the continuance of social units ensured from one generation to the next? (I admit at the outset that how they managed to synœcize into the Badaga community is a question that remains difficult to answer.)

Indian caste society has usually been described in terms of joint family, lineage, clan and *jati* (subcaste), but in the Badaga case, one that today fits a caste model imperfectly, we will refer to the following categories instead. These are their social units, listed in order of increasing breadth and numbers:

1. Joint patrilocal family (exogamous; belongs to one village)
2. Minimal lineage (exogamous; occupies one village)
3. Minor lineage (exogamous; occupies one village)
4. Major lineage (exogamous; occupies one or several villages)
5. Maximal lineage (exogamous; occupies one or several villages)
6. Patrilineal clan (exogamous; widespread)
7. Phratry (mostly endogamous; widespread)
8. Moiety (mainly endogamous; Nilgiri-wide)
9. Badaga community (traditionally endogamous; Nilgiri-wide)
10. Fifteen *kolas* or septs (exogamous; in popular belief these are South India-wide).

Individuals usually claim membership in every one of these units.

THE JOINT PATRILOCAL FAMILY

The Badaga family is always patrilineal and with a few exceptions patrilocal: the descent is in the male line. Because of the power its numbers command a joint family is also the ideal, and every third generation typically passes through this desired state. Thus a young couple establish their new home in the village of the groom's father. Their children, if male, should remain in the same house with their parents, or be married later into another village if female. The young men take brides from villages of affines (whom we might also call in-laws), bring them to the parental home and raise their children there. At this juncture there would be three generations living under the same roof as a joint family: (1) unmarried grandchildren, (2) unmarried daughters, married sons and their wives, (3) the parents.

On the death of the founding father the brothers are expected to leave his house and establish separate homes nearby. This dispersal of the household has three causes – architectural, legal and psychological. The first is that a Badaga house contains only two or three fairly small rooms (Diag. 7; Hockings 1999: 34-36, figs. 1.1–1.3; Noble, in Hockings 2012: 52, fig. 21 E); and by the time that three generations, two of them with spouses, are occupying a single house there is an acute shortage of space – a situation which would only have been aggravated by polygyny. The legal cause of dispersal is the tradition of ultimogeniture: Badaga customary law requires that the *youngest* son inherit his father's house and at the same time take care of the widowed mother (cf. Rivers 1906: 559-60). Financial provision should be made for all the older brothers to build separate houses. The psychological causes are the total lack of privacy and the elder brothers' uneasy feeling of indebtedness to the youngest brother who legitimately owns the house. A further complication is that in recent years one brother who works in an office has become increasingly unwilling to share his relatively high income with his extended peasant family of small farmers. In this manner large joint families are no longer so common in the present day as they were even half-a-century ago and earlier too: thus today an average Badaga household might contain only 5.5 members, but the range in household size is from one to perhaps twenty. (It should be remembered that a household is not exactly the same unit as a biological family in all cases, for it sometimes will contain a distant relative or even a servant, and thus is a residential, not a biological, unit.)

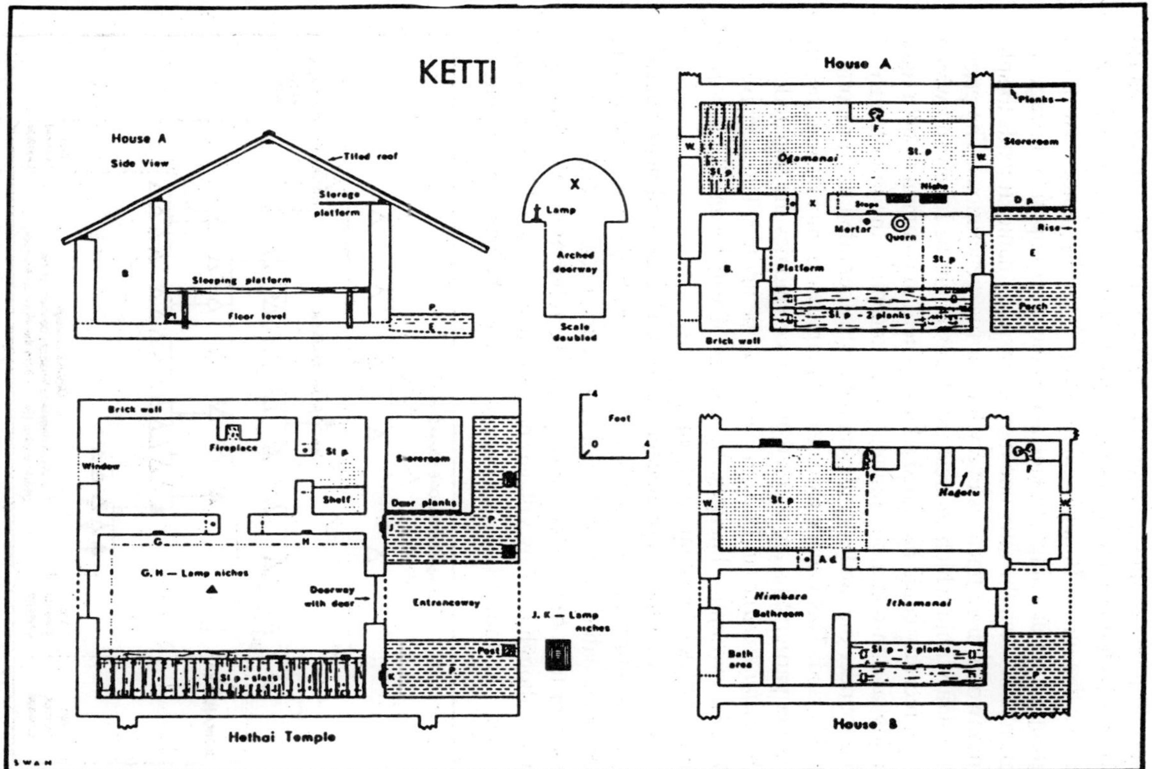

Diagram 7: Flan of two houses and the Hette temple in Ke:ti

LINEAGE

Several joint families agreeing on precisely how they are descended from a common male ancestor consider themselves a *minimal* or a *minor lineage* (in Baḍagu, *guppu*). This is an exogamous patrilineal group living in a single village and is the most important lineage for members, often the only one they know of by name. It tends to split into two or three lineages every four or five generations. The *guppu* is a unit within which interest-free loans might be found and which even recently could have had a buffalo herd in common. It no longer holds land in common, although at its inception the joint family of the founder did, and each descendant is still entitled to a proportion of his land. This lineage tends to hold family ceremonies together. If further participants are wanted at such ceremonies the remainder of the *major lineage* (in Baḍagu, *kutti*) can be invited. This consists of at least two minor lineages the leaders of which can all trace their ancestry back to a common founder.

Very often the major lineages in one or in several neighbouring villages summate to a maximal lineage (in Baḍagu, *kuḍumbu*) and knowledgeable members can often trace their actual descent from its founder too. All levels of lineage can be referred to by a founder's name, though in many villages no more than one level is now recognized. The minor lineage commonly bears the name of the line of

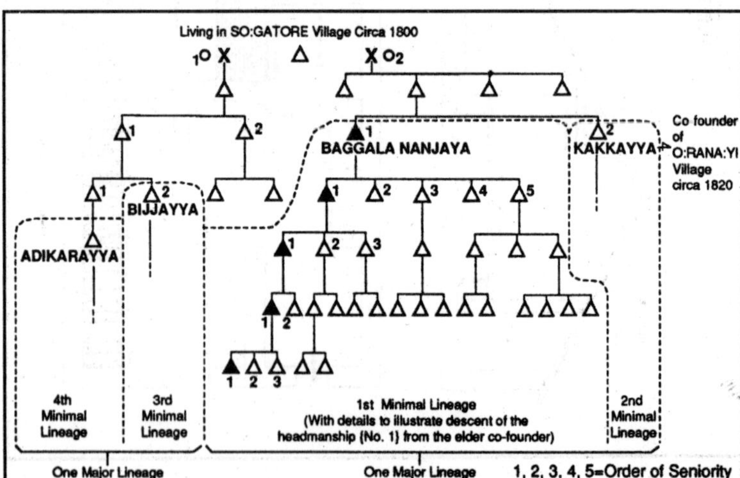

Diagram 8: O:ranayi village: A maximal lineage

work-yards (the *ke:ri*) that front the houses along which its members live. Lineages of all levels may usually be invited to attend family ceremonies.

From the example in Diag. 8 it is seen that a maximal lineage has a depth of about seven generations. As at that village, the maximal lineage is very often co-terminus with the village, which explains the exogamy of most villages. There are, however, some exceptional villages, notably those of the Oḍeyas and Toreyas, and the Gauḍas of So:lu:ru commune and Hasanu:ru, which contain several distinct lineages from *different* clans within each village; so that, although exogamy still marks the lineage, it is not a necessary practice within those villages.

There was traditionally a strong sense of lineage solidarity, strongest at the minor level but still significant at the maximal. In case of a dispute with someone outside the villager's own lineage, be it minimal, minor, major or maximal, his fellow members are usually willing to support him even if this means agreeing to false evidence. Such behaviour may help to keep land and other property within the lineage, and it can also uphold the good name of a lineage and the village it inhabits. Solidarity is also expressed when a man needs to sell some land. Traditionally he should offer it first to other members of his minimal or minor lineage, then to his major lineage, then to his maximal, then to any other inhabitants of his village, then to people in neighbouring villages. Only in the unusual case when nobody in this sequence would buy may he offer the land to Badagas from elsewhere. The land surrounding each village is typically owned by the various families of that village only.

CLAN

Several maximal lineages make up the *clan* (in earlier terminology, the *sib*; in Baḍagu, *ku:ṭa, kola/kula*). Like the lineage, the clan is exogamous, but is rarely confined to a single village. A lineage embraces all the patrilateral descendants of a known common ancestor (Schusky 1965: 77), whereas a clan, which is made up of two or more lineages, is a unilinear kinship group in which actual descent from a common male ancestor is now only a presumption.[2]

At this level of social organization the clan unit is spatially widespread: two Badaga clans are confined to a single village each (only among Kumba:ras); others are represented in clusters of nearby villages, while over half of the 44 clans are Nilgiri-wide in occurrence (Heidemann 2006: 141-67).

Clans are relevant in the arrangement of marriages, for there are fixed rules about which clans may intermarry; for example, Adigaris may marry Ha:ruvas, but never Kaggusis. Clans may also form a community of interest for the pursuit of really serious disputes. In 1897, for instance, the Ha:ruvas of two different lineages in neighbouring villages were in dispute over which should have precedence during the annual firewalking ceremony at Me:lu:ru. After reaching a compromise whereby each group celebrated the festival on alternate years (Francis 1908: 340), the whole Ha:ruva clan laid claim to a higher status than Oḍeyas, Adigaris or Kaṇakkas. A schism within the Ha:ruva clan has not emerged since (see below, pp. 111, 238).

PHRATRY

Among the Badagas, two to fourteen clans form a larger unit that I call the phratry. Most of these phratries and some of the clans have been called *sects* or *subcastes* by previous authors, if only because they are large named social units.[3] It is manifestly confusing, however, to apply the same term to two quite distinguishable kinds of social unit. A phratry is usually defined as a grouping of two or more clans whose members assume a conventional bond of kinship which, though undemonstrable, is at least supported with a story of their common origin. In the Badaga community most of the phratries are non-exogamous, but in specific cases exogamy is tolerated; and no Badaga phratry is totally endogamous (Lowie 1948: 338; cf. Diag. 9). The phratries each carry a distinguishable subculture. The smallest in size, the Be:ḍas and Kumba:ras, are divided into two clans, identifiable simply as agnates and affines. Phratries with more than about a thousand members have a larger number of clans and thus a more complex internal organization. In this respect the four thousand or more Christians mark the extreme of complexity.

MOIETIES

Some small societies, among them the Todas and Australian aboriginal tribes, are divided into only two phratries, which are then called moieties (from the French word for 'half'). Other societies, notably in lowland areas of the South Asian subcontinent, have a number of endogamous phratries that are ranked into long-lasting social hierarchies; such units, called *jatis* or subcastes, may summate to castes or *jati*-clusters (Mandelbaum 1970: *passim*).

Badaga society, consisting of 44 clans and 10 phratries, is now in the anomalous position of being to some extent a moiety organization, to some extent a *jati* organization. This situation has perhaps arisen because two different social models were available to the Badagas for emulation, a Brahminic one known to them from lowland caste society and – unique in India – a tribal one represented by Todas' social organization. Their situation became yet more complex when in the nineteenth century Westernization also began, and a tenth Christian phratry grew out of six of the others. This complexity has not been properly appreciated, for though several earlier writers have described Badaga society as a hierarchy of subcastes none has considered it to have moieties. Even so, the neighbouring Todas possess a well-known moiety system. In their case there are now 15 exogamous patrilineal clans, 5 in Töwfıḷy (Teivali) moiety and 10 in To·ṟθas̱ (Tarthar). Each moiety is endogamous, and To·ṟθas̱ has a ritual superiority over Töwfıḷy which is expressed by ownership of the most sacred grades of temple and buffalo; the priests who used to sacrifice buffalo calves belong to Töwfıḷy.[4]

The Badagas show much more cultural diversity than the Todas, largely because the former are a community many times larger, who arrived at various periods from different places and from varying Kanarese caste and religious backgrounds. Nevertheless, we may consider them (at least for the sake of argument) to have two well-defined, culturally heterogeneous, ranked moieties, one vegetarian and the other not. As we have already seen, the act of eating meat placed some ancestral groups definitively in one moiety, where they have since remained. In this connection it is worth noting that while both Toda moieties are vegetarian, it is only the priests of the lower moiety (Töwfıḷy) who killed calves (some parts of which they did once cook to eat; Walker, in Hockings 2012: 175-77), and who also sacrifice the more sacred buffaloes at a funeral. A further parallel between the two neighbouring societies is that, just as Todas of Töwfıḷy moiety must perform certain priestly functions for To·ṟθas̱, so men in the Ha:ruva and Oḍeya clans perform a priestly role only for clans of the other Badaga moiety. Among the Todas a kind of secondary marriage is permissible between otherwise endogamous moieties (Rivers 1906: 699-700); among Badagas formal marriages may sometimes occur between the usually endogamous moieties, so long as the man or woman from the meat-eating moiety abstains from meat while in the presence of a vegetarian spouse.

It is important to note that the present trend in Badaga society is towards total endogamy of each moiety: Ha:ruva, Adigari and Kaggusi marriage with Gauḍas has been decreasing in the past century, while Lingayats recently have avoided marrying into the Ha:ruva families which also have marriage connections with Gauḍas; yet the traditional hypogamy and hypergamy are both still permissible, if uncommon. Were the Badagas moving towards a caste model of society, one might expect hypogamy to disappear (something almost unknown in caste societies), and further culinary distinctions to be adopted. For example, distinctions might then be made, as elsewhere in India, between those who eat beef, those who take mutton and chicken but no beef, those eating eggs but no meat, and those solely vegetarian. Yet no such complication is emerging: people are strengthening the boundary between households of vegetarian and non-vegetarian diet, but no finer distinctions are drawn. The moiety of vegetarians includes all of the clans noted for their religious orthodoxy, while the much larger non-vegetarian moiety includes most of the better educated, somewhat Westernized and economically influential families, including Christians.

SEPTS

The clans are reputedly distributed among 15 septs which, we are told, cross-cut all south Indian society. In theory every clan of each Hindu caste is affiliated to one or more exogamous *kolas*; the Badaga clans were of the same *kolas* even before leaving Mysore, and indeed all of their *kolas* are still identifiable among various castes there (Nanjundayya & Ananthakrishna Iyer 1930-35). *Kola* has thus to be defined as a sept or patrilineal descent group, 'a group of persons, all of whom believe themselves to be related, owning some relation to an object animate or inanimate, and exhibiting the taboo-behaviour towards it. . . . There does not appear to be any larger organization comprising the various kulas' (Srinivas 1942: 32).

Table 4: Distribution of the Badaga phratries among the fifteen septs

Su:riya (sun)	former chieftains from Mysore; some Oḍeyas
Chandra (moon)	servants of the former rulers; Kongaru
Barata (finger)	some Oḍeyas
Bra:ma (god Brahma)	Ha:ruvas, and Kumba:ras
Beḷḷi (silver)	some Oḍeyas, Kaggusis, Gauḍas of Jakkata and Neḍuguve; some Toreyas of Kaige:ru area; some Be:ḍas
Selandi (spider)	some Oḍeyas and Gauḍas of Hulikal and 'Kongaru' Gauḍas – both descended from Oḍeyas
Ko:ve:ri (Cauvery R.)	some Oḍeyas, some Adigaris, and Toreyas descended from those Adigaris
Maṭure (sweetness)	some Oḍeyas (also called Ma:ntu)
Kasturi (musk)	some Gauḍas of Ke:ti, Me:lkunda, and Kiekunde; some Adigaris; some Toreyas of Ebbuna:ḍu
Malliga (jasmine)	some Kumba:ras and Be:ḍas
Maduve (marriage)	some Oḍeyas; Gauḍas of Poranga:ḍ (Heidemann 2006: 91-98, 108, 129, 137)
Ma:ṇikka (gem)	Kaṇakkas (who claim their sept to be Ma:nta); some Gauḍas of Jakkana:ri; some Toreyas
Samundi (champac flower)	some Kumba:ras
Ma:ri (goddess Ma:ri)	Gauḍas of Todana:ḍ
Na:ga (cobra)	some Toreyas of Kappaṭṭi area

Their distribution, a few elders recall, is as in Table 4. Although today few, even among the elders, know the details of their septs, in earlier days they were important, especially before their society took on its present structure, and when marriages were to be arranged between families from clans not well known to each other; '. . . exogamy having progressed, if we may say so, more rapidly than social differentiation, it was necessary to call into question an increasingly large number of clans, to adapt the old institutions to the new rules' (Lévi-Strauss 1968: 480, trans.). In the reworking of social thinking after settling on the hills, Badagas might well have found family membership in these already long-established septs a helpful guide; the rule of sept exogamy and the wide knowledge of their names protecting against in-breeding between families from the same descent group. For the Oḍeya phratry, its membership in seven septs remains, as we shall see, the basic way of organizing marriage rules.

It is interesting that a distribution of the Badaga phratries in terms of these septs (Table 4) suggests that there are two grand connubia or 'marriage fields' in Badaga society, one of them made up of all those groups, Lingayat or otherwise, that had once been associated as *servants* with the Woḍeyar rulers of Mysore; and a second group, of Gauḍas, Ha:ruvas and Toreyas whose ancestors, if anything can be generalized about them, came into the Nilgiri Hills rather as *refugees* from Mysore. It will be noticed that there is a good deal of complementarity of distribution between the smaller groups with membership in only one to three of these exogamous septs.

Formerly the septs were quasi-totemic, as was common throughout India.[5] One old lady of Selandi (spider) sept asserted to me that its members should never kill a spider; Oḍeyas of Beḷḷi (silver) sept may not wear silver ornaments; Toreyas, however, no longer have any special relation with the cobra, though some of them belong to Na:ga (cobra) sept and were formerly forbidden to kill it.

The Badagas do not distinguish between what Lévi-Strauss (who follows S.V. Karandikar, 1929) called big and little *gotras* (septs). Elsewhere in India 'big' *gotras* are said to be of recent Brahminic origin and few in number; whereas 'little' *gotras* 'appearing sometimes as territorial groups, sometimes as lineages, as clans or subdivisions of a clan, sometimes patrilineal and sometimes matrilineal, are . . . the object of exogamous rules of great complexity' (Lévi-Strauss 1968: 478-79, trans.). Clearly the Badaga septs are 'little' *gotras*. As such they were concerned, not with political divisions or different schools of ritual, but solely with the arrangement of marriage alliances. Each of their 15 septs is distributed through one or several clans. On the other hand, the Oḍeyas belong to seven septs, but other phratries to as few as two septs.

JATI, MARRIAGE PREFERENCE AND ROLE AMBIGUITY

Although it is possible to view this society as a pair of moieties, the phratries, like social units in nearly every part of India, are ranked by members into a hierarchy about which there is considerable if not total agreement.[6]

All Hindu Badagas agree that the Christians are now the lowest phratry, and this estimation is reflected in disapproval of intermarriage and absence of formal interdining between Christians and the higher phratries during the twentieth century. There is also agreement that the Toreyas are next lowest; higher groups should neither dine nor intermarry with them. At the other end of the scale there is near-universal accord on the supreme position of Oḍeyas. Though the great majority of the community are not Lingayats themselves, they cite the purity of an Oḍeya's vegetarian diet and the orthodoxy of his sectarian observances as support for his high rank. Many also say that the Oḍeyas were descended from ancient Virashaiva Lingayats, reached the Nilgiris before any other Lingayats did, and came there as priests, for which reasons too they merit primacy.

Nobody disputes with the Christians or the Toreyas for their lowly position, not even the Kota tribesmen who have found themselves ranked lower still. On the other hand there has long been a movement to give the Ha:ruvas higher status than the Oḍeyas: this springs from that minority who support a pro-Ha:ruva and pro-ceremonial music faction. The mechanics of upward mobility for Ha:ruvas, a vegetarian group since its inception, have been to abrogate marital links with lower clans. The Ha:ruvas may marry Gauḍas (who are non-vegetarians), Koṅgaru (vegetarians), or Kaṇakkas and Adigaris (both of them Lingayat vegetarians). Recently the frequency of marriages with Gauḍas has decreased noticeably, for the Ha:ruvas are shifting away from their lower-status affines while becoming more closely linked through marriage with Badaga Lingayats, although not adopting Lingayat religious practices themselves.

Mandelbaum (1970: 20) once described the Badagas as a *jati*-cluster. It is true that the units often identified as subcastes are now thought to constitute a hierarchy; but *none* of the ten is totally endogamous like a *jati*. Hypogamous marriages occur almost as regularly as hypergamous ones, a state of affairs not found between *jatis*, especially as marriage may take place between vegetarian and non-vegetarian Badagas. The ceremonial and economic links that one expects between *jatis* are of no consequence here, except at the top of the hierarchy: Oḍeyas and Ha:ruvas do have attenuated ritual roles to play for the rest of the community, although over the past eighty years these have been almost abandoned. Such linkages between the groupings are slight when compared with the traditional economic and ceremonial ties that had existed between any Badaga village and its nearest Kota neighbours. These facts do not really justify calling the Badaga community a hierarchy or cluster of *jatis*;

the concept of *jati* is unnecessary to this analysis. 'Phratry' is the usual word by which anthropologists identify a grouping of clans, and there is no need to depart from that form here, especially as by doing so we might conjure up images of multi-caste villages, *jati* endogamy and *jati* occupational specialization which have no place in Badaga social organization, although they are otherwise widespread in India.

M.N. Srinivas (personal observation, 1965) was probably right in suggesting, however, that at some point in the past, perhaps a couple of centuries ago, the Badagas adopted a caste model of society (or revived memories of the old Mysorean one) and attempted with only moderate success to fit their collection of lineages to it; indeed this perhaps was their act of synœcism. The inadequate fit that they achieved is reflected both in recent shifts in the ranking and in the ambiguous position that the claim to Brahminic status has brought to the Ha:ruvas. This group long ago adopted the 'sacred' thread,[7] a vegetarian diet, and the role of priests, but they have no initiation ceremony, no *śrāddha* for the dead and – having been illiterate – no Sanskrit or other holy writings. In the mid-nineteenth century they were still quite ignorant of Hindu scriptures (BEMS 1867, no. 28: 73). They now find themselves caught between a pair of models, as it were, for while they are trying to develop the image of orthodox Brahmins other Badagas find that model much less appealing than a new Westernizing model already being upheld by Christians and by the large, dominant and increasingly well-educated Gauḍa phratry, a model that displaced their older tribal model nearly a century ago. A more general ambiguity is expressed by shifts in the ranking of the hierarchy, as certain Badagas attempt to achieve a more convincing accord between the recently learnt Brahminic ideals and local needs. Since the Badagas have shown no willingness to modify customary marriage patterns, they are obliged to accept the anomaly of a hierarchy relevant only for ritual and not for marriage purposes: this sets them off from the usual model of caste society, in which the units of the hierarchy of purity are clearly delineated by marriage rules.

Another explanation for the lack of concern about status congruence when a marriage is being arranged is that the social status of a young girl is determined by the village where she lives. Girls before puberty are for many purposes treated as children of the entire village, rather than of one particular family. Once any girl has attained menarche (in earlier days, before that) she should be married into another village, where she will become identified with her husband's family and where her status is determined only by the clan and the affluence of that family, never by her own father's. The same attitude towards women is reflected in the kinship system, where only the males' generation level is important in determining relationships. The generation level of a woman is that of her husband and could actually change if she married successive husbands from different generations.[8] Although a cross-cousin is preferred, a Badaga may marry women, either concurrently or sequentially, from his aunts' or nieces' generation levels as well as from his own: such co-wives would all attain the generation level of their husband by these marriages. It is this outlook on women that permits Badaga marriages even between differently ranked clans, without any idea of hypergamy being advantageous or hypogamy reprehensible.

Marriage between cross-cousins is the ideal, but because a young man's spiritual guidance is the responsibility of the mother's brother that man's daughter is less preferable as a bride for the youth than the father's sister's daughter. The mother's brother, who is called a *guru*, has a superior status to his nephew's, yet as giver of a daughter in marriage he would occupy an *inferior* position in the eyes of the groom and the groom's parents. This is because the bride's father feels under some obligation to the family who will be looking after his daughter. As one old man explained, the feeling is expressed in the newly emerging practice of offering gifts of many thousands of rupees to 'bribe' a youth into a marriage. The likelihood of role ambiguity in cases where a man marries his *guru*'s daughter tends to be avoided either by searching out a more distant, classificatory cross-cousin, or by choosing the daughter of a mother's brother *other* than the spiritual guide, or else by marrying a father's sister's daughter. (Only among the Toreyas is marriage with a classificatory niece permissible: usually a father's brother's daughter's daughter.)

Role ambiguity may also affect the women in a household where a man has married his *guru*'s daughter. In that situation the bride's aunt (a father's sister) will also be the husband's mother. The bride, relying on her father's influence over his own sister, may choose to quarrel more with her than in the alternative case where a man has married his father's sister's daughter: the latter should be more timid and controllable, and hence more appreciated by her new family.

A further reason for preferring marriage with a daughter of the father's sister is the need for reciprocity in bride-exchange between exogamous villages. If a man marries his mother's brother's daughter, he is then *taking* a girl from the same village, lineage and family whence his own father also *took* a wife. On the other hand a reciprocal relationship has been honoured, Badagas feel, when the youth *takes* his bride (the father's sister's daughter) from the same village, lineage and family to which his father's father *gave* a daughter in marriage. Since bride-giving is thought to be vaguely demeaning, this reciprocity allows the families to maintain their relative social standing (for more on marriage rules, see Hockings 1982).

Another factor entering into the choice of a bride is expressed in the proverb, 'Get a girl from a far-away place; get a cow from a nearby place!' (Hockings 1988: 292, no. 535). It is generally felt that a woman from a distant village who is a classificatory cross-cousin will make the best of wives, as she may not take too many liberties with affines who were not previously well-known to her, and at the same time she will be unable to run home to her parents too often; in short, she is likely to remain in the marital home and work effectively there. An example of an ideal marriage with a classificatory father's sister's daughter is to be seen in Diag. 11 (p. 205: the man marked X). The principle of 'equivalence' of brothers in this kinship table makes X's wife a cross-cousin to him.

One study based on census materials from 1961 and 1971 found that, among 182 Badaga marriages,

> 1.10 per cent were uncle/niece marriages
> 23.62 per cent were MBD (mother's brother's daughter) marriages
> 3.85 per cent were FZD (father's sister's daughter) marriages
> Thus 27.47 per cent were marriages with first cousins,
> and 28.57 per cent were consanguineous marriages of some form.
> (The inbreeding co-efficient was 0.019; Roychoudhury 1980: 171)

In Chapter 15 (pp. 280-85) we will examine the manner in which the modern Badaga community is tending towards a class society. We should nonetheless note here that already by the nineteenth century a class of 'gentry' (*manetana*) had emerged in each village. This is the term I have chosen for the families descended from the village founders and including all of the headman. As will be seen, these people had higher social status than others and a peculiar status in Badaga law (to be explored in Chapter 11).

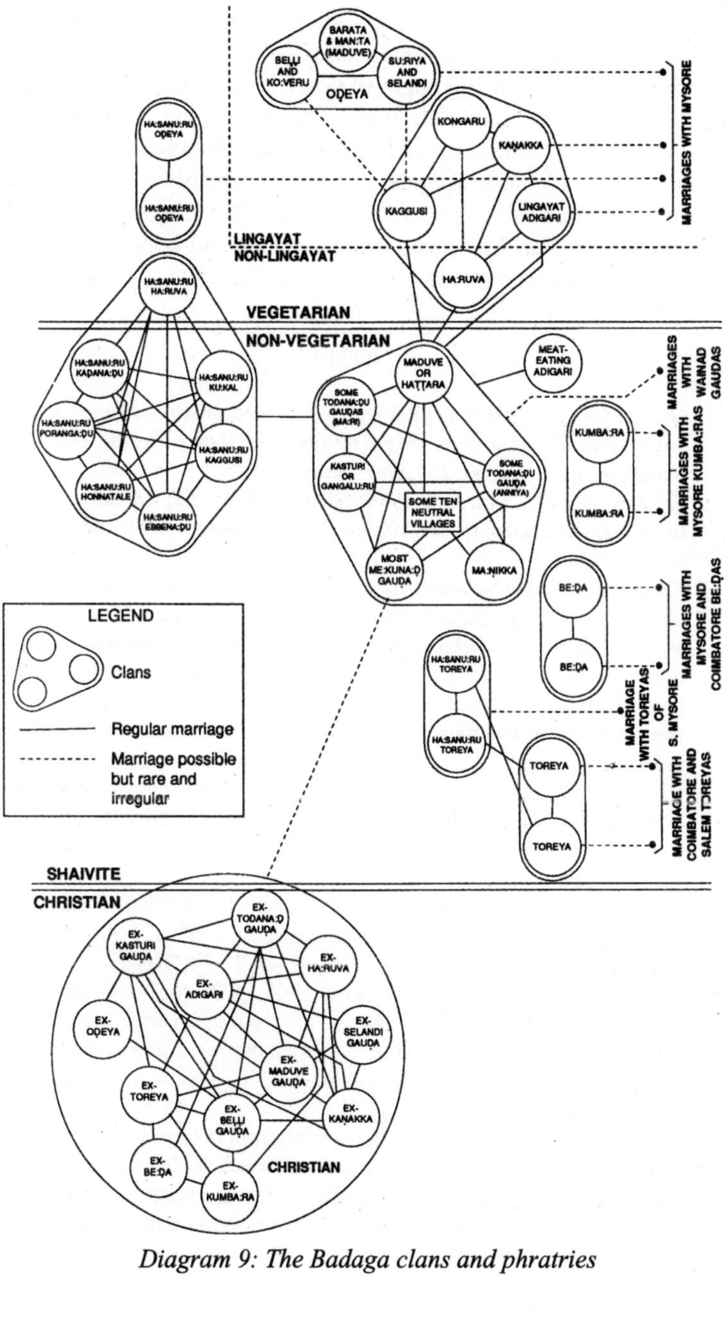

Diagram 9: The Badaga clans and phratries

The marriage system that now links the 44 Badaga clans into 10 phratries is a very complex one and calls for a clarifying diagram to accompany the following pages of description. Each of the circles in Diag. 9 represents one clan, while the intervening lines link clans that customarily intermarry. Clans have been grouped into phratries. The dotted lines mark irregular but still acceptable patterns of marriage. Subcultural divisions found between the Lingayats and other Shaivites, between Christians and Shaivites, and between the vegetarians and meat-eaters, have also been indicated.

NOTES

1. Grigg 1880: 219. Their factual legends, devoid of supernatural elements, are in sharp contrast to the origin myths of such tribes as the Toda or the Santal; cf. Rivers 1906: 184, and Orans 1965: 5.
2. Gillin 1948: 439; Murdock 1949: 66; Firth 1951: 53; for fuller information on Badaga kinship, see Hockings 1982; 1999: 73-99; and 2012: 92-97.
3. Several competent scholars have argued that the various tribal groups, including the Badagas, constitute a Nilgiri caste system. If so, it is quite an atypical one. Zvelebil apparently had a Pauline conversion: '. . . in my 1979 publication, . . . I maintained that the tribes "are, in fact, jātis, participating in a hierarchic pattern of ranking." The truth is that – with the exception of the Baḍagas – the Nilgiri communities manifest social, political, economic, religious and psychological traits which are in contrast with jāti characteristics' (Zvelebil 1982: 49). On the same page, however, he asserts 'Baḍagas should not be designated and defined as a tribe. They are a Hindu caste' (n. 115). But a caste has necessarily to be located socially amongst other castes!
4. Rivers 1906: 36; Emeneau 1937: 103, where the number of clans given for Töwfıḷy is incorrect; see also Lévi-Strauss 1968: 125. On the priests who make sacrifice, see Rivers 1906: 39-42, 71-72, 276-85, 354.
5. Srinivas 1942: 32-38; Lévi-Strauss 1968: 477. As Nanjundayya and Ananthakrishna Iyer (1930, vol. 3: 177) put it, 'named after material objects, with the usual prohibition against cutting, using and sometimes touching such objects'. For the taboo on killing snakes, see Breeks 1873: 104.
6. Diag. 9 roughly illustrates the hierarchy, from bottom to top. A stranger to this community might hear claims of much higher ranking than the speakers would dare voice to members of other Badaga clans; here we will only present the most widely agreed-upon ranking. (The existence of a hierarchy does not *ipso facto* make this a caste society.)

7. Ward 1821: lxxi; Hough 1829: 88. Their thread has only one strand, unlike that of Brahmins.
8. Note, for example, the wives of Hucci in Diag. 5, on p. 44. The Badaga kinship terminology is of the Dakota type (Hockings 1999: 88-89).

CHAPTER 6

The Organization of the Phratries

OḌEYAS

The majority of Badagas would rank Oḍeyas as the highest and purest phratry in the community.[1] They occupy a dozen villages that are scattered across the plateau, some very close to the villages of lower phratries. Their hamlets are by no means all exogamous. There are perhaps seven thousand Oḍeyas, distributed among three unnamed clans, or seven septs. These *kolas* or septs, with their variant names and deities, are listed in Table 5.

Table 5: Descent of the Oḍeya septs

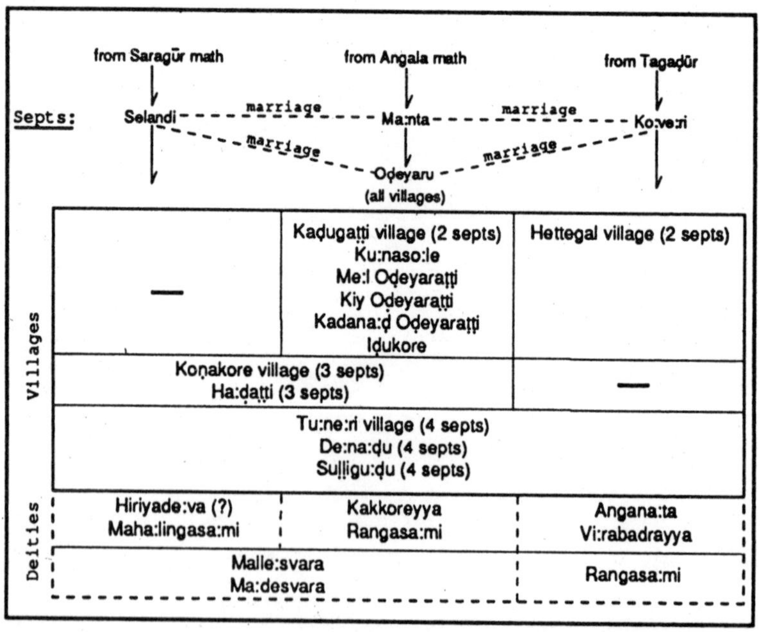

Because the clans themselves are not actually named, the confusing practice has grown up of referring to them either by the names of various villages where they are found *or* by the names of their constituent septs. Further identification of the clans is to be found in the unusual feature of their recognizing clan deities (Table 5). Thus most of the Oḍeyas of Tu:ne:ri, De:na:ḍu, Koṇakore and Suḷḷigu:ḍu belong to Selandi sept, and all worship Maha:lingasa:mi; but those of Hiṭṭegallu and Iḍukore worship Rangara:ma (Rangasa:mi – a Vaishnavite god). As with the Lingayat Mallavas of Coorg (Srinivas 1942: 36-37), Oḍeyas who *worship the same god* may not intermarry: septs and clans are each exogamous.

Oḍeya marriages are arranged between members of any two of the three unnamed clans, even if between inhabitants of the same village. Marriages also link those of the Nilgiris with those of Hasanụ:ru (see pp. 130-31). Over the past century marriages have been contracted with Lingayat girls from the Oḍeya caste of Mysore who, unlike Badaga girls, brought a dowry and were often well-educated: outsiders from the plains have thus increasingly been entering this community. Some intermarriage with Kaggusis has also occurred, and there are a few cases of Oḍeya girls having married Kaṇakkas.[2]

Oḍeyas, however, cite not only their supposed royal origins[3] but also the longer time they have lived in the Nilgiris as reasons for the near-absence of intermarriage between them and the other Lingayat clans. Initially, too, they were suspicious about whether these immigrants really were Lingayats; and furthermore the fact that people of these other three clans readily marry certain non-Lingayats was obviously not lost on the Oḍeyas. Apparently the Oḍeyas had established their position as a self-perpetuating phratry in the Nilgiris before the other Lingayat clans arrived. Locally they are considered a conservative and orthodox Lingayat group, in the sense that they abide strictly by whatever prescriptions and proscriptions of the Lingayat creed are known to them. Lingayats of Mysore might regard them as rather unorthodox, though, for these Badagas were illiterate until the past century and so were not able to read Lingayat scriptures, or even to follow the religious calendar properly (BEMS 1867, no. 28: 73). One does not hear of the Oḍeyas having traditionally celebrated any of the annual Lingayat festivals of Mysore, namely Chaitra, Vaisakh, Srāvan, Bhadrapāda, Answayuja, Kartik, Māgh, or Phalgun (Nanjundayya & Ananthakrishna Iyer 1931, vol. 4: 110).

In the past Oḍeyas did not accept food from Ha:ruvas or from any socially inferior phratry but would eat in the inner room of any other Oḍeya house (Grigg 1880: 220). Their food may only be cooked in metal vessels, not earthenware. Other Badagas take meals (always vegetarian) only in the outer, less sacred part of a Oḍeya house. Members of the Nilgiri tribes accept food from the Oḍeyas too, but are not allowed to pass beyond the veranda into the house.

KONGARU

These people, like Ha:ruvas, wear a single thread without *linga* and are vegetarian. They probably belong to the Chandra sept, and intermarry with Kaṇakkas, Ha:ruvas and Kaggusis. There are altogether just four villages of Kongaru.

HA:RUVAS

Like the Oḍeyas, the one clan of Ha:ruvas numbers about six thousand people.[4] They occupy about six villages, but this does not imply that those villages are unusually large, for often there is only a single Ha:ruva family who live permanently in some Gauḍa village. Perhaps half of Ha:ruvas are so distributed, as they have traditionally served as priests in Gauḍa and Toreya temples. Of the five clans making up the phratry to which they belong (the only one that is unnamed), Ha:ruvas alone have challenged the Oḍeyas for primacy in the Badaga social hierarchy. The ramifications of this claim will be explored when recent factions are discussed (pp. 236-38).

Ha:ruvas are vegetarian Shaivites but not Lingayats. For over a century they have been claiming that before leaving Mysore they had been Brahmins and that they should therefore be treated as such today.[5] This Brahminization, reminiscent of the nineteenth-century Kherwar movement among the Santal tribe (Orans 1965: 36-37), has been primarily an attempt to gain higher rank. Little of Ha:ruva behaviour accords with that of true Mysorean Brahmins, however. The three indicators in support of their Brahminhood are the observable facts that they are vegetarians, they wear a white thread across the left shoulder, and they have acted as temple priests for the great majority of Shaivite Badagas.[6] Despite these arguments, the subculture of the Ha:ruvas is for Brahmins a most atypical one: they have no special ceremony for investiture of the sacred thread and do not consider themselves 'twice-born'; the thread itself consists of only one strand instead of the customary three; until the past century they were totally illiterate in Sanskrit, Tamil and Kannaḍa; and they are altogether exogamous. They are in fact like many another Badaga clan in matters of marriage, having unions with other clans of dissimilar subculture, especially the Kaṇakkas, and even intermarrying with meat-eating Gauḍas.

If a Ha:ruva girl marries a Gauḍa then no meat is ever cooked in his house, and his wife remains a vegetarian. If her husband wants to eat meat he may arrange to have some cooked elsewhere and eat it away from home. The children of the union are fully Gauḍas and will usually be non-vegetarians. When the Ha:ruva woman dies her household might revert to a non-vegetarian diet. It has been reported that, on the other hand, 'If a Badaga [i.e. Gauḍa] woman marries a Haruva she has to give up meat-eating and, to cleanse her, a red hot iron is put to her tongue.'[7] 'After this she would not dare to eat meat . . . she would lose her eyesight' (Karl 1945: 3). From this dire threat we can tell that a woman married into a Ha:ruva family is expected to accept its dietary norms, whereas a Ha:ruva girl marrying into a socially lower clan is not expected to follow their diet (Tignous 1911: 117). A Ha:ruva girl who marries into a Lingayat family does not change her diet but will have to wear the *linga* if it is offered her and to behave as a Lingayat in ritual matters. When a Ha:ruva man marries a Lingayat girl he continues to wear his thread while she usually continues to wear the *linga* if it has already been given her (Pl. 16).

Ha:ruvas are willing to accept food in the inner and more sacred room (where household gods may be installed) of any other Badaga group, except the Toreyas. They would not demean themselves by entering a Toreya house; and they would probably be offered food only in the outer room of a Oḍeya house. Oḍeyas never accept food in a Ha:ruva home as they consider Ha:ruvas inferior; but the other three Lingayat clans will eat in the inner room of a Ha:ruva house. Even meat-eating Adigaris, who are no longer Lingayats, may be offered vegetarian food in the inner Ha:ruva room. The same holds true for visiting Gauḍas and Kaggusis, people who might often visit if related to the Ha:ruva household by a marriage. Until the 1950s the Ha:ruvas would also allow Todas, Kuṟumbas, Iṟulas and Kasava tribesmen to eat in the outer room, although Kotas were thought too polluting to pass beyond the entrance; so since that time only Todas have been allowed into the house.

ADIGARIS

The vegetarian Adigaris are a Lingayat clan numbering perhaps six thousand people who inhabit sixteen villages scattered across the plateau. Though they should only marry with Ha:ruvas or Kaṇakkas, in the past century some Adigari men have married girls from Lingayat families in Mysore villages. It is rare on the other hand for a girl to go from the Nilgiris to Mysore in marriage. There have also been a few irregular cases of vegetarian Adigaris marrying the meat-eating Gauḍas (but never meat-eating Adigaris).

The Adigari villages come closer to being a corporate group than any of the other clans, except perhaps for the two tiny phratries of Kumba:ras and Be:ḍas. This solidarity stems from the fact that the Adigaris, alone of all the clans, hold an 'annual reunion'; for every November they go down to the village of Nellitore, on the edge of the Coimbatore Plain, to worship at the place where a Lingayat saint was drowned. It was from this point that the original six Adigaris started up into the Nilgiris.[8] It is still obligatory for at least a few men from each Adigari village to attend this annual function, to which members of other Badaga clans are also welcome.

Despite this demonstration of Adigari solidarity there have been several defections from the clan and its Lingayat values. In one village (Sakkata) Adigaris married with Toreyas a few generations ago and now are treated as Toreyas although sometimes called Adigaris. In one other Gauḍa village (Śo:lu:ru) the Adigaris have intermarried with meat-eating Gauḍas. In both of these situations the *soi-disant* Adigaris are no longer vegetarians or Lingayats (Metz 1864: 50-51). The three other meat-eating Adigari villages do not dine with Toreyas, but they may take a meal in the inner room of a Gauḍa house. In two villages of vegetarian Adigaris the *linga* (Pl. 16) is not worn, but the inhabitants retain the name and status of Adigaris and belong to the same clan, although they are not considered Virashaivas.[9]

Adigaris and Kaṇakkas will eat only in the houses of Oḍeyas, Ha:ruvas and Kongaru, where they can feel sure of being given the correctly prepared vegetarian dishes. Adigaris, like Kaṇakkas, admit

Ha:ruvas, Kaggusis and other Lingayats to the inner room for meals (Oḍeyas would refuse to eat with them). The meat-eating Adigaris, Gauḍas and Toreyas, along with Todas, may only eat in the outer room, while other Nilgiri tribesmen should not enter the house at all.

KAṆAKKAS

There are perhaps six thousand Kaṇakkas. Although now agriculturists like all other Badagas they once were the only literate men in the Nilgiris (Grigg 1880: 221). Their name means 'accountant', and refers to their former position as village accountants under the Ummattūr régime. Though the Kaṇakkas are Lingayats and today have a status equal to the Adigaris', there are some Badagas who whisper darkly that the Kaṇakkas were in origin Tamilians, unlike all others (Metz 1866a: 144). The Kaṇakka clan themselves would not own to this, perhaps because negative experience with Tamil Nadu officials has led many Badagas to look down upon the Tamilian.

Kaṇakkas intermarry with Adigaris, Ha:ruvas, Kongaru and Kaggusis, and during the past century some have married women from Lingayat families of Mysore villages. A few instances of Kaṇakkas marrying Oḍeyas have been cited above. As Kaṇakkas and Adigaris intermarry much more frequently among themselves than with any other clan, and as both are Lingayat groups, the two groups are now accorded equal status by all other Badagas. The rules for Kaṇakka commensality are precisely the same as those of Adigaris.

KAGGUSIS

Among the smaller clans is the Kaggusi one, numbering about four thousand. These people inhabit eight villages; they are vegetarians and Lingayats, but instead of wearing a personal *linga* they have one sacred *rudrakśa* bead on a string round the neck, and do a daily *pu:ja* to that. Their marriages are mainly with Gauḍas, though also with Kaṇakkas, Kongaru and occasionally Oḍeyas (rumour also recalled a misalliance long ago with a Kota). As soon as Kaggusi men reached the plateau and married Gauḍa girls they left off wearing the *linga* and kept it in their houses, as they still do. It is of note that Adigaris will not marry Kaggusis on the grounds that, as the Kaṇakkas *do* marry them, the Kaggusis must be fictive 'brothers' to the

Adigaris (although the two in fact belong to different septs); yet no such argument stops the Adigari from marrying a Ha:ruva, though logic dictates that it should. An explanation lies in the higher status that Adigaris accord to Ha:ruvas.

Kaggusis allow vegetarians and the meat-eating Gauḍas into the inner room for a meal, but they feed members of the lower meat-eating phratries in the outer room. People from other tribes may eat only on the Kaggusi veranda.

GAUḌAS

At least three-quarters of the entire population is Gauḍa, so that this particular phratry is commonly called *Baḍaga*. At a rough estimate it numbers near 100,000.[10] I prefer to use the correct but not widely recorded name *Gauḍa* (spelt *Gowder* in earlier days), as it obviates the confusion that can arise in calling one phratry and also the entire community by the same name. The word *gauḍa* also points to their origin amongst the Kanarese farmers and cattle-breeders known by that name.[11]

It appears that the Gauḍas have six clans, based on their original septs, plus ten 'neutral' villages which may have marriage relations with any other Gauḍa village, thus forming a sort of non-exogamous seventh clan. The six clans can roughly be categorized as follows:

Beḷḷi (silver)	Gauḍas of Jakkata and Neḍuguve
Selandi (spider)	Gauḍas of Hulikal; 'Kongaru' Gauḍas
Kasturi (musk)	some Gauḍas of Ke:ti, Dimbaṭṭi, Me:lkunda, and Ki:ekunda (also called 'Gangaḷaru')
Maduve (marriage)	Gauḍas of Poranga:ḍ (also called 'Haṭṭara'; Heidemann 2006: 91-98, 108, 129, 137)
Ma:ṇikka (gem)	some Gauḍas of Jakkana:ri
Ma:ri (goddess Ma:ri)	some Gauḍas of Todana:ḍ including Anniya lineage

The Gauḍas occupy about 400 hamlets; so, unlike a member of a small phratry, no Gauḍa will expect to have friends or relatives in every village. Often one cannot be too certain if a particular *distant* village is in his own or another clan, which could raise difficulties if a marriage is being arranged with a village into which the groom's lineage or village has not previously married. Otherwise, the Gauḍas can assign every village with which they have marriage connections to one clan or another (aside from some special cases).

It appears – and informants confirm this – that the unwieldy size of clans with close to twenty thousand members, on average, calls for different kinds of marriage solution. The first employs divisional boundaries – the only situation where we find the larger pre-British political divisions of the Nilgiris being relevant in the arrangement of marriages. Gauḍas observe a rule that clan exogamy is essential only for marriages that are arranged between two villages *within* the same division (*na:ḍu*). If the village is in any of the other three divisions, and if there is no known precedent of a marriage with that particular village, then it is usually *treated* as a member of another clan even though one might argue that it belonged to the *same* clan, were the villagers to trace out a network of other known marriage connections that indirectly link the two villages. If, in one's own division, two villages A and B have both had marriages with village C, then A and B usually belong to the same clan and call themselves 'brothers'. But if the villages A and B are in different political divisions then the fact that at some time they had both married people from (or into) village C – which might be anywhere in the three other divisions of the plateau – is considered irrelevant. In practice, where a history of marriage with C could be demonstrated for both A and B, villagers would usually rationalize that knowledge by saying: 'After all, the connection is too distant to matter; we are not marrying our own blood.' In effect they are giving up the ideal of clan exogamy in these cases while retaining the more proximate ideal of village and lineage exogamy. Their clans have now become so large that Gauḍas can no longer look upon them as corporate groups. This adjustment in thinking is necessary because the old names for the clans have often been forgotten and because the detailed knowledge a Badaga carries of his kinship – often embracing more than three hundred people – coupled with the tremendous accumulation of relatives that has come from numerous births and frequent remarriages could otherwise make the old ideal of clan exogamy fatally unrealizable.

There is another manipulation to surmount this problem. There are ten non-exogamous Gauḍa villages that are in a sense of 'neutral' clan affiliation: that is, they may arrange marriages in their own village or with any Gauḍa clan without generally being accused of marrying within a prohibited degree. These thus form a sort of safety-valve: the precedent of a marriage with one of these villages can be used to validate any other village's membership of a particular clan. This is possible because the six clans are not generally referred to by names now (although at least some of them still were early in the twentieth century): they are identified only by reciprocal terms meaning 'agnates' and 'affines' (i.e. 'our clan' and 'another clan'). These rather special villages thus act as a kind of reservoir of youths and girls eligible to *any* Gauḍa village in need of spouses.

Although the vast majority of Gauḍa marriages occur within this complicated system of clans and neutral villages, a number of permissible marriages have also been arranged with other phratries. Ha:ruvas marry into Gauḍa families, although in recent times with decreasing frequency; the meat-eating Adigaris, a small clan, have no marriages outside the Gauḍa phratry, to which they therefore belong in sense if not in name.[12] A recent development has been the marriage of a few Badaga Christian girls with Gauḍa men, usually those with college education. Christian girls enjoy a certain reputation among urbanizing Badagas for their comparatively high level of education and their somewhat 'freer' interaction with men. When a Christian girl marries a Hindu Gauḍa today her patrilineal ancestry must still trace back to a clan other than her groom's.

Gauḍas, like Badaga Christians, are usually meat-eaters. They are willing to eat in the houses of any other phratry but the Toreyas and the Christians. Adigaris, Kaṇakkas and Oḍeyas offer Gauḍas food in the outer room only, whereas Ha:ruvas and Kaggusis allow them to eat in the inner room. Such dining occasions will usually arise when Gauḍas visit families related to them through marriage. In each of these cases the Gauḍas receive only vegetarian food; more generally the vegetarian phratries do not eat with non-vegetarians. Toreyas may be given food in the outer room of a Gauḍa home, but meat-eating Adigaris (who may marry Gauḍas) eat in the inner one.

KUMBA:RAS

Few Badagas know of the existence of this phratry, so small are its numbers. Kumba:ras have only about eighty households, perhaps 500 people, who live in two villages near Male Ko:ṭe, where they were once employed as potters (whence their name). Each village is an exogamous clan; when possible, alliances are arranged between the two. As one village contains about four times as many families as the other the larger village has to look elsewhere for most of its spouses, however. They no longer intermarry with other Badagas but with the several thousand families of Kanarese Kumbāras living in and near Mysore city who are believed by the Nilgiri Kumba:ras to share a common ancestry with them. The Kumba:ras living on the Nilgiri Plateau nevertheless consider themselves as Badagas and are so recognized by their neighbours, since they bear a Badaga culture identical with that of the Gauḍas. Among those people who do know the Kumba:ra villagers many consider them to be Gauḍas, though only at Me:lu:ru have they been absorbed into the Gauḍa phratry.

The traditional occupation of Kanarese Kumbāras was potting,[13] and although these Badagas no longer know the craft there are any number of broken sherds stratified at a depth of 2 or 3 m. in the ramparts of the old Male Ko:ṭe fortification (see pp. 52-58) to testify to this former industry. On the basis of their presumed (if servile) connection with royalty the Kumba:ras claim to be the highest of all Badaga phratries; other Badagas knowing anything about them rank them below Gauḍas but above Be:ḍas and Toreyas. Some of the Kumba:ras are vegetarians, but most are not. Their rules for commensality are the same as those of Gauḍas.

BE:ḌAS

Another small phratry neighbouring on the Kumba:ras, the Be:ḍas, also number about eighty families divided between two clans. Their two villages near Male Ko:ṭe each include members of both clans, and thus are not exogamous (Metz 1864: 47-48; Francis 1908: 350, 370). Though they no longer marry with any other Badagas they too are undeniably Badagas. These people either marry into the other Be:ḍa clan or arrange marriages with Kanarese Bēḍas (who are not Badagas) coming from Mysore city or Tiruppūr (now the headquarters of Tiruppūr district, in Tamil Nadu).

The Be:ḍas, as we have seen, believe they came to the hills as hunters in service to a chieftain of Ummattūr, in the late seventeenth century; the word *be:ḍa* means 'hunter' (Burrow & Emeneau 1984: no. 5527; Hockings & Pilot-Raichoor 1992: 435). Although now only farmers, the men supplemented their diet until about 1950 by hunting on the jungle slopes with bow and arrow. As they are eaters of meat and traditionally takers of life they are ranked by other Badagas as lower than Kumba:ras though still above Toreyas. It is worth noting that Kumba:ras and Be:ḍas, like other non-Lingayat villagers, have their own 'commune Toreyas' who in the past acted as messengers for the headmen. Most Badagas know so little about Be:ḍas that they erroneously think of them as a group totally absorbed into the Gauḍa phratry. There are in fact two Gauḍa villages descended from unions of Gauḍas with Be:ḍas. The Be:ḍas follow the same rules for commensality as Gauḍas. Very recently the central government has accorded the Be:ḍas the status of being a Scheduled Tribe – unique among all Badagas; this aligns them in official thinking with Todas and Kotas.

TOREYAS

The Toreyas were universally regarded here as the lowest of Badaga phratries, but they had yielded that position to the new Christians by 1900. In former times they were the poorest and least educated of Badagas (Harkness 1832: 112). Although there are certain meat-eating Adigaris who have become absorbed into one Toreya village, the phratry is now endogamous. It numbers perhaps 25,000 people and occupies 26 villages.[14]

Like all other Badagas they have traditionally been cultivators, but in addition to this they held a customary role of messengers and 'commune servants', even in the Be:ḍa villages, whence their low social status. Certain Toreyas are perhaps until now appointed (except in Lingayat villages) for specific duties at festivals and some public ceremonies, particularly funerals.[15] For this they used once to be given a quarter-rupee and three measures of grain by each household. In some Toreya villages, however, it is the Kuṟumba watchman who holds these duties.[16] It is recorded that in the nineteenth century Toreyas were also 'weaving a kind of sackcloth',[17] but today neither they nor anyone else can recall this activity.

Alone of all phratries the Toreyas are (or were) under a certain disadvantage in the Badaga judicial system. In villages where other Badagas also live they may find that, while being permitted to bring cases to the village or commune council and to sit through its deliberations, they must not take part in the discussion that leads up to the headman's decision. A Toreya village headman who is excluded from a meeting of the commune council might not complain about such demeaning treatment in the way that any other headman in the commune undoubtedly would. The depressed status of Toreyas is symbolized by the fact that during the great memorial ceremonies for a deceased generation (*manevale*) the Toreyas built a separate, smaller catafalque for their ancestors beside the main one (Hockings 2001: 62). Most recently the state government accorded the Toreyas – and no other Badagas – Most Backward Caste status.

Many of the 26 Toreya villages are adjuncts to Gauḍa villages, set off from them by a mere stone's throw, as at Ke:ti; but a group of nine Toreya villages on the eastern edge of the plateau are so isolated spatially that their only close contact is with Oḍeyas of De:na:ḍu (Heidemann 2006: 102-05, 160; see Map 4).

Toreyas have two clans, and in many villages both of them are found. Despite the well-known precedents in other phratries, they have not married non-Toreyas.

The Toreyas can be offered vegetarian food in the houses of all higher phratries, and meat in those which habitually eat it themselves. Recently some Gauḍas have interdined with Toreyas on an equal footing in their inner rooms, although traditionally none of the other groups would allow Toreyas into the inner, more sacred room; they were expected to eat in the outer one. 'If they should eat food with other Badagas, the Toreyas must clear away all remnants of the feast – nobody else will help' (Benbow 1930: 11). No other phratry, not even the Christian one, will accept food in the house of a Toreya (Tignous 1911: 117). In terms of the commensality rules that pertain elsewhere in India the Toreyas may therefore appear to be a low or even untouchable caste; and it is true that, Christians apart, they are considered the lowest of the Badaga phratries. There is nevertheless a Badaga rule that 'foreigners' and plainsmen may not enter the inner room of *any* Badaga house: they may be offered food only on the veranda or in the outer room. Badaga commensal rules, valid as much among the Toreyas as among higher phratries, have sometimes come as a surprise to visiting Brahmins, who could find themselves excluded from the more sacred room or from receiving food there. Badagas, even Toreyas, do not generally recognize high ritual status when it is found outside the Nilgiri social system. Plains Brahmins of course would rationalize the rebuff by considering the Badagas as Śudras, through whom no Brahmin would pollute himself by accepting their often non-vegetarian food.[18]

HASANU:RU BADAGAS

The twelve villages of this community, lying in the low Biligiri Rangan Hills some 40 km. northeast of the Nilgiris, belong to eleven clans that are distinct from those of the plateau. These clans form three phratries – Oḍeya, Gauḍa and Toreya. A clan of Ha:ruvas is found within their Gauḍa phratry.

The two Oḍeya clans rank highest in the Biligiri Rangan Hills; they intermarry with each other, with Oḍeyas of the Nilgiri Hills, and recently with the Oḍeya caste inhabiting villages near Śāmarājnagar (not far away in southern Karnataka). Like all other Oḍeyas, those of the Hasanu:ru area are vegetarian and Lingayat. They allow the Ha:ruva clan to eat in the inner room of their houses, but for the past century, since they began intermarriage with Mysore villages, these Oḍeyas have stopped allowing other Badagas (non-vegetarians) to eat in their houses.

At the other end of the social hierarchy are two clans of Toreyas, who intermarry chiefly with the two clans of Nilgiri Toreyas, but also with neighbours of the opposite clan in Ko:ṭa:ḍa, their village near Hasanu:ru, and in some cases these Toreyas have intermarried with the Torea caste found near Śāmarājnagar, a nearby town.

Between these two poles are four Ha:ruva families and about 115 Gauḍa families (my 1970 figures; the Oḍeyas numbered about 25 families then, and Toreyas 20). The Ha:ruvas and Gauḍas are divided into seven clans (Diag. 9), generally identified by their place of origin in the Nilgiris. Members of each clan may intermarry with any of the other six clans, and also with Gauḍas of the Nilgiris. However, because of their common origin, the Gauḍas of Ku:kallu clan, for example, may not marry Gauḍas from Ku:kallu village in the Nilgiris: both villages belong to Anniya lineage.

There is a sort of hierarchy within this phratry, Ku:kallu clan and the Ha:ruva one ranking higher than the others. Ku:kallu dominates because of its size, for it consists of some 25 families, as compared with the four families in each of the four smallest clans (my 1970 totals; nothing more recent). It is the leader of Ku:kallu clan who settles most of the disputes in these twelve villages, though each of them has its own headman. When neither he nor family elders were able to resolve difficult disputes in the past, the headman of Ku:kallu commune in the northeastern Nilgiris was asked to adjudicate.

The twelve villages contain a population of about 1,000 Badagas, together with several hundred Iṟula tribesmen. While no intermarriage occurs between the two groups, there have been stray cases of Badaga men keeping Iṟula mistresses.

The comparable situation of a peripheral Badaga community who live in the Wainad will be discussed below (pp. 169-70).

NOTES

1. Jagor 1876: 202; Francis 1908: 130-31. 'At a funeral the Badagas in general take off their turbans, but the Wodearu [Oḍeya] keep theirs on. Every Native, not even excepting the petty hill-chiefs [headmen], must bow down before them and pay them adoration'; Metz 1864: 48-49. During the great memorial ceremony the Oḍeyas were honoured with a bed on which they were invited to sit; Belli Gowder 1923-41: 14.
2. There have also been a few irregular marriages of Oḍeya girls to men living in Mysore State and the Kollegal Hills near Hasanu:ru; see pp. 295-96, below.
3. Grigg 1880: 220; Francis 1908: 130-31; Thurston & Rangachari 1909, vol. 1: 72-73. The name *Oḍeya* actually means 'owner, lord, master, ruler'; Burrow & Emeneau 1984: no. 593; Hockings & Pilot-Raichoor 1992: 99.
4. In a sample of about 38,000 Badagas resident in Poranga:ḍ, Heidemann found that only 3 per cent were Ha:ruva; 1997: 129; 2006: 125.
5. Ward 1821: lxxi; Hough 1829: 88; Metz 1864: 54; Grigg 1880: 221; Francis 1908: 131. The claim was based upon their membership in the Bra:ma sept.
6. Kittel 1894: 1650 gives the Kannaḍa *Hâruva* as meaning 'Brahmin'; Burrow & Emeneau (1984: no. 4091b) translate it as 'Brahmin' or 'seer'.
7. Benbow 1930: 9. This claim is dubious, since the pollution of meat normally cannot be removed from a woman, only from a man.
8. Metz 1864: 50-51, 63-64; see above, p. 35. *Adigari*, meaning 'powerful man', was once used as the title of a village headman or magistrate appointed by the local chieftain, acting for the ruling power in Mysore.
9. Since about 1960 some of them have taken to wearing the *linga* again.
10. In a sample of about 38,000 Badagas living in Poranga:ḍ, Heidemann (1997: 129; 2006: 125) found that 73 per cent were Gauḍa.
11. Gauḍas, in Mysore, are a branch of the Okkaliga castes; Thurston & Rangachari 1909, vol. 2: 269-72. Another use of the word *gauḍa* is a title for the headman, and by extension as a common Badaga male title; this also accords with the usage of the Gangadikāra Okkalu of southern Mysore; Nanjundayya & Ananthakrishna Iyer 1930-35, vol. 3: 175.

12. Most Badagas now consider these Adigaris to be Gauḍa, as they do also Be:ḍas and Kumba:ras.
13. An art they are said to have taught the Kotas.
14. Thurston & Rangachari 1909, vol. 7: 176; Nanjundayya & Anantha-krishna Iyer 1931, vol. 4: 637-39; see above, pp. 46-47. Toreyas of the Hasanu:ru area now intermarry with those of Mysore. Most cloth was woven by Chettis on the Coimbatore Plain. In a sample of some 38,000 Badagas living in Poranga:ḍ, Heidemann (1997: 129; 2006: 125) found that 15 percent were Toreya, but they are more numerous in that *na:ḍu* than in any other, being concentrated in its easternmost villages, where they were perhaps once based to follow their palanquin-bearing duties between the plateau and the plains (Map 4).
15. In 1972 the paramount chief in Tu:ne:ri told me that he still had an *u:r Toreya*, who was then paid Rs. 1.25 and one *kolaga* of grain each year by every household in Tu:ne:ri commune. This man would carry messages anywhere in the Nilgiris for the chief. Funerals are public events in Badaga culture, organized by the village as a whole; Hockings 2001: *passim*; 2012: 347-52.
16. See below, pp. 161-65. Belli Gowder 1938-41: 11 gave his gratuity at a funeral as 'a sum of Re. 1.25 along with ten measures of rice'.
17. Harkness 1832: 10, 109; Breeks 1873: 14. It may be that these writers confused the Toreyas with Kaikolans, however: twelve male and nine female Kaikolans were enumerated in Todana:ḍ early in 1821; Grigg 1880: 26. They were a low-status caste of weavers and musicians from Coimbatore, among whom one woman of each family was dedicated in a temple to the art of prostitution; Thurston 1906: 29-30; Nanjundayya & Ananthakrishna Iyer 1930-35, vol. 1: 214-15; 'Miles' 1951: 200-02.
18. Here a note about commensality with other non-Badagas. The Oḍeyas and other Lingayats never allow a Nilgiri tribesman to enter beyond the veranda; neither may any non-Lingayat visitor coming from the plains enter. Ha:ruvas and all lower phratries permit Todas and until recently Kuṟumbas, Iṟulas and Kasavas to eat in the outer room. Kotas and any lowlander thought to be a Hindu untouchable are too polluting to be allowed past the veranda.

CHAPTER 7

Badaga–Kota Interchange

THE INTERDEPENDENCE OF THE PLATEAU COMMUNITIES

Until a decade after World War I had concluded, the Badagas were as intimately involved in their traditional system of economic and ritual interaction as were the other main participants, viz: the Todas, Kotas and Kuṟumbas. Throughout the whole of the nineteenth century, from the first rough description of the Badagas in 1812 (Keys) until Tignous' account in 1911, there seems to have been no essential change in the organization of this complex relationship; but since World War I the Badagas withdrew more and more from obligations and privileges which had traditionally been theirs. What then were these duties and privileges? How complex was their system of interchange? Why did everything attenuate?

The socio-economic relations linking these groups can be summarized in the perhaps over-simplified way shown in Diag. 10.[1] The system of interdependence outlined here involved a complex, standardized and widely accepted division of labour rather like the *jajmani* system (Wiser 1936: *passim*; Beidelman 1959: *passim*) which used to be regularly encountered in multi-caste villages elsewhere. In order to understand the full complexity of this system, we need to reconstruct it from several types of observation. Details are discussed at length by several writers, are still known to the oldest villagers and to a slight extent might still be observed in a few of the Nilgiri villages. Recently, however, with the cash economy becoming universal among all these communities, and the proportion of Badagas to Todas and Kotas having risen rapidly (Appendix 2), this relationship has diminished to the point where it is today a mere shadow of what it was prior to 1930. The breakdown is apparent in all parts of the Nilgiris, though in different localities it proceeded at differing rates, depending partly on the accessibility of a bazaar.

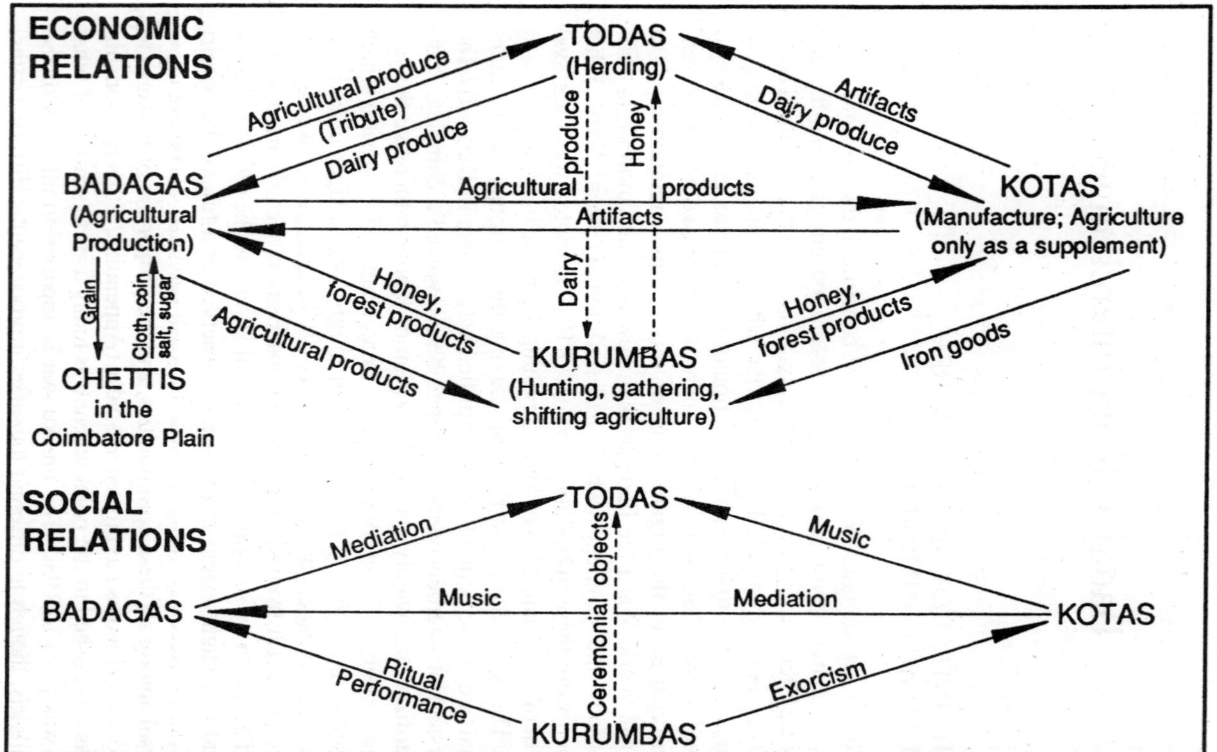

Diagram 10: Economic and social relations among Nilgiri communities

BADAGAS AND KOTAS

The ties linking the Badagas and Kotas have always been closer and more complex than those between any other pair of Nilgiri communities, largely because the Kota products were almost indispensable, and Kotas can perform a wider range of services than can any other group; the Badagas, in contrast, practised nothing but farming. The inter-community ties are essentially a relationship of mutual obligation which binds a specific Badaga family to a specific Kota one and are inherited on either side through the males. A Badaga can never shift to a new Kota partner unless the old one agrees to it at a joint meeting of their village councils, which has rarely happened. Traditionally the Kota produced certain types of artefact for a Badaga, who in return gave him grain and cloth on occasion. Because of the great disparity in numbers between the Badagas and Kotas,[2] though, it became necessary early in the twentieth century for each Kota family to maintain such ties with perhaps 50 to 100 Badaga households. In each case, whether or not the services required were those from a woman and whether or not the initial request came from a woman, all mediation between two associated families took place between the male heads of each.

There are in the entire Nilgiris only seven Kota villages: these are widely and evenly dispersed, being on the average 14 km. apart (and further by road). One village on the outskirts of Gu:ḍalu:ru is in the Wainad, below the slope west of the Nilgiri Plateau; the larger two of the indigenous political divisions each contain two villages; and the remaining two divisions of the plateau have a single Kota village each. This distribution of their settlements, whether originally so intended or not,[3] results in some Kota workers being conveniently accessible to all of the Badaga and Toda settlements; for there is not a hamlet anywhere on the plateau that would be more than a morning's walk from a Kota village. Normally each Badaga village is linked with whichever Kota village happens to be closest.

The usual pattern for activating the exchange relationship is for the Badaga to request his Kota partner's *services* whenever the need arises, but to order his *products* once each year; while the Kota in turn comes for a dole of clothes and foodstuffs once a year (Harkness 1832: 78-79; Ranga 1934: 72; Hockings 2012: 118-19). There existed a general understanding that the Kota man should enquire annually of each Badaga partner what items might be required in the

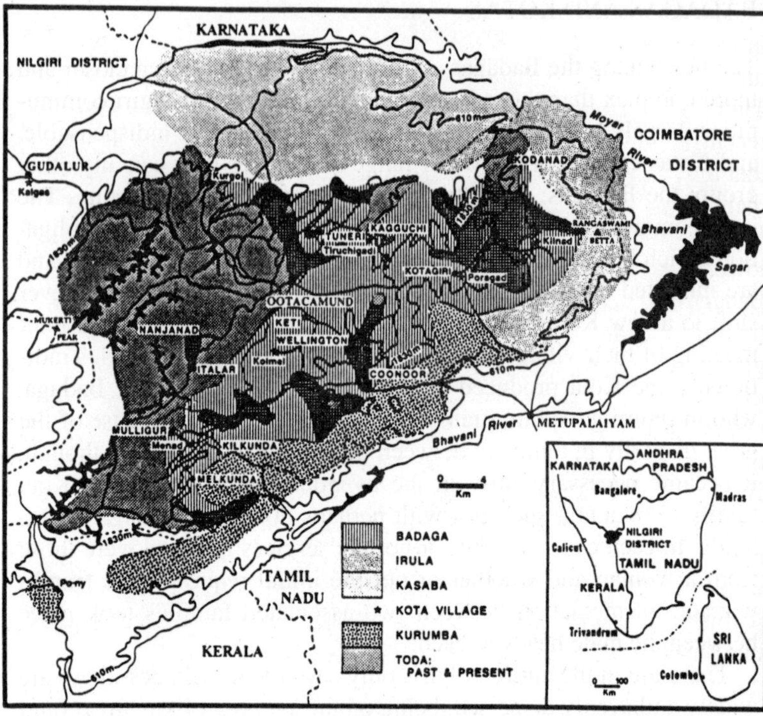

Map 6: Distribution of the Nilgiri ethnic groups

coming months. The Badaga then gives him a list of items, while the Badaga's wife passes on to him another list of things required from the Kota's wife. The Kota then announces that he will be returning on a specific day (generally a Monday, the weekly holiday) just before the major Kota festival of Kambaṭṭara:ya in early January, and the Badaga knows that he must have gifts ready for the Kota on this occasion. On that day the man usually comes with his wife and children, bringing the ordered goods if they are now ready. These particular Kotas then are considered guests of the partner's family, though their lower status prevents them from entering the Badaga house. The Kotas are fed on the veranda. Formerly a visiting family would eat simultaneously out of a single cloth, but in the twentieth century that came to be regarded as a disrespectful means of serving food; and so it was then given rather more acceptably on one large plantain leaf instead.

The traditional remuneration for Kota goods and services was not in cash – rare in the Nilgiri economy until the mid-nineteenth century – but in food grains, potatoes and mustard (King 1870: 34; Thurston and Rangachari 1909, vol. 1: 85; Jagor 1914: 47-48). More recently, however, Badagas preferred to pay cash for specific items that they required; and some even bought goods at fixed prices from their Kota partner's stall in the market at Ootacamund, Coonoor or Kotagiri. The traditional Kota dress was a skirt-like cloth around the lower parts of the body and a cloak: both were annual gifts from the Badaga partner, who had in turn acquired them from his Chetti trading partner (see below, pp. 182-84). Quantities of the two chief grains, little millet and finger millet,[4] could also be given. Whether the Badaga gave grain or cloth, or both, was a matter of personal preference. The actual volume of grain given was seemingly not fixed: it varied with the Badaga's harvest each year, according to Badagas, but according to Kotas should have been a quarter of the yield.[5] The Kota would arrange to supply a quantity of articles proportionate in value to the gifts he had received; and it is said that he was capable of remembering what each of his fifty or more Badaga partners had given him on his last visit: '. . . if a Kota family felt that the Badaga families for whom they provided tools and music were not giving them a rightful share of the crop at harvest, a Kota council could be called which might decree that those Badagas were to be boycotted until they paid up properly' (Mandelbaum 1960: 275).

Instances did sometimes arise of a Kota partner dying and leaving a wife but no son; or a wife died and her widower had no woman in the house. Then a Badaga might want some article from the remnant of his Kota partner's family while there was actually no appropriate person left to make it. If he wanted a man's product the widower could make it, and if a woman's product the widow might still make it, of course; but otherwise the surviving Kota would be obliged to maintain the relationship by arranging for some kinsman to produce whatever it was the Badaga needed.

KOTA PRODUCTS AND SERVICES

The Kota friend was until recently the only source for a Badaga's metal goods. The items which Kotas have regularly manufactured in their smithies, first from local iron ore and later from imported scrap metal, were various kinds of knives (Thurston & Rangachari 1909, vol. 4: 8), adzes, crowbars, pickaxes, sickles, hoes, axes, hammers, iron cooking-basins, skillets and ploughshares (Hockings 2012: 313-14); and long ago they also produced stirrups, horse-bits, bows and iron-tipped arrows. Kotas were once gold- and silversmiths for the Badagas, too, and still occasionally supply them metal ornaments. In addition to manufacturing this variety of articles, the Kota partners were expected to repair them when necessary. Now they are normally given cash for any repair work done, and that is rare.

A second category of products over which the Kotas formerly held the monopoly is that of leather. Although not even members of the highest Badaga phratries object to handling leather goods, only the Kotas have applied themselves to the polluting task of converting buffalo hides into leather articles. The goods they have regularly prepared were horse saddles and bridles, leather ropes for ploughs and tethers (Metz 1864: 131-32; Thurston and Rangachari 1909, vol. 4: 7), leather nets once used in trapping, and possibly sandals and water bags. It is worth remarking that while Badagas do not find it spiritually polluting to handle the leather on drums, they do think it demeaning to play Kota drums; and so such instruments have never been sought from the Kotas.

Pottery is a further item over which the Kotas held the local monopoly until the past century. Archaeological surface finds indicate that three centuries ago the two hamlets of the Kumba:ras, a tiny Badaga phratry located on the northern edge of the plateau, were producing many kinds of wheel-made pottery (see above, p. 127). But since that time pot production has been entirely in the hands of Kota women who, it is said, had initially learnt this art from some Kumba:ras (Mahias, in Hockings 2012: 725-27). Items that they regularly supplied the Badagas included household and dairy vessels, oil lamps, and clay smoking-pipes. Unlike other Kota manufactures, their new pots passed through quite an elaborate purificatory ritual by Badagas before coming into daily use.[6]

The Kota partner was also in earlier times the producer of leaf-umbrellas and of a wooden device not unlike a nutcracker which Badagas use for castrating young bulls. A curious item with which Kotas must supply their Badaga partners when they come upon it is the bezoar, a hairy ball that accumulates in the paunch of some buffaloes. Eating a little of this is believed to make a baby strong, brave and manly; and thus all Badagas – whether vegetarian or not, and even if quite cognizant of its polluting origin – will feed some of it to their newborn sons, if tradition still holds.

Some Kotas are adept carpenters. Back when Badagas were still using ploughs they got these from their Kota partners, who made them from timber supplied by the Toda partners of the Badagas. Kota men sometimes made the heavy wooden pounding-stick once found in virtually all Badaga households: in this case the wood was first obtained from the jungle slopes by the Pālu Kuṟumbas of one particular settlement, Ba:ni, who passed it on to the Toda who had asked them for it. This Toda would then give the timber to the Toda partner of the Badaga needing the pounder. He in turn passed it on to the Badaga's Kota partner to whittle into a pounder. This was the most complex traditional network we know of within the Nilgiris, although there may well have been other comparable ones.

Kota partners were also employed to help build houses or cattle-sheds for their Badaga partners. In this case, too, if the Badaga's Toda partner were a relatively affluent man he would supply timber for the purpose. If the Kota were an affluent man he might give food to his own helpers who carried the timber from the Toda source. Similarly, the Badaga partner might get the timber that was needed for a Kota's house. There was in fact considerable flexibility in these intertribal connections.

When a Badaga house is being built the Kota partner has to place a piece of iron in the foundations to drive away bad spirits; ghosts and demons abhor iron (as elsewhere across the Old World). A comparable ritual at the completion of a new Badaga cattle-shed requires that the owner's Kota partner bring a crowbar and lay it across the threshold over which the first cow[7] to enter must step.

The Badagas literally hold a house-warming ceremony in a newly built house, when the hearth is first built. The Kota partner of the owner must also attend this, bringing a new pot with him. This is essential, for grain has to be boiled in it during the ritual. Another Kota man will also be less directly involved in this ceremony, as the mother's brother of the house-owner also has to bring another pot for the same purpose from *his* Kota partner.

Until the past century Kota men were usually requested to thatch Badaga houses. This service has, however, been discontinued: in 1900 or a little before, thatch was replaced by tiled rooves, which were found to be more convenient, permanent, safe and prestigeful; but generally Kotas do not lay tiles.

For at least the past century Badagas and Kotas have been building their houses of bricks (from the Basel Mission). Kota bricklayers have built Badaga houses, while Badaga bricklayers have also built Kota houses. In either case the traditional ties would not always be involved, if only because so very few Badaga or Kota men could lay bricks properly. In these situations payment would usually be made in cash according to recognized rates for the labour performed.

BADAGA PRODUCTS

Apart from the annual grant of grain and cloth to Kotas, their Badaga partners used to give them whatever cattle died. 'All the cattle that die in the villages are carried off by the Kotas, and feasted on by them . . . and at no time do the Kotas thrive so well as when there is a murrain [babesiosis or another infectious disease] among the herds of the Todas and Badagas' (Metz 1864: 128).

Though Badagas and Todas used to exchange cattle on occasion, no such trade ever took place between Kotas and Badagas; indeed until the mid-nineteenth century these other two communities would not allow Kotas to own any buffaloes, and after they did get some they still did not milk them (Reclus 1891: 192; Thurston & Rangachari 1909, vol. 4: 7). The Kotas would eat every Badaga or Toda buffalo that died, however, or would kill and eat an ageing beast (normally a bull) given them for the purpose; but it is noteworthy that once they started keeping herds they would never eat any of *their own* buffalo carcasses.[8]

Another item for which the Kotas looked to the Badagas in the nineteenth century was opium. Good-quality opium was produced on the Nilgiris at that time, but the Badagas seem to have held a monopoly on it. Recently anyone could buy poppy capsules illicitly in the town markets (Thurston & Rangachari 1909, vol. 4: 9); I have seen them in Toda homes (Mahias, in Hockings 2012: 717-19).

IRREGULAR SERVICES

There are certain services which Kotas are called upon to render only if some unusual situation arises. Thus Kotas do not normally help their Badaga partners to harvest the crops; yet if a Badaga had difficulties in harvesting a large crop he might until recent years ask his Kota partner's family to help. An agreement would be made for the Kotas to receive perhaps one-fourth or one-fifth of the harvest, in addition to the usual yearly gifts.

Once in a lifetime a Kota should make a ceremonial visit to the house of each Badaga partner's married daughter. At a pre-arranged time the Kota, perhaps accompanied by his wife, should go there and present the daughter with some woman's implement, generally a sickle. In return for this – and on behalf of her husband, not her father – the woman gives the Kota at least one item of cloth, most commonly a loincloth.

Another service which Kota friends might be expected to render irregularly, with or without any money changing hands, has been the supply of sexual partners. Affairs between Badaga men and Kota girls are supposedly forbidden (and certainly no intermarriage has occurred), since the Kota would pollute a Badaga in a ritual sense. Nevertheless a Badaga (even a Lingayat) might occasionally ask his Kota partner to get him a Kota girl. Badagas sometimes claim that these girls have no objection in general to such arrangements as they believe that any offspring of these affairs, although brought up as Kotas, will have some of the admired qualities of the higher-status Badaga. No opprobrium was attached in times past to Kotas said to have Badaga fathers. On the other hand, intercourse between Kota men and Badaga women was seemingly impermissible.

Just as there are situations in which a Badaga has to call on his Kota partner for irregular services, so are there times when the Kota may need his Badaga friend's help. In general these occur in four kinds of situation. One is when a Kota wants to borrow something – usually money – that is not available in his own village. Since 1800 the Kotas, like the Badagas, have been increasingly involved in the cash economy, for they have had to pay land taxes and buy musical horns and scrap iron from lowland towns, transactions that required ready money. Secondly, a Kota might ask his Badaga partner to help him arrange for a reputable Badaga therapist, to give him medical treatment (Hockings 1980b: *passim*). Thirdly, since not all Kotas have had regular Toda trading-partners, a Kota might have to ask a Badaga partner to arrange for some needed timber from that Badaga's Toda friend. Lastly, Badaga elders may help arbitrate disputes between Kotas, just as Kota headmen in former times might sometimes become the judges for a serious dispute in the nearby Badaga communes.[9]

BADAGA RITUALS

The role of the Kotas in Badaga ritual has been, at least until 1930, a crucial one, since custom required that Kotas provide the music at Badaga funerals, weddings and certain festivals (Ward 1821: lxxvii; Harkness 1832: 78-79).

Funerals (unless for Christians) always take place in the village of the dead Badaga (Hockings 2001: *passim*). Whether they involve the Lingayat practice of inhumation or the general Shaivite practice of cremation, the funerary ritual is not considered to have been completely performed unless a Kota band has arrived to play dance music and lead the cortège. Thus as soon as a Badaga person has died his village's headman must send out word of the funeral plans, not only to other Badaga villages with which there are relationships but also to the Kota partner of the deceased. This man then arranges a party of eight Kota musicians to play at the funeral (Pl. 15). The partner himself attends the ceremony but usually does not play an instrument then, for he is in mourning for his friend. The band regularly consists of two flutes, two drums, two tambourines (which are beaten with sticks) and two large brass horns. The bandsmen go immediately to the bereaved house and there play music for dancing.[10] It is a rule that the corpse should not be removed from the house until this performance has begun. However, if the funeral is to be on a lavish scale, word of it may have to be sent great distances, in former days by messengers on foot, and the Kotas would then have to play for two or three days before the main obsequies began. Each time a party of visitors arrives from another village the Kota band go out with the headman a short way to welcome them. At night the Kotas light a fire on a veranda for warmth and sleep there if need be. If the dead man were rich his Kota partner might honour him by bringing *two* bands of musicians, who take turns in playing through the night as well as the day. Once the corpse has been brought out to the yard in front of the house, the music is played there for several hours while Badaga men dance around the catafalque (a thing that is rarely if ever constructed nowadays; see Pl. 9 and 13). Each time the corpse is moved on for the next stage of the complex ritual it must be preceded by the band. When the corpse has finally been disposed of the Kotas return to their homes; they have not set foot on the burial or cremation ground, and have never entered a Badaga house (Hockings 2001: 12, 14, 28, 38, fig. 7; 2012: 347-50).

There are certain articles that a Kota is required to bring to the funeral of his Badaga partner. If the deceased was a male of a meat-eating (and so formerly a hunting) phratry, the Kota produces a roughly made bow-and-arrow to be burnt with the corpse; but if the deceased was a vegetarian male of the Lingayat sect a small hoe is brought instead, and this has to be used for the first strokes in digging the grave.[11] It is carried anticlockwise once around the catafalque on the head of a near male relative of the deceased and is then kept underneath the corpse (which is lying on a cot) with other gifts.[12] If the deceased was a woman the Kota partner brings two toe-rings, one for each second toe. In the nineteenth century the Kotas also provided a dead woman with a pounding-stick (Metz 1864: 77); today a rough one is made by her relatives instead.

The Kota partner is often requested to supply a band of musicians for a Badaga wedding if this is to be a public one. (Many weddings are held privately, 'within the family circle', just to save expenses; in which case that Kota might still come, but without musicians.) At an ostentatious marriage their musical services might be required for several days; but while the attendance of Kota musicians at a funeral is imperative, it is for the groom's family to decide whether or not to have them at his wedding. The Kota partner may also be invited to a naming or an ear-piercing ceremony, and should certainly be asked to a bull-castration.

In the early years of the past century the Kota man would receive from his Badaga partner a total of Rs. 2 or its equivalent for each day the band played at any ceremony. Later in the twentieth century it became common for less than a complete band of eight musicians to attend (Pl. 15); but each bandsman would be fed and given Rs. 5 a day, even more if the donor were wealthy. The Kota partner, however, got nothing in return for the gifts that he had to bring to a funeral.

In each commune the Badagas were supposed to hold a massive memorial ceremony (*manevale*) whenever one generation level had altogether died out, or else when sixty years had elapsed since the previous ceremony (Hockings 2001: 61-64; 2012: 14-17). These events would began on a Sunday and lasted for eight days, during which many thousands of Badagas from all over the plateau would turn up. On these rare occasions the Badaga headman informed the headman of at least the nearest Kota village (indeed, he had to seek that Kota's permission), and he arranged for all the men and boys of that village to play their music at the ceremony. For this purpose the Kotas divided themselves into numerous bands of eight men each, and thus the dance music could be kept going day and night for the entire period, with several of the groups playing simultaneously in different spots. At the end of this ceremony these Kotas would all lead the memorial procession to the cremation ground, where a cot was burnt up, along with sticks on it representing every member of the deceased Badaga generation. The Kotas were fed by the commune for the duration of the ceremony; after their performance each participating Kota village was given one male buffalo, and a measure of rice or other grain was also given to each player. All of these expenses, together with the cost of entertaining Badaga visitors and erecting the great catafalque, were borne in common by a standard levy on each Badaga household.[13] After 1936 (that one in Tanga:ḍu) the whole event was found to be too costly to perform any more.

KOTA CEREMONIES

Just as the presence of Kotas at these Badaga rituals is obligatory, so are there Kota rituals that require Badaga attendance.

When there is a death in the family of a Kota, his various Badaga partners should come to the funeral with some male relatives and friends. Yet although these Badagas are expected to attend they actually play no part in the ritual: they must simply put in an appearance and make a gift to indicate their sympathy for the bereaved family. Formerly, if a Badaga was rich this gift would be a male buffalo to be killed during the funeral; if poor he would give Rs. 5 or 10, or the equivalent in grain (Thurston & Rangachari 1909, vol. 1: 85). The Badaga men pay no formal respects to the corpse; and they stay neither for the ceremonies nor for the exciting buffalo capture and sacrifice. Usually they are offered tobacco or cigars by the Kotas, but cannot accept food.

Badagas are also expected to attend the Kambaṭṭara:ya (Kamatrayn) festival every January in the villages of their Kota partners (Breeks 1873: 44; Thurston & Rangachari 1909, vol. 4: 14-17; Řezničkova, in Hockings 2012: 487-90). Some days prior to this the Kotas will already have received their annual gift, which commonly includes new clothes for the festival and perhaps also a temporary loan of jewellery. When the Badaga men go to a Kota village on this occasion they are accompanied by some of their female relatives. On arriving a Badaga party will halt just outside the village until the Kotas come with their musicians to escort them in. Again, the Badagas are not there to take part in the ritual itself; but once this has been completed the visitors are expected to dance and to generally enjoy themselves. After a few hours of this the Badagas return home for they could not pollute themselves by accepting the food of Kotas (Metz 1864: 130-31).

To repeat, all of the above-described interaction was very much curtailed after about the year 1930, although in some villages more rudimentary ties remained until later in the twentieth century.

NOTES

1. Adapted from Zvelebil 2001: 148 (originally 1955: 243-44). In fact a number of other tribes are interrelated socially and economically with these four, and so an adequate account would embrace close to a dozen communities; Bird-David 1997: *passim.*
2. Roughly one Kota to every hundred Badagas in 1980; see Appendices 1 and 2.
3. The Todas claim that 'the Kotas are . . . artisans specially brought up from the plains to work for them'; Thurston & Rangachari 1909, vol. 4: 7. For the location of Kota villages, see Map 2 above, pp. 39-40.
4. Respectively *Panicum miliare* and *Eleusine coracana.*
5. Emeneau 1946: 257. Harkness (1832: 109, 135) noted: 'Each Burgher [Badaga] community now pays . . . at the rate of eighty measures [probably 65 litres] for each plough of land'. But at Kotagiri the Kotas got 182 litres from a village. Later Breeks noted that from each village the Kota would get from 37 to 74 litres of each kind of grain grown (1873: 42).
6. Thurston & Rangachari 1909, vol. 1: 85. The Oḍeyas alone will not cook in earthenware.
7. Nowadays any small piece of iron is used; the cow is always a gift of the Badaga's wife's father.
8. If a Toda or Badaga animal strayed into a Kota herd for one or more nights it would be returned to the owner, but the Kotas would make a point of never eating that particular animal. On nineteenth century practices, see 'Rifle' 1872: 32. During the latter half of the twentieth century the Kotas abstained from eating buffalo flesh in a bid for greater respectability (Verghese 1966: 105-06).
9. Emeneau 1946: 261; Mandelbaum 1955: 241. Each Kota village constitutes a commune separate from each contiguous Badaga commune but

answerable to the *pa:rpatti*, who is the Badaga head of that division (*na:ḍu*) of the plateau.

10. The music and dance are performed upon the *ke:ri*, the work-space in front of every house. These bands look identical to those of the Mēdas and Poleyas of Coorg; Srinivas 1952: pl. opp. 192.
11. More practicable tools are used for the real work; Hockings 2001: 33, fig. 2a; 2012: 313-14.
12. Today the Kota simply borrows an old hoe in the Badaga village and then covers it with mud as a gesture 'to make it into a new hoe'; Hockings 2001: 33, fig. 2a.
13. Belli Gowder 1923-41: 15. The last time these rituals were performed was in 1936, in Tanga:ḍu, when each household had to contribute a minimum of Rs. 30; see Pls. 11 and 12, and Hockings 2001: 61-64; 2012: 14-17.

CHAPTER 8

Badaga–Toda Interchange

BADAGAS AND TODAS

Until quite recently every Badaga family maintained an exchanging relationship with one Toda man; some still do.[1] This relationship is inherited on either side by a son from his father and usually links (or did link) a certain Toda to an entire Badaga village. This connection is structurally different from the ties between Badagas and Kotas, as specific Toda women are not formally involved in it in the way that Kota wives are; for in what was formerly a polyandrous society like the Todas' the fact that a woman might simultaneously have several husbands could mean that if she were associated with the Badaga partner of each one she would become overwhelmed by the requirements of these multiple loyalties. In practice the same Toda man has normally been partner to all the Badagas in one village, and some have even been linked with everyone in half-a-dozen neighbouring Badaga villages. Toda culture has apparently changed less than have either the Badaga or Kota culture during the past century-and-a-half. Indeed Fenicio, writing in 1603 ([1906]: 723), describes the same economy and the same kind of interdependence with Badagas that Rivers was to observe precisely three centuries later.

In the earliest days of European contact, Harkness had noted:

> A very good understanding exists between these two tribes, the Tuda assuming to himself a superiority which the Burgher [Badaga] has no inclination to dispute; and the former, content with this privilege, willingly yields to the latter the palm of superior civilization and domestic economy; which he would think dearly bought if at the expense of any portion of his natural liberty, or of his freedom to range, when and where he pleases, over his native mountains. (1832: 39)

In 1963 an elderly Toda summarized the present situation: 'The Badagas now consider themselves superior to the Todas as they have risen financially. The Todas do not accept the Badaga superiority. Todas are superior because they do not eat flesh, while Badagas do.' But further questioning revealed that the attitudes that had been recorded by Harkness still pertain. (A vegetarian tribe is very rare.)

The nature of the status difference between the two communities is indicated more precisely in their customary salutations, which are still sometimes performed:

Whenever a Toda meets a Badaga *monegar* (headman) or an old Badaga with whom he is acquainted, . . . the Toda stands before the Badaga, inclines his head slightly, and says "*Madtin pudia*!" ("*Madtin*, you have come.") The Badaga replies "*Buthuk*! *buthuk*!" ("Blessing, blessing") and rests his hand on top of the Toda's head. This greeting only takes place between Todas and the more important of the Badaga community. . . . The salutation is made to members of all the various castes [phratries] of the Badagas except the Torayas. It has been held to imply that the Todas regard the Badagas as their superiors, but it is doubtful. . . . The Todas themselves say they follow the custom because the Badagas help to support them. It seems to be a mark of respect paid by the Todas to the elders of a tribe with which they have very close relations, and it is perhaps significant that no similar sign of respect is shown to Toda elders by the Badagas. (Rivers 1906: 630; cf. Walker 1986: 29)

Although Badagas in the past were motivated to maintain links with the Todas out of economic considerations, those links were apparently tinged with some distrust. While Ku̲rumbas have been regarded by all the neighbouring communities as highly dangerous sorcerers, many Badagas and Ku̲rumbas have believed that Todas too possess some lesser skill in sorcery; and it is this suspicion that may in part explain why some Badagas have kept up the exchange relationship even when they might have preferred to drop it.[2]

There is no doubt that the Badagas believe in the powers of the Toda sorcerers. I was told [in 1902] of several definite instances in which misfortunes were believed to have been brought . . . in this way, and there is little doubt that, in one case, the supposed author of the death of a child was murdered by the Badagas.

If a Badaga suspects magical influence of this kind he may consult one of the Toda diviners, showing that the Badagas believe in Toda divination as well . . . (Rivers 1906: 635; cf. Thurston 1906: 320; 1912: 234)

Even certain natural catastrophes have in the past been attributed by Badagas to the supernatural powers of Todas:

> When any epidemic prevails among the Badagas or a murrain [disease] decimates their cattle, their first endeavour is to discover the Todas, to whose enchantments the calamity may be attributed . . . the whole male population of two neighbouring Toda munds [hamlets] were taken before the [paramount] chief Badaga of the district and accused of having killed the cattle by means of sorcery [*ca* 1847], the Badagas threatening at the same time to withhold their usual tribute of grain unless the murrain immediately ceased. The Todas readily consented to stop their enchantments. . . . Shortly after, the disease abated and the simple Badagas at once viewed this as the result of their compact with the Todas. (Metz 1864: 21-22)

Metz once rescued a Toda from fifty Badagas who were on the point of hanging him for suspected sorcery; but later on Badagas did indeed murder a Toda 'sorcerer' after one of their children had died (BEMS 1855, no. 15: 39; Metz 1864: 34; Rivers 1906: 261; Francis 1908: 144; see below, pp. 232-34). Emeneau has recorded a Toda text referring to violence done by Badagas for other reasons against Todas in times long past (1984: 357-58); while, on the other hand, Liudmila Shaposhnikova referred to a case during the 1960s when a Toda murdered a Badaga over a matter of rent that the Badaga owed for land (1969: 174-77).

BADAGA PRODUCTS

The 'tribute' of grain, called *gu:ḍu*, is well documented by earlier writers. Fenicio (1603 [1906]: 727) mentions that at the start of the seventeenth century the Todas were subject and *paying* tribute to the Badaga headmen. One should note that all later authorities speak of the Badaga headmen paying Todas, though; perhaps the Italian, who worked through a Malayali interpreter, was misinformed. In 1832 Harkness said (110) that the Badagas were giving grain to the Todas 'rather as a free gift, than as tribute'. Ouchterlony, writing in 1848 (38), considered it rent for the land (Shortt & Ouchterlony 1868: 15; cf. Grigg 1880: 328); but he suggested enigmatically that it was also meant to buy off Toda men who might have an interest in Badaga women, who come to the village 'and demand, in their right as temporary husbands of women of the naad, the "goodoo . . ."' (Ouchterlony 1848/1858: 283). The Todas themselves think of the *gu:ḍu* as a rent for certain hamlet sites that their ancestors gave to the Badaga settlers. This accords with the fact that certain Badaga villages traditionally did not pay anything to the Todas (Grigg 1880: 328).

The *gu:ḍu* was not exactly a rent for land anyway, for when Badagas sold land to European planters there was never any stipulation that the new owners should give something to the Todas; nor did the Todas advance such claims against those Europeans.[3] Furthermore there is no record of Todas objecting to the government's levy of its full revenue assessment on the Badaga lands from which the *gu:ḍu* came (Breeks 1873: 12-13).

The amount of *gu:ḍu* varied, possibly from one part of the plateau to another or from harvest to harvest. Harkness noted that around Kotagiri the Badagas reserved about 36 litres for the Todas, half of that for the dairyman-priest; but elsewhere much less was given.[4] In 1848 Ouchterlony noted that the contribution varied 'according to the circumstances of the inhabitants, the owner of a rich house giving usually 1 cundagum = 20 kollagums [= 74 litres]; and those less opulent from $^1/_2$ to $^1/_4$ cundagum . . .'[5] However, he noted that even though the Badagas professed to give one-sixth of their harvest, they in fact gave 'not above one-half of this proportion, if even so much, especially in the item of wheat which is so profitable to them' (Ouchterlony 1848: 17; Shortt & Ouchterlony 1868: 15). From this it appears that grain prices in the town markets were so high in 1847 that the Badagas chose to short-change Todas for the sake of extra cash income. In 1873 the *gu:ḍu* was said 'formerly to represent about $^1/_{10}$ or $^1/_8$ or $^1/_5$ of the gross produce' (Breeks 1873: 9, note; Grigg 1880: 333). This indefiniteness of the amount given was discussed by Marshall too:

> . . . as no very accurate accounts are kept . . . this foraging [in the Badaga villages] stands with the Toda in lieu of sport . . . ; it being to the interest of the Badagas to postpone and shirk payment of grain as long as possible; whilst . . . the state of the Toda stores, and his natural persistency combined, are urging him on to repeat the visits. . . . The result being that the Toda gets exactly as much grain as will just satisfy his actual necessities. (Marshall 1873: 79)[6]

Ouchterlony traces the origin of the grain gift to the earliest Badaga settlement on the hills. He attributes the subsequent decrease in the amount to a lack of deference on the part of the Badagas:

> . . . some Burghers or "Buddaghars" came up the Hills and . . . asked permission to settle also and obtained it on condition of the payment of the "goodoo" or tribute of $^1/_6$th of their entire harvest. More . . . soon followed the first comers; the amount of the "goodoo" became extensive; the habits

of the Todars changed . . . the deference of the Burghers for them diminished, and with it the amount of the "goodoo", which received a great acceleration in its decline by the coming of Europeans . . . ; the Burghers observing their indifference to the alleged claims of sovereignty of their hitherto feudal landlords, gradually assumed the position of donors of the "goodoo" of free will, and as a charity; and hence reduced its amount as the circumstances of . . . harvest, or their own wants and inclinations, directed. Upon this footing . . . the "goodoo" appears at present to rest. The Burghers profess not to desire to be relieved from it as a tax, because to give it as a donation to the Todars has become with them a time honored custom. (Ouchterlony 1848: 52-53; Shortt & Ouchterlony 1868: 53-57)

Rivers, among others, suggested that Badaga fear of Toda sorcery was one reason for the continuing payment of grain.[7] But he added correctly that Todas did own some disused dairies in the middle of Badaga fields, and that if the Todas became too estranged from Badagas they might re-assert their claims over these sites and so cause a few Badagas to lose their farmland. Another reason claimed for the continuing payment is that it might encourage Todas to restrain their herds from trampling the Badagas' fields (Breeks 1873: 13; Lawley & Penny 1914: 206; Emeneau 1971: 45, 751). All such arguments are denied by modern Todas, who now mention the great distance between most Toda grazing and Badaga lands, the non-existence of Toda sorcery, and the absence of any usable Toda dairies in Badaga farmland today. In the Toda view *gu:ḍu* was never compulsory but was an annual gift the Badagas used to make them in return for help rendered by Todas and for disused hamlet sites the Todas had once presented to certain Badaga immigrants long ago.

Ever since 1900 the grain given has not been enough to feed the Todas, so that they have also bought grain and rice at the bazaar (Breeks 1873: 13; Rivers 1906: 632-33). Some modern informants say the Toda associated with a Badaga village could expect roughly 4 litres of inferior-quality grain from each household there, but this would still vary with the donor's generosity. Some Toda songs refer to 'one four-anna piece from each house' and one measure of grain (Emeneau 1971: 165, 167-68). The system of *gu:ḍu* was still operating in certain villages late in the twentieth century, mostly those closer to the grazing lands of Todana:ḍ. Few Todas nowadays consider it worth the trouble or the indignity of going to each house and trying to get their annual due, while few Badagas see it as being a duty rather than mere charity to give visiting Todas anything.

It was traditionally in September when Todas would go to collect this grain – either little or finger millet or, in the twentieth century, home-grown potatoes or paddy rice imported from the plains. They would decide among themselves how to divide up the task of collection, and then one Toda would go to each village and visit every house. Where practicable he ought to be the traditional partner of those particular Badagas (Emeneau 1938: 103). Until early in the twentieth century it was not even necessary for him to call at every house because the Badaga headman himself would collect the grain together from the donors beforehand.

There are other items which Todas regularly expected from their Badaga partners as well. Two centuries ago, before the Ootacamund bazaar came into being, much of their cloth came from Badagas.[8] This and the materials for embroidery had initially been supplied by a Badaga's Chetti partner, or else bought directly from an itinerant Chetti (see below, pp. 182-84). In the days before the cash economy Todas could obtain from their Badaga partners salt, crude sugar, and perhaps tobacco, which had been bought in the plains during the annual trading expedition there.[9] One item which Todas, like Kotas, might rarely get from Badagas was opium (Hough 1829: 96, 104; Walker 1986: 25); today some buy poppy capsules in the market, but have long ceased getting them from any Badagas.

TODA SERVICES AND PRODUCTS

In turn, certain necessities of Badaga life regularly came from the Todas. Of major importance was dairy produce, mainly clarified butter but also milk and buttermilk.

A few types of basket, among them the winnows, were traditionally supplied to Badagas by Kuṟumbas; but the majority, including the huge grain-storage baskets (*balla*), were made for the Badagas by their Toda partners, out of various types of split creeper. Certain baskets on the other hand were obtained from Kuṟumbas by Todas who would then weave strong edges to these before passing them on to their Badaga partners (Rivers 1906: 630-31; Emeneau 1938: 103).

Prior to the past century, before thatched roofing fell into disfavour among Badagas, it was the Toda partner and his friends who brought the bundles of reeds needed for thatching (Puyravaud, in Hockings 2012: 902-03). Until recently the Todas also brought split creeper and wood needed for building the heavy wooden beds of the Badagas. Other wooden and cane items were supplied when asked for: the milk-churning stick made of cane, timber for ploughs and roofing, threshing-sticks and walking-sticks with incised decorations (Hockings 2012: 982-83). Flutes are sometimes made by an Iṟula who trades them to a Toda, or sometimes the Toda makes one himself to give to his Badaga partner. Until the beginning of the last century Todas also made and supplied umbrellas woven of leaves. Cylindrical vessels used for milk and necessary in certain Badaga rituals, and in earlier days grain measures, were articles made by Todas out of wide sections of bamboo. Not only were the Badaga partners provided with such things, but sometimes a Toda would also bring a gift of fresh bamboo shoots, a great delicacy that would always draw a return gift of grain.

Cloth was formerly supplied to Todas through the Badagas, but there are two circumstances in which Todas might still give Badagas an embroidered cloak (Pl. 4). The rarer of these was when a Badaga headman needed one; for the distinctive Toda cloak was in the past virtually a symbol of office for Badaga and Kota headmen, and would also be worn by other elders as a mark of respectability. It is also a custom for Badaga corpses to be covered with an embroidered cloak, obtained from his Toda partner by the husband of the daughter of the deceased. The embroidery is done by a wife or mother of the Toda (in a very shoddy manner if it were intended for a Badaga funeral; Balaram, in Hockings 2012: 916-19). A coarse kind of cloth used once to be woven from the fibres of five species of local nettle, these having been supplied by Todas. Even today a bundle of these fibres (called *mañji*) should be offered to a female corpse during a Badaga funeral, and comes from the Toda associate.

Irregular Transactions

As a general rule Badagas, Kotas and Todas would shift their cattle to new grazing areas independently of each other, at the start of each year. During the nineteenth century the Badaga herds were sufficiently large that each village would 'have usually two substantial cattle pens, or more according to the size of the village, with high, rough, dry stone walls, and barricaded entrances' (Pharoah and Co. 1855: 483; see Pl. 11).

At present, however, Kota and Badaga cattle are so few that it is rarely necessary to move them at all; but some Todas still practise transhumance within the limits of the plateau, occasionally with Badaga cattle mixed among their own. It was formerly common for Badagas to take part in the annual migration of the Toda buffaloes; or sometimes they entrusted their buffaloes to the Toda partners, to take them to better summer grazing on the southern edge of the plateau (Ward 1821: lxxiii; Rivers 1906: 133, 137; Ranga 1934: 24; Walker 1986: 27). There Todas would intermingle their own herds with the Badaga buffaloes and enjoy the use of their milk, until they were to be returned home at the approach of the June monsoon. They were easily separated again, as the Toda ones came to the call.

Badagas and Todas have sometimes exchanged buffaloes in order to get others of more useful age or yield.[10] This barter only involves female animals and is typically the exchange of one buffalo of good yield for two of lower yield. The Todas may also get non-sacred buffaloes from Badaga friends when they suddenly need the animals for sacrifice at a Toda funeral, or alternatively sell them to Badagas when they need cash. Any difference outstanding after such transactions was formerly paid on the Badaga side by grain, cloth, or gold and silver ornaments; and on the Toda side by various bamboo and basketry articles. More recently any differences have been made up with money alone.

Todas sometimes ask their Badaga partners for financial loans. In the nineteenth century if the request produced no immediate result they would mortgage buffaloes to wealthy Badagas as security for a loan (Marshall 1873: 130). In the late twentieth century one could still find a few Badagas lending money, but usually out of fear of the Todas' sorcery.

Although it has not occurred within living memory, 'It was formerly a common practice for rich Badagas to hire forty or fifty Todas to go on wife-stealing expeditions, and carry off by force the wives of other Badagas' (Metz 1864: 75). Today, while the practice of stealing wives may still occur very occasionally, assistance from the Todas is no longer required, it seems. A parallel situation when gangs of Badagas used to help Todas steal wives was also recalled. In either case the assistants each received a few rupees.

Sometimes when a Badaga wants to indulge in some illicit sexual activity he may ask his Toda partner to lend his own wife or find him a Toda girl; but as Toda women were generally rather free in their interaction with non-Todas it was normally no problem for the Badaga to importune a girl himself. Todas on the other hand have had virtually no opportunity for intercourse with Badaga women. (Such at least is what reliable Badagas have stated; Toda men deny any such relations between the two communities.)[11]

Badagas are very fond of betting; and so when they meet informally a Badaga and a Toda sometimes have a bet over the possibility of their performing some athletic feat, such as lifting a boulder up to shoulder height (Rivers 1906: 597-98).

Medicine is another matter that can bring the Todas and Badagas together. Although Todas did have therapists in their own tribe they occasionally went to Badagas noted for particular kinds of cure.[12] A Badaga partner may help the Toda arrange treatment; but the therapist himself/herself would usually expect some fee or gift from the patient.

Todas are considered moderately powerful sorcerers, despite their own recent disclaimers.[13] It was for this reason that the parties of Badagas who went to massacre Kuṟumbas always included one or two Toda associates to deliver 'the first blow' (*Calcutta Monthly Journal* 1836: 54). This practice has never recurred since 1900; nor have Badagas murdered a Toda sorcerer since that time.

Most affluent Todas (affluent because of illicit land rentals, and more recently because of farming profits)[14] now live in Badaga-style brick houses instead of the customary thatched huts, as the houses are more spacious and comfortable (Noble, in Hockings 2012: 57, fig. 23). The habit began a century ago (Rivers 1906: 29, 634; Noble 1997: *passim*). The Badaga-style houses (distinct from the modern government-financed housing) are built in a Toda hamlet by Badaga men hired for the purpose, though not necessarily by a Toda's Badaga partner.

Ritual Interaction

A common setting for interaction between the two communities is ceremonial. Thus once a year some Todas donated one or two buffaloes to Hette's sacred herd at Be:rage:ṇi, the only Badaga village with a sacred herd attached to its temple (Francis 1908: 316; Noble 1976: 116). And for the annual hunting ceremony of Be:ḍa Sa:mi

(Noble 1968: 149-50) held by both Badagas and Kotas, the Toda used to bring clarified butter to smear on the weapons. On some Badaga festival days the Toda may be required to bring the sticks and make fire by friction, or perhaps bring a new milking vessel.

Even so, no very crucial part is played by either community in the ceremonies of the other. A Badaga partner and his family or friends will often be invited to the naming, wedding or funeral of a Toda. The Badagas at these times will eat Toda food provided it has been prepared in a separate pot (Rivers 1906: 323, 634-35).[15] Similarly Badagas may invite their Toda partners and friends to weddings, funerals and certain of the annual festivals, to most of which the Todas are required to bring some useful present, such as a new pot (in Toda, *puθ aḍy foṛy*). On these occasions the visiting Todas or Badagas should be fed, and it is also appropriate for the hosts to make small gifts; yet gift exchange is not requisite to all ceremonies.

Once a year each Badaga village holds a ceremony at which the cattle are given salty water. The Toda man or men who are the usual associates of men in that village are invited on this occasion to take whatever coarse salt is left over from the ceremony (Hockings 1968: 414).

The Toda, like the Kota partner, has also an obligation to visit the married daughter of each Badaga partner once in a lifetime. He will send word of his intention; and then comes and presents her with a buffalo heifer or perhaps something even more valuable. In return she gives him a cloak and possibly some other clothing.

All Todas from nearby hamlets were invited to attend the great memorial ceremony (*manevale*), in which Badagas honoured one generation of their dead; indeed it could not take place without permission from some Todas of the neighbourhood. These local men brought cane to use in the catafalque and were offered five coins (Rs. 1.25) in return. A Toda associated with the Badaga village might opt for the special duty of sitting at the major village entrance and receiving each group of visitors. He would ask every group if they included any important man – one carrying some administrative portfolio or a member of the gentry.[16] If there was such a man in the group the Toda told them all to wait while he brought the commune headman to welcome them, along with some Kota musicians. Otherwise he conducted the visitors to the place where a great catafalque had been erected. The Toda was fed while performing the service, and afterwards got a gift. Todas may have had a similar role during the funerals of the Badaga divisional headmen. Their main duty seems to have been policing the immense crowds that always attended the ceremonies (Lütze 1887: 14; Hockings 2001: 62; 2012: 14-17; see Pl. 11 and 12).

As was mentioned earlier,

> At the present time [1902] the amount of grain supplied by the Badagas is not sufficient for the needs of the Todas, and both grain and rice are bought by the Todas in the bazaar. All the grain used by the *palol* [priest] must, however, be that supplied by the Badagas; but if more grain is required than the Badagas supply, it is possible that other grain may be used, though it is always in this case procured through the Badagas. The rice used at a *ti* dairy [highest-grade temple] must also be procured through the Badagas. (Rivers 1906: 632-33)

This statement suggests that there used to be a separate category of Badaga associate for the priest of the *ti·* dairy-temple. This supposed institution was elaborated upon by Rivers:

> The supply of grain is far from being the only duty of the Badagas to the *ti* dairies. Each *ti* has one or more special Badagas, each called *tikelfmav*, or "*ti* help Badaga," who acts as intermediary between the *palol* and the Hindus. The earthenware vessels used in the inner room, the various garments of the *palol*, and other objects are made by Hindus [i..e., the Chettis], from whom they are procured by the *tikelfmav*. I did not learn of any material recompense given to the Badagas for these services . . .[17] (1906: 633, and cf. 98, 630)

But reliable Toda informants have assured me that there was no such institution, even in the nineteenth century. For one month a year the now derelict *ti·* at Ö·nṭöw was indeed occupied by the priest (*poḷ o·ḷ*), and until the middle of the twentieth century local Badagas gave him grain during the ceremonious feeding of salt to the Toda herds there at Ö·nṭöw. (That *ti·* was surrounded by Badaga fields.)

Before 1900 the Badagas received clarified butter produced from the milk of sacred buffaloes (Metz 1864: 41; Grigg 1880: 195; Macleane 1893: 905). One priest explained to Marshall (1873: 145) that this clarified butter from the *ti·* dairy, '. . . which we don't eat ourselves, I sell to the Badagas, who in return supply me and my family with grain, clothes, and a little money'.[18] Further, 'The *palol* wears garments of the kind called *tuni*, of a dark grey material made at Nulturs [Nellitore] in the Coimbatore District'.[19] These were sometimes brought to the priest by a Badaga who had previously acquired them from his Chetti trading partner, but could really be supplied by anyone. The black *tüṇy* cloth, a fabric quite different from ordinary Toda clothing, is also used to enshroud a corpse, and was obtained from Badagas for that purpose as well (Rivers 1906: 236-37). One further item got through Badagas was the above-mentioned vessels to be used in the sacred *ti·* dairy (ibid.: 90).

An irregular Toda ritual that a few Badagas may attend is the re-building or rethatching of a temple. A day or two beforehand some Badaga elders from nearby villages should be invited by their Toda partners. At one such event in 1963 several Badagas made offerings of silver to the Toda temple and quietly made vows before it.

Sometimes when Toda men expect to be busily occupied at some such ceremony they now hire Badaga youths to prepare the food; Toda women could not do this. It is just a matter of convenience, however, and not a traditional element in the bonds between the two communities.

Although Badagas are often invited to a funeral, 'The only part played . . . is that the bell called *tukulir mani* may be kept by a Badaga or a Kota' (Rivers 1906: 633; cf. Walker 1986: 29). This ancient bronze bell has to be tied round the neck of a sacred buffalo as a part of the ritual before it may be sacrificed. Some Badagas do help of their own volition with the Toda's pyre, and in the nineteenth century they actually used to carry the Toda headman (*maṇega:r*) to the ceremony (Ling 1892: 76).

A frequent guest at Toda council meetings of both a judiciary and a non-judiciary nature is the headman of Tu:ne:ri village, who is paramount chief of the Badagas (see below, p. 193). His advice is well regarded by the Todas, and he is expected to help mediate in complex Toda disputes whether or not Badagas are also involved in them (Rivers 1906: 550, 633; Walker 1986: 28, 254). Formerly the headman of Ba:kola, who was a divisional headman (a *pa:rpatti*) of the Badagas (Pl. 9), would also attend those meetings.

NOTES

1. Only four of the 16 Toda clans keep up the relationship, and it has been totally abandoned by Christian Todas and Christian Badagas; cf. Emeneau 1939: 101. I am indebted to T. Mutiken, a Toda (1924-2004), for his patient criticism of these pages on Toda/Badaga relations.

2. '. . . were it not for the hold which the Todas have upon them by the pretended use of witchcraft, they would doubtless refuse payment of their accustomed tribute'; Metz 1864: 21; cf. Marshall 1873: 145; Grigg 1880: 328.
3. Ouchterlony 1848: 59; Shortt and Ouchterlony 1868: 59-60; Breeks 1873: 12-13. Ward (1821: lxxiii) stated it was paid to Todas because they were 'the hereditary claimants of the soil'. We should note that during the second half of the nineteenth century the government allowed the Todas Rs 150 annually, as 'goodoo' or compensation for former Toda lands now being used by the Europeans in Ootacamund Municipality; Grigg 1880: 302, 329-31, 333-41; Price 1908: 227-28. Similar compensation was paid for Toda and Badaga lands in Coonoor Municipality; Francis 1908: 343. On the legal status of *gu:ḍu* and Toda land rights, see Sutton 2009: 16-27.
4. Harkness 1832: 108, 110-11. He presents (135-36) a general figure of 2.25 litres – probably what each household gave the Todas.
5. Ouchterlony 1848: 59; Shortt & Ouchterlony 1868: 59. Kotas claim it should be one winnowful (4 litres) per household; Emeneau 1946: 257.
6. Cf. Shortt & Ouchterlony (1868: 59): 'Sometimes the offerings . . . are not considered sufficient, and sometimes they refuse to give anything at all, when confusion ensues; the Todars . . . entering their houses and laying them under contribution by force.'
7. Grigg 1880: 195; Rivers 1906: 261; Francis 1908: 144; cf. Metz (1864: 41): '. . . they stand in fear of the supposed power of the Palaul to kill their cattle by sorcery'.
8. Toda men and women wear the *pu·txuḷy* – a large cloak intricately embroidered by the women (Pl. 4) – over a loincloth.
9. On occasions when the Todas did not join Badagas and Kotas in this venture.
10. Rivers 1906: 634. Toda songs often refer to buffaloes obtained from Badagas for funeral sacrifice; e.g. Emeneau 1971: 6, 79, 307, 448.
11. Basel Mission 1905: 305 records how a Badaga Christian teacher, who had relations in 1903 with a Toda girl and later with his own mare, was disciplined. Emeneau 1971: 613 cites the case of a Toda woman 'raped by a Badaga'. One other report of wife exchange between Todas and Muḍugas has not been substantiated by recent investigation; von Fürer-Haimendorf 1954: *passim*.
12. Rivers 1906: 323, 634-35; for details of Badaga therapy, see Hockings 1980b.
13. Grigg 1880: 212; cf. Metz 1864: 123; 'Rifle' 1872: 32; Stokes 1883a: 6. They were from one particular clan nicknamed 'Kuṟumbas-cut-people'.
14. Francis 1908: 272; Thurston & Rangachari 1909, vol. 7: 115; Shaposhnikova 1969: ch. 22; at present very few Badagas rent any land from Todas.

15. Those of the high-status Ha:ruva and Lingayat clans eat only the milk products, not cooked food, if they visit any Todas. For an instance of a Toda priest putting butter on the Badaga ceremonial spear, see Emeneau 1971: 5, 744.
16. There is a kind of upper class among Badagas, which I call the gentry: families claiming direct descent from the founder of their village. It is from these families that the headmen usually come; see above, Diag. 8, and pp. 280-81.
17. Cf. Walker 1986: 27-28. The fact that Badagas or anthropologists may go right up to the *ti·* enclosure while Todas stay 100 m. away perhaps led Rivers to presume that his Badaga guide for the day had a special relationship with the *poḷ o·ḷ*!
18. The sanctity of the milk from sacred buffaloes has been lost once it is made into clarified butter, and so this can be sold; Emeneau 1938: 104, 112.
19. Rivers 1906: 103. A less reliable source claims the *poḷ o·ḷ*'s cloth was woven by the Toreyas of Jakkana:ri, near Kotagiri; see Macleane 1893: 905. On the culture of Jakkana:ri itself, see the detailed analysis given in Heidemann 2006: 201-446.

CHAPTER 9

Interaction with the more Remote Tribes

BADAGAS AND KUR̲UMBAS

The Kur̲umbas have been conventionally treated in English writing, including censuses, as being one of the five main tribes found on the Nilgiri Hills, the other four of course being known as Toda, Kota, Ir̲ula and Badaga. Actually the Kur̲umbas (Pl. 16) are a cluster of six tribes, a fact that only became apparent some thirty years ago. These groups are the Jēnu Kur̲umbas (or Kāḍu Nāyakas), Bëṭṭa Kur̲umbas, Muḷḷu Kur̲umbas, Pālu Kur̲umbas, Ālu Kur̲umbas, and Muḍugas (Kapp and Hockings 1989).[1] From the point of view of the Badagas, Todas and Kotas, however, they can still be viewed as a single unit.

The Control of Sorcery

Geographically the Kur̲umba hamlets are much more isolated from the Badagas' than are the Todas' or Kotas', and the various Kur̲umba tribes occupy separate territories on the lower slopes; nevertheless certain of the Kur̲umbas have long had a crucial role in the Badaga community. A Badaga family does not have a specific Kur̲umba partner, but each commune would appoint a particular Kur̲umba[2] to act as guardian and watchman to all of its constituent hamlets. This is a lifelong appointment that passes from father to son (or else to a brother's son if he had none himself). It involves warding off magical attacks from *other* Kur̲umbas with the watchman's own sorcery. As with Toda sorcery, these 'magical attacks' were once a common way of interpreting crop failures and animal diseases as well as most human ills. A Kur̲umba watchman is expected to spend a part of the time in his Badaga commune, where he generally lives on the veranda of the headman's house.[3] If he does not appear there very often the Badaga inhabitants nonetheless believe he is magically present each night or else knows by clairvoyance what is going on in the villages; yet his visits tend to be frequent, for he is fed by the commune. The standard annual remuneration to the Kuṟumba watchman should be 3.7 litres of wheat or millet from each household, given at harvest-time. Cloth might be given during some Badaga festivals. This at least was the traditional situation (Hockings 2012: 853-58).

Many Badagas still believe that the Kuṟumba is the most effective of all south Indian sorcerers (though some Kuṟumbas now give the palm to the Paraiyans of Kerala). Kuṟumbas can kill victims at a distance with a spell, it is believed, can secretly remove the internal organs from the living, can violate women without their knowledge, can enter a locked door, and can change into an insect or any sort of mammal.[4]

Until perhaps four decades ago Badaga charges were often levelled against Kuṟumbas; even today the suspicion popularly directed towards them is still strong. Formal charges of witchcraft, handled by Badaga commune councils, used to unite the Badaga community against an external threat of (or target for) aggression; and the massacres that sometimes followed such charges in the nineteenth century were clearly a tension-reducing activity for the Badagas:

> In 1836, no less than fifty-eight Kurumbas were murdered, and a smaller number in 1875 and 1882. In 1891, the inmates of a single Kurumba hut were said to have been murdered, and the hut burnt to ashes, because one of the family had been treating a sick Badaga child, and failed to cure it . . . . Again, in 1900, a whole family of Kurumbas was murdered, of which the head, who had a reputation as a medicine man, was believed to have brought disease and death into a Badaga village. The sympathies of the whole countryside were so strongly with the murderers that detection was made very difficult, and the persons charged [in a lawcourt] were acquitted. (Thurston & Rangachari 1909, vol. 1: 86, and Thurston 1912: 233-34; he partly quotes from Stuart 1901: 5; see below, pp. 232-34)

Br. Metz also wrote on this tension:

> When I first commenced by missionary labours on the Neilgherries, and whilst I was considered by the natives as their great friend, my object having been then but imperfectly understood, I was repeatedly asked to rid them of the Kurumbas, that is, to get them hunted down like wild beasts and exterminated, and they would remember my name with gratitude for ever. (1864: 123)

Some Badagas claim that until the mid-twentieth century a Kuṟumba council would sometimes authorize Kuṟumba youths to go out for a few weeks and practice the sorcery they had learned. At such times the Kuṟumba watchman would warn all the Badagas he was supposedly protecting that this was occurring, and that they should not leave homes after dark or take needless risks; nor should they blame him for any deaths, as each youth was permitted by the tribal council to kill one man. Since the Kuṟumbas could also kill each other it was believed that no young sorcerer would try his skill against members of a Badaga commune that was protected by some more powerful or senior Kuṟumba, since the latter might well retaliate out of revenge against his fellow tribesman.

Exchange of Goods and Services

Despite the tension-fraught nature of the relationship, the Kuṟumba watchman was no mere predator on the paranoid fears of Badagas; for he did engage in economic exchange with them, too. Kuṟumbas were expected to supply the communes with three kinds of basket: two types of winnow (Pl. 13) and a large flat basket to hold grain while drying. They also provided 'their' Badaga communes with some rare kinds of timber found on the jungle slopes, especially the hard false frankincense wood (*Hardwickia binata*) needed for pounders. In the past honey, tamarind, bees-wax and knotted nets were regularly supplied by the Kuṟumbas, along with some leaf umbrellas and sleeping mats made of split cane or reeds.

One duty a Kuṟumba might exceptionally perform for Badagas was to treat certain maladies that the Badaga therapists were unable to cure. Some male Kuṟumbas became noted for their abilities to cure specific ailments, either by herbal medicine or by spells, and a Badaga might arrange for treatment by them through the village's Kuṟumba watchman (Thurston 1912: 233; Hockings 1980b: 189). Fees or costly presents would be expected for any such favour. The Badaga village Be:ragallu has a name derived from the Kuṟumba *báre+kállu*, 'lines + stone', referring to flat stones nearby that were covered in etchings and other marks. In earlier times these would be 'read' by a Kuṟumba in an effort to ward off buffalo diseases.

The Kuṟumba watchman may still play a necessary role in the ritual of his Badaga commune but Badagas have no part whatever in

Kuṟumbas' ritual. An Ālu or Pālu Kuṟumba must participate in the sowing and harvest festivals: these are the two most important ones in the annual cycle. In the former, he must make certain ritual utterances and cut the first furrows with a plough – recently with a mere ploughshare – at an early morning ceremony in January, and then he must sow the first seeds. In the harvest festival, which comes in July, he must sacrifice a buffalo calf early one morning in a Badaga's field. Two days later he leads a procession of Badagas to their temple, where he assists the priest with preparations for the ritual. Then two days after this he must make a wreath of millet sheaves, attach it to a stone arch (representing a temple gateway) and then reap the first grain of the harvest. Kuṟumbas now claim it was they who initially taught the Badagas of old about these two ceremonies. During the memorial ceremony (*manevale*) for a generation that had passed away, the commune Kuṟumba also had an active part to play. On the second day of that huge event (a Monday) he was to bring along a bamboo ladder for use in building the catafalque, and he also cut the first bamboo pole to be used in this construction. On the following Sunday and Monday he sacrificed two goats (seemingly their only recent role in Badaga culture). His own role throughout all of these rare ceremonies was that of an accessory priest, and for this he would receive some Rs. 15 (Ward 1821: lxxvi; Birch 1838: 103, 105; Francis 1908: 154; Belli Gowder 1923-41: 13-15; Noble 1976: 118-20; Kapp & Hockings 1989: 237-38; Hockings 2001: 62; 2012: 14-17).

Although he does not help at any other Badaga ceremonies it used to be considered a wise precaution to invite that Kuṟumba's attendance at any auspicious ceremony, such as a wedding, first pregnancy or naming, and then make him some small gift that might help avert the ever-threatening malice of Kuṟumbas. For any Badaga funeral he might also receive a payment (Thurston & Rangachari 1909, vol. 1: 86-87; Jagor 1914: 47-48); although Kuṟumba sorcery could not disturb such an inauspicious ceremony.

At Pannamaḍe hamlet, which adjoins Hulikal, the Badagas have a temple for Raŋgana:ta, a Vaishnavite god, and during his annual festival there local Kuṟumbas beat drums and play music. There are certain situations in which Kuṟumba musicians perform at a Badaga wedding or funeral in place of the Kota band, too (Grigg 1880: 211). Traditionally it could happen either when a dispute had at least temporarily alienated a Badaga family from their Kota partner or when an epidemic was rampant in that Kota's village. Nowadays, when most Badagas have stopped inviting Kotas to any of their ceremonies some do invite Kuṟumba musicians instead while others dispense with the music altogether. If the Kuṟumba watchman is asked to arrange for a band of musicians, his own Kuṟumba village headman should notify the Kota headman that they will be playing at a certain Badaga village; and the Badaga who invites them should first get permission from that Kota headman to do so.[5] This set of rules is no longer followed, since the feelings of Kota headmen are not respected now that Badaga-Kota relations have in general been broken off.

Until the 1930s when the institution of commune watchman began to lose currency, the Kuṟumba got a quarter-rupee each month for every pair of oxen in the commune, or more often its equivalent in grain.[6] At harvest time he would also receive the same sum or else 6 litres of new grain collected from each household by the headman's assistant. In addition, he and his family would be fed whenever they were in the commune.[7] The Kuṟumba could also rely on Badagas to satisfy all of his clothing needs, for which purpose the headman would first collect grain from the villagers with which to purchase the cloth by barter from the visiting Chetti trader. An early claim that the commune Kuṟumba should inherit a Badaga's estate when there were no traceable heirs (Harkness 1832: 109, note) has never been recorded since, and would not be possible today.

In pre-British times the Kuṟumba watchmen got their only salt and crude sugar from Badaga friends who made annual expeditions to the plains for such needs. This latter activity had generally ceased by 1825, however.

When their Kuṟumba watchman dies the headman of the Badaga commune should collect various gifts from the villagers and take them, or have them sent, to the bereaved family. This used to be imperative to secure the goodwill of the family from which the next watchman would also be drawn.

BADAGAS AND IṞULAS

The tribe that is conventionally identified in English writing as Iṟula (in Baḍagu, *U:ruvi*) is in reality a cluster of five tribes, as Zvelebil (1981: 522-23) has demonstrated: the Mele Nāḍu Iṟula, Vĕṭṭe Kāḍu Iṟula, Ūrāḷi, Śolaga, and Kasava. The only Badagas who now have any regular contact with Iṟulas are those near Hasanu:ru and some living in the most easterly sector of the Nilgiris. In this latter area Badagas tend (erroneously) to treat the Iṟulas as a section of the six Kuṟumba tribes, and hence their interrelationship approximates that between Badagas and Kuṟumbas elsewhere on the plateau.

One of the highest mountains (1788 m.) in that particular area is Rangaswami Peak (Metz 1864: 65-66; Nicholson 1898: 426-27; Noble 1976: 124; Zvelebil, in Hockings 2012: 754-57; see Pl. 2), important in Nilgiri culture because it is crowned by a Vaishnavite shrine (actually two megalithic circles of unknown antiquity).[8] This is controlled by Iṟula priests who, unlike most south Indian tribals, are Vaishnavites. The two monoliths inside the stone circles stand for the god Ranga and his wife, to whom some of the local Badagas make a yearly offering of plantains, milk and coconuts:

> The hereditary pújári is an Irula, and on the day fixed by the Badagas for the annual feast, he arrives from his hamlet . . . bathes in a pool below the summit, and marches to the top shouting 'Góvinda! Góvinda!' The cry is taken up . . . and the whole crowd, which includes Badagas, Irulas and Kurumbas, surrounds the enclosures while the Irula priest invokes the deities by blowing his conch and beating his drum, and pours oblations over, and decorates with flowers, the two stones which represent them. That night two stone basins on the summit are filled with ghee [clarified butter] and lighted, and the glare is visible for miles around. The ceremonies close with prayers for good rain and fruitfulness among the flocks and herds, a wild dance by the Irula, and the boiling . . . of much rice in milk. (Francis 1908: 340; cf. Ward 1821: lxii; Breeks 1873: 70; Macleane 1893: 373)

While Badaga contact with the Iṟulas used to be less frequent than with other tribes on the Plateau, one of the major 'sanskritizing' influences in the Nilgiris was clearly constituted by the Iṟulas, until the late nineteenth century. As Metz noted (1864: 133), 'They come up now and then . . . and divert the inhabitants with obscene theatrical performances representing passages in the life of Krishna, whom they call Govinda'. The Abbé J.A. Dubois (1817 [1906]: 196) pointed out how in the early 1800s Rangasāmi Peak (Pl. 2) was a place of pilgrimage for Hindus from the nearby plains, who 'have made it a *punyasthala*, or place of virtue . . . As it is very difficult to reach the top of this mountain, a view of the summit alone . . . is considered sufficient to remove the burden of sin . . . .' Those stalwart pilgrims who did clamber up the peak could well have influenced the local Badagas to some extent in pre-British times. For such services as their Krishna dramas and the occasional medical therapy I̱rulas used to obtain grain from Badagas, a gift which was probably a kind of *douceur*, for I̱rulas were also considered to be sorcerers, though less effective than the Kuṟumba. Some Badagas living close to I̱rulas probably had a more regular exchange relationship, giving grain to the Irulas in return for honey, beeswax, timber, nets and other jungle products (Grigg 1880: 215-16; Macleane 1893: 373). Like the Kuṟ-umbas, I̱rulas may be asked to play music at Badaga ceremonies when Kotas cannot be appealed to for a band. I̱rula women living in the twelve Badaga villages near Hasanu:ru have sometimes become mistresses of those Badagas too, but not elsewhere.

BADAGAS AND KASAVAS

Although it was once suggested (Thurston and Rangachari 1909, vol. 3: 256; Noble 1968: 69) that the Kasavas ('labourers') are merely I̱rula tribesmen who had moved into the labourers' settlements in plantations over the past century or so, their geographical distribution does not support this. Kasavas are a northern I̱rula tribe only found along the Moyar Ditch just north of the Nilgiri Plateau, whereas the other local I̱rulas only live south and east of the plateau (Noble 1968: 6, fig. 2; Řezničková & Hockings, in Hockings 2012: 463-65). But no doubt they are people of very similar culture. Possibly the 'labourer' title dates back to the Middle Ages when their area of residence had had a much more dense and urbanized population.

The Kasavas performed a service for the more northerly Badagas analogous to that which the Todas perform for those living farther south: Kasavas take Badaga cattle down into the Moyar Ditch for grazing and breeding (Francis 1908: 209; Noble 1968: 69-72). A Badaga owner occasionally visits his herds there, and several dozen Badaga families now live there permanently (Davidar 1997: 184-88); but traditionally the Badagas' animals were regularly tended by a Kasava family who together received perhaps Rs. 6-10 weekly, as well as vegetables and grain, for doing this. In addition they got a ration of rice, an annual supply of clothing and occasional gifts, for example, at a Kasava wedding. The livestock camps (called *huṇḍi*) of Kasavas are mainly used for breeding, but large numbers of cows and buffaloes would have been sent there by the Badagas when the grazing on the hills was sparse. More generally,

Dry cows are taken down, and good milk yielders are brought back up. . . . Milk and buttermilk [from Badaga cattle while in the Moyar Ditch] may be consumed by the Kasuva caretakers. Clarified butter carried up by Badagas or Kasuvas is either sold or consumed by Badagas. (Noble 1968: 72)

Be:rage:ṇi, the only Badaga village with a sacred herd attached to its temple (Francis 1908: 316), had throughout at least the twentieth century and perhaps earlier kept its hundred buffaloes permanently in the Moyar Ditch under the charge of Kasavas because of shortage of grazing around Be:rage:ṇi itself (Hockings 2012: 127). The herders were paid out of the temple funds.

As with Kuṟumbas and other Iṟulas, a Kasava band might come to Badaga ceremonies in place of the usual Kota one. Aside from this, there are two annual events that have brought the two communities together in considerable numbers over the past half-century. First, there is a complex *pu:ja* to the goddess Śikkamma at her Kasava-owned temple at a *huṇḍi* beside the Moyar Ditch, held every March. This is one among several frontier shrines which are located on the ancient boundary between Mysore State and the Nilgiris. Over ten thousand Badagas and most of the Kasavas will attend. On the next auspicious day following, the same crowds walk into Ma:siniguḍi nearby, for a festival to honour Śikkamma's elder sister, the goddess Ma:siniamma, who holds a strong reputation there for bringing prosperity to the people. The highlights of both events are a *pu:ja*, a free meal, perhaps a Badaga drama, and a noisy night-time procession with the goddess' image mounted on an elephant that is dramatically lit up with electricity (Davidar, in Hockings 2012: 566-67).

BADAGAS AND ŪRĀḶI IṞULAS

The Ūrāḷi Iṟulas (in Badaga, *U:ra:yi*) are a tribe of gatherers and shifting cultivators who inhabit jungles on some southern slopes of the plateau; nowadays however many of them work on plantations. They have had no regular connection with Badagas, but since they are feared for their sorcery they can depend on alms from Badaga villagers should a crop failure force them to wander up onto the plateau, as it occasionally has done in the past. Under some unusual circumstances Badaga men might pay a band of Ūrāḷis to perform music at a ceremony when for some reason Kotas cannot be invited (Řezníčková, in Hockings 2012: 966-67).

THE WAINAD GAUḌAS AND THEIR NEIGHBOURS

Wainad Gauḍas are Badagas who settled on the lower plateau some two centuries ago. Near them are various other non-Badaga groups: Kotas, Chettis, Paṇiyas, Iṟulas, Kuṟumbas and until 1925 even a few Todas. The Gauḍas, a dominant community in the area, cultivate dry and irrigated rice. They now claim it was the desire for rice which had prompted their ancestors to move down into the Wainad from Badaga villages on the Nilgiri Plateau (Hockings 2012: 980-81).

The community consists only of Gauḍas, except one village that also has some Toreyas (now calling themselves Gauḍas, however). The 951 people (as counted in 1963; perhaps 1,500 nowadays) live in two communes, each made up of a few hamlets containing one lineage; and there are also seven unaffiliated villages, hence a total of 21 hamlets. Each village has a council, and for complex legal cases a council of all the Wainad communes is held at Pandalu:ru town. This system thus parallels that of the Nilgiri Badagas but does not link up with theirs: cases cannot, for example, be referred to the paramount chief of the Badagas in Tu:ne:ri, and he does not invite Wainad Gauḍas to his councils. The head of the all-Wainad council is someone noted for his justice, called the Great Headman (*doḍḍa gauḍa*); he is selected from any of the communes. Each commune is headed by a man termed the *jammaka:ra*, under whom there are two or three lesser headmen (*kuḍiya:re*). Both of these offices are inherited fraternally; i.e. they pass from brother to brother in order of seniority, then on to the eldest brother's eldest son, and so on. Each *kuḍiya:re* is responsible for the descendants from one particular Nilgiri *division*: in Ko:lepaḷḷi, for example, there are two such headmen because its population is descended from Todana:ḍ and Me:ḳuna:ḍ villagers. As in the Nilgiri hills proper, a legal dispute passes up this hierarchy from the *kuḍiya:re* to the Great Headman if necessary.

These Gauḍas have maintained some marriage connections with Nilgiri Gauḍas, even with families of the gentry. Several communes still intermarry with the Nilgiri Badagas of Śo:lu:ru; but more generally all of the communes here marry endogamously *or* exogamously within the broad Wainad community. Their constituent hamlets, just single lineages, are however always exogamous.[9]

There is a nineteenth-century reference to trading parties of Wainad Gauḍas regularly visiting the Me:kuna:ḍ village of Ke:ti (and presumably elsewhere on the plateau too), bringing with them buffaloes and gold dust 'for sale' (BEMS 1854, no. 14: 41). The nearby Kota village of Kollimale would no doubt have been involved in making the gold into Badaga jewellery, ear-rings and finger-rings.

These Wainad Gauḍas had no connection with a few Todas who, until the 1920s, lived on the edge of the Wainad, but some do maintain an exchanging relationship with the Kotas there, and also with certain I̱rulas and Kuṟumbas. The Kota partner from Gu:ḍalu:ru should provide pottery as well as a pole used in Gauḍa funerals, to which he should also bring Kota musicians. He traditionally would help, too, with house building (Ranga 1934: 26). In return he got an occasional buffalo. I̱rulas and Kuṟumbas may also provide music for the funerals. Like the Paṇiyas, they are valued as basket-makers, but have no reputation for sorcery here as they do elsewhere. (The Kuṟumba watchman institution described above was not extant in the Wainad, so far as we know.)

Gauḍa landowners have a special relationship with the Paṇiya tribe, some of whom were their prædial slaves.[10] As if to justify this situation some Wainad natives claim that the Paṇiyas originated as African slaves who escaped from two British ships in Calicut harbour during the reign of Tipu Sultan; but it is more likely they were local tribals or slaves (*paṇya*) who had escaped across the border from the small state of Coorg.[11] These labourers, whose services could be bought along with the land (Thurston & Rangachari 1909, vol. 6: 58), and whose serfdom there was inherited patrilineally, worked without real wages in return for regular meals, housing and clothes. Some of the more progressive farmers gave them a little pocket-money as well, and usually paid their marriage expenses. In 1976 the Government made a serious effort to release all such people from bondage, and further legislation to this end was developed over the next two decades (Hockings 2012: 848-50).

TRADITIONAL INTERCHANGE: A SUMMARY

Each of the main ethnic groups here – Badagas, Kotas, Todas and the several Kuṟumba tribes – was linked with each of the others through patrilineally descending partnerships (cf. Diag. 10, p. 134). The men involved supplied each other with specific goods and services, supplementing their own economic activity and also symbolizing their social interrelationship through ritualized interaction.

Only the Badagas produced a real surplus of grain before modern times; Kotas and Kuṟumbas grew hardly enough crops for their own needs and Todas never grew anything. Thus the Badagas alone were in a position to pass out grain to the Todas, Kotas and Kuṟumbas at harvest-time. They were also to some extent the suppliers of cloth, sugar and salt for these tribes. While Badagas thus played a major part in the economy of the Nilgiri tribes, their role in the rituals of these groups was minimal, probably because the form of the rituals antedated the arrival of the Badagas on these hills.

Todas specialized in dairy produce, just milk and clarified butter. These they provided on occasion for Badagas, Kotas and Kuṟumbas. Todas were also able to supply Kotas and Badagas with a variety of cane products: beds, flutes and certain baskets (Pl. 13).

The Kotas possessed some buffaloes and did cultivate grain, too. But they also made various artefacts for the Badagas who gave them cattle carcasses and grain and for the Todas who gave them clarified butter. The Kotas were the Nilgiri specialists in carpentry, pottery, leather-work, metal-working, thatching and ceremonial music. Their participation in Toda and Badaga funerals was essential.

By comparison with the Kotas, the Toda and Kuṟumba tribesmen maintained relatively simple relationships with the Badagas. Most Kuṟumbas were kept distant from the other hill peoples because of their area of residence and their reputation for infallible sorcery. The commune Kuṟumbas, or watchmen, were appointed by a Kota or Badaga commune to protect its members from Kuṟumba sorcery, however. The loyal watchman was rewarded with a dole of grain at harvest, with new cloth whenever he needed it, with meals when he was with the Badagas, and in fact with anything else that he might wheedle out of his employers by supernatural threats or promises.

NOTES

1. Kapp (in Kapp & Hockings 1989: 233) thought that the Ūrāḷis were one of seven groupings of Kuṟumbas, but more recent research by the late K.V. Zvelebil treats them as one of five subgroups of Iṟulas.
2. *U:r Kurumba*; Breeks 1873: 53-54.
3. No Kuṟumba is allowed in a Lingayat house, as he is believed capable of polluting it. Other phratries allow him as far as the outer room and consider him less polluting than a Kota.
4. Harkness 1832: 84-85; Metz 1864: 116-117; Anonymous 1879: 148-49;

Thurston & Rangachari 1909, vol. 1: 86, and Thurston 1912: 232-33; 'Miles' 1951: 71. For a particularly fanciful account of this sorcery in the nineteenth century, see Blavatsky 1930: 120-32, 198-204, 213-25. Early in the last century one up-to-date old Kuṟumba lady was 'experimenting with flying'. I have elsewhere suggested that Kuṟumba sorcery is derived from Buddhist sorcery, and as such is a relic of the Buddhist presence in south India, which otherwise evaporated about a thousand years ago; Hockings 2012: 853-58.

5. Badagas have asserted it would be immoral or liable to bring misfortune were Kuṟumbas and Kotas allowed to play music together on the same occasion.
6. Metz 1864: 116; Thurston and Jagor, however, have stated this to be the *annual* tax paid by each Badaga family; see Thurston & Rangachari 1909, vol. 1: 86-87; Jagor 1914: 47-48. According to Kotas it should be 'four annas and a meal paid by each house'; Emeneau 1946: 257.
7. Ward 1821: lxxvi; Harkness 1832: 109; Metz 1864: 116. Around Kotagiri each family gave their Kuṟumba 18 litres; cf. Harkness 1832: 135, note. Elsewhere he was thought to get about one-sixtieth of the harvest; Harkness 1832, 57. Even earlier his share was put at 15-37 litres per farmer, plus 'as many of the sheaves as he can well bear away on his shoulders'; Ward 1821: lxxvi. The Kuṟumbas accepted cooked food from Badagas, uncooked food from Todas, but none from Kotas; Macleane 1893: 222.
8. Though the Badagas are Shaivites there are also Vaishnavite temples in a few villages, managed by Shaivite priests; see p. 29, n. 17 and p. 164.
9. Marriage, which is rarely polygynous, involves payment of a bridewealth of Rs. 100, refundable upon divorce; for an instance of marriage between Śo:lu:ru and the Wainad Gauḍas, see Emeneau 1971: 611.
10. Ranga 1934: 55-59; Noble 1968: 174-75. This relationship was ended by Government action in 1976.
11. Moses 1964: 10; Srinivas 1965: 20-22; Paṇya is also a section of the Yerava tribe in Coorg.

CHAPTER 10

From Barter to Marketing, from Millet to Cash

ORIGINAL STATE OF THE ECONOMY

We know little about the Badaga economic system before the arrival of a few British officials in 1819, except that the exchange of goods and services outlined in the previous three chapters was undoubtedly in operation.[1] It is nevertheless worth surveying the available sources since the pre-monetary economy of the period preceding the impact of European economic ideas has till now been influential on Nilgiri cultures, despite their monetization for well over a century. Some of the most detailed information lies in the traditions of the Badagas. Because of the high degree of correspondence between tales coming from different parts of the plateau, their content seems to be factual rather than legendary, and can go a long way towards explaining the many vestiges of this indigenous economy that one can observe even today.

The earliest mention of Badagas in the Nilgiris is by Fenicio, who reports an encounter with both Badagas and Todas. The 'Badegas' told him they had only three villages on the plateau, but this information might be misleading.[2] Fenicio mentions a village called Melcuntaõ – the modern Me:lkunda – which at the beginning of the seventeenth century already had a population of at least 100, with a mixed-farming economy. The Italian man tells us that these Badagas had cattle, poultry, goats; that they grew lentils, 'rice' (presumably a millet), mustard seed, garlic and wheat; and they also ate honey. At this early date the Badagas were not self-sufficient as they gave the Todas 'rice' in exchange for buffalo ghee. He added that Badagas also carried this clarified butter to a place called Manaracathe to sell (Fenicio 1603 [1906]: 723). This place is evidently the Mannar

Ghat or escarpment track, which runs from Malabar to the Sunda-paṭṭi Pass, and then leads up the south side of the plateau to Me:l-kunda village.[3] Whether coinage was involved in such transactions we are not told; but it seems unlikely. The same description might very well have been penned by another visitor to the area two centuries later.

Nothing was, however, written about the following two centuries of life on the Nilgiris, although that was the period when the Badaga community expanded to over 300 villages and consolidated itself. The next mention of Badagas occurs in Francis Buchanan's survey of 1800 (1807: 246-47), where this Scotsman mentions briefly their having ploughs, practising swidden cultivation and collecting jungle produce, including honey and bees-wax.[4]

From about 1809 to 1812 several British men explored the hills.[5] Casual visitors, these people apparently had no impact on the local economy. The 1812 expedition, however, was sent to survey the area quickly and report back to the Collector of Coimbatore under whose charge the tract had nominally rested since the Treaty of Seringapatam in 1799. Keys' short report (1812) contains some valuable material to add to what little we may glean from Fenicio, Buchanan and the oldest traditions of the Badagas themselves.

In 1819 the first European settler, Mr John Sullivan (Pl. 16), an official from London, came to the plateau and immediately set in motion a train of events that quickly and significantly transformed the indigenous economy into a monetized one (Hockings 2012: 881-88). Over the succeeding years the European population slowly increased; but it was only after 1838, when coffee was first introduced (Muthiah, in Hockings 2012: 214-17), that Britons had any commercial reason for taking up residence in the area. Long after that date the great bulk of Europeans – who never amounted to more than a couple of thousand, anyway – remained in the three towns they had founded on the plateau, so that their influence on the rural economy may well have been marginal. By the 1830s there is however some evidence of an attempted modification of Badaga farming that can be attributed directly to the British presence: English-style ploughs were introduced in Ke:ti in 1830, and in 1837 a number of these were distributed to Badaga farmers. However, 'Towards the end of 1839, it was reported that the experiment had proved a complete failure, and it was consequently abandoned' (Price 1908: 224). Other introductions were more effective, though, for John Sullivan worked hard and almost single-handedly to improve the quality of life for *all* Nilgiri residents (Hockings 1989c: 336-41; 2012: 881-88). Yet in general, however, what O'Malley has observed for the India of Moghul times is also an accurate enough summary of the Nilgiri situation throughout the entire nineteenth century:

> The only contact with the villages was by means of local officials having their head-quarters in the towns, who were responsible for the patrolling of the main routes, the suppression of organized crime, and the realization of the land revenue. So long as it was paid, and so long as there was no disturbance of the peace endangering the general security or outbreaks of crime preventing the safe passage of travellers and merchandise, the villages were left to manage their own affairs, with headmen and councils of elders to try their petty cases and village watchmen to prevent petty crime. (O'Malley 1941: 12)

A detailed view of the economy up to the year 1830 (when a large part of the plateau was transferred from Coimbatore to the Malabar administration) can be reconstructed from several reports, mainly British ones.[6] These provide us with a list of Badaga produce which can be amended slightly by modern informants.

The main items[7] cultivated by Badagas at that time were wheat, barley, Italian, finger and slender millets, prince's feather (or amaranth), panic-seed, chick pea or Bengal gram, mustard seed, black gram, peas, pepper, poppy, rose-mallow seeds, a bean, garlic, onion, fenugreek, pumpkin and gourd (the first six of these were grains).

The main animal products in this period were cow and buffalo milk, clarified butter (made more by Todas than by Badagas), hides (prepared by Kotas from Badaga cattle), bullocks used in ploughing and threshing, and a few large poultry. No sheep were kept, though both Fenicio and Birch had noticed goats in the hills (Fenicio 1603 [1906]: 723; Keys 1812: li; Birch 1838: 103).

Materials gathered from the jungles included kitchen fuel, honey, bees-wax, hay, wild flax, gentian, sandalwood, rattan cane and black dammer or resin.

Items usually imported and exported by Badagas are also listed in the same sources. The imports were coarse cloth, salt, tobacco, iron bars for the Kota blacksmith (Thurston & Rangachari 1909, vol. 4: 8), coarse sugar made from a palm sap, trinkets and coinage.

Exports from the hills then included wheat, barley, some superior millets, bales of millet and barley hay and wild flax (all used for fodder), poppy capsules and opium, honey, bees-wax, garlic, onion, mustard seed, pepper, fenugreek, clarified butter, hides, sandalwood, gentian, rose-mallow seed, cane – and coinage paid in land taxes to an official at Daṇṇayaka Ko:ṭe.

MARKETING BEFORE 1825

Until the British encouraged sundry traders from the plains, including some Parsis, to establish a weekly bazaar in Ootacamund around the year 1825,[8] there *was* no market-place on the plateau itself, nor any cattle fair, and coinage did not circulate much among Badagas. Nevertheless they did participate slightly in the market economy of the plains early in the nineteenth century. Depending on the position of their villages, some went down the eastern slopes to the market of Ka:ramuḍu (in Tamil, Kāramaḍai), others chose a route down the northern slopes to the Mysorean town of Gundlupet (Guṇḍulupēṭe), and those in Kundena:ḍ went southward (as in Fenicio's day) to Sundapaṭṭi, a small market in the westernmost corner of the Coimbatore Plain.[9] This reflected a common geographical situation:

> The juxtaposition of different ecological zones, in particular the links between highlands and lowlands, means exchange systems are important and finds expression through specific marketplaces often at the intersection of zones. Any such gathering is also significant for social interaction, including marriage brokering, and some sites are also associated with religious functions so that the market per se is linked to a broader celebration as a festival. (Funnel and Parish 2001: 90-91)

Apart from visiting Ka:ramuḍu (they called it *Kongu*, meaning 'plains') Badagas never had any occasion to travel extensively on the Coimbatore Plain: it was foreign, Tamil-speaking country. Guṇḍulupēṭe was just called *Pe:ṭ* – 'a place where people come together', hence a market; or as some say, 'a place where cattle gather'. It has long been a major cattle market in southernmost Mysore.

Early each March the Kanarese Chettis along with other villagers of Ka:ramuḍu held a festival to honour the god Rangana:tan,[10] after which there was a large cattle fair and general market. A delegation of Badaga men from villages in the eastern part of the Nilgiri Plateau attended that festival every year.[11] They would first of all assist in dragging the chariot of the deity along, to acquire religious merit, then would barter goods for coinage or whatever else they needed.

There seems to have been no fixed date for the annual visit of more westerly villagers to Gunḍulupēṭe, but it coincided roughly with the Ka:ramuḍu expedition. In both cases Badaga men obtained provisions for their main harvest festival, the Great Festival,[12] which falls in March or April, and salt for the ceremonial feeding of their cattle in March (Hockings 1968). In Gunḍulupēṭe the Lingayats could also purchase personal *lingas* (Pl. 16) at a monastery. In view of the very long walk from these markets and the 1,500 m. ascent, it is not at all surprising that the items bought were small and fairly valuable.

All three trading expeditions were organized on the same principle. Permission to go was first obtained from the village headmen, then preliminary arrangements were made as to which men would go and the time of their departure. The Badaga headmen would then send a message to neighbouring Kota headmen, thus giving Kotas an opportunity to join the party, for the Kotas did not organize their own expeditions. Todas sometimes also joined too, trading clarified butter and honey for tobacco, trinkets and cloth. The clarified butter was much appreciated in the plains, and was 'transported great distances, even as far as Bombay' (Hough 1829: 72). The trading party would be at least twenty-strong; sometimes hundreds went together – after carefully taking off all their valuables. This precaution was important to the participants because of the dangers, real or imaginary, which they could anticipate as they passed through steep jungle tracks infested with tigers, elephants, wild buffalo, wolves, leopards, brigands and Kuṟumba sorcerers.

Until the 1830s certain Badagas, generally commune headmen, walked once every year to the fort at Daṇṇayaka Ko:ṭe, below the eastern slopes (Pl. 2).[13] The plateau formed a part of the Daṇṇayaka Ko:ṭe *taluk* (revenue division) from Tipu Sultan's administration up to 1830. This was a convention important only for the collection of land revenue from the Badagas and Kotas. Each farmer was assessed a fixed rate by the officers, according to the total rather than the cultivated area he held; the rate would not decrease if some fields remained uncultivated one year. Traditions tell of occasional visits by Tipu's officers to extract payment from the unwilling villagers (Metz 1864: 119; Grigg 1880: 312, 325; Emeneau 1946: 255). In 1799, once Tipu had been killed in battle, the plateau passed quietly into the hands of the East India Company by the Treaty of Seringapatam, and for over twenty years the British continued to collect the

Nilgiri revenues at Daṇṇayaka Ko:ṭe (Pl. 2) without colonizing the plateau or even visiting it. The tax estimates were now based not on acreage but on a farmer's wealth. Each year therefore the headmen carried their collected taxes down in coin. While at that fort they could also no doubt visit the nearby market towns of Sattiyamangaḷa or Seremoge (Metz 1864: 5).

A major reason for the trading expeditions was to sell enough of the new harvest or other produce to get the coins needed for this tax payment, even though this could be paid in part with opium (Francis 1908: 290; Price 1908: 224). Coinage was hardly in circulation on the plateau at the time, especially because there was no market there until 1825; yet coins still had a ceremonial use. Ward (1821: lxxiii; cf. too Rivers 1906: 361-62) mentions gifts of a quarter or a half rupee to Todas on the occasion of Badaga weddings. Rupee coins also reached the Todas, presumably from transactions with Badagas and from those trading expeditions, since a number of the coins still displayed in the Toda funerial ritual are East India Company silver rupees of the late eighteenth century, or even a few Archduchess Maria Theresa (1717-1780) dollars. As further evidence of the ceremonial circulation of coinage, Ward (1821: lxxi) also discusses the Badaga bridewealth,[14] and the payment of 20 Canteroy *fanams* (tiny gold coins totalling nearly Rs. 6; Hockings & Pilot-Raichoor 1992: 127) to a mother when, after divorce, she gave the custody of her newborn child to her former husband. To judge by somewhat later Badaga practices, it is very likely that a gift of coins[15] was already an integral part of most family ceremonies. Such a gift was actually a delayed exchange: it implied that a return gift was expected later, whenever similar circumstances arose. By 1848 only the East India Company's coinage was in circulation, though a good deal of it was also hoarded by burial or made into ornaments (Ouchterlony 1848: 72; Shortt & Ouchterlony 1868: 72). It was an ancient custom: with finds of Roman coins in India, 'many of them have loops or apertures so that they could be worn as ornaments, suggesting that they were not circulated but hoarded as treasure' (Gurukkal 2010: 138).

This pattern of coinage circulation was very slow and uncertain, for it depended on the occasional celebration of weddings and other family events. Coins clearly had a ritual value for Badagas and were important in this period as a symbolic link between various social units (as to some extent they still are). We have no definite evidence that coins were used for payment of fines to the headmen as early as the eighteenth century; but throughout much of the nineteenth century a regular schedule of fines was maintained in Badaga judicial practice (see below, pp. 194-95).[16] Coinage did not define values in a local Nilgiri market, but acted as a convenient and reliable way to store credit acquired in the lowland markets where, from 1799, the British pursued a policy of fixing the local grain prices by currency values.

By the start of the nineteenth century the Badagas had become 'terribly impoverished', and most were heavily in arrears with payment of land revenue. Nevertheless, as Grigg noted, 'The rates of assessment were undoubtedly low', were based on acreage, and 'varied with the appearance of the crop at harvest-time' (1880: 312; Francis 1908: 268). During the first thirty years of British rule a decline in these payments set in. Thus during 1799-1813 the average annual revenue from the entire plateau was Rs. 14,762, but over the next thirty years it fell to Rs. 6,000 (Grigg 1880: 292; Francis 1908: 268). In 1801 it was Rs. 13,425; in 1811, Rs. 15,067 (Grigg 1880: 314); but in 1821, Rs. 9,000 (Mackworth 1823: 123-26); and by 1830 it was down to Rs. 6,000 (Baber 1830: 314). There were several reasons for this decline, the most general one being the minimal administrative control over the plateau that could be exercised from Daṇṇayaka Ko:ṭe; Sullivan justly attributed the low revenue to lack of a proper road (Grigg 1880: 280-81, 314). The tax-farmers who operated for some time on the plateau, from 1807,[17] were too demanding of the dues they had paid the East India Company for the privilege of collecting, while in some other years the commune headmen were too slack about the collection. The drought of 1805-07, the general shortage of coin, the after-effects of Tipu's plundering of Badaga villages: all perhaps contributed to the decline in the payments, if not the actual fortunes, of the Badagas at this period.

Despite a British policy of fixing grain prices there were fluctuations from year to year. Sarada Raju's study of economic conditions in Madras Presidency during the first half of the nineteenth century clarifies these fluctuations. She does not offer any specific data for Coimbatore District (which then included the Nilgiris); nevertheless she may be justified in her view that on a long-term basis the trend was similar in all districts (Sarada Raju 1941: 227). As her statistical data for the Presidency adequately confirm (ibid.: 228-30),

> . . . prices were high in the first few years of the nineteenth century. The country had just emerged from a protracted period of war and anarchy during which rival armies and plundering bands had laid whole districts desolate. Cultivators who had fled to the jungles and hills were but gradually returning to their neglected fields. . . . The period was also marked by a number of scarcities, more or less severe. The very first year, 1799-1800, witnessed a severe dearth and again between 1805 and 1807 occurred another famine, when prices ruled very high. After this prices were persistently low . . . from 1807-8 to 1850-51 prices rose above the [analyst's] base only on seven occasions; and these were famine years.
>
> When the pendulum swung back, low prices ruled till 1812, when two dry seasons caused a scarcity which lasted till 1813-14. But with the coming of the rains, a lower level was reached and we hear frequent complaints of the "continued low price of grain" . . . All the Collectors remarked about it, affecting as it did the ryots' [peasants'] ability to pay the revenue. (Sarada Raju 1941: 231-32)[18]

While several seasons of adverse weather, mentioned by Sarada Raju. did give rise to famine conditions in the Coimbatore District, which was one of the driest in the Presidency, it is very unlikely that famine also occurred on the Nilgiris at those times. Because of their wetter climate the Badagas have always been able to subsist whenever famine ravaged the South Indian plains (Grigg 1880: 34). Even so, Badagas were undoubtedly affected by the occasional lowland famines and by fluctuations in the grain prices, since they were selling their grain surplus in the nearby lowland markets. We need hardly point out that they would have made unusually good profits from sales in the famine years, but they might also have been taxed more heavily in those years. Active participation in lowland markets was difficult in those times, however, since there were no roads up into the Nilgiri Hills, wheeled transport was thus out of the question, and the heaviest loads were what a man could transport on the backs of oxen in hessian sacks, or perhaps on horseback.

MARKETING AFTER 1825

Around the year 1825 the handful of British settlers, through their few municipal officials in Ootacamund, began to encourage traders from elsewhere to develop a market in that small town and provided government-owned land for the purpose (Price 1908: 233; Eduljee, in Hockings 2012: 683)). By the end of 1827,

. . . advances had been made to [immigrant] natives to open bazaars . . . in the place so that 'the market is now well and regularly supplied with every essential article' . . . a public establishment of palanquin-bearers was kept up; and . . . villages were beginning to spring up at the foot of the passes. (Hayavadana Rao 1908: 115; cf. Grigg 1880: 288)

The traders in those early times were Chettis who came up from Meṭṭupe (Meṭṭupāḷaiyam), Ka:ramuḍu and other nearby plains villages or towns.[19] A market in Ootacamund was held only on the Monday and Tuesday of each week; then every Thursday the same traders went to a market in Seremoge, and on Friday they were in Ka:ramuḍu. In these latter places they would collect the produce from the surrounding Chetti-controlled villages, and then on Friday night they would start out by bullock-cart back up the long Coonoor pass to the plateau. Their merchandise included rice, salt, coconut, spices, crude sugar, and other foodstuffs.[20] As the climb was entirely uphill the bullocks rested all day Saturday and Sunday on the slopes (Pl. 15) and travelled during the nights. Later on in that century wealthy Chettis built free rest-houses (choultries) by the roadside for these tedious journeys. The carts regularly reached Ootacamund on a Sunday evening after a 48-hour haul. After two days of trading the Chettis left with their loaded carts around four each Tuesday afternoon. By Friday morning they were back in Ka:ramuḍu to repeat the weekly cycle and to barter their Nilgiri acquisitions for further produce, to take back up to the hills. Mondays and Tuesdays in Ootacamund, Thursdays in Seremoge, Fridays in Ka:ramuḍu, and Saturdays in Meṭṭupe are however still called 'shandy days',[21] and in the later twentieth century it was still customary for Badagas to visit the Nilgiri towns on Monday, the weekly holiday, and to send truck-loads of farm produce to Meṭṭupe or Ka:ramuḍu every Friday.

According to modern Badaga informants their forebears did not use cash at the Ootacamund market in the first two decades of its existence. They exchanged the products of their own lands for the foodstuffs brought up by the Chettis. Thus too the Plateau was exporting a variety of goods to Ka:ramuḍu and beyond, particularly clarified butter, onions, honey, coriander, millet hay and opium.

The initial period of barter in the bazaar passed as this town got a few regular shops. Later in the nineteenth century coinage came into use in the local market, now open every weekday, and a government superintendent would fix the day's prices there (Ouchterlony 1848:

72; Price 1908: 187). One could even borrow money there at 2 or 3 per cent per month interest (depending on the security). The habit of hoarding money drew criticism from officials like Ouchterlony:

> . . . large amounts are expended in Ootecamund . . . ; the payments are all made in silver, which disappears, and can never be traced again, whether it is carried away and hidden, or converted into ornaments, . . . it disappears from circulation. (Ouchterlony 1858: 37, line 5466)

The transition to the exclusive use of coinage in the market took a very long time, for ninety years ago Gáymard was still able to remark that when they made their weekly trips to town some Badagas did not carry a purse but instead a basket or sackful of grain, which they would exchange there for essential things like pimentos, salt, utensils and cloth (Gaymard 1924: 2-3).

ITINERANT TRADERS ON THE PLATEAU

Both before and after these town bazaars had been established the Badagas maintained another time-honoured kind of link with the lowland economy. Chettis from villages lying directly east of the Nilgiris used to come up onto the plateau once a month on foot for petty trading. Badagas call them Regional Chettis (*na:ḍu cetti*), in reference perhaps to the restricted range of each man's trading itinerary. Although living in a Tamil-speaking area their native tongue is Kannaḍa. Their settlements in and near the towns of Seremoge, Meṭṭupe and Ka:ramuḍu were concerned with petty trade, weaving and cultivation. The Chetti man and his family would weave cloth in their home for the Badagas; and till the advent of the Ootacamund bazaar these people were the regular source for cloth among the entire Nilgiri population.

Chetti merchandise consisted of cloth, lamp-wicks and various trinkets, which were exchanged for grain or cash when available. Since the early nineteenth century these traders had also been making and bartering iron measures of volume, artefacts that had previously been made out of bamboo by the Todas.[22] The Nilgiri system of measures differed significantly from that of southern Mysore, presumably because these Chettis and officers at Daṇṇayaka Ko:ṭe were imposing the standards of Coimbatore markets on the Badagas.

Each Badaga village had a traditional bartering relationship with a particular Chetti man, inherited on either side by the son from his father; and despite the vast economic changes since the inception of this system some centuries ago the relationship continued until recently, modified however by a very considerable drop in the number of clients and volume of trade. During the ten days of his visit the Chetti would work through two or three villages a day, restricting himself to the two dozen or more villages of his recognized circuit, and would then return to his home in the nearby plains. After twenty days of work there he would return to the plateau and repeat this circuit. Contiguous territories would be covered by different Chettis often from the same village, so that one could send a message to his own Regional Chetti by contacting another one on tour in the hills. Although a Chetti might sometimes bring his wife with him all dealings occurred between him and the Badaga men. If the Chetti's wife accompanied him, it was only to strengthen the bonds of friendship with Badaga trade associates, through making conversation with the Badaga womenfolk. During nights on the plateau the Chetti slept in the outer room of a Badaga friend. He was allowed to eat in that room as well, but was expected to wash his own plate, an act which marked his lower status.

The relationship between Badagas and Chettis was very different in character from that linking Badagas with either the Todas or the Kotas. Until well into the twentieth century these latter linkages were crucial for the flow of necessary goods to members of these three communities; whereas trade with Chettis was never anything more than a convenience which in early times saved Badagas from extra journeys to the plains and more recently to the nearest bazaar. The Chetti is considered a foreigner as he is from the plains. Usually his Badaga friends need not visit his village: for there is no ceremonial gift-exchange between the two, and scant participation in each other's rituals. This contrasts with the intensity of the traditional relationships uniting the peoples of the plateau (Diag. 10, p. 134).

We know of only two occasions when the Chettis and Badagas had some ritual interaction: one in the plains, the other on the hills. Perhaps two centuries ago, and certainly before British suzerainty in the area, the Chettis of Ka:ramuḍu, acknowledging that they were becoming wealthier because of trade with the Nilgiris, built a larger temple to their god Ranganātan and started the annual chariot-dragging festival in his honour. It was this festival day that the Badagas always chose as the time for their yearly trading expedition; the trading was preceded by a mandatory participation in the ceremonies, thus making this a ritual as well as an economic link between the two groups (Nicholson 1898: 352; see above, p. 176).

Secondly, one of the major Badaga festivals, which honours the deified *sati* Hette[23] ('grandmother'), is held just in Be:rage:ṇi village, where there is a special building called Weaving House that belongs in common to the whole village. Several days before the annual festival their Regional Chetti would come up from near Seremoge to sit in this house and weave a year's supply of new clothes for the priest. These items were a loincloth, turban and shawl, all of cotton, for the making of which the Chetti got a fixed amount of cash from temple funds (Francis 1908: 317; Heidemann 2006: 184-90). These men would not otherwise weave while touring the plateau.

IMPACT OF BRITISH IDEAS ON THE BADAGA ECONOMY (1799-1850)

During the first half of the nineteenth century British administrators took a number of steps which moved the Badaga subsistence economy decisively, if unintentionally, into the purview of a monetized market economy.[24] The ceding of the Nilgiri Plateau to the East India Company by the Treaty of Seringapatam in 1799 was the first step in this process. Though it was to be another twenty years before any Britons actually settled on the plateau, the demand of land-revenue payment became more insistent and regulated than it had been under Tipu Sultan's tenuous reach (see above, p. 57). Badagas must therefore have been obliged to trade more persistently with the lowlands to acquire the coinage now being demanded at the Daṇṇayaka Ko:ṭe treasury every year.[25]

A second point of impact on the Badaga economy was the Company's policy of fixing grain prices. The rigid control of prices, attempted by the District Collectors throughout Madras Presidency, must have encouraged the Badagas to market grain in the Coimbatore Plain (which lay within that Presidency), where they could feel somewhat confident about getting satisfactory prices for their goods and not being cheated. Had the grain prices been more of a gamble the Badagas would have been less inclined to produce a surplus of grain and carry it the long distance down to the market.

When the pioneering John Sullivan (Pl. 16) came up to the hills in 1819 he gave Badagas superior seed grains from Europe, as well as seeds of various European vegetables.[26] This increased grain production somewhat, and started Badagas growing vegetables they were unaccustomed to eating. Peach, plum, nectarine, apple and pear, all were introduced at this stage. And as the foreign population increased so did the demand for locally grown British fruits and vegetables. A few Badaga farmers, being able to supply them, were thus drawn further into the market economy. Although imperial military occupation is rarely of great benefit to indigenous peoples, in this case the fact that Ootacamund had been designated a 'military bazaar' from 1832 to 1841 meant that 'considerable cultivation of vegetables for the market' – meaning for European residents, including soldiers – occurred (Francis 1908: 118-19; Price 1908: 117).

One area in which the British tried to effect early changes, without success, was in formal education. Already in 1820 or 1821 John Sullivan had founded a school at the Oḍeya village of De:na:ḍu, directly overlooking Daṇṇayaka Ko:ṭe, but this effort (prompted no doubt by a need for local clerks) was apparently a failure (Ward 1821: lxx; Hayavadana Rao 1908: 113). But then in 1830 Sullivan founded another school at Ku:kallu, again in the northeast of the plateau, to teach Badaga pupils the Tamil and Kannaḍa languages. Another was probably founded by the Church Missionary Society in 1830 at Dimbaṭṭi (Moses 1964: 11). Among the few youths who did acquire some education, there was an attitude which is still voiced today and portended changes in the occupation pattern: they considered themselves fitted by this schooling for a lifetime of something better than manual labour (Harkness 1832: 69-70).

Another school, the first to use English as a medium, was formed by a former judge and devout Christian, George J. Casamajor, at Ke:ti in 1845. This place, as we shall see, became the local headquarters of the Basel Mission in the same year, by Mr. Casamajor's bequest, and a school has been there more or less constantly ever since (Hockings 2012: 119-21, 179, 467-68). In his time parents had to be paid one anna a day before they would send their sons to the school.[27] It was only in the latter half of the nineteenth century, after the Mission was well established at Ke:ti and elsewhere, and several more schools had been founded that education became at all popular with Badaga villagers. For this achievement German pertinacity can take some credit; yet after 1856 Badagas had begun to realize that literacy in Tamil was the one sure road to jobs in the local bureaucracy, and hence began to value schooling for their children (Anon. 1879: 149; Grigg 1880: 423; see below, pp. 257-63).

In the early days of European settlement Britons regularly needed day-labourers to do sundry jobs in the developing Nilgiri towns. A large population of lowland immigrants, coming mainly from Coimbatore District (Cederlöf 1997: 48), now lived and worked in these towns, but Badagas were also occasionally hired by British residents and paid a daily rate in cash. Around 1827, nonetheless, it had been observed that 'The hill people are so independent . . . that no temptation of wages will induce them to engage . . . as coolies, and they are only prevailed upon to work from a conviction that, refusing to do so, Government might make some just demands against them for increase of rent [land revenue]. . . .' [28] Yet by the 1840s there were many Badaga families earning a certain amount over a few months of each year from townspeople, from gardening, and probably from the new Mission too (Ouchterlony 1848: 64; Shortt & Ouchterlony 1868: 64). Their economy was now monetized, even though the majority of families were still dependent on farming for their food requirements. The farming day was a busy one, with a clear division of labour between men, women and children (Jagor 1914: 41-42; Hockings 2012: 91-92).

EXPANSION OF THE MARKET ECONOMY (1850-1900)

During the second half of the nineteenth century, it would seem, far-reaching economic changes which had been triggered by the British settlers introduced the concept of competition and the importance of valuation to the Badagas; for there is scarcely an indication of any competitiveness in their indigenous exchange activities or bartering practices before about 1840.

The opening of coffee (1840) and then tea (1854) plantations on the plateau called for a great deal of manual labour; immediately Badaga schoolboys left to work in these locations (BEMS 1858, no. 18: 93; BEMS 1860, no. 20: 59); and so by the 1860s many Badagas found themselves competing for the first time with lowland immigrants in a labour market.[29] Each group constituted one-half of the work force (Grigg 1880: 399) but the British estate owners preferred Badaga workers to immigrants because of their health and diligence. These labourers were paid in cash, not grain.

Secondly, the hundreds of Europeans now on the hills were requiring substantial quantities of cabbage, carrot, potato, radish, and other European vegetables that some Badaga farmers were able to supply. Their tradition of intensive farming in small fields was readily adapted to the new cash crops (Shortt & Ouchterlony 1868: 35); and their venture was helped by a climate not unlike that of northwestern Europe. (Tennyson – without ever going there – was later to muse on 'the sweet, half-English air of the Neilgherries'.) Soon potato cultivation was to become an important cash-earner, the harvest being hawked door-to-door in the towns (*South of India Observer* 13 [17 Sept. 1879]: 7). Although European ploughs had never caught on, Mr. A. Jamieson, a long-time Scottish curator of the local Government Botanical Gardens, wrote a manual on potato cultivation for the benefit of Badaga farmers, and he distributed new seed to them (*South of India Observer* 11 [10 Nov. 1877]: 5).

In the latter half of that century a wide variety of indigenous farm products also came onto the local market.[30] These foodstuffs were local varieties of wheat and barley, Italian, finger and slender millet, prince's feather (or amaranth), mustard seed, coriander, chick pea (or Bengal gram), garlic, onion, fenugreek, as well as milk, poultry and eggs. Though officially suppressed in 1854, and again by the Opium Act of 1878, opium continued to be produced (Ouchterlony 1848: 27-28; Baikie 1857: 92; Metz 1864: 153; 'Geofry' 1881: 132; Benson 1895: 432-33; Price 1908: 224; Mahias, in Hockings 2012: 717-19). Foodstuffs introduced by Europeans but now being grown by Badagas included those shown in Table 6.

Trade imports to the Nilgiris in the late nineteenth century included four key products also imported in pre-British times – sugar, salt, cotton cloth and tobacco. In addition, various other Indian goods began to arrive only during the latter half of the century: almond, betel or areca, cattle, clarified butter, coconut, coriander and other spices, dried fruits, furniture, gunpowder, lime, limes, finger and Italian millet, oils, peas, poultry, rice, salted fish, scrap metal, sheep, sulphur, toddy, tools, turmeric, and wheat. And there was a variety of European articles arriving on the Nilgiris in the later nineteenth century, among them groceries, guns, wines, spirits, beer, clothing, candles, pottery, glass, hardware, shoes, books and stationery.[31]

Among the exports from the plateau at this time were some that had also been exported in pre-British days, namely opium, wheat and bees-wax. But the more important exports of the later nineteenth century were coffee, tea, potato, barley, as well as resin, silk and hides.

Table 6: European introductions of food plants

Grains	*Root-crops*	*Vegetables*	*Fruits*	*Stimulants*
Barley (new variety)	Beetroot	Artichoke	Apple	Coffee
Fiorin grass	Carrot	Asparagus	Blackberry	Tea
Italian rye	Mangold	Cabbage	Brazil cherry	Tobacco*
Lucern (for fodder)	Parsnip	Cauliflower	Capers	
Oats	Potato	Celery	Citron	
Wheat	Radish	French beans	Gooseberry	
	Swede	Kidney beans	Lemon	
	Turnip	Kohl rabi	Loquat	
		Leek	Nectarine (new variety)	
		Lettuce	Orange	
		Peas	Peach	
		Savoy cabbage	Pear	
		Sea kale	Plum	
		Spinach	Raspberry	
			Strawberry	
			Tomato	

Note: * Reputedly a Toda import (Baikie 1857: 95).

NOTES

1. 'There are no manufactures on the hills and much less of trade'; Keys 1812: li, perhaps exaggerating; cf. Hayavadana Rao 1908: 108.
2. See above, p. 40. It may be mentioned that both Ptolemy (i.e. Claudius Ptolemaeus, *ca* 100-168 CE) and the *Periplus Maris Erythriæ* (*ca* 70 CE) refer to a town that was called Νελκυνδα in Greek; but this was most probably Nirkundram, near Kottayam in Kerala.
3. It connects with the most westerly part of the Coimbatore Plain, in the upper valley of the Bhavāni, as well as with Malabar District; Hayavadana Rao 1908: 105; Hockings 2012: 384, 888-89. One of the two men who accompanied Fenicio was Fr. Schipano, who had been working as a missionary at Manna:ru in 1596; Schurhammer 1957: 13. Fr. Fenicio's name, it might be noted here, has been repeatedly misread as Ferreira, Ferreiri, and also Finicio; Price 1908: 1, note; cf. Hockings 1996: 57, no. 1663; Walker, in Hockings 2012: 314-21.
4. He did not ascend the hills but made his enquiry at the foot, on the

Coimbatore side; Grigg 1880: 277; Hayavadana Rao 1908: 106; Price 1908: 2.

5. Burton 1851 [1991]: 270-71; Metz 1864: 6; Balfour 1884: 1099; Hayavadana Rao 1908: 107, n. 1. Among these people was Col. Alexander F.P. MacLeod who spent some months in military movements in the Wainad in 1804; several Badaga boys born on a day of his visit were hence named MacLeod. But before all of them Arthur Wellesley, the future Duke of Wellington, had been in the Wainad (1800); Metz 1864: 6; Grigg 1880: 312; Price 1908: 10. Other early visitors included Dr. Lacy G. Ford (in 1809), Capt. Henry Bevan (1812), William Morrison (1812), and William Keys and C. McMahon (1812); Hockings 2012: 334, 421-22, 468-69.
6. Keys 1812: li; Sullivan 1819: lv; Macpherson 1820: lvii; Ward 1821: lxiii, lxv; Leschenault de la Tour 1822: 261; Baber 1830: 315; Harkness 1832: 136-37; Birch 1838: 103; 'Stocqueler' 1845: 579; Price 1908: 8; Sarada Raju 1941: 107-08; Hockings 1989c: *passim*. On the partition of the district, see Grigg 1880: 290-91, 303; Hayavadana Rao 1908: 117.
7. Botanical identifications for the species referred to in this study, here arranged alphabetically, are as follows: almonds (*Terminalia catappa*), barley (*Hordeum hexastichon*), betel or areca nut (*Areca catechu*), black dammer or resin (from *Canarium strictum*), black gram (*Phaseolus mungo*), chick pea or Bengal gram (*Cicer arietinum*), coconut (*Cocos nucifera*), coffee (*Coffea arabica*), common millet (*Panicum miliaceum*), coriander (*Coriandrum sativum*), country bean (*Dolichos lablab*), fenugreek (*Trigonella fœnum-græcum*), finger millet (*Eleusine coracana*), flax (*Linum mysorense*), garlic (*Allium sativum*), gentian (*Gentiana pedicellata*), gourd (*Lagenaria vulgaris*), great millet (*Andropogon sorghum*), Italian millet (*Setaria italica*), Italian rye (*Lolium italicum*), lime (*Citrus aurantifolia*), mustard (*Brassica juncea*), oats (*Avena sativa*), onion (*Allium cepa*), panic-seed (*Setaria pallidifusca*), peas (*Pisum arvense*), pepper (*Piper schmidtii*), poppy (*Papaver somniferum*), potato (*Solanum tuberosum*), prince's feather (*Amarantus paniculatus*), pumpkin (*Cucurbita pepo*), rattan cane (*Calamus* spp.), rice (*Oriza sativa*), rose-mallow (*Hibiscus esculentus*), sandalwood (*Santalum album*), slender millet (*Panicum miliare*), tea (*Camellia sinensis*), tobacco (*Nicotiana tabacum*), turmeric (*Curcuma longa*) and wheat (*Triticum dicoccum*).
8. Hayavadana Rao 1908: 115. This area, now built upon, was until recently the playing-field between the Lawley Institute and the Botanical Gardens.
9. Baikie 1857: 25. In the mid-nineteenth century the Sundapaṭṭi and Manna:ru Passes provided a safe short-cut for smugglers between Coimbatore and the Malabar region; Ouchterlony 1848: 75; Grigg 1880: 19, 291; Hockings 2012: 888-89.

10. Nicholson 1898: 352. One should note that the deity is a Vaishnavite one; its chariot-dragging festival is still held. See above, p. 183.
11. After crossing the Bavāni River in a rattan coracle covered with skins; Mackworth 1823: 118-19; Grigg 1880: 295; Hockings 2012: 224-25. The legend is that one of seven Badaga brothers, soon to settle Hulikal, had a vision of a snake in a basket suckling from a cow. Then the man heard the voice of the god Rangasa:mi, telling him to worship in this place. Once the market had been opened in Ootacamund, Ka:ramuḍu ceased to have much importance for Badagas; Francis 1908: 340.
12. *Doḍḍa habba*; on the salt ceremony, see Hockings 1968: *passim*.
13. This fourteenth-century fortress, now submerged by the Bavāni Dam, controlled the important Gajaḷaṭṭi Pass which links southern Mysore with the Coimbatore Plain; Nicholson 1898: 425-27.
14. Ward erroneously calls the sum a dowry.
15. Later in quarter and one rupee denominations; but until the past century a gold Canteroy *fanam* was still placed in the mouth of the dead.
16. In the amounts of Rs. 1/4, 1/2, 1, 3, 6, 12, 24 and 48.
17. Also the case in some other districts of Madras Presidency; Buchanan 1807: 247; Grigg 1880: 286, n. 1.
18. The years 1803-1805 were a period of drought in the Nilgiris; Grigg 1880: 279, n. 2.
19. There were as yet no Moslem traders; Sait, in Hockings 2012: 625-26.
20. Cloth was not among the trade items. The Coonoor Pass or ghat was completed in 1833; Grigg 1880: 17. In her novel *Love in the Hills*, set in Coonoor, Fanny Penny, who was a resident there, describes the ghat road: 'Transport by cart is cheaper than rail; and though we haven't nearly as much traffic on the road [*ca* 1913] there is still a regular service. Between this [town] and Burliar I met no less than a dozen carts all loaded with stuff of various kinds. . . . A good deal of it was grain for the Ooty bazaar. . . . The cattle were resting at Burliar for the day. They will come on about midnight and work slowly up the ghat at not more than a mile and a half an hour, if so much. . . . It is only the first driver of a string of carts who is obliged to keep awake to guide the cattle; and he need not be very wide awake, for there is only one road, and it as as well known to the cattle as to the men.' (Abstracted from Penny 1913: 177-79, 194-95); cf Hockings 2012: 384-87, 562-68.
21. Shandy (Anglo-Indian) means 'market', from the Tamil *cantai*; Winslow 1862: 401.
22. Foodstuffs were usually traded by volume rather than weight, as scales were never used in or near the Nilgiris; Hockings 2012: 983-84.
23. On the important myth of Hette, see Hockings 1989a: 223-28; 2012: 410-14; Noble 1976: 116-17; and Heidemann 2006: 169-212.
24. For a more nuanced analysis of the British impact on this district than space here permits, see Philip 2003.

25. Even though there was no tax farmer on the plateau to harass them till 1807; Buchanan 1807: 247.
26. Harkness 1832: 138, note; Shortt and Ouchterlony 1868: 17; Grigg 1880: 455-56; Francis 1908: 167; Price 1908: 23; Hockings 1989c: 338-41; 2012: 881-88. According to Metz 1864: 5, Sullivan reportedly came to the Nilgiris 'at the solicitation of the hill-people themselves'. In a letter to the Board of Revenue, 1819, he indeed explained that 'the inhabitants are extremely anxious to have their lands measured, under an idea that they are paying more than they ought to do'; Grigg 1880: 280. Another early influence on Badaga farming may well have been the experimental farm for European crops operating at Ke:ti from 1830 to 1836; Metz 1864: 6-7; Grigg 1880: 456-58; Macleane 1893: 403; Francis 1908: 203, 441; Hockings 1989c: 340; Sutton 2009: 27-32.
27. In 1901 Ke:ti's became the first Badaga high school; Metz 1864: 8-9; Francis 1908: 332; Moses 1964: 13. (An anna was Re. $^{1}/16$.) On the use of Badaga land by Europeans in Ke:ti, see Sutton 2009: 27-32.
28. Grigg 1880: 288, quoting from a report of Dec. 1827; yet Harkness 1832: 111, remarked that 'The poorer Burghers form the only class of labourers now to be procured on the hills. . . .'
29. BEMS 1848, no. 18: 93; 1860 (no. 20): 59; Shortt and Ouchterlony 1868: 64; Grigg 1880: 510-11; Watt 1889: 465; Francis 1908: 171, 178; Jagor 1914: 48; Tanna 1970: 17, 37. The first tea grown experimentally in the Ke:ti Valley farm was by Asst. Surgeon A.T. Christie, beginning in 1833, from Chinese cuttings. But he died in Nov. 1833, and so his experiments with tea, coffee, mulberry, and the making of ice ended. 'When the farm was closed in 1836 and its buildings were lent to the Governor of Pondicherry, as a residence, Mr. [Georges-Samuel] Perrottet, the French botanist found that the plants had been half-buried by ignorant gardeners and were consequently in a bad condition. . . . In 1840, samples of Nilgiris tea made from plants growing at Ketti and Billikal were sent by Mr. J. Sullivan to the Agro-Horticultural Society, Madras' (Gopalakrishnan 1995: 525). In 1838 the first coffee plants were imported from Mysore. Then in 1854 Mr. Mann began an experimental plantation near Coonoor. More tea cuttings were brought from China in 1856 (despite its having been found growing wild in Assam), and commercial plantations were opened at Dunsandle and Thiashola in 1859; Macleane 1893: 403; Watt 1893: 448; Price 1908: 128; UPASI 1956: 1-4; Muthiah 1993: 26-27, 134-35; and Muthiah, in Hockings 2012: 895-99.
30. 'Stocqueler' 1845: 579; Ouchterlony 1848: 2, 5, 28; Baikie 1857: 38, 92; Markham 1862: 367; Metz 1864: 99, 152-54; Shortt & Ouchterlony 1868: 71; Grigg 1880: 465-67. See the list above, p. 189, n. 7.
31. It is unclear how much of these items were for consumption by the Europeans: they were the prime market, despite their small numbers.

CHAPTER 11

Administration and Law

CUSTOMARY LAW

Until the end of the nineteenth century the Indian Penal Code and the British system of local administration seemed to present little direct relevance to Badaga villagers; for they had their own uncodified law and their own headmen and councils to administer it.

Three periods are distinguishable in their legal history: one prior to the advent of the British when something akin to *lex talionis* was operative; a second period when Badagas still had full control of their legal procedure but nonetheless operated it under the ægis of the British; and a third period, from about 1900 to the present, when litigants played off the Badaga system against the magistrate's court in an attempt to win cases through obscuration.

There are no records for the phase of *lex talionis*, but a rough account of the procedure is provided by legend. A village council sat in judgement and stipulated a time and place for punishment of the guilty. The man who had assaulted someone was to be kicked or beaten by him, the rapist had to offer his wife to the aggrieved husband, and the murderer was hanged by the family of his victim.

By the beginning of the nineteenth century this legendary pattern had given way to one that is with some modification still recognized. It originated before coinage was circulating in the Nilgiris, since the earliest fines, as among the Todas, were paid in buffaloes and not in rupees. Even though there are no written records the procedure can be described in some detail because of its relative recency.

Headmen and Administrative Boundaries

As we know, the Nilgiri Plateau was for centuries divided into four areas, viz: Todana:ḍ, Me:kuna:ḍ, Poranga:ḍ and Kundena:ḍ.[1] (These were rather different in their boundaries from the modern administrative *taluks*, two of which are not even on the plateau.) It may be of some significance that the Kota divisions were also rather different; for they too recognized Wainad and Poranga:ḍ with much the same boundaries, but what the Badagas called Todana:ḍ they called Me:kuna:ḍ ('western region'), while what the Badagas regarded as Me:kuna:ḍ (and later Kundena:ḍ too) the Kotas called Doḍḍana:ḍ (roughly, 'important region'). In each of the Badaga divisions there are several communes,[2] each made up of from one (as Ta:mbaṭṭi, Bandime, Ba:muḍi, Sakkata) to forty-two (Ta:ndana:ḍu) contiguous villages. These hamlets may belong to any one of the seven plateau phratries, and one of them, not necessarily the largest or even of the highest phratry, has permanent precedence and gives its name to the entire commune. Its headman is also head[3] of the entire commune; under him are the headmen[4] of all the other villages. The divisional headman[5] is a hereditary position in one family of a chosen village. From time immemorial it has been the village headman of Tu:ne:ri, in Todana:ḍ, who has functioned as paramount chief[6] of the entire Badaga community.[7] Because of the extent of their duties the divisional headmen and the paramount chief do not also function as the headmen at all other levels, just for their own villages. All of these offices are normally inherited patrilineally, save when the eldest son is deemed unfit and then another relative is chosen by the council to replace him in the office. However, there is some evidence that from time to time the political boundaries of the communes have shifted, as new villages came to the fore and became the heads of new communes in some areas. Poranga:ḍ has had an unusually fluid organization over the past century or more (Heidemann 2006: *passim*).

At each of these levels – village, commune, division and the entire community – the relevant headman can call together a council (a *ku:ṭu, manda*) of respected men to judge disputes. Every case has to pass up this hierarchy of councils, so that only when the lower councils have failed to solve them satisfactorily do the most complicated land and marriage disputes and murder cases reach the paramount council. A dissatisfied disputant may appeal a council's decision to the next higher level of council, but high-level headmen check that a case brought to them has first passed through the lower-level councils. Badaga law had the unusual provision that if a higher level of headman considers the judgement given at a lower level to be in error he could fine the headman responsible for that decision. This was in the past a check against favouritism, though bribery was still a possibility. In reality, 'Redress of grievances is not always obtained by litigation alone' (*South of India Observer* 1877, 7 March: 3).

Procedure

In a dispute between two parties from the same village their headman (*gauḍa*) called a council of the heads of each household, one of whom would be his deputy (*gauṇḍike*). When litigants came from neighbouring villages the case would first be heard by the commune council, which was made up of all its village headmen. If one of the parties was a Kota his headman would also take part in the council. The proceedings would begin with statements from the contending parties. Male witnesses might then be brought to support these statements. Females and serfs[8] never appeared before the councils, but if their evidence were considered important it would be heard in private by the headman in charge. Toreyas could make statements and attend the meeting but used not to take an active part in the council's deliberations.

A man's family and lineage would usually support him in any dispute and provided the most usual 'witnesses'. Beside their testimony other kinds of admissible evidence included written receipts, even re-enactments of the event, oaths testifying to a man's innocence, and pronouncements uttered by a god through the mouth of a man in trance.[9] If necessary a postponement was allowed, for additional evidence to be brought. Presentation of the evidence was followed by a council discussion, after which the headman in charge voiced his opinion and determined punishment. It was not unusual to punish both parties in a dispute.[10]

Crime and Punishment

The following tentative list of traditional punishments suggests the sanctions that were (until the twentieth century) commonly placed on various crimes:

Planned murder of a Badaga adult – hanging
Unpremeditated killing – Rs. 48 fine, or servitude to the victim's family
Causing someone to commit suicide – Rs. 48 fine
Failure to obey an important order of the headman – ostracism

Failure to pay a fine – ostracism

Rape of a father's wife – ostracism or Rs. 48 fine Rape of a son's wife – Rs. 24 fine or less Rape of a brother's wife – minimal fine	Reduced if the woman had consented – i.e. a case of adultery

Man beating victim with leather – Rs. 24 fine, or head shaved

Woman beating victim with a broom – Rs. 24 fine, or else made to parade through the village with a basket of ash on her head

Minor misdemeanour – bow down inside the circle of the council (i.e. the minimal punishment)

Attempted suicide – not considered an offence.

The preceding was never a fixed scale of punishments but rather a guide to how an offender would be treated in those times, 'all else being equal'. In each case the punishment could be mitigated according to the circumstances of the crime and the social identity of the criminal. A poor man would be fined less than one of the gentry; and any man might plead poverty or haggle with the council to have his fine reduced. This is equally true today.

LOCAL ADMINISTRATION

Since the start of the nineteenth century Badagas were ruled indirectly by the British but contact with them had very little effect in the earliest years. The Badagas habitually avoided the British legal system and its officers, and their own customary system continued to operate effectively until the end of the nineteenth century when they subtly adapted their legal thinking to avail themselves of the Imperial system as well. The first recorded instance of Badagas going to the lawcourt was, however, as early as 1840, as a result of a boundary dispute between Bikkaṭṭi and Ellena:yi, two villages on the main roadway halfway between Ootacamund and Coonoor. As Lt. H.V. Conolly,[11] the Collector of Malabar, had noted at the time: 'Formerly all differences were settled by the Burghers [Badagas] themselves. The influx of strangers, and the altered state of their society, has led them, as appears from the present instance, not to be always satisfied with this simple mode of administering justice,' i.e. that of the traditional headmen and councils (Grigg 1880: 304).

Village government under the British administration perpetuated the existing hereditary headmen, certain of whom received the title of *maṇega:r*. The *hierarchy* of traditional headmen did not enter into the British scheme for local government, however; a *maṇega:r* was typically an *u:r gauḍa*, a commune-level headman. In the early days of their administration the British thought it enough that a *maṇega:r* be one of the gentry who was respected by the Badagas; but by the end of the nineteenth century the role of headman had been split up: a *maṇega:r* was appointed in the main communes by the District Collector,[12] but the Badagas would still select their own headmen at both the village and the commune levels.[13] The chosen *maṇega:r* was usually a literate man, no longer merely somebody with prestige (Grigg 1880: 366). In addition, the British appointed an accountant (*karaṇam*) to maintain village records. Both of these roles,[14] held by Badagas now responsible to an outside authority, were new to Nilgiri society, but were not honoured in the spirit expected by the British administrators. Henry B. Grigg, who was the Collector in 1880, noted with perhaps only a little exaggeration that

> The vaguest notion of their duties as village magistrate or police officer prevails among the headmen. So far from their understanding that it is their duty to repress such crime, they seem to regard it almost as a sacred duty not only to countenance and shield the wrong-doers, but even to aid in the perpetration. (1880: 411; cf. Francis 1908: 295; *South of India Observer* 1877, March 7: 3)

The power and influence of the *maṇega:r* were vastly greater in the nineteenth century than recently. Some of the old tales depict him as a sort of itinerant autocrat, as for example: '. . . when he visited any village within his jurisdiction, the monegar had the privilege of having the best women or maids of the place to share his cot according to his choice'.[15] Girls were only one kind of bribe that might quietly be used to secure his sympathies: clothes and feasting were much commoner. The autocracy of these local officials is well illustrated by 'stories . . . of a Monegar of one village who ordered an individual who had disobeyed his orders to be covered with a slab of stone' (Natesa Sastri 1892: 831-32). 'Folklore has it that for slight mistakes sometimes capital punishment was awarded. . . . Whipping and burning of the fingers with oil were common punishments' (said Belli Gowder 1926). Much must have changed, for in 1972 the then paramount chief, Pada Gauda, told me that the qualities of a good chief are that he be honest, trustworthy, and willing to sacrifice for the people.

Just as alien as the British notion of a headman's role was the idea of electing a council; and yet a supposedly elected *panchayat*[16] became the official organ of local government shortly after the First World War. (Its duties today are to provide certain facilities, notably the up-keep of roads and paths, water supply, community radio, maintenance of land records and birth and death registers, and the supply of information about local governmental activity.) Despite the appearance of village *panchayats* and of a state police outpost in some villages, the organization of celebrations and the settlement of disputes have remained very much in the hands of the traditional headman, his festival committee and his council. Any criminal cases should be reported to the police and are usually handled in a law-court, but civil and petty criminal cases can either be settled by the village council or by an official *panchayat* court.[17]

A sensational case of a communal assassination reveals the recent interplay between powerful religious forces and an essentially alien, Tamilian-dominated police force. I summarise the events from contemporary newspaper reports:

> Early in 1987 the council of a Gauḍa village excommunicated and fined Ka:li and her family because she was believed responsible for various acts of sorcery. Around February her family requested police protection because of ugly accusations. It was agreed that she and her family would continue to live in — village without interfering with others, while two police constables from the town were posted there by a Superintendent of Police.
>
> The 40-year old sorceress, Ka:li, was staying in her brother's house when, early on April 2, the two constables went off to town. Immediately a group of villagers of both sexes went to this house, seized Ka:li there, tied a rope around her neck, dragged her out of the village for the best part of a mile and then stoned her to death.
>
> Her brother, evidently powerless to stop all this, now called the police in. They recovered the body, and a special party was set up to track down the killers. When the police arrived in the deserted village, however, the normal population, which the press put at 1600, was nowhere to be found. In the following days barely 30 people remained in the village, maintaining that they had no idea where the rest were hiding. Eventually, though, the police arrested eight Badaga men and seven women and charged them with this murder.
>
> About two weeks after the murder the Police Superintendent, along with Akkamma Devi, a respected Badaga lady who was a former Member of Parliament, and several others convened a meeting to try and stabilise the situation of Ka:li's family members in the community. Other villagers were very frank with journalists afterwards about why it had been necessary to kill the sorceress: women openly said that Ka:li had deserved to die. The

family was said to have 'traditionally' engaged in sorcery, and had equipment for it in their house. It was Ka:li who had dried up the water sources, causing repeated crop failures. A young woman had not conceived, even after three years of marriage, thanks to Ka:li's powers. One youth said he had lost his job with a state-run bus company because of her. Some women complained that their daughters had been eating vast quantities of chilli powder because of her sorcery. The headman sided with village opinion, asserting that only after the arrested persons returned home could amity be restored with Ka:li's family.[18] (Based on Radhakrishnan 1987, etc.; name changed)

It is not just that a village council sometimes has to deal today with a state police force and the lawcourts. The multiplicity of procedures available exposes Badagas to three different legal systems: their own indigenous one, still influential in establishing precedents; the present-day village council which will settle disputes according to a majority opinion – an opinion voiced, however, by the headman and modified by the knowledge that the case may then be taken together with the decision before a court of law; and finally the ever-popular hierarchy of government lawcourts.

Throughout the long history of administrative changes it has remained true that at the core of any Badaga village community is a centralized leadership, holding both secular and sacred authority, represented in the dual roles of headman and priest. These males, commonly occupying hereditary and thus stable positions, stand for power and purity respectively. Annual ceremonies conducted by the priest for the community regularly highlight the authority of the headman too. In the wider Hindu polity, their two roles were paralleled by those of king and Brahmin; which perhaps helps explain why some of the Badagas still support myths that they were 'related to' rulers (Oḍeyas, Kumba:ras), or that they had 'originally been' Brahmins (the Ha:ruva case). History does not really give support to such claims, yet they are an appropriate legendary statement of the power and purity expressed in the two public roles.

The goddess Hette is another central symbol of purity. In her case the underlying meaning of this story about a woman who became an unconventional *sati* is not so much that women too can be models of purity in themselves but rather that without such an ideal of womanly purity the very integrity and ethnic identity of the entire Badaga community might somehow be compromised. So genuinely Badaga children must always have a proper Badaga mother, as the legend of the heroine Hette confirms symbolically (Hockings 1989: 223-28; 2012: 410-14; Heidemann 2006: 169-212).

THE RECENT AMBILEGAL SITUATION

At the present day, with such a confusion of courts, officials, regulations, police intrusion and legal options, how can a Badaga choose which legal medium to use? The prime consideration is apparently not the seriousness of the complaint but the good repute of a man's village; which is why in the sorcery case described the entire village population disappeared from view. Even recent cases of murder and suicide have been handled entirely by the traditional Badaga council in the village where the acts were committed (murders sometimes being covered up by asserting they had been suicides); a procedure that contravenes Indian law, for any such criminal offences should automatically be reported to the police and then examined in the magistrate's court.[19] However, whether siding with the victim, the malefactor or neither, Badagas prefer to settle such matters through the headman and his council, thus protecting the village name from the dishonour of a police investigation and loose gossip, not to mention press reports. For the same reason they also try to stop a case from reaching the higher levels of their own traditional councils.

Despite this restrictiveness, it is now very common for a case that has already been judged by the village council to be taken to a lawcourt by whichever side has lost; hence we may characterize the present procedure as 'ambilegal'. There are two factors which may prevent the loser from appealing his case to a magistrate: one is the high cost of solicitors and of perhaps bribing various petty officials; the other is the common knowledge that the decision of the village council, though often not very impartial, can be used as evidence in court, whereupon in something like '98 per cent of cases' (in the estimate of one seasoned observer) the magistrate will just restate that decision.

Though he usually upholds the village council's decision, it is not in itself legally binding. So while appealing to the village councils is normally cheaper this is done less often now than before the Second World War. As disenchanted and Westernized litigants turn to the magistrates more often, the old hierarchy of councils is proportionately sapped of power to enforce its decisions.

A case taken from my notes may help illustrate how an individual could, in the mid-twentieth century, try to manipulate the two judicial systems to disadvantage an opponent.[20]

Two brothers, Kallan and Jo:gi, lived together with their wives and children as a joint family in a Me:kuna:ḍ village and, as was the custom then, also held joint ownership of their land, each farming as much of it as he wanted. In 1948, Jo:gi, the elder brother, died leaving his two young children and wife in the care of Kallan. One of these children was a daughter who would leave the family at marriage and would not be entitled, under Badaga custom, to any inheritance from her dead father. But Nandi, the dead man's son, would in time demand a half of the joint family's estate. Kallan knew this very well, for he could easily see how most joint families were breaking up into nuclear families; and he also recognized that with his wife, two sons and two daughters he would be making a much greater drain on the family resources than would Nandi and his mother. Kallan therefore decided soon after Jo:gi's death to secure title – under the Indian legal system – to much more than the half of the family land which he could justly claim when Nandi demanded its division, as he undoubtedly would in due course. Already arguments had arisen between Kallan and the widow over who should cultivate each part of the land.

Kallan realized that he could expect no support from his village council, for they would probably take the just side of his victim, and Kallan himself was not wealthy or powerful enough to bribe them into doing otherwise. He therefore decided to get a legal agreement registered for transfer of land to himself without either the boy or his mother knowing about it. He mustered two men and one woman to act as witnesses, giving them handsome bribes for their services and secrecy. Two of them belonged to a different phratry than Kallan's, and all were unrelated to his family. At the land registrar's office in Coonoor, far from their village, the woman witness claimed that *she* was Jo:gi's widow, and that Kallan had loaned her some money against the security of about three-quarters of the land she had title to since her husband's death (i.e. on her son's behalf). The government official registered an agreement that if the sum of money supposedly lent her was not repaid within ten years the land would automatically become Kallan's property. The official did not investigate whether the woman really had any title or whether she was indeed Jo:gi's widow. As she could not write, she set her thumb-print to the document.

Kallan continued to let Jo:gi's real widow use the land she needed, hoping that she would die within the next ten years; and after eight years she did in fact pass away, presumably of natural causes. By this time her son Nandi had attained legal majority and soon found himself faced with the perennial problem of Badaga farmers, shortage of money. He went to the local cooperative society and obtained a loan of two thousand rupees against a pledge of two acres of what was assumed to be his land. The cooperative society casually enquired if the land was encumbered, but as nobody suspected that it was the loan was granted.

That year Nandi's potato crop was ruined by disease, and he was unable to repay the loan within the stipulated time. The cooperative society thereupon made preparations to seize the two acres that Nandi had pledged; at which point Kallan decided to step in, as the land was covered by his spurious agreement. He even announced that he would sue the society in court for trying to seize land that legally belonged to him. This was the first time that Nandi and the village learned about the transfer agreement registered some twelve years earlier.

In revealing the existence of that document and telling Nandi that his mother had made the agreement while he was a small boy, Kallan failed to take note of one important fact: one of the men whom he had paid to act as false witness at the registration was now the president of the cooperative society! This man, Maḍia, now did what seemed best for his society and – without mentioning his own role in the matter – tipped off Nandi about the falsity of Kallan's agreement. Maḍia advised the young man to take the case to the magistrate's court and charge Kallan with false representation. This would not be difficult, for the woman who had posed as Nandi's mother was still living, and her thumb-print could thus be checked with that on the document. Such a sophisticated method of demonstrating the falsity of a document would be beyond the capabilities of the village council, and would probably win scant support for Nandi's case there. (Undoubtedly Maḍia had his own reasons for not wanting the matter discussed in his village.) But unfortunately Nandi had no money to initiate a hearing in the magistrate's court. He did not take the matter to his own village council either, for he knew the council has little power left to enforce its decisions, and the likelihood was high that Kallan would be able to bribe its members.

Whether bribes were in fact given or not, the council did discuss the case and advised Nandi to repay the money his mother had supposedly borrowed from Kallan. This was their compromise solution, offering Kallan a financial inducement – the money which he had never really lent – and offering Nandi tenure of the two acres he had pledged and cancellation of Kallan's spurious agreement. Kallan was apparently willing to accept this, for he was then urging Nandi to repay the supposed loan but under no circumstances go to a lawcourt. Now it was up to Nandi to solve the problem (still at stalemate when I last enquired in 1975). The solution which he chooses must be couched in the current ambilegal idiom. If he were to attempt a solution purely in the traditional idiom or purely in the lawcourt idiom, without taking into account the alternate system and Kallan's possible manipulation of it, then Nandi's chances of ultimate success would be slim. (Names have been changed)

The point which the case of Kallan and Nandi underlines is that the introduction of British procedural law in the nineteenth century did not simply offer Badagas an alternative, or even a more effective approach, for solving conflicts in their community. The procedure in a lawcourt must have seemed capricious to a villager: it operated on the assumption that all individuals were equal before the law, and that the proceedings must work directly towards a just decision; so whether a man was a Toreya or a member of the gentry was deemed irrelevant to how he would be treated. His past history and his family's reputation were similarly not taken into consideration. To Kallan and Nandi, therefore, as to many of their Badaga contemporaries, the lawcourt is less a mechanism for dispensing impartial justice than a possible means of revenge and a process for overcoming one's opponent (regardless of who might actually have been in the right).

A more recent case involving three brothers and their three wives opposes a manipulation of traditional marriage practices against a manipulation of the legal process, when one wife seeks to get a legal divorce on the grounds of bigamy. I summarise the case from documents presented in court in 1986.

Lakshmi, wife of Bomma, accused him, his second wife Maṇi, and ten other relatives who served as witnesses to their marriage, of an offence under section 494 of the Indian Penal Code, claiming that they had performed a marriage which was a 'bigamous marriage . . . void under section 17 of the Hindu Marriage Act, 1955.'

Bomma said in defense that one brother, Ra:man, was married but had no children. He therefore wanted to take a second wife, and so it was he, not Bomma, who had married the girl named Maṇi. Lakshmi alleged, nonetheless, that Maṇi was really married to Bomma, by formal rites performed at 5.30 one morning, according to 'all ceremonies prevailing in the Badaga community'; and for that reason she was seeking a legal divorce from Bomma on the grounds of his bigamy. Bomma denied that he was actually married to Maṇi, but had his own story to tell the court.

A year before, Lakshmi had left home without Bomma's knowledge, leaving behind her marriage emblem, the *ta:li*, with his younger brother Ajjan. She went to the town, withdrew Rs. 15,000 from their bank account, and left her nine-year old son there with an acquaintance. Then, joined by Ajjan, and taking her seven-year old son along, she went off to several towns around Coimbatore District, namely Pāḻani, Dindigal and Kodaikanal, staying in hotels (which were named) with Ajjan as though he were her husband. After living together for four months, their whereabouts came to be known back in the Kundena:ḍ village, and an elder went to Dindigal where he found them in a rented house and brought the three of them home.

Having regained both his sons, Bomma let his mother take care of them. Meanwhile his wife was living with her mother, shunned by the other villagers because of her bad reputation. This remained the situation when the case went to court the next year. There Bomma maintained he would still take his wife back if she apologised to the villagers for her behaviour. 'I am ready to take her back and give her all rights and live with her for the sake of my children's future, for she is my uncle's daughter and secondly Ajjan is my own brother,' he said. (Based on legal papers; all names changed)

In short, it was a conflict between Badaga custom, specifically the ancient practices of polygyny and fraternal polycoity, and the Indian Penal Code. The use of a lawcourt can involve an opponent in crippling legal costs and the prospect of these costs may frighten him into compliance with what is wanted of him. Threatening to go to a lawcourt after receiving unfavourable treatment from the village council can also be used to undermine the authority of the elders and cast aspersions upon the village's respectability. For well over a century Badagas have had a saying that runs: 'If you prefer a complaint to a magistrate, it is as if you had put poison into your adversary's food' (Metz 1864: 92; Grigg 1880: 224; Hockings 1988: 211, no. 311a). That belief is still voiced today; but in the interim the Badagas have learned how to apply the poison effectively.

POLITICAL CHOICE

Even before Independence some Badagas were involved in political activity. About 58 of them were directly involved in such movements as the picketing of shops selling toddy and foreign cloth, and some went to jail in pre-Independence times (Gopalakrishnan 1995: 231-49). When Mohammed Ali Jinnah addressed a public meeting in Ootacamund, restating his lasting conviction that 'There must be Pakistan!', it was Badaga men who argued with him to give up his quest to partition India (Gopalakrishnan 1995: 227).

For the past eight decades Badagas have been elected to seats in the state legislature, and for the past six there have also been Badaga Members of Parliament. In recent times (as an effect of earlier reversals) the Congress Election Board and some other parties have been careful to choose candidates who were Badagas, since this is a major block of voters in the Nilgiris constituency. Until 1967 the electorate was clearly more interested in the candidate than in his party's platform; but in 1967 this preference was reversed, owing to opposition party propaganda and the failure of previous Congress representatives to satisfy educated young Badagas.

The first Badaga to enter provincial politics was H.B. Ari Gowder, a university-educated Gauḍa (Mulley, in Hockings 2012: 79-81) His village was close to the European towns of Wellington and Coonoor, and his father (a former cowherd) was involved in lucrative construction work on the railway. Ari served for three terms as a member of the Madras Legislative Council before the Second World War, and then had three terms in the Madras Legislative Assembly. He was defeated by a Congress candidate in 1946, but in 1952-57 served another term as an Independent M.L.A. In his early political career he was an Independent but with leanings towards the Justice Party (which tended to support British rule and oppose the dominance of the provincial administration by Brahmins; cf. Dirks 2001: 242-43); and ever after he remained an Independent, despite a general sympathy amongst most Badagas for the Congress movement. This man clearly achieved much political influence and some charisma by entering public life in 1924 and capitalizing on the wealth and popularity of his father, H.J. Bellie Gowder. Up to his death on 27 June 1971, he was undoubtedly more powerful among Badagas than their paramount chief.[21]

As Diag. 11 indicates, Ari Gowder's relatives followed him into the political arena. In the 1957 elections for the State Assembly his sister's husband was elected, and in 1962 the Communist candidate was his nephew; in the same year his brother's wife, the first Badaga woman to graduate, ran for Parliament on the Congress party ticket and was elected. In 1967 she was defeated by a former Congressman, a well-educated Gauḍa from the Ke:ti area who represented the rightist Swatantra Party; and this was the first time since Independence that a winning Badaga candidate was from a party other than Congress. In the State Assembly election of that year Congress also lost to an Independent and a D.M.K. (Dravidian Progressive) candidate (both Badagas). As a result the national Congress government, which the electorate held responsible for the poor rice ration, tried to regain favour with Badaga voters by locating in the Nilgiris during the later 1960s a German agricultural development project, a French-supported film factory and a protein products factory, suppo-

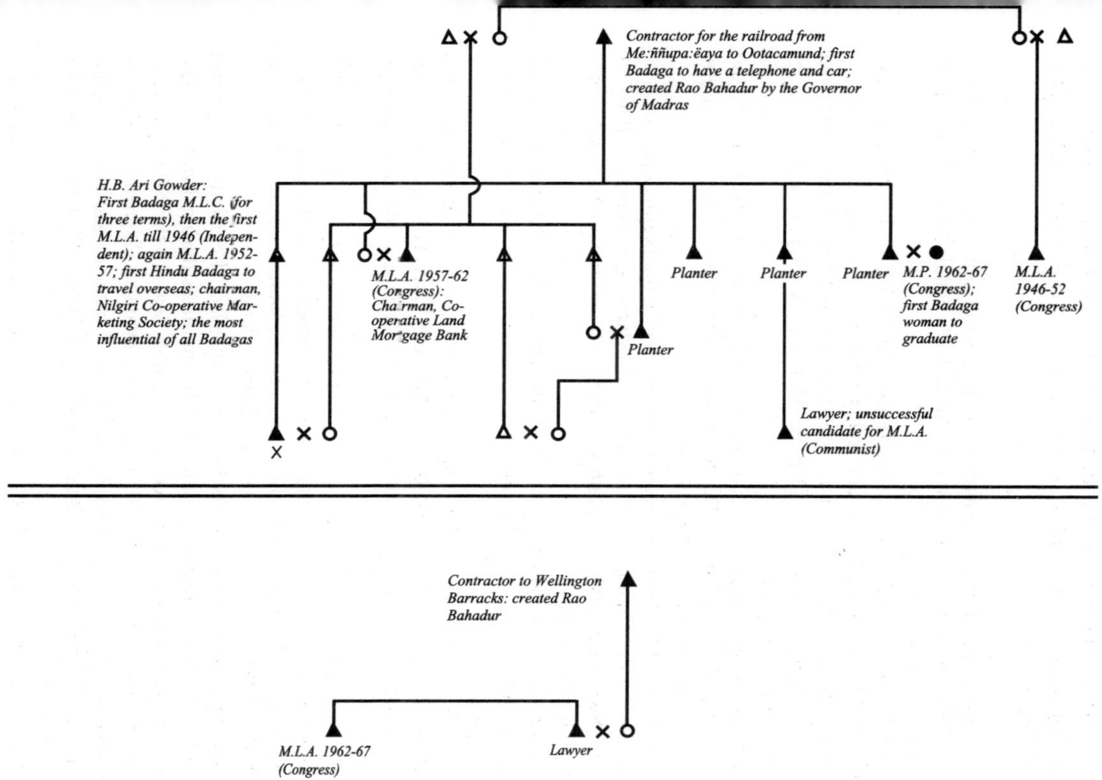

Diagram 11 : The Corridors of Power

sedly to improve the farm productivity and employ the pool of Badaga graduates locally. (Several other industrial endeavours, along with the expanding educational system, have also helped them.)

A brief synopsis of the history of elections in this district has been provided by Gopalakrishnan, who edited the most recent District Gazetteer:

> The major political parties contested in the district in the first General Elections 1952, were the Congress, and All India Scheduled Caste Federation, besides Independents.
>
> During the second General Elections held in 1957, the Congress and Dravida Munnetra Kazhagam and Independents were in the fray.
>
> In the third General Elections, of 1962, the political parties contested were Swatantra, Communist, Dravida Munnetra Kazhagam and the Congress, besides Independents.
>
> For the fourth General Elections of 1967, the contest was among the political parties viz. the DMK, Swatantra, Communist Party of India and the Congress, besides Independents.
>
> During the fifth General Elections held in 1971, the political parties contested were the Communist Party of India (Marxist), Communist Party of India, Swatantra, DMK, Bharathiya Jan Sangh and Indian National Congress (Organisation).
>
> In the sixth General Elections, 1977, the DMK, INC, INC(O), Janata and the All India Anna Dravida Munnetra Kazhagam contested, besides Independents.
>
> For the seventh General Elections of 1980, the political parties which were in the fray were the DMK, CPI, All India Dravida Munnetra Kazhagam, Janata Party (Jayaprakash Narayan), and Congress (Indira) besides Independents.
>
> The eighth General Elections were held simultaneously for [Tamil Nadu] Assembly as well as Lok Sabha during December 1984. The parties which contested in the three Assembly and one Parliamentary seats were the DMK, AIDMK and Congress besides Independents.
>
> The ninth General Elections for the Tamil Nadu Legislative Assembly and for the Lok Sabha were held on different dates during 1989. . . . The political parties which contested for Assembly seats of the Nilgiris district were the Congress, DMK, All India Anna Dravida Munnetra Kazhagam (Jayalalitha Group), All India Anna Dravida Munnetra Kazhagam (Janaki Ramachandran Group) and Bharathiya Janata Party, CPI, CPI (U) besides Independents.
>
> The Nilgiris Parliamentary Constituency, was contested by . . . candidates belonging to Congress and DMK Parties. Besides Independents . . . (Gopalakrishnan 1995: 1252-53)

Despite the wide range of contesting parties, it should be noted that it was Congress which won the Nilgiri seat for the Parliament (the Lok Sabha) in all of these elections except in 1971 (DMK) and 1977 (ADMK, two regional parties). Badagas have in general tended to support the Congress party, although in 1998 the sole Badaga candidate was a tea planter, supported by the Bharatiya Janata Party, who won that election as M.P.

State Assembly elections have had a more complicated history. In two seats, Ootacamund and Coonoor, the electorate was largely Badagas. Congress gained the seats until 1967, when Swatantra took Ootacamund and the DMK Coonoor. After that the DMK or ADMK took both seats in the 1970s elections; but in the 1980s elections Coonoor continued to be held by DMK or ADMK, while Ootacamund was taken by Congress each time (Gopalakrishnan 1995: 1288-90). In 1998 a Badaga was again returned as the M.L.A. for Ootacamund, representing however the DMK Party.

MODERN LAWS

Certain pieces of legislation often regarded as true milestones in the modernization of Indian society have affected the Badagas little, and these we need review only briefly. The Hindu Widows' Remarriage Act, 1856, had no effect on Badagas since there was never any interdict against remarriage of their widows. The Hindu Women's Right to Property Act, 1937, has always been ignored by Badagas, and the women have never challenged their traditional treatment: property is usually inherited by males. Nor does the Hindu Marriage Act, 1955, receive due recognition from Badagas: marriages are still not always monogamous and are occasionally contracted with grooms below eighteen or brides below fifteen. Kotas and lowland Harijans, although supposedly protected by the Untouchability (Offences) Act, 1955, have not been allowed into Badaga temples and to my knowledge are normally served with separate 'untouchable' glasses when they drink at a village teashop.

People in Nilgiri villages may not be ignorant of such legislation, and indeed there are now Badaga lawyers aplenty yet there certainly remains some resistance to the idea of integrating the official system of law and administration into Badaga culture. Even more resistance can be found among the Todas, Kotas and Kuṟumbas, however.

NOTES

1. Meaning, respectively, Toda division, western division, Europeans' division (from *ferangi*, 'Franks') and peak division (from Tamil *kunṟu*, 'mount'). Why one division should have been named after Europeans is not clear, unless it be a reference to seventeenth-century Jesuits who may have entered this area from Sattiyamangaḷa and Meṭṭupe, where they were then active (near the eastern foot of the Nilgiris; Société des Missions-étrangères 1933, vol. 12: 234-35; Hockings 2012: 719-20). The name Porangana:ḍu/Poranga:ḍ is certainly ancient. Grigg (1880: 13, n. 1) and Macleane (1893: 678) derive this name, however, from Tamil *periya Raṅga*, 'great god Ranga', who is indeed worshipped in this area; cf. above, pp. 164, 166. Throughout the nineteenth century these territorial divisions were adopted by British administrators, but in 1882 they were superceded by the three *taluks* (Gudalur, Ootacamund, Coonoor) that became four in 1973, but otherwise are still recognized today (although two more have been split off from these).
2. A commune can be defined as the smallest administrative unit above the village, consisting of a number of contiguous villages under one headman and council; cf. definition in *The Oxford English Dictionary* 1933, vol. 2: 698. The commune used to be found in Serbia, and as the *tambon* it is a basic administrative unit in Thailand; there the headmen of the villages constituting a *tambon* elect one of their number to be commune chief.
3. *u:r gauḍa*, or *naṭṭame*. An exceptional area near De:na:ḍu, on the eastern rim of the plateau, was so isolated and broken in terrain that it was only around 1960 that the nine Toreya villages there formed a commune and elected a man from Tumbimale as their *u:r gauḍa*; before that they had recognized as a higher authority the headman of De:na:ḍu, a Oḍeya who was also the *pa:rpatti* (see below, note 5) for Poranga:ḍ.
4. *haṭṭi gauḍa*; small villages may do without a headman for years.
5. *pa:rpatti*, or *si:me gauḍa*; Thurston & Rangachari 1909, vol. 1: 80-81.
6. *na:ku beṭṭa gauḍa*, often referred to as *Tu:ne:ri maṇega:r*. It is only since James W. Breeks became the District Commissioner, around 1870, that these paramount chiefs were also recognized as *maṇega:rs* by the administration, and one of them, Pāda Gowder (Gauḍa), then became the only Badaga member of the District Board; see Pl. 9.
7. Much the same system of headmen has been noted in the South Canara, Coimbatore and Coorg Districts; see, respectively, Thurston & Rangachari 1909, vol. 2: 269-72; Nambiar & Bharathi 1965: 10, 63; Srinivas 1965: 57-59.
8. Until some sixty years ago wealthy Badaga households had Badaga serfs, mainly from the poverty-stricken area of Kundena:ḍ, who were children bound to serve for a period of from five years (in the case of

pre-puberty girls) to a maximum of twenty-one years (in the case of some youths). In return they received food and housing, and their parents were paid a sum of money. Those in servitude were generally well treated, being like children of the households where they worked. Harkness (1832: 115) notes they were paid Rs. 2 or 3 *per annum.*

9. Such divine utterances have not been given credence in the past century, but oaths have. The scale of oaths, in order of increasing severity, is this: (1) to assert 'it is true!' (2) to pull up some grass with the fingernails and throw it onto the meeting-ground; (3) to touch the ground with one hand; (4) to put a cloth one is wearing on the ground and step over it; (5) to lay one's child on the ground and step over him – if a false oath, the child will magically die; (6) if non-vegetarian, to sacrifice a goat at the temple; (7) to visit the temple at a set time and swear one's innocence before the god. Divine punishment ought to fall on whoever breaks such oaths.
10. If after disposal of a case further evidence came to hand the headman could reopen the discussion and perhaps reach a different decision; this might protect him from being fined for a faulty judgement by a higher headman.
11. Lt. Henry Valentine Conolly, then the Collector of Malabar, disarmed the Mappilas in March 1855, collecting 7,500 knives. But then he was rather dramatically murdered on 11 Sept. at his bungalow in Calicut by three Mappilas (or Moplahs), one aspect of the long-running outbreaks of 1835-1922 in Malabar. His murderers, Valassery Emalu, Puliyankunnath Thenu (who had both escaped from prison one month before), and Haiderman the hairdresser, were all shot dead by government forces led by Maj. Halley and Capt. Davis, after being six days on the run.
12. Grigg 1880: 366; Natesa Sastri 1892: 831; Thurston and Rangachari 1909, vol. 1: 79-80. The Collector was always a university-educated, male British career official.
13. These received the title of 'sub-manegar' and a small salary from the British administration.
14. Officially these two roles entailed the following: 'The head of the village [*manegar*] is the representative of Government in the village. He is the village magistrate and head of the village police. He is the collector of the revenue of the village over which he presides, and has also to perform [miscellaneous small] duties. . . . The karnam, who is entrusted with the keeping of village accounts, is subordinate to the head of the village. He should help and advise the head . . . in every way. He is the clerk of the head of the village in his capacity as village munsif [*manegar*] and Magistrate. He has to prepare reports, accounts, statements, etc., which it is necessary to put in writing . . .' (Madras 1958: 1).
15. Thurston & Rangachari 1909, vol. 1: 80; Jagor 1914: 48. This reported

but unusual treatment was not obligatory and was indeed rarely possible because a *maṇega:r's* rounds were short and could not have kept him away from home at night. Moreover, a *maṇega:r* with a penchant for girls would quickly have lost his reputation.

16. The India-wide term for a village council. The distinction between civil and criminal law is made explicit in the Indian Penal Code, which in this matter closely follows English common law.
17. The *panchayat* members are supposedly elected every four years; their position is prestigeful but unpaid. The chosen representatives tend to be relatively well-educated but rarely village headmen. The powers of this court, which is at the lowest level in the hierarchy of lawcourts, are: '. . . to take cognizance of and try specified offences of a trivial nature and abetment of such offences committed within the local limits of their respective jurisdiction. Such offences are affray . . . , voluntarily causing hurt . . . , assault or using criminal force . . . , theft . . . , and mischief . . . , insult . . . , some nuisances . . . and generally any other offence under the Indian Penal Code or any special or local law which is punishable with fine only or with imprisonment for a term not exceeding six months or with both' (Madras 1958: 50).
18. Apparently related to this incident was another: some six months after the murder nine girls aged 7-12 from this same village suffered seizures in which they blacked out or behaved oddly. They were thereupon taken to the Coimbatore Medical College, where hysteria was diagnosed, evidently a delayed reaction to having viewed the assassination.
19. It is supposedly the headman's duty to decide whether a case should be taken before a magistrate.
20. This case remained unsettled in 1975 (all names used here are fictitious ones).
21. 'Satchit' 1940: 15; Dharmalingam 1962; see Diag. 11. For H.J. Bellie Gowder and his son Ari Gowder, see Mulley, in Hockings 2012: 79-81, 125-26. Just before his death H.B. Ari Gowder (1893-1971) corrected what I have here written about his life.

CHAPTER 12

The Eve of the Modern: a Stressful Epoch

A CHRONOLOGY

Badaga social history since 1812 is recorded in sufficient detail, in English, for us to delimit confidently an especially stressful period for them in the nineteenth century and examine its relationship to the formation of factions and religious revitalization movements. There are four questions to answer: (1) What was causing the stress? (2) What steps did Badagas take, in the face of stress-producing situations, to bring the society back to its previously perceived stability? (3) Did these steps amount to what A.F.C. Wallace (1956: *passim*; 1966: 158-63) has called revitalization – namely a cult movement that reinvigorates, as it were, a society which has undergone too much stress? (4) If so, what new institutions arose from this cult behaviour; or if not, why did revitalization fail to occur?

It had been a quarter-century since the arrival of the British. Then published sources tell of some local disaster confronting the Badaga people almost yearly from 1846 to 1907 – a lifetime of unusual stress that threw more difficulties into the path of the slowly modernizing community than at any other time since records had begun.

To begin with, a succinct chronology of this time of troubles is presented below. Items about missionary endeavour have been included because their ideas were seen by the Badagas as strange and often very upsetting, and seemed a serious threat to the integrity of the Badaga community. (It will be noticed that matters that might be viewed as the 'causes' as well as others that are clearly the 'effects' of stress, or its manifestations, have been included here.)

1845 Four Germans from the Basel Mission began preaching in many Badaga villages; such itinerant preaching continued until 1914.

1847 The mission took over a school already open in the central village of Ke:ti and began persuading local parents to send more children there; Badaga parents objected to losing their children's labour, and a *douceur* had to be paid for school attendance. Other mission schools started nearby in Ka:ṭe:ri and So:gatore. Epidemic among Badaga cattle; Toda sorcery held responsible. Badagas in fear of the magic of Br. G.H. Weigle, who was vaccinating some 700 of their children against smallpox; in fact the only medically-trained missionary, he was the first person to vaccinate in the Nilgiris.

1849 The mission schoolmaster and the son of a Badaga headman were involved in some (unspecified) 'misconduct'. The headman prevented children from attending the school or communicating with missionaries, and that school was closed for six months. Another one opened in nearby Sulligu:ḍu. Some smallpox prevalent.

1850 Ambivalent feelings towards missionaries was shown in the account of a village that begged Br. J.F. Metz to visit them, but then vacillated and asked him not to, as the village god might run off.

1851-53 Three typhus epidemics killed over five hundred Badagas. More opposition to Evangelists. Jakkatala lost much land for the army barracks. *St. Luke's Gospel*, first book ever printed in the Baḍagu language (1852).

1854 Cholera and typhus epidemics among Badagas. Government made production or sale of opium illegal; this had been an important marketable item for Badagas, and some of them were addicted.

1855 Smallpox epidemic killed over a thousand Badagas. A temple for Jesus Christ built by them. One Badaga presented himself for baptism but died before this could occur. Government prohibited their firewalking ceremonies (Pl. 8).

1856 A missionary rest-house burnt down by Badagas. From this year until 1887 British government authorities continuously planting further tracts of land with eucalyptus trees.

1857 Mission school re-established in So:gatore and another in Ba:kola. Stories of widespread rebellion in North India during the Indian Mutiny caused increased hostility among some Badagas towards missionaries and indirectly prevented a conversion. Drought in the Nilgiris.

1858 The first Badaga convert to Christianity, Abraham Nerkambe (formerly Halaiya), was driven from his Adigari village, which itself was ostracized; much opposition to his conversion, even from his wife. Large drop in school attendance coinciding with the conversion, and the legal takeover of some government schools by the Basel Mission. Crops partially destroyed through drought; it was blamed by Badagas on a curse from the Christian preachers, but by the missionaries on Badaga idolatry.

1859 Continuing drought. By now, ten mission schools opened.

1862 Model jail opened in Ootacamund. Paper currency now legal.

1863 Legislation to stop private parties clearing swiddens to farm in the reserved forests. Famine and some migration of Badagas away from their native villages; it was blamed on the missionaries, who were preaching that Christ was responsible for all that happens. The continuing conversions were usually attributed by Badagas to sorcery; very low school attendance. A further government order prohibiting the annual firewalking ceremonies.

1864 A Badaga 'oracle', when questioned by villagers, indicated that the 'English god' was dangerous and evil-intentioned. Consecration of a Protestant chapel at Ne:rikambe, an Adigari hamlet near Ke:ti.

1864-84 Land Settlement; registration of all land-holdings, and the real end to swidden farming.

1865 Famine on the Nilgiris and elsewhere; drought blamed by Badagas on their gods losing power. Some headmen now pulled down their temples and built new but bigger ones, for the first time in brick. A promise reportedly made by the god Vi:rabadrayya to come to the plateau to cure the sick and destroy the missionaries; but many Badagas disappointed that he never came.

1868 The local newspaper, the *South of India Observer and Agricultural Times* (founded just two years before), doubtless reported that the Pharmacy Act had been passed: this established a category of Dangerous Drugs that included opium – a traditional Badaga product, up till that point thought of as a harmless recreation.

1873 A Badaga living near Wellington became a death-bed convert to the Roman Catholic faith. First sight of steam engines at Meṭṭuppāḷaiyam, on the Coimbatore Plain.

1875 Massacre of 18 Kuṟumbas by Badagas armed with axes; this in retaliation for a fever among the Badagas.

1876 Monsoons failed. Cholera epidemic among Badagas.

1877 Smallpox and cholera epidemics and dysentery on the Nilgiris and famine in South India (including the north of Poranga:ḍ). Grain prices double; heavy immigration of starving, unemployed people from the plains north and east of the Nilgiris. Revenue survey of Badaga land completed. Among Badagas much loss of faith in the efficacy of Hindu rituals, and some Christian conversions.

1878 Famine continues. Opium Act, to suppress its production and sale.

1880 183 Badagas now converted since 1858, and the process continued slowly; ostracism and physical fighting still at each conversion.

1882 Madras Forest Act defined forest boundaries and further restricted the cutting of timber; from now on more and more land declared as 'government reserve'. Family of a Kuṟumba sorcerer killed by Badagas and Todas, after 3 sudden deaths in a Badaga headman's

	family. Major Hindu/Moslem riots in Salem and elsewhere.
1884	Conclusion of the Final Land Settlement in the District (1881-84). Drought in the Nilgiris, followed by crop failure.
1887	Some smallpox. School attendance decreased following a series of conversions. A Kuṟumba shot by a Badaga whose wife it was believed he had bewitched.
1889	First mission school opened in Kundena:ḍ, at Bikkaṭṭi, by request of 'a friendly Badaga'.
1890-1910	'Bible women' (i.e. South Indian Christians) were active in trying to convert Badaga women, but with very little success.
1891	Massacre of Kuṟumbas by Badagas.
1892	Famine in Madras Presidency. Age of Consent to Marriage Bill.
1897	Opium-eating noted to be on the increase: prohibited, although an old Badaga narcotic. Factions among Ha:ruvas over who should have precedence in walking over fire at their Maha:linga festival.
1900	Typhoid epidemic and famine among Badagas; massacre of Kuṟumbas by Badagas. Earthquake in the Nilgiris and Coimbatore.
1901	Conversion of Kereha:ḍa headman's daughter; attempt to isolate the Badagas of that area from the rest of their community.
1902-03	Epidemic of bubonic plague among Badagas.
1904	Police used to suppress the Badaga persecution of a new group of converts. After this date there was no further physical harassment of Christians. Another earthquake. First cars seen in the district.
1904-05	Plague among Badagas. Huge and grand *manevale* at Kadana:ḍu.
1906	Minor earthquake in the Nilgiris; houses shook. Much higher rate of intoxication than in previous years. By now there were about eight hundred Protestant converts. From this year onwards there was a 'Badaga Christian Poor Fund' distributed from Ke:ti.
1907	Factional disputes among converts: some Badaga Christians petitioned the Ke:ti presbytery committee to have two separate cups at Communion, 'one for the Badagas and one for the Tamil Christians': they claimed that the Tamilians still ate carrion. The Tamil Christians denied this, and presbyters refused the request.

The cut-off date of 1907 in this sketch of 60 years is rather arbitrary; but it is clear that the misfortunes which had for so long dogged the Badagas became considerably less frequent beyond this date.

FACTORS LEADING TO STRESS

Biographical material in publications of the Basel Evangelical Mission and in the minutes of Ke:ti parish (Basel Mission 1905: *passim*) for the latter part of the nineteenth century leaves no doubt of a deep disturbance in Badaga society during this period. Three distinct factors were responsible: natural disasters, unfavourable reforms in the land legislation, and the increasing influence of the missionaries.

Land Legislation

Late nineteenth-century censuses (1871-1901) show steady increase in the population (both Badagas and others; cf. Appendix 2), which implied a need for more farmland. Given the steady British demand for plantation land, the government responded however with several moves intended to conserve land and forests. So they stopped traditional swidden farming in 1863 (people had cleared as much land as needed and farmed it for just a few years, up till then). This practice seemed wasteful of land, and was thought to cause soil erosion. Not unrelated was the need for more plantation land, for cheap labour, and for land from Jakkatala to build the new army barracks.[1] As a check on the wasteful use of land officials made a register of all holdings in the district, the Final Land Settlement (1881-84): it was the basis for annual assessment of land taxes. Holdings were restricted to a maximum of 500 acres (202 ha.). Even the cutting of timber in jungles was halted by the Madras Forest Act of 1882. The main requirements then were lumber to build houses, cattle-sheds, and for ploughs and beds, while some rough-cut timber was also needed for fencing and funerals. By the early twentieth century the funerals and house rooves were needing ever more timber, just because of the continually burgeoning population (Hockings 1989a: 209).

In the years 1863-82 British legislation thus changed the whole complexion of the farm economy and prompted doubts among many Badagas about the very survival of their community, culture, and lands. The situation was aggravated over this period by a continuing extension of eucalyptus, cinchona, tea and coffee plantations – and the sight of steam engines (Prabhakar & Gadgil 1995: 166, Map 2).

> The competition of the planters, the profiteering of local revenue officials and the changing terms of the agrarian economy created stress in Badaga society. Disputes over 'boundary, grazing and rights of way' became increasingly common and in 1883 three Badagas of Davaney [Da:vaṇi] village were arrested and charged with murder after they beat to death a man who 'in spite of warnings, continued to use a footpath, the right of way through which was disputed'. (Sutton 2009: 72)

Missionary Activity

The sense of uncertainty about the immediate future was further aggravated by foreign missionaries attempting, without much success, to convert Badagas to Christianity. The Basel Evangelical Mission had established its first local station in Ke:ti village, on a large property given by George J. Casamajor, a retired judge.[2] In 1867 another station was set up in Kotagiri. In 1888 a Roman Catholic priest began proselytizing, with scant success, among some of the Protestant converts. In 1909 the Basel Mission set up a third outpost at Kallaṭṭi (Harvest Field 1909, vol. 20: 477-78; Tignous 1911: 156).

> The Mission was properly commenced in 1846 by the Rev. G. Weigle, who was then visiting the Nilgiri Hills for his health, and was completing his revision of the Canarese [Kannaḍa] Bible. . . . Miss. Weigle was soon joined by other labourers, and in a few years the settled staff at Kaity [Ke:ti] consisted of three missionaries, Messrs. Buhler, Metz and Moerike, who had made the Badaga language their special study. . . . [T]he missionaries soon found that little opportunity existed for public preaching, and that they could best reach their ignorant charge [*sic*] by domestic visits and conversation. They have therefore maintained a constant system of itinerancy, and it is believed that but few of the natives on the hills have never heard the gospel from the lips of these indefatigable wanderers. (Mullens 1854: 61)

Of the four pioneers mentioned here, three were graduates, one of them in medicine (Schlatter 1916: 51). Mullens adds (idem) that 'by gifts of medicine and attention to the sick, they had an access to the Badagas superior to every thing else.' This evangelization went on for decades in the hands of these Germans, and the extent of Badaga opposition to it was seen in 1856, when they burnt down the mission's rest-house at Kallaṭṭi (BEMS 1856, no. 16: 27, note). At about the same time Br. J. Friedrich Metz noted that 'some parties were so hostile to me that they intended bribing a Kurumba to kill me by sorcery. . . . In one place the Badagas created a disturbance, and refused me admittance into their village . . .' (1864: 137). This could be construed as a local reflection of the Great Revolt (otherwise the Indian Mutiny) that was taking place in northern India. Yet it should be emphasized that, in general, 'The storm of the Mutiny raised only a couple of ripples in Madras' (Butterworth 1923: 267), and neither of them came near the Nilgiris. North India was like another land.

In 1858 nonetheless the very first Protestant conversion did occur, and from then onward the ranks of these Christians slowly increased

(Hockings 1999: 179, fig. 8.2), prompting a realistic fear among Badagas that their society would be split along religious lines into two factions or parties, each avoiding the other. Nothing comparable had ever occurred among the Todas or the Kotas, nor had anyone in the Nilgiris been converted to Islam.[3] In the view of Badaga Hindus the techniques of proselytizing were as unsavoury as they were materialistic: the converts were told to renounce polygamous wives, and not to marry Hindus, and they were presented with comely Christian brides converted, sometimes, from communities other than the Badagas (or so modern informants claim). Furthermore, the missionaries occasionally arranged grants of land for converts who were denied the use of their family's customary farmland; such men often received loans from mission funds at the low interest rate of 6 per cent; after 1906 the Badaga Christian Poor Fund could sometimes sustain the poorest of them too; missionaries also could help converts to obtain employment with European families, plantations or officials.[4] Though the Christians were always viewed as outcasts, their existence still threatened to subvert the traditional values of Badaga culture, and to some extent did so.

The itinerant preaching that the Germans did in the early years of the mission's work continued until they were expelled from India as 'enemy aliens' in 1915 (Metz 1865: 83-87; 1867: 95-97). The ideal of their evangelistic programme was for someone to visit every village in turn, with a catechist. But there were some 435 Badaga villages on the plateau (Appendix 3), and as missionaries were so few, their health sometimes poor, and travel by no means easy (the journeys being of necessity mostly on foot), a village might be visited only once a year, and for a few days at most (Hockings 2012: 195, fig. 68). Sometimes the missionaries were welcome, sometimes not. Some of these Germans approached the villagers in an arrogant manner which could have done nothing to attract Badagas to their faith. They commonly turned up at ceremonies, especially funerals, to preach to the large crowds at those events (just as St. Patrick had done in Ireland 1400 years before; BEMS 1849, no. 9: 23; 1850, no. 10: 23; 1851, no. 11: 34; 1853, no. 13: 38; 1859, no. 19: 69; 1869, no. 30: 74; 1875, no. 36: 37; 1879, no. 40: 75). It was while preaching at one firewalking ceremony that Br. J.F. Metz, an obese figure (Pl. 16) who had been nicknamed 'Three-quarters God', lost face by declining their well-meaning invitation to demonstrate the superiority of his religion by walking across the fire.[5]

As another of these German missionaries recalled:

The proclamation of the Gospel, which was repeated again and again in every village with scarcely any exception, met with an increasing opposition, till at last it became a great trial of faith and patience to go on preaching to the same well known and apparently hopeless generation. From the proverbially timid Badaga we even heard expressions like these: – 'You have ruined our country, why do you come to us? – stay at home!' (Mörike 1858: 96)

Apparently, though, the missionaries could and did capitalize on the misfortunes that all too often struck at the Badaga community. On one occasion of drought, in 1859, for example, the missionaries blamed that disaster on the continuing worship of idols; and on another dismal occasion Metz reported: 'The famine may have helped to awaken in many a fear of the wrath of God. . . . Especially one day, after four Badagas had been burned in one house . . . people were eager to hear the Word and ask questions about it, so that it was quite refreshing to me' (BEMS 1866, no. 27: 78-79). In 1855 missionaries had prompted the Presidency's government to issue a ban on Badaga ritual firewalking (Pl. 8). This move back-fired, however, for a village had burnt down at about the same time, and this was taken to be a manifestation of the Badaga deity's wrath towards the missionaries (BEMS 1855, no. 15: 39).

The mission schools were another important means of evangelizing. Indeed it has been said, 'One could call the Mission on the Nilgiris a School-mission' (Schlatter 1916: 215, trans.). So a mission school had been founded at Ke:ti in 1845, and by 1859 nine others were in operation. At first the Badaga parents in the neighbouring villages were given a small coin (one anna a day) as inducement to send their unconverted children there rather than have them work in the fields. The schools were intended to create a favourable impression among the Hindus; but the missionaries had to record that the frequent changes of local schoolmasters, their indifference to teaching, their loose morals, and the periodic closure of the schools led to a halting literacy but scarcely any conversions.[6] No 'industrial training' was given at these institutions. One permanent day-school was established by the mission in 1871, yet these drawbacks remained.[7] Only in the 1880s did some Badagas begin to appreciate the merit of the schools: the number of permanent Mission schools on the Nilgiri Plateau 'was only 3 in 1879, but 21 in 1889, and 36 in 1899'.[8]

Whatever one might think about their motives for evangelization, the missionaries (and in most Protestant cases, their families too) were quite significant agents in the introduction of modern Western ideas to the Badagas; so perhaps we should not rush to judgement. Even in such a small area as the Nilgiris, 'Generalizing about missionaries, however, is not possible. They include verticalists, who limit themselves to preaching, and horizontalists, who are dedicated to practical work, and they vary from cultural relativists to fundamentalists' (van der Geest 1996: 797). As was suggested before, the nuclear families of the Germans and Swiss, as well as the high status of their housewives, their firm sense of discipline and cleanliness, and the strong emphasis on education, work and worship, may well have served as a role model for some Hindu Badaga families even in the nineteenth century (Hockings 1999: 242).

Natural Calamities

A third, quite unpredictable source of tension was the frequent and varied natural disasters, whether drought, epidemics, earthquake, or famine. Badagas were not slow to attribute these calamities to the doings of the Mission.[9] Yet on a few occasions the disasters were so intense that they prompted hundreds of people actually to turn to the German missionaries for sustenance. In 1877 especially, the general South Indian famine and crop failure led to a steep rise in food prices in the Nilgiris and to a heavy immigration of indigents from the plains. Beggars came to Ke:ti by the hundred, and the missionaries had to restrict their alms-giving to the old and the sick. The mission established some relief-work for Christians and distributed rice to the congregation; and this clearly prompted many, especially the relatives of previous converts and those already familiar with the Gospel, to forsake Hinduism. 'Their idols, some said, had been of no use to them in this calamity, they would now follow the God of the Christians.'[10] The missionaries were of course glad to enlarge their flock, yet by the tail end of the nineteenth century some of them were becoming more realistic about the motives prompting Badagas to convert. Thus the first Badaga pastor in Kotagiri, Jacob Kanaka – a former Lingayat – noticed that 'The larger number of the famine-converts came from the village Tandanadu, the abode of a heart-hardened people and the seat of idol-worship in this district.' [11]

Indeed it would be no exaggeration to say that Badagas came to the mission more often for temporal than for spiritual aid. In the late nineteenth century mission staff felt many were willing to convert, yet seemed 'more concerned about their debts of money than those of sin; they promise to embrace Christianity if their debts will be paid by the Mission' (BEMS 1849, no. 9: 45; 1850, no. 10: 23; 1897, no. 58: 53-54; Lütze 1899: 50). The missionary was commonly sought out in times of sickness, after herbal therapy had failed. Food was often begged from mission people too. Thus, for example, one hungry Hindu Badaga asked a Christian woman for food, and she remarked on the risk of her polluting him. The man answered: 'In your Bible it is written: If thine enemy hunger, feed him; if he thirst, give him drink. Therefore consider me as your enemy and act in accordance with your Bible.' So the woman had to give the knowing heathen food (BEMS 1906, no. 67: 82).

Instances of spiritual aid being sought by Hindus from a missionary should also be noted, however, and especially at times of sickness and death: 'You are our Padre . . . if you only look at the sick or put your hand on their heads, they will feel relieved' (BEMS 1905, no. 66: 68).

REACTIONS OF THE BADAGAS TO EVANGELIZATION

Missionary activity and the other stress-producing factors we have mentioned led to a wide variety of reactions among nineteenth-century Badagas. Some attempted to incorporate Christianity into their own religion or to bolster that religion so that it might seem as effective as Christianity; some attacked or intimidated the converts; some threatened the missionaries; some massacred the supposed Kuṟumba sorcerers; some took to opium or liquor; many became involved in factional disputes; while quite a few people ignored the vehemently held wishes of their relatives and did convert.

Conversion (1) was at one end of a spectrum of reactions that also included (2) quiet acceptance of much in Christian teaching, without formal conversion; (3) ambivalent feelings leading a man to seek and appreciate temporal help from the missionaries, but only when he could not possibly do without it; (4) ignorance of Christianity and a wary avoidance of the missionaries; (5) ostracism and threats of violence directed against missionaries, converts and even potential converts; (6) physical violence, making use of fire, fists, sticks, stones and blunderbusses against converts.

Let us review these patterns of stressful behaviour now.

Attempts to Syncretize Christianity and Hinduism

One reported pattern among Hindu Badagas exposed to proselytization was the attempt to syncretize the two religions. As early as 1849 – a decade before any conversion – some people were praying to the 'God Jesus', and in 1850 one headman was heard invoking Jesus among other gods as he knelt on the bank of a stream at a Hindu ceremony (BEMS 1850, no. 10: 23; cf. BEMS 1854, no. 14: 41). Then, as later, Christ was thought of as *another* Hindu god, perhaps an *avatār* of Vishnu.[12] Even the missionary might be incorporated into Hindu thinking: the man could be called '*Shiva kandidhone – Swāmi kandidhone*', the one who has seen Shiva (BEMS 1849, no. 9 45). Br. Metz, for example, visited the village where a woman had just before committed suicide by swallowing opium (the common method among Badagas in those days). As he had previously condemned her for leaving her husband and taking a lover, he was now treated with great circumspection: the frightened villagers took Metz for either a sorcerer or a god (Metz 1864: 71-75).

The 'Christian temple' was another case of syncretism. In one village Badagas claimed that a vision of Christ had appeared to them and told them to believe the preachers. These people promised to build a Christian temple, which they did around 1855. In it they enshrined a *New Testament* in the Tamil language (which scarcely anyone could then read). A rumour soon developed that every night Jesus came to taste the milk and bananas offered on his altar. But when Metz visited that village in 1863 he found the temple fallen into disrepair and the village nearly deserted. He blamed this on the current famine; but the Badagas tended to blame the famine on *him*. This was the occasion already alluded to, when the Badagas interpreted the preachers' explanation of Christ's supreme authority as meaning that Christ was responsible for the death and starvation at that time (Metz 1864: 69-70; Reclus 1891: 239-40).

In the same year the Badagas of that particular village went to a temple for divination and asked: 'Is he who is called Jesus Christ a good Swami [lord]?' The response though was negative (Metz ibid.:

71; Reclus idem). Another instance of Hindu practices being directed at the mission was cited by Br. Gottfried Wieland (see Mulley, in Hockings 2012: 193). A child in Ke:ti was sick; its Hindu father promised to give Rs. 5 to the Christian God if He would cure the child. Since the child later did recover, the missionary was indeed given the coins (BEMS 1907, no. 68: 68). Such action is traditional and quite routine in Hindu temples all over India.

On one occasion the boys rushed from a school in consternation when a missionary asked them to repeat a prayer after him, fearing that, 'If we say the *mantroum* of the Christians, Christ will hear, Christ will come, Christ will carry us off!' (Reclus 1891: 239-40).

In general we may say that Badagas found Christianity to be of some relevance to them only when they could treat it as an aspect of their own form of Hindu religion; as they did, for example, when they equated their goddess Ma:riamma with the eponymous Virgin Mary venerated by the Roman Catholics (Metz 1866a: 142). The manner in which the spiritual message of Christianity was presented led to some wild misunderstandings of what Christianity stood for. Most Badagas simply could not comprehend why anybody should want to be converted. They asked Metz (1864: 138) if the new converts '. . . would soon mount horses and ride about like Europeans, and whether they had got plenty of money by the change?' Clearly some Badagas were viewing conversion as a process of social mobility whereby one should adopt the behaviour patterns of Europeans and abandon those of Badagas; and in this they were not altogether mistaken, as the upward mobility of some Christian converts soon illustrated.

Hindu Reformers

The European missionaries were not, as it happened, the only ones to adopt an aggressive posture in the conversion arena. The actions of these aliens prompted a counter-movement of Hindu proselytizing, using similar evangelizing methods to make the Badagas and other communities into more orthodox Hindus. These Brahminic missionaries belonged to the Hindu Tractate Group of Madras city (now called Chennai), and they visited a number of Badaga villages to distribute pamphlets and even set up their own short-lived schools (BEMS 1854, no. 14: 41; Eppler 1900: 306).

A Hindu reform movement that developed without any apparent support from outside emerged in the village of Eḍapiḷḷu in 1892. There the young men formed an organization called the Society of Virtuous People (or *Yeḍapuḷḷu Sajjana Sangha*; BEMS 1892, no. 53: 77-78). Among various proposals they advocated cleanliness of body and home, education for girls, an end to tattooing, cessation of lavish spending and of dancing to music at the funerals, discontinuing the use of drugs and intoxicants, and general adoption of monogamy (except that if one wife proved barren a second wife could be taken, but the first should remain with the husband). The account of this society shows it aimed to put right the various 'evils' of Badaga life that Europeans had for so long been condemning. (One automatically thinks of the close parallel between this organization and the Arya Samaj in northern India, also active in the last decades of the nineteenth century.) It is worth noting that, while nothing further was heard of the Society of Virtuous People, the village of Eḍapiḷḷu did become strongly Gandhian in the 1930s – when Mahatma Gandhi had visited the neighbouring towns of Wellington and Coonoor, and villagers took part in picketing the local toddy shops and places selling foreign cloth.[13] Today that village still retains something of this idealism, has a well-balanced mixed farming economy and an optimistic outlook on the future – a combination of factors that was not common in Badaga villages. It was also the first village to send a Badaga to the United States for postgraduate training, in agriculture; this was Y.B. Morachan. It would appear therefore that Eḍapiḷḷu, lying close to Coonoor, has been quite a progressive community for well over a century.

The Destruction of the Temples

Building and destroying temples were equated in Badaga thinking with establishing or destroying a religion. In one village, as we have seen, Badagas sympathetic to some aspects of Christianity built a temple to Jesus in which they placed the *New Testament* they had been given. In another village Metz knew some Badagas who were willing to pray with him but who would not openly call themselves Christians. They even asked him to pull down their Hindu temple. When Metz suggested it would be better if they showed their faith by doing this themselves, they refused, but did remove the *pu:ja* offerings at the temple and kneel in front of it while the missionary prayed with them (Metz 1864: 135-36). At Me:lu:ru the original round temple for Mahalingasa:mi was destroyed by local villagers, and a square stone one built in its place (Pl. 5).

In 1864 a Protestant chapel was consecrated in the Badaga hamlet of Ne:rikambe, not far from Ke:ti (Hockings 2012: 642), and in 1865 famine hit the Nilgiris. Some of the Badaga leaders felt this had happened because their gods were not properly honoured, and so during the next few months many villages went through the unprecedented steps of tearing down their temples and building new, bigger ones in their place. By this means the people hoped to regain the favour of the gods and counteract the influence of the mission. Until that time the temples were commonly thatched, and made of 'sun-baked mud' (King 1870: 6). Thus it is noteworthy that brick, a novelty which until then had rarely been used in Badaga building at all and, ironically, was only available from the Basel Mission's brickyards in Mangalore, was the material chosen for all these new temples; stone was the more usual material of the twentieth century. In one large village several temples were destroyed by the headman and four new ones built, two of them for gods who had not previously been worshipped there.[14] The process of rebuilding temples continued for several decades and affected 'almost all the villages' (BEMS 1870, no. 31: 22-23; 1905, no. 66: 66). Badaga houses also were commonly being rebuilt in brick now.

Sanctions against Conversion

Social pressures were constantly being exerted upon converts, their close relatives, and any other Badagas who seemed receptive to the missionaries' message. Many cases could be cited from the mission publications of Badagas who wavered in their attitude towards conversion. Metz for example commented that

> . . . the people of a village can be really affected by the love of Christ, when it is preached to them. . . . But when I come again on my next tour . . . I find that in the meantime they have been so frightened by Satan and his tools that they hide in their houses when they hear that I have come, or run away when I ask them to listen if only for an hour. They fear to be convinced by my sermon and to have to suffer for it from their relations. (BEMS 1870, no. 31: 22-23)

In some instances men waited till they were dying before openly requesting baptism (BEMS 1878, no. 39): 63. People were always very reticent, understandably, to become the first convert of their village. They would often promise to become Christians if only their friends or relatives would lead the way. And thus Metz would complain:

> . . . there are Badagas who will readily kneel down with me and offer up a prayer in which their wants were often expressed more forcibly, than they probably would have been by many a nominal Christian, and who, for several years, have discontinued idol worship; but when I ask them to go one step further . . . they immediately refer me to another, and say that if he will set the example, they will follow it; and if I appeal to him, he puts it off with a similar excuse. (Metz 1864: 135)

Their over-riding family problem was explained by several local men to the preacher: 'What you say is true; but were we to follow your advice, we should have no hope of getting wives for our sons' (BEMS 1853, no. 13: 39; 1856, no. 16: 34; 1858, no. 18: 92). Intermarriage between Hindus and Christians remained for a century unthinkable. Fear of ostracism was great, and it held men and women back from entering the Christian fold, even if they might otherwise have been tempted. This was probably true in many South Indian communities.

The biographies of some converts vividly convey the extent to which the Hindus tried to force converts back into their old ways. The following slightly abbreviated quotations from missionary magazines offer a representative pair of case histories.[15]

> (1) [Mada, baptized as Mark] . . . had a wife and a little child. . . . The wife had promised to join him [in Christianity]. But on his return from Church the first Sunday, he found the door of his house locked, and his wife did not dare open it for him. Next day his father-in-law came, and took her and her child away to Adhikarhatti. His whole house was pillaged, and property to the value of several hundred rupees was taken away; even his potato field was dug up by his father-in-law. Shortly afterwards Mada's wife returned and was about to fulfil the promise she had made her husband before his conversion that she would also become a Christian. But next day her brother took her away by force, and after a few days she was sold [i.e. married after payment of bridewealth] to another husband. Only the little babe was left to Mada [as was normal at a Badaga divorce].
>
> The bereaved husband then tried to get back his wife and his property by the help of the law. . . . But the [Moslem Police] Inspector treated the

Christian witnesses with marked rudeness and would not listen to their evidence. Their depositions were sometimes taken down contrary to what was affirmed, in spite of [the missionary] Mr. Lütze's protests, while the witnesses of the opposite party were fully heard and recorded. Mada's wife was constantly surrounded by heathen Badagas, and when her husband asked her whether she had left him of her own free will or by compulsion . . . she could only reply as she was told by the Badagas. . . . At last the police declared that the defendant [her father] had committed no unlawful action, and the case was dismissed. . . . Heathen neighbours and relations promised [Mada] their assistance to get back his wife and property, on condition that he returned to caste; Kalla especially pledged himself to that end. Mark [Mada] hesitated and wavered. . . . He stayed away from divine service, and when Kalla carried off Mark's wife by force from the neighbouring village and brought her back to him, when most of the plundered property also came back, he gave way. . . . (BEMS 1893, no. 54: 87-88; *Harvest Field* 1894, ser. 3, vol. 5: 546-51; Lütze 1894: 22-23)

(2) About the beginning of 1893, several young men of Kerehada . . . came repeatedly to Mr. Lütze, mostly at night, to express their willingness to become Christians. They were Kalla, . . . Karcha, the son, and Konga, the nephew of the *headman* of the village. They broke caste and openly spoke against idolatry and heathenism. . . . After some time Karcha and Konga asked [the missionary] to lend them some money to clear off their debts, which prevented their joining the Christians. Mr. Lütze had his suspicions, but Joseph, Kalla's cousin, said it would be wrong to hinder the victory of the gospel; he borrowed the money himself and lent it to the young men, getting a bond from them for the same. Then the three young men came to the mission-house at Kaity [i.e. Ke:ti] and openly joined the Christians. . . . The news spread like wild fire, and from the villages round to a distance of 15 miles people were flocking into Kaity sitting down inside and outside the mission-compound and trying to persuade the three young men to return to caste. For ten days the entreaties and tears of their female, and the promises and entreaties of their male, relations continued, and repeated endeavors were made to carry them off by force.

At last the young men could stand it no longer. On the 7th April 1893 Karcha and Konga stole away, and four days afterwards Kalla followed them. By the intrigues of the headman they were after a month re-admitted into caste, and Kalla even succeeded in enticing back his son Madya (Immanuel). The poor boy is now a drunkard and totally ruined. 'It is better to be ruined body and soul than to be a Christian,' that is the opinion held and expressed by many of the heathen. But the heathen Badagas, especially the headman . . . , were not satisfied with these successes. He induced the backsliders to deny the receipt of the money lent to them by Joseph and to force him to return the bonds. Joseph was threatened by them with a cudgelling and with death if he did not return the bonds. Moved by fear he at last returned them. But his tormentors were not satisfied; they refused acceptance of the bonds. Twice Kalla lay in wait for good-natured Joseph . . . , dragged him to a safe place and beat him mercilessly, and Karcha lodged a complaint against Joseph accusing him of fraudulently eliciting a bond from him without paying him the money. He brought false witnesses, who swore to the truth of the complaint. . . . But the case was decided in favour of Joseph. Cheerfully Joseph and Isaiah returned that day from Coonoor to Kerehada. On the way they found Titus of Chogatorre [i.e. So:gatore] and invited him to spend the night with them. So the three men wended their way home, followed at a short distance by Isaiah's daughter and his brother-in-law. Just after they had crossed a deep [stream] . . . Karcha, armed with a cudgel, rushed forward from behind a rock and knocked the three men down. Kalla, Konga and Mark [Mada] also came forth from their hiding place, while the *headman* of the village with his servants was seen standing at a little distance encouraging the assailants. But as Isaiah's daughter and his brother-in-law called for help, they had to retire. Joseph and Titus were so injured, that they were unable to work for a whole month. Isaiah's arm had to be bandaged. When the assault was inquired into by the police, the assailants turned round and brought a complaint against their victims, whom they represented to have been the aggressors, and sued for Rs 2,000 damages. This time, however, they were convicted and punished. Daniel also, the brother of Kalla, who had so greatly rejoiced at his brother joining the Christians, had to suffer from Kalla's spite. He drove him, his sick wife and his children out of their own house and locked it. After they got it back, he reaped Daniel's barley crop and filled his verandah with the straw. A few days afterwards the house was partially burned down. In consequence of this, Daniel's wife's illness was so aggravated that she died after long suffering. . . . (BEMS 1893, no. 54: 88-90; my italics)

It is clear from many such recorded cases that the converts, their fellow villagers and even the missionaries were regularly being subjected to a lot of stress during the latter part of the nineteenth century. Attempts to make the converts return to their former life were sometimes legalistic and sometimes not, sometimes violent or else merely argumentative. Much of the behaviour that marked these feuds drew its form and inspiration from the older practice of ostracism. Even before the British came to the Nilgiris Badagas had been in the habit of banishing members of their community for certain categories of crime and anti-social behaviour (see p. 195). Such people would then have to clear some patch of land in the jungle and create a new home there, or else find a distant village willing to accept them. Attempts to exclude the converts from their own villages fitted this pattern and prompted the mission to allocate land near its Ke:ti compound for some of the new converts. Male converts who later went back to Hinduism could be readmitted to the Badaga community by a ceremony involving shaving the head, cutting a thread of the loincloth, and purifying the tongue by burning it with a heated golden wire or some charcoal ('Miles' 1951: 70).

Violent opposition to almost every conversion characterized the relations between Hindu Badagas and the mission from the time of the first conversion in 1858 to 1904, the last year in which some conversions 'roused a storm of persecution which could only be suppressed by the help of the police' (BEMS 1904, no. 65: 68-69).

At about that time a rumour was circulating among Badagas and elsewhere in southern India that just before Christmas the Christians sacrifice a human and offer the head on their altar; a Freemasons' Lodge in Wellington was said to preserve the skeletons.[16]

But these were by no means the only reflections of the stressful behaviour in the nineteenth century. As we shall see in the following chapter, widespread personal disorientation developed, groups of Kuṟumbas from time to time were massacred, the religious scene was coloured briefly by the cult of Vi:rabadrayya, and for the first time factionalism became an important feature of village life.

NOTES

1. Despite getting some compensation, most Jakkatala villagers were very unhappy about the long negotiations (1848-52) that had deprived them of close to 350 ha. of good land; Francis 1908: 342; Sutton 2009: 35-40. On the Land Settlement in the Nilgiris, see Sutton 2009: 48-84.
2. Grigg 1880: 421-22; BEMS 1900, no. 61: 104. The old mission house, still standing, was built by Lord Elphinstone for his residence in 1840; Grigg 1880: 458; Macleane 1893: 403; Francis 1908: 331; Sutton 2009: 27-32; Hockings 2012: 179, 467-68. One of the missionary occupants ca 1869-73 was Br. Johannes Hesse (1847-1916), father of the famed writer and Nobel laureate, Hermann Hesse; Hockings 2012: 408-09.
3. Somewhat more recently one Badaga was converted to Islam and was being trained to proselytize that faith on the Nilgiris; BEMS 1901, no. 62: 96.
4. Thus two days after the first Badaga conversion, the missionary wrote: 'I went with Abraham into the coffee plantation yesterday in order to present him to his master as a Christian and to ensure his work as a planta-

tion supervisor there'; Mörike 1858: 93, trans. Basel Mission (1905) has full details of the frequent loans that were made against pledges of land.

5. Metz (1864: 55) reflected: 'Challenged to perform a similar miracle . . . I replied that a much greater wonder than that, was, that I should not cease to love such squalied [*sic*] fellows as they were; and that too, in spite of all the abuse they daily heaped upon me. . . . When a recent order was issued prohibiting the practice [of firewalking] . . . I had to submit to the most dreadful execrations, showered upon me as the originator of the order'; cf. BEMS 1849, no. 9: 45; 1853, no. 13: 39. On Br. Metz, cf. Hockings 2012: 592-53. The outrageous Madame Blavatsky, who came to Ootacamund a decade after Metz had already left (and was doubtless quoting the District Forest Officer, Gen. Henry R. Morgan, who was in those days rumoured to have been her lover), pictured how Metz 'washed himself only once a year, lived only on dairy products, and finally became so fat that he began to suffer from dropsy' (Blavatsky 1930: 101; cf. Hockings 2012: 144-45).
6. BEMS 1849, no. 9: 44; 1863, no. 23: 50-51; Metz 1864: 8-9, 56; Grigg 1880: 424-25; Stokes 1882: 177; BEMS 1887, no. 48: 98. By 1864 boys could earn three to five rupees monthly on coffee plantations; this, and the usual parents' contention that 'they have become old without knowing [how] to read or to write and could do their work as well as their forefathers', explain the initial unpopularity of schools; Metz 1864: 9, note; cf. Grigg 1880: 425. Problems with 'loose morals' long continued among the Christian population, as when in the Ke:ti neighbourhood an early twentieth-century teacher got another unmarried one pregnant; the man involved was a church elder.
7. Ke:ti was probably the third Badaga village to get a school. One had been established at De:na:ḍu in 1820 or 1821 and another at Ku:kallu around 1830; Ward 1821: lxx; Harkness 1832: 69-70; Hayavadana Rao 1908: 113.
8. Eppler 1900: 306-07; in these years there were respectively 69, 497 and 967 students. See BEMS 1886, no. 47: 88; 1887, no. 48: 98. In 1904-05 there were 39 Badaga schools, with 1,222 pupils; Thurston & Rangachari, 1909, vol. 1: 64.
9. The epidemic of 1863 was attributed to Jesus, 'because the missionary had but lately been preaching that not a hair, not a bird, can fall to the ground without his [Jesus's] express will and his sovereign command'; Reclus 1891: 238.
10. BEMS 1877, no. 38: 15. At this same period, Br. William Stokes, an Anglo-Indian, claimed that most of the converts 'embraced the Christian religion from conviction and not from unworthy motives, as is very often the case in the plains where large numbers are gathered in'; BEMS 1873, no. 34: 32, and Grigg 1880: 422.
11. BEMS 1900, no. 61: 110; such a shift in attitudes was not confined to

one village.

12. BEMS 1883, no. 44: 80. It must be remembered that the Badagas were then rather ignorant of Hindu scriptures; BEMS 1867, no. 28: 73.
13. One Eḍapiḷḷu resident, M. Jogi, served four months in the Central Jail in Coimbatore for picketing toddy shops in 1930-31; Gopalakrishnan 1995: 238-39. On Gandhi's brief visits to the Nilgiris, see Hockings 2012: 375-76.
14. Metz 1863: 134; BEMS 1865, no. 26: 70-71; Metz 1866b: 119; Stokes 1882: 174; Sawday 1884: 12-13; Francis 1908: 130; Tignous 1911: 116. To meet the cost four rupees were levied from each household. Prior to this time Badaga temples had been round thatched structures; Pl. 5; also in Breeks 1873: pl. LXXV; BEMS 1904, no. 65: 68, plate; Noble, in Hockings 2012: 60, fig. 24.
15. There are many comparable anecdotes in the presbytery minutes and the various mission periodicals.
16. Schad 1908: 134; Butterworth 1923: 208, presents a similar tale. Since fresh skeletons were supposedly collected every Christmas, Badagas near there would only walk around in groups after dusk during November and December, for fear of the European headhunters. The lodge in question was Anchor of Hope; Hockings 2012: 546.

CHAPTER 13

Widespread Disorientation

PERSONAL DISORIENTATION

One finds a number of references in the Nilgiri literature to opium and intoxication. Opium had been produced and taken by the Badagas as early as 1812 at least, when there was an 'official' reference to it (Keys 1812: li; Macpherson 1820: lix). But strong liquor was seemingly unknown to them until three decades after their first contacts with the British (Marshall 1873: 82). It was noted in 1820 that no intoxicant was distilled, drunkenness was unknown, and opium chewed only in moderation (Macpherson 1820: lix). Though opium continued to be taken (Young 1827: 42; Mahias, in Hockings 2012: 717-19), locally made intoxicants were still unknown to the Badagas in 1834 (Ainslie 1834: 36). By the time the Basel Mission became active among them, however, they found opium-eating to be widespread (Metz 1864: 132; Gover 1871: 87; Anonymous 1879: 149), even though its manufacture had been outlawed by the British in 1854 and again in 1878 (Price 1908: 224). Opium-eating occasionally became a problem in the Christian congregation too, even as the ultimate release from this stressful world (Metz 1866a: 142), and it continued for long as a solace for Hindus. It was stated to be on the increase at the turn of the twentieth century (BEMS 1897, no. 59: 64; Basel Mission 1905: 119, 129-30). Drinking also became an increasing problem at that time: thus in 1892 the Society of Virtuous People at Eḍapiḷḷu tried to halt the use of liquor and drugs there (BEMS 1892, no. 53: 77-78; Basel Mission 1905: 170-72, 179). In 1905, a year of plague, some Badagas near Kotagiri decided that their whole community was being ruined by drinking, and '. . . pledged themselves to their goddess Hette to give it up and to excommunicate [i.e. to ostracize] everyone who transgresses this covenant' (BEMS 1905, no. 66: 68). The next year, in Ke:ti, Br. G. Wieland noted that drinking alcohol was increasing rapidly among the Badagas (BEMS 1906, no. 67: 63). The anecdotes in Chapter 12 show a specific instance (in 2) of acute stress apparently leading to alcoholism; the Ke:ti parish minutes (1905) contain other examples.

Although none of the mission sources suggested the correlation, it can hardly be doubted that the increased use of opium and liquor in the latter half of the nineteenth century was generally related to the higher frequency of stressful situations in the lives of many Badagas during that period (as outlined in the previous chapter).

THE MASSACRING OF KU<u>R</u>UMBAS

There were several occasions, in the years 1824, 1835, 1875, 1882, 1887, 1891 and 1900, when Ku<u>r</u>umbas were massacred by parties of Badaga men.[1] The techniques of killing varied from case to case, but usually involved burning down a hut or even a whole hamlet – to make the slaughter seem accidental.

Thus in 1875 a head Ku<u>r</u>umba had bewitched a Badaga woman into loving him and had supposedly caused a fever among Badagas. He was killed in a gun duel, while altogether six households of Ku<u>r</u>umbas near Tumbimale were massacred with axes. The story was immortalized in the epic ballad of *Kadare Gauḍa* (Hockings 1997a: 297, 301-09, 312-13). In the gruesome case of 1882 the family of another sorcerer were impaled and burnt alive:

> On the 1st of May Madia, the son-in-law of the headman of the Badaga village of E— . . . died. And as some time ago two of the children of this man had died, suspicion fell upon the Kurumba priest Molle Sevana as having caused the deaths of the two children through sorcery. This priest was living at the foot of the mountains, in Sirur. So when now the father suddenly died, nobody was in any further doubt that this priest was planning to destroy the whole Badaga family. The funeral celebrations of the Badagas, which are quite ceremonious, were planned for the 7th of May and, because of that, people began the extensive preparations on the Saturday, sending out messengers in all directions in order to invite people from the neighbourhood and from far-away places.
>
> At the foot of the mountains there lived some Irulas in the same place where the local Kurumba priest Molle Sevana was living: according to custom, they were all told of Madia's death and invited. When some of the Irulas came to him, the Kurumba excused himself from going because of illness. So when these Irulas were asked by the E— headman where the Kurumba Molle Sevana was, they answered as they had been told, and the

headman replied in the following way: 'Let him carry on like this: we will take care of him because he is trying to act like the Almighty!' Even other Badagas who turned up at every funeral were mentioning that they were in no doubt nobody else but the Kurumba could have killed Madia.

On Sunday evening the Irulas went back to Sirur, and no one seems to have reported to the Kurumba what had been said about him in E—. While the Irulas were sitting together in their yard after having finished their dinner, they saw two Todas and some Badagas passing by, who mentioned to them that they had been in the plains. Because it was already late the Irulas invited them to spend the night with them; but they refused the invitation with the remark that they were planning to stay overnight on the other side of a small stream which passed the village nearby.

About midnight the Irulas were awoken by cries which could clearly be heard coming from the hut of the Kurumba Molle Sevana, situated only a few hundred feet away. They immediately ran into the bushes and from there could see what happened without being observed. A large fire was burning in front of the Kurumbas' hut and several Badagas were standing around it while two Todas carried the body of the Kurumba out and threw it near the fire. The corpse, covered with a blanket in which the Kurumba had been sleeping, was then tied to a long pole and they proceeded to walk towards E—, one and three-quarter hours away. Two Badagas and two Todas were carrying the load on the pole. Two other Badagas were leading the pregnant Kurumba woman, each by one arm, and dragged her uphill while she was constantly screaming and begging them to let her go. One Badaga took the Kurumba's youngest child on his shoulder, and some others brought the various possessions of the killed man and were driving the two older children before them. They thus climbed the steep mountain path uphill from Sirur in bright moonlight. A number of Irulas followed the procession at some distance in order to see what would happen next.

When they reached E— they could see a large fire in the middle of the funeral ground. It was quite clear that new wood had been added after the corpse of Madia had been burned, for the Kurumba should not be burnt with the Badaga. The Irulas who were hiding in the nearby bushes could clearly observe everything without being seen. The corpse of the Kurumba was thrown into the fire just as he was bundled up. After that the Kurumba's wife was impaled on a long pole by a Badaga, followed by the impaling of the children one after the other. The screams of the mother and the children could be heard for some time coming from the flames, until they ceased. When everything was over and daylight started to reappear, the Irulas went back to their village. (Stokes 1883a: 6-7, 11-12, trans.; the village identity has been concealed)

Common to such killings was the fact that they followed closely on some catastrophe in the Badaga village responsible for the carnage, and also that one or two Todas were always involved. According to Badaga witnesses at the ensuing court trials, these Kuṟumba sorcerers had caused deaths or epidemics in a Badaga village, either of people or of buffaloes, and their sorcery might be halted by the massacre only if a Toda, also considered a sorcerer, were to strike the first blow against the unfortunate Kuṟumbas.

Thus, for example, a Badaga killed a Kuṟumba out of fear of his sorcery after epidemic disease had attacked both the Badaga village people and their cattle and a great part of the murderer's family had died. The heavy sentence that was given the man by a local British magistrate was incomprehensible to the community and it reportedly 'gave much encouragement to demonology, and tended greatly to increase the insecurity both of themselves and of their cattle' (Harkness 1832: 83-84). We might cite this as an early example (*ca* 1828) of Badagas' insecurity being unintentionally aggravated by inscrutable British official practice. Then, a few years later, several Todas were condemned for having massacred a reported 58 Kuṟumbas who they thought responsible for a buffalo epidemic in 1835.[2]

Occasionally Todas were also accused of witchcraft by Badagas. The relationship between the accusation and the feelings of stress is dramatically illustrated in another incident:

> One day a respectable man interrupted Br. Metz by remarking that through his new doctrine their gods had lost much of the respect and reverence in which they were formerly held and this he said was the cause of the great drought and all their misfortunes. . . . Just at this time he was interrupted . . . by a body of people dragging a dead calf along with them and accusing a Toda boy of having killed it by witchcraft.[3]

The last known instance of Badagas killing a supposed Toda sorcerer, around 1895, was in retaliation for the death of a Badaga child (Rivers 1906: 261; Francis 1908: 144).

FACTIONALISM

There is no published evidence of any kind of factional division among the Badagas until the late 1850s. The question that this raises must therefore remain unanswered: was the emergence of factional disputes really a reaction to the stresses of crossing the threshold into the modern world, a world which introduced the Badagas to a cash economy linked with international markets, a code of law that put them theoretically on an equal footing with everyone else, opportunities for schooling and literacy, pressure to change their faith, obligations to pay taxes and obey unpredictable foreign officials? Or was the periodic factional restructuring of the community an integral part of Badaga life, something that had occurred for as long as Badagas had existed? We have no means of knowing.

There are two different types, or different scales, of faction, but both are designated by the same Badaga word.[4] First, there are what might be called 'personal' factions or feuds, which stem from strong differences of opinion in a single village about someone's personal grievance. The second type embraces most Badaga villages, each of them taking one side or the other in some dispute of general concern to everybody. Descriptions of the Badaga reaction to the earliest religious conversions suggest that this type of faction grows out of what is initially a dispute confined to a single village (BEMS 1889, no. 50: 67-68; Anonymous 1894: 547-51; Eppler 1900: 153-55).

From these nineteenth-century descriptions several reflections might be culled of the process by which factional behaviour gets started. However, because of the evident partisan attitude in early mission writings, a more recent example of faction formation is preferable. The following case is a summary of my informant's account (the name is fictitious). What happened there prompted the formation of two factions, although the division was probably founded in part on earlier experiences and previous disputes.

> In 1963 when one village was preparing to perform a funeral the headman asked every household there to donate three meals for the expected visitors. One man, Ajja, however, was requested to prepare four meals, perhaps by mistake; and he did as asked, only to find that nobody came to his house to eat them. Why this was so is not clear; but apparently Ajja was not a very pleasant person to get along with. He demanded a refund of the cost of the meals from the general village funds, but the headman decided to do nothing about it. This impasse quickly divided that village into two separate communities.
>
> At first only three households closely related to him supported Ajja; but after another funeral in the village, other people belonging to the same lineage as those three households found themselves drawn into Ajja's faction. At this point the village council led by the headman forbade any women to help members of Ajja's faction with such tasks as working in their fields. Because of this proscription a number of women were forced to join Ajja's faction: they perhaps had no strong feelings about the actual dispute, but were too poor to forego the Rs. 1 1/2 they were earning as daily labourers.

Thus within a few weeks from the start of the grievance typical factional behaviour was characterizing interaction in this village: no one was supposed to talk to members of the opposite faction or to visit their houses and eat with them. In effect, what had been a single village now took on the organization of two non-communicating but interdigitated villages. And so within two months following the initial funeral arrangement there was a complete breakdown in village cooperation at the celebration of any festivals: each faction celebrated its own separately from the other.

Yet some ten weeks after the dispute had begun there were already signs that the factional structure was falling apart. No longer could a rigid separation be maintained between the two factions. Members of one were paying supposedly secret visits at the back doors of friends in the opposite faction; but everybody knew what was really going on. Already it was acceptable behaviour to talk to members of the other faction on the street, so long as no interdining with them occurred. The break-up of the factional division was spear-headed by women from other villages who had married into this one: in several instances there were pairs of sisters from another village who were married to men of opposite factions here. In such cases the sisters felt seriously inconvenienced in being socially separated by a dispute that was not really their concern; and so they took every opportunity to meet secretly and interact with each other across the cleavage that was still separating their husbands. Nobody in the village really expected these factions to become more rigid: slowly but surely these kinship ties were bringing the two sides together.

By comparison with such frequent and short-term factional disputes as this example, the all-Nilgiri factions are few but long-lived. Altogether only a half-dozen of these are known, and only two of them antedate the twentieth century.

The first major factionalism we know of, and certainly the most important if judged by its effects, was that engendered by the conversions that split the community into Christians and Hindus. The second major dispute in Badaga history emerged in 1897 and, like the first, was still the basis for a factional cleavage in the 1960s, until resolved by a lawcourt. Whether this dispute was triggered by the tensions which mission activity and other trials of that period generated is nowhere clearly indicated in our sources. Initially it was only a dispute over which Ha:ruvas should walk first on the fire during their annual festival for the god Maha:linga at Me:lu:ru – those of Maṇuhaṭṭi or those of Tanga:ḍu.[5] (By 1897 both of these villages had mission schools, but Tanga:ḍu, though ritually inferior, was much wealthier than Maṇuhaṭṭi.) As the dispute grew, the entire

Ha:ruva clan consolidated to claim superiority in status over the Oḍeyas and all other groups. The Ha:ruvas and certain other Badagas who supported them – pre-eminently in the Gauḍa villages of Kundena:ḍ division – believed the Ha:ruvas had been of the high Brahmin *varṇa* before they had left Mysore to settle in the Nilgiris. In support of this belief they cited the facts that they belong to the Bra:ma sept, they have always been priests for the non-vegetarian Badagas, they are strict vegetarians themselves, and also they wear a thread across the shoulder. Opponents of the Ha:ruva claim included the majority of Badagas. They perhaps recognized that the Ha:ruvas have no knowledge of Sanskrit or any other sacred literature – for until the twentieth century they were all illiterate; furthermore, there is no ceremony for investiture of the 'sacred' thread and no concept of being 'twice-born'. But the argument most generally used against the Ha:ruvas' claim was that they are only priests in Badaga temples, including the one at Me:lu:ru, because the non-vegetarian phratries *appointed* them to act in this capacity; just as they had appointed certain Todas, Ku̱rumbas and Toreyas to act in special economic and social roles for the benefit of an entire village. In modern times the Gauḍas commonly assert that the Ha:ruvas are equal in status with the Gauḍas, amongst whom they find spouses.

Although it is the Oḍeyas whom the Ha:ruvas contested for ritual superiority, there has not been any open clash between Ha:ruvas and Oḍeyas. This is not too surprising though, considering that Oḍeyas are Lingayat while Ha:ruvas are not; Oḍeyas never employ Ha:ruva priests; Oḍeyas do not intermarry with Ha:ruvas at all, and do not live near those who triggered the dispute; and thus Oḍeya-Ha:ruva interaction has always been minimal.

The main clash in this dispute was between Ha:ruvas and most of the lower-status Gauḍa phratry, who resented the Ha:ruvas' claim. Only a minority of Gauḍas supported the Ha:ruvas; the remaining villages had not only denounced Ha:ruva pretensions but over half-a-century ago broke off their ceremonial relations with them too. In most Gauḍa villages the Ha:ruva priests were supplanted in their duties by non-Ha:ruva members of the village; Gauḍa marriages with Ha:ruva men or women ceased, and already married couples were sometimes peremptorily divorced by the village headman; formal interdining with Ha:ruvas was also halted; and occasional fights would break out, particularly at some festivals when the customary

Ha:ruva priests tried to perform their ritual duties and members of the anti-Ha:ruva faction tried to stop them.

The Ha:ruva dispute has never been altogether resolved, although the paramount chief was able to mediate it in some villages and at least two community-wide meetings resolved to end it, in 1957 and 1972. In the earlier decades of its history it was marked by the usual fights, lack of intermarriage or interdining between disputants and even by resort to the British Indian legal system. (A case against Ha:ruvas was carried, I was told, as far as the Privy Council.) More recently the dispute has cooled to the point where it might only become relevant in the arrangement of marriages. This also seems to be the present case with the erstwhile conflict between Hindu and Christian Badagas. In either instance marriages now may sometimes occur across the cleavage, and without arousing much opposition.

In summary we find that Badaga factions arose from and gave expression to a situation of stress in the community (Hockings 2012: 310-13). Yet only one of the half-dozen important factional disputes arose directly from the stressful experience of evangelization.

THE CULT OF VI:RABADRAYYA

So far, we have seen several types of reaction to evangelization and certain calamities, without finding any movement meeting Wallace's criteria (1966: 158-63) for a successful revitalization of a culture. So let us now review what is known about the cult of the Oḍeyas' god Vi:rabadrayya, since this was a kind of eschatological movement.

> A rumour was spread that the God [V]Irabattaraya,[6] born of a white elephant, would come up to the hills within some months bringing to each [Badaga] a true Linga, & consuming Mr. Metz with the breath of his mouth. Even the Todas, ignorant as they are of Vishnoo & Shiva, accepted the mark of Shiva on their foreheads, that they also might be acknowledged by the God as his followers when he would appear. This excited such a sensation among the people, that for some time the proscribed Missionary had the utmost difficulty to get a hearing. But the appointed term elapsed & the god did not make his appearance. At last the news was spread, that Irabattaraya was in Satyamangalam, a town at the bottom of the mountains, performing the same wonders, as Mr. Metz was in the habit of relating of Jesus Christ. Multitudes of sick people, dressed in white, descended the mountain but came back uncured & disappointed; and after a few weeks the god had disappeared. The impostor appears to have been a Mohammedan juggler.

But the people were not yet satisfied. An embassy consisting of 20 men was dispatched on a 5 days' journey into Mysore to ask the old god of the Badagas when he would come up? This frenzy has now passed away. . . . (BEMS 1865, no. 26: 70-71; similarly Metz 1866b: 119)

Yet more telling details about the saintly Vi:rabadrayya's incarnation in a nearby village of the plains were provided for us, however, by a local British elephant-catcher,[7] who described it as

an amusing pious fraud which was practised on the credulous villagers near Morlay [Muraḷi] by three sharp fellows from the Hyderabad country. The very simple means they employed were as follows: They arrived at Hurdenhully [Haradanaḷḷi] a village near Morlay, and took up their abode in a tope, or clump of trees. One was represented to be an ascetic on a pilgrimage from Kási (Benáres) to Rámêshwaram, the holy cities of Northern and Southern India; the other two were his attendants. The holy man soon attracted the attention of the people by the austerity of his religious observances. He had long, unkempt locks, a rag round his loins, and his body was plentifully besmeared with cow-dung and ashes, after the manner of Indian devotees. He spent his time in sitting apart in a reverential attitude, muttering incantations and invocations, and appeared to be wholly wrapped up in the contemplation of divine things. His companions attended to his few wants, and took care to extol his great piety, his advanced religious state, and unworldly spirit, in the villages near. Hundreds of people soon began to visit the Gooroo (spiritual guide) and to pay their reverence to him.

At last it began to be rumoured about that his long contemplation of sacred things had gained this holy man the Divine approval, that supernatural powers had been granted to him, and that he proposed a descent to Pátárla (the regions existing under the earth . . .), and a return after seven days. This produced tremendous religious interest for many miles round. An abundant harvest was just over; it was the dry weather and the people had nothing to do; so thousands flocked to bow before the saint who, unmoved as ever, appeared to be in a rapture of contemplation. Charitable contributions of grain poured in from all sides, and after being offered to the still oblivious Gooroo, were cooked for the consumption of the attendant crowds. After a few days, moved by the spirit, he transferred the scene of his devotions to some open ground a mile distant, and here, under the directions of his two companions, his newly-attached disciples commenced the excavation of a hole in the ground, about five feet deep and three in diameter, which was to be his starting-point for the lower regions. Over this was built a substantial earth-work shrine, with a small door at one side; surmounting the whole was the figure of a bull, the emblem of Shivite worship, in clay. At a distance of about twenty feet from this structure the two attendants erected a small hut of branches: this was carefully closed in with cloths, and during the few days when the shrine was being prepared, the man of ashes spent the whole of his time in it, fitting himself (it was supposed) by renewed diligence in prayer for his projected visit to the other world.

The public excitement was kept up at all hours by incessant tom-toming and horn-blowing, and the charitable and well-to-do ryots [peasants] who were present distributed food gratuitously to the daily-increasing crowds. At last the eventful day for the mystical disappearance arrived. The chief men amongst the multitude pressed round the shrine as the Gooroo approached it chanting a song of adoration, and implored his blessing. The devotee then entered the hole below the shrine, and it was securely closed and thenceforth sedulously watched day and night pending his resurrection, and in accordance with his parting instructions.

During the intermediate time interest in his performance was kept alive by exciting news of his having been seen first at Bissalwadi, a hill five miles to the west; shortly afterwards, in the jungle ten miles in an opposite direction. . . . Whilst public speculation pointed to some particular direction as a probable one for his next manifestation, a messenger would suddenly arrive in camp with news regarding the ubiquitous one which set all calculation at defiance. The fact that he was wandering about the country instead of being in Pátárla [the Underworld], does not appear to have struck any of his believers as a departure from his original undertaking; it was possibly thought these flittings were the performances of his disembodied spirit.

At the expiration of the appointed seven days the expectant multitude was massed round the shrine, which at a given signal from the inside was opened, and the wonder-worker calmly stepped into the daylight, shaking the soil from his matted locks, and merely seeming a little dazed by the glare of day. He was received as a god, and seated on the figure of the bull. A blanket was spread at his sacred feet by his companions, who regarded this as a favourable opportunity for making the collection. . . . One eager worshipper after another now pressed forward to touch the holy feet with his forehead, and drop his coin on the rapidly-increasing pile on the blanket. Some gave as much as thirty or forty rupees; and a sum of upwards of £200 was thus contributed.

The holy man then made a progress from village to village, levying further contributions with a cupidity scarcely consistent with his unworldly character. He stated the object of his pilgrimage to be the collection of funds for constructing a well for travellers at one of the entrances to Rám-éshwaram, and that the amount already subscribed was insufficient for the purpose. If any one declined to contribute, his holiness resorted to the effective practice known in India as "Dherna", which consists in the claimant's seating himself at the entrance of a house, and vowing neither to eat, drink, nor go away until his request is complied with. To avoid incurring the sin of allowing such a sacred character as our hero to suffer at his door, the persecuted tenant was generally impelled to purchase his departure.

The Gooroo and his two friends shortly proceeded on their pilgrimage. I should mention that the hole into which he had descended had been filled in immediately on his reappearance, in accordance with some superstitious representations made by his attendants, and some months elapsed before the sequel of the story transpired. It was during the following rainy season that some of the ryots [i.e. peasants] of the neighbourhood noticed that the earth had sunk in an extraordinary manner about the scene of the wondrous achievement, and an examination of the place showed that the devotee and his companions had dug a small burrow or tunnel, merely sufficient to admit of a man's squeezing himself along it, between the shrine and the adjacent place of his retirement; this had been done before the Gooroo's entombment, and the work had now collapsed. Through it the Gooroo had made his way after his descent, and had effected his escape after nightfall. He had then shown himself here and there, with what result has been seen, and had managed his reappearance by the same means. (Sanderson 1878: 44-47)

This cultic activity, which flared up briefly in 1865, seems to have contained features of both the Christian and Hindu religions. If, as Metz asserted, this *guru* was claiming to perform the miracles of Jesus, one is left in doubt as to whether the Vi:rabadrayya cult drew some of its inspiration from an earlier contact with Christianity, or whether instead missionaries in nearby Sattiyamangaḷa during the 1860s had somehow prompted this anti-missionary movement.[8]

CONCLUSION OF THE STRESSFUL PHASE

In asking whether Badaga reaction to stress either restored an equilibrium or amounted to a revitalization movement, we must recall the features of revitalization outlined by Wallace and Fuchs.[9] Wallace's view of revitalization as a social process stems from the general hypothesis that under certain circumstances a particular sequence of events is likely to follow.

First, Wallace says (1966: 158-63), a society is in a 'steady state' when disorganization and stress remain tolerable to most people. Certain social groups may find some stressful incident intolerable but their restricted 'correction' does not overthrow the entire social system. Then increasingly large numbers of people may encounter stress from climatic or biotic change, from war and conquest, social subordination and acculturation. There follows a sharp rise in crime, illness, alcoholism and anti-social behaviour. A third phase occurs when some people attempt to restore an equilibrium by certain socially dysfunctional means, such as by attacks on 'scapegoat' groups. Individual aberrations become institutionalized efforts to eradicate The Evil.

Once such severe 'cultural distortion' has occurred the society can usually return to a 'steady state', Wallace has written, only through a revitalization process. This involves several recognizable characteristics, he states: (1) a code is formulated, transforming the stressful conditions into an ideal society; (2) the code is preached in an evangelistic spirit to attract converts; (3) the movement becomes organized with the formulator of the code, the disciples and the sympathetic followers; (4) the code is adapted to face outside threats and to clarify ambiguities; (5) a large part of the population is converted and control of the communication networks is won, thus achieving the goals of the movement and drastically reducing the symptoms of anomie; (6) the movement changes from being an innovative one to being a routinization and maintenance force.

We recognize that Wallace's impressionistic concepts of steady state and social equilibrium leave the reader in serious doubt about how one is to identify these conditions on the ground. If, however, we assume Badaga society was in a 'steady state' prior to the impact of the British (an assumption predicated on our ignorance of the society prior to the early nineteenth century!) then a phase of cultural 'distortion' had arisen by the middle of that century as the Badagas became increasingly uncertain about their future. Ecological change induced by the new land laws, epidemic diseases, acculturation, deforestation and some subordination to the ruling caste all produced stressful effects on the social system of the Badagas. Some cases of alcoholism and opium addiction followed, as well as the sporadic attacking of opposite factional groups, both Hindu and Christian, within the community, and of Kuṟumba sorcerers outside it.

The stage was thus set for a revitalization movement, but what came along? – the cult of Vi:rabadrayya. This cult was formulated by someone, perhaps a non-Badaga Moslem, around 1865, and word of it was spread to many Badaga villages by disciples and gossips. Followers by the hundred made a pilgrimage to where the god was supposedly residing; and afterwards the cult collapsed in disillusionment for reasons that are evident: it appears that no one of sufficient charisma had arisen and stayed to fuse Badaga sentiments in this particular cult; nor had it proved possible to institute an on-going movement in support of the cult and its anti-European goals. This cult had all the makings of a revitalization movement but failed for want of a sustained leadership. It is nonetheless worth pointing out that the next ten years were marked here by no social disturbances of any kind among the Badagas. Then 18 Kurumbas were killed.

If an inability to become routinized was a mark of the Vi:rabadrayya cult it was even more true of the earlier syncretic cult of Jesus Christ, as well as of the temple-rebuilding fervour. Indeed no Hindu religious activity in the nineteenth century successfully revitalized this community; the Badagas recall no great charismatic leaders in their recent past (except perhaps the mid-twentieth-century politician, H.B. Ari Gowder; see above, p. 204).

Yet a new 'equilibrium' had been achieved by the early years of the twentieth century; or at least the stress became much less acute. The Hindu Badaga community continued to be a distinct, mainly endogamous group, with its own characteristic language and culture, yet beside it there emerged a Christian community. What then had happened to relieve the tensions that I have documented? Several features of the changing social condition can be mentioned here as at least a partial answer.

Accommodation of the Christian Community

After the final outburst of protest in 1904 the Hindus were no longer openly antagonistic to every new conversion (BEMS 1904, no. 65: 68-69). The community of Christian Badagas was by then so large, so influential with the Europeans, so well schooled and hence so powerful locally that it could no longer be threatened and attacked with impunity. The Badaga Christians came to be seen as a caste, separate and inferior to Badaga Hindus. Having thus been unconsciously assigned a position in the social organization of the Nilgiris, the Christians no longer posed such a biting question about the continuance of Badaga society. After the expulsion of German missionaries in 1915, early casualties of World War I, the Basel Mission on the Nilgiris passed almost immediately into the hands of the rather less evangelistic Wesleyans. A stable family and behaviour were so encouraged among Christians that they indeed became something like a reference model for the remainder of the Badaga community in these respects. Then the first schoolteachers, the very first college graduates, the first government clerks, the first factory workers, and even the first published writers among the Badagas were Christian.

Major Factions Became Permanent

Like the division between Christians and Hindus, and another one between Lingayats approving of marriages with Kanarese girls and those who were opposed to it, the factional division between Ha:ruvas and those who did not acknowledge their claims to Brahminic status became a persistent feature of Badaga social organization. Even in recent decades every lineage has belonged to one or the other of these factions. We might wonder whether the rapid increase in the Badaga population over the past century or more led to a growing awareness of impersonality in the community, which this and later factional splits have counteracted by 'dismissing' large sectors of the society as unfit for interaction. If the population of the undivided Badaga community in 1871 was just under 20,000, then there has scarcely been any growth in *scale* when we consider that recently this would still be about the order of people with whom a Badaga could potentially interact *within* each of the several factions that cross-cut the community during the twentieth century.

Health Improvements and Economic Growth

The hazards of famine and epidemic disease which the Badagas of the nineteenth century faced posed less of a problem for them in the twentieth. Virtually no living Badaga has known starvation. Their standards of health have much improved and public health facilities, especially mass inoculations, have decimated the earlier scourges. The modern practice of piping fresh water into the villages, too, has caused a great improvement in health (Grigg 1880: 185, n. 2; also Hockings 1980b: 10-15).

The development of a mixed cash-crop farming economy and slight industrialization from the time of the First World War have been crucial factors in the improvement of Badaga living conditions. While there are still many families that are landless or very poor, the opportunities for earning cash are so much wider than they were one century ago that a general famine is not a serious or recurrent threat any more.

Education, too, has broadened the Badagas' view of society and is now very popular with them. Even kindergartens have been opened recently in several villages. As early as 1887 it was noted that they had themselves built six schools out of their village funds.[10]

The community thus managed to overcome the social and economic difficulties which, when not ameliorated, have often triggered some kind of revitalization movement.[11] No successful revitalization did occur among Badagas even though several small and localized cults showed some potential for it. Instead the people were able to survive their period of frustration, accept the existence of a separate Christian community and move from subsistence into a cash-crop economy which allowed them to improve their standard of living significantly even though the ratio of people to farm acreage was rapidly increasing. Thus we can say that while the society is in no sense static today it has managed to reduce its tensions and achieve something like a 'steady state' based on a cash-crop economy, rising expectations, and the institutionalization of certain social divisions that were the major cleavages during the time of troubles in the latter half of the nineteenth century: a big step towards modernization.

NOTES

1. Breeks 1873: 65; Grigg 1880: 299, 411; Stokes 1883a: *passim*; Francis 1908: 155; Thurston & Rangachari 1909, vol. 1: 86; Tignous 1911: 155; Belli Gowder 1923-41: 50; Hockings 2012: 577. I have been told of a much more recent instance (not well substantiated, however) in which Badagas burnt down a Kuṟumba hamlet near Manjakombe because of the excessive demands for food that one Kuṟumba watchman had been making.
2. *Calcutta Monthly Journal* 1836: 54; Grigg 1880: 299 implies that the perpetrators were never caught.
3. BEMS 1858, no. 18: 91-92; the Toda was rescued by Metz; see Metz 1864: 22-24, 34.
4. *kaćći*; Hockings & Pilot-Raichoor 1992: 120; cf. Burrow & Emeneau 1984: no. 1099 for cognates.
5. Wieland 1900: 86. The Maṇuhaṭṭi priests thought themselves superior as their service was done inside the temple, whereas Tanga:ḍu's priests remained in the outer precincts. The Tanga:ḍu Ha:ruvas, who by then included several contractors and were distinctly wealthier than Maṇuhaṭṭi

people, held that firewalkers should proceed in order of seniority; and in 1897 the seniormost candidate was an old man from Tanga:ḍu. After that the festival was celebrated by the two villages on alternate years; see Francis 1908: 340, and Jogi Gowder, no date: 3-5. In a few years the rift had widened, apparently over a marriage quarrel: a Ha:ruva from Maṇu-haṭṭi had asked for the sister's daughter of a Gauḍa headman. The latter arranged her divorce, and she married the Ha:ruva. He, however, had agreed to pay six rupees worth of finger millet for the divorce but never did, precipitating a long court case and a rift between Ha:ruvas and Gauḍas. About 1940 the Gauḍas of Me:lu:ru successfully wrested the fire-walking ceremony from the now reunited Ha:ruvas of Maṇuhaṭṭi, Tanga:ḍu and two other villages, causing the latter to celebrate the festival on alternating years at two of their villages, but never more at Me:lu:ru (Francis 1908: 340). In effect, these Gauḍas had refused to acknowledge the ritual superiority of the Ha:ruvas whom they used to marry, and also have won themselves legal recognition as owners of a temple which had previously employed Ha:ruva priests. On firewalking, see Pl. 8 & Hockings 2012: 327-32.

6. 'Virabhadra, sometimes called Munniyappan, is an incarnation of Siva's anger . . .'; Elmore 1915: 63.
7. George Peress Sanderson (1848-1892), the son of a missionary, was in government service as a resourceful elephant-catcher. He is believed to have been the archetype for the character of Petersen Sahib in Kipling's short story, 'Toomai of the Elephants' (in *Second Jungle Book*, 1895), which led to the 1937 film *Elephant Boy*, directed by Robert J. Flaherty.
8. We may recall that by the early eighteenth century the Sattiyamangaḷa population was largely Christian, as a result of proselytization there from 1643 onwards by some Jesuit Fathers, notably the Tuscan, Roberto de Nobili (1577-1656). Persecution by Tipu Sultan, a Moslem (1749-99), forced the entire town's population to revert to Islam or else Hinduism (Société des missions-étrangères 1933, vol. 12: 234-35; 1938, vol. 17: 632-33). The London Missionary Society maintained a catechist there in the late nineteenth century, yet by 1891 there were only 28 Christians in a population of 3,574; Nicholson 1898: 424-25.
9. The process of revitalization, though of concern to Max Weber (1946, 1947), was first clarified and labelled by Wallace 1956: *passim*, & 1966: 158-63; cf. Fuchs 1965: 1-20.
10. Anonymous 1887: 122. 'The increasing prosperity of the Badagas is unquestionably inclining them to seek instruction for their children'; Grigg 1880: 426.
11. Fuchs 1965: 1. He presents many examples of such movements from all over India.

CHAPTER 14

The Twentieth Century: Developments within the Madras Presidency

We have seen how some aspects of Badaga culture have undergone impressive change, how the economy was monetized, how national systems of law and administration were to some extent adopted by Badagas, how a stressful period was endured, and how a nuclear Christian community became a permanent feature of their social organization; all this well over a century ago. We will now examine other religious changes that have come about, what has happened to the Christians, how education has developed, and how the society adjusted to the new patterns of communication, commerce, marriage and residence during the twentieth century.

GROWTH OF LINGAYAT TIES WITH MYSORE

Until the twentieth century the minority of Badagas who were Lingayats were mostly illiterate, knowing little about their religious faith as it was being practised in the old Mysore homeland. Perhaps once or twice a year a Lingayat *guru* would come to the hills from nearby Angala or Nanjangud (Nanjaraguḍi) monasteries, selling *lingas* and performing ceremonies for the families (Harkness 1832: 137); whatever he taught people about Lingayat belief would have been transmitted by word of mouth. Over the past century, however, Badaga Lingayats were mostly literate, and some became avid readers of books on Lingayat philosophy. Cheap bus transport also enabled them to visit easily the Nanjangud temple (not far from Mysore city) and other places of pilgrimage, and so to meet well-informed monks and priests in towns of Karnataka state (former Mysore).

One fruit of this increased contact was that quite a few marriages occurred between Badaga Lingayat men and Kanarese Lingayat girls, beginning about a century ago; there were even a few of the more conservative Oḍeyas who took this step. However, this move for forming marital ties with Mysore did not find ready acceptance among most Badaga Lingayats, even though they thought Kanarese brides would usually bring a substantial dowry with them. For much of the twentieth century this particular matter was the subject of a bitter factional dispute within the Lingayat segment of the community (see pp. 250-51). They would argue that as people from even the lowest castes could be converted to Virashaivism (although they seldom are), there was a danger that girls brought from Karnataka were really descendants of Untouchables converted to the faith. For upwardly mobile Badagas, that was no easy pill to swallow.

THE NEW FACTIONS

By the late nineteenth century there may have been several different intra-commune or intra-village factional disputes of which now no record exists; small inter-family feuds were undoubtedly common, and among the Christians these were already recorded in the monthly minutes of the Ke:ti parish's lay committee; but there were only two factional divisions of Nilgiri-wide scope, one separating Hindus from Christians, and one disputing the relative superiority of Oḍeyas and Ha:ruvas (see above, p. 111). During the twentieth century these divisions remained, while other ones arose alongside them.

The Oḍeya-Ha:ruva dispute was intensified by another conflict which began on 14 Sept. 1930, and quickly assumed Nilgiri-wide proportions (Benbow 1930: 11, 13). It concerned the question of whether, during a Badaga funeral, it was dignified to dance beside a corpse to Kota music (Pls. 9, 13 and 15; Mandelbaum 1960: 302-03; Hockings 2001: 13-18). Those who supported the Ha:ruva claim to superiority wanted to continue this traditional use of Kota music; while those opposed to the Ha:ruva faction and also to the use of Ha:ruva priests were equally opposed to having the music at their funerals. The latter group, who formed the majority faction, felt that such music was an indignity to both mourners and Kotas, and also that dancing was an indignity to the dead since as an expression of joy it was inappropriate, un-Hindu, and 'uncivilized' in this context.

Those who still wanted to have the dancing, a conservative minority, felt it had been an integral and time-honoured element in their culture, and that to discontinue it would be to dishonour and even jeopardize the deceased with an incomplete funeral. The new-found opposition to what had always been an essential part of the mortuary ritual arose indirectly from contact with Tamilian culture and a consequent shift in Badaga cultural orientations, and found its leaders in the first Badaga M.L.C., H.B. Ari Gowder, and his father Bellie.

Today few if any Badagas invite Kotas to play either at funerals or at weddings and festivals, and most of their economic connections have also been severed. This has had the effect of increasing the social distance between themselves and what they see as their more backward and polluting Kota neighbours, who are categorized by the government as a Scheduled Tribe (Emeneau 1938: 104-05; Mandelbaum 1960: 302-03). Some who eschew Kota musicians at ceremonies are willing to tolerate Kuṟumba or Iṟula musicians, but most view these as no different in this context than Kotas. In dropping the practice of dancing at funerals while adopting anniversary ceremonies for the dead and such festivals as Ma:rgaḷi, Ka:rttige and Di:pa:vaḷi, modern Badagas have been striving for upward social mobility by taking on the model and assuming the conduct of more orthodox Shaivite Hindus. Most Kotas meanwhile show no interest in playing funeral music or otherwise underpinning the old Badaga culture. They too have their college graduates, tea planters and well-to-do families who are all looking for a better style of life than that their ancestors had known. Performing at funerals of another ethnic group has simply become an under-paid anachronism for them.

Another factional dispute that lasted for nearly a quarter-century prior to Independence (1947) was a political one: Badaga political behaviour at that time took the form of a factional division. Most villagers were not at all concerned with national political matters but the more informed hamlets – those with higher literacy and closer links to the towns or mission schools – tended to be aligned either with the Indian National Congress and the Independence movement or with the Justice Party and a reliance on the British administration of India (Dirks 2001: 242-43). The most aggressive phase in this factional history, when most villages became involved, was from Gandhi's salt *satyagraha* in 1930 up to the outbreak of war in 1939. A recent *Gazetteer* lists 58 'Freedom Fighters' from the district who were Badagas: many of these men took part in the Civil Disobedience movement during the 1930s, or became imprisoned under the Defence of India Act in the 1940s (Gopalakrishnan 1995: 231-49). During that period the two political factions would not eat together or talk to each other, would sometimes maintain different headmen (Heidemann 1997: 63), celebrate festivals separately, forbade intermarriage across the cleavage and sometimes would even give way to outbreaks of violent fighting.

Just as the dispute over use of Kota music reinforced an existing factional division over the status of Ha:ruvas, so this political dispute became yet another facet of the same old quarrel: those who supported the Ha:ruva claim also supported the Indian National Congress. The reason for this is quite clear: in Madras Presidency the short-lived Justice party was an anti-Brahmin party; its support depended largely on opposition to the supposed preponderance of Brahmins like Nehru in the Congress, and to the ease with which the small Brahmin minority here was seeming to get the lion's share of government employment, to the envy of many non-Brahmins.[1] In this area the dispute over Ha:ruva superiority thus took on a political colouring for some: those opposed to Brahmins in general and *ipso facto* to the Ha:ruva claim were in support of the Justice Party.

Before the Kota music factions and this political division arose, a factional feud had split the Lingayats, while not involving other Badagas: it was triggered by some marriages with Lingayat girls of Mysore (see above, p. 248), the first of which occurred in an Adigari family around 1890. Those who favoured marriage with Mysorean girls felt that it might raise their status to have connections with the city of Mysore and its *Umland*, particularly as this was an area with many monasteries and an orthodox interpretation of Virashaivism, where the Badaga bridegrooms would receive the blessing (*ubadeś*) of a high-status *guru*; a dowry could also be expected from many a prosperous Mysorean family. Most Lingayat Badagas knew that the Lord Basava himself had taught that all men and women are equal, that caste distinctions and endogamy are all social evils, rather than divine prescripts. The Badagas who have since about 1925 opposed these marriages contend that, because Lingayat philosophy countenances conversion from any caste, the girls' families might originally have been in low or even polluting castes; yet once converted, there is no means of checking on their ancestry. Although such marriages have actually been rather rare occurrences, the factional split they engendered has been marked by more violence than most. Its culmination came one day in 1944 when a thousand or more Lingayat men in one place waged battle with sticks and rocks until restrained by the police. For many years the two groups had not intermarried or dined together and had litigated against each other; after this fight the temples in the feuding Kaṇakka village were sealed and festivals were only permitted under police surveillance, separate times being allotted for each side to use the temples. For over a decade this village maintained such a heated division that each faction had its own headman and council. As one proverb puts it, 'If there is a break in the head "mother" [village], the village will have two [commune] markers' (i.e. *akka bakka*; Hockings 1988: 350, no. 680). In this particular case the dispute was resolved around 1959, and members of the two factions since then have been able to dine together and support a single headman and council.[2]

A factional dispute over these unconventional marriages, which only concerns Lingayats, or a dispute over political affiliations, that concerns primarily the more well-informed villages, are examples of a faction type that is neither community-wide nor confined to a single village: it is an intermediate type involving particular interest groups.

The Christians form another interest group providing some more recent examples. In 1955 a Badaga Christian studying at Madras University wanted to join its Badaga Students' Association, and shortly afterwards one other Christian posed the same problem. As this Association had always tacitly been a Hindu organization two factions emerged, one accepting Christian members, the other not. They celebrated their Annual Day on two separate occasions for as long as these Christian Badagas remained in the University.

Another case concerned the Christians alone. Half a century ago a majority of the Badagas along with some Tamilians in a Christian village decided it was disrespectful for the minister to wear shoes while conducting a church service: they apparently reasoned from the fact that it would be unthinkable for a Hindu priest to wear shoes in a temple. For some time this congregation was divided, and those opposed to shoes in the church would neither wear them there nor attend the service of a minister wearing shoes. The dispute later subsided and the two sides resumed inter-dining, worshipping and talking together. In the final analysis, people thereafter wore shoes to church if they wanted to, though for awhile some of the ministers judiciously refrained from doing so (despite the cold stone floors).

In another Christian village an unusual three-way split developed between converts who came from the Gauḍa, Kumba:ra and Be:ḍa phratries. Each group claimed that they were socially superior to the other two categories. In this village as a result little intermarriage occurred across the boundaries between ex-Gauḍas, ex-Be:ḍas and ex-Kumba:ras. They normally interdined but could refuse to do so during sacred festivals. They had no objection, however, to attending the same church service together. Somewhat similar 'retrospective' factions also appeared in the past in the small Roman Catholic community of Badagas, between ex-Hindus and ex-Protestants; and also in the Protestant community, around 1918, between Wesleyans and the ex-Basel Mission converts (Société des Missions-étrangères 1928, vol. 7: 573; Périé 1933: 100).

We thus find that the factional divisions have been a deep-seated feature of Badaga social organization in modern times. Even when people are converted to Christianity or go to a distant college cleavages may still occur among them that are marked by a rigid pattern of antagonistic interaction. One is tempted to see in this an urge for a periodic reorganization of the society, one which helps make the components of the social organization visible to members. Heidemann (1997: 63) suggests factions are the last resort of the traditionalists when their authority has been undermined in most respects by British influence, or, more recently, by state government authorities. Yet by late in the twentieth century the importance of local factions had diminished to the point where even the most influential men in one would go to funerals and talk with members in the other.

THE CHRISTIAN COMMUNITY

A historical survey of the evangelization of the Badagas reveals to us four distinct phases in their changing of cultural orientations:

1. *Ca 1834-57*. Negative orientations towards values of the outgroup were rigidly maintained by both the villagers and the foreign missionaries (see above, pp. 220-230). While several Central Europeans began to preach their Christian ideals in some villages and some Badagas were curious enough to listen not a single person was

converted, and there are no signs that Hindu orientations were modified in any significant way.

2. *1858-ca 1904*. This period saw the number of Badaga Christians slowly swell from one to just over a thousand. Converts were drawn from three social categories:

(i) poorer men attracted towards mission-held land, employment with European undertakings, perhaps even the chance of monetary disbursements or the charms of young Christian brides;

(ii) close relatives of people already converted;

(iii) boys and girls, especially orphans, who were receiving their education at mission schools.

All of the earliest conversions of Badagas angered and frightened fellow villagers, who were unable to tell why people should change their cultural orientations at all, or what the future social impact of such change might be. Despite the few conversions, both Badagas and missionaries held a negative attitude towards each other's ideals and company. Often a conversion brought an immediate retaliation from the convert's own village: either he was punished with ostracism, robbery, divorce, arson, or violent assault, or else he was captured and taken back from the mission to his old home. While there are no indications that any convert was made a prisoner in his natal village, it is clear that he was set free there after his enforced return in the expectation that he would automatically remain 'where he belonged' and revert to his former cultural orientations. In some cases this procedure did work; in others, he returned to the mission later on. The relatives of important men, mainly members of the gentry, usually met with much greater opposition to their becoming Christians than did poorer, less influential Badagas of either sex.

3. *Ca 1904-47*. It was during this half-century that the Christian community became recognized as a distinct caste-like grouping inferior to Badagas but superior to Kotas, and patterns of interaction between Hindu and Christian Badagas became formalized. But now that the latter were a separate social group, Roman Catholic priests (most of them from French provinces) were active here, mainly in converting Protestant Badagas, and thereby split the Christians into two culturally very similar but structurally opposed groups.

From the start of the twentieth century, then, the Christian community was viewed by other Badagas as a distinct stratum, and rigid patterns of interaction were formalized. This marked a big change from the general pattern of Hindu opposition in the late nineteenth century. During 1904-47 the Hindus, like Christians before them, became increasingly dependent on an economy and a labour market which ultimately were controlled by the British. As a result partly of this, partly of assigning the Christians to a separate phratry status, the former acts of violence towards Badaga Christians came to an end in 1904. As many Hindu Badagas now found it advantageous to show outwardly friendly attitudes towards the British, they could not at the same time be openly hostile to those following the religion of the British. As one Catholic priest said, 'The Badagas are not hostile to the Catholic religion; on the contrary, they willingly visit our churches and pray to our Saints, especially in places of pilgrimage. In 1938 a well-to-do Hindu Badaga built at his own cost a shelter for [Christian] pilgrims at Kotagiri' (Béchu 1948: 67).

Once Christians had become a separate phratry (with 12 clans; see Diag. 9, p. 115), and once the German missionaries had been expelled from India in January 1915, French Catholics as mentioned became very active – mainly in converting Protestant Badagas, in the absence of their German pastors – and thus split the Christians into two opposed groups, each one maintaining a self-righteous and antagonistic stance not only towards towards all Hindus but also towards the other Christian Church (Tignous 1911: 156; *Illustrated Catholic Missions* 1916, vol. 2: 8; Périé 1933: *passim*).

The first Catholic baptism, by Fr. Pottier, of a dying old Badaga near Wellington was recorded in 1873, just 15 years after the first Protestant conversion (Béchu 1948: 65). But then several subsequent converts apostasized. During the 1890s Fr. Robin did some itinerant preaching, much as the Basel missionaries had been doing over the preceding half-century. Thus he visited Lingayats in O:rana:yi, near Kollimale, for example, an area that was already being visited with some regularity by sisters of the Franciscan Missionaries of Mary in Ootacamund, who were much appreciated because they would bring medicine and cared for the sick (Tignous 1912: 156; Franciscan Missionaries of Mary, in Hockings 2012: 554-56). The local Catholic priests were active at first just within Ootacamund and Coonoor towns: as well as building churches, a school for 'native' boys was founded in Coonoor in 1865, and one for girls in 1875. St. Joseph's College was established in Wellington in 1885, then moved to Coonoor in 1890. Then in 1894 Fr. Foubert built a small chapel near the Badaga village of Hulikal; and 14 years later a

Badaga man was baptised there. Altogether, during the period 1892–1916, about a dozen Badaga families were baptised by the French Fathers Foubert, Robin, Deniau, and Gudin.[3] Although this Church had been catering for some time to the Tamilian plantation labourers working near Coonoor and around Hulikal, it was only during the period 1916-22 that a permanent Catholic foothold was established in a rural Badaga parish, and again in the Ke:ti area, right beside the scenes of Basel Evangelical successes, and thanks to the Missions-étrangères de Paris (Hockings 2012: 682-83). Now Fr. Foubert built a small chapel and presbytery there in Śa:ntu:r, baptising about fifty Badagas before he died. His successor, Fr. Tignous, continued this activity and built schools in several of the villages. It was he who got the Franciscan Missionaries of Mary to open St. Michael's Convent in 1927, also at Śa:ntu:r; to this convent a dispensary, an elementary school, and a girls' orphanage were attached (Béchu 1948: 111). In 1924 the Bishop of Coimbatore, Msgr Augustin Roy, came and baptised the Ke:ti headman and 38 other converts, thus bringing the Badaga Catholic total here to about a hundred. So when Tignous died in 1930, the Catholic Church was well established in the Ke:ti Valley and, perhaps with some hyperbole, the good Father was hailed as 'the Apostle of the Badagas' (ibid.: 67). The following year the church of St. Michael Archangel was built in place of the former chapel (with French financing) by Fr. Périé. Yet there were to be setbacks: 'No sooner had the church been completed, than a revolt arose among the local Badaga Catholics on the occasion of a mixed marriage of which they disapproved.' (Following on this, Fr. Périé was transferred to Gu:ḍalu:ru parish; ibid.: 67, 82). The school and other facilities near Ke:ti continue in operation to this day (ibid.: 65-69). By 1924 there were about a thousand Badaga Protestants and a hundred Roman Catholics (Société des Missions-étrangères 1924, vol. 3: 466). By 1938 the latter group had increased to 360.

4. *1947 till today.* The conversion of Hindus to either Christian sect virtually ceased with Independence, or of Protestants to Catholicism. But it was not the whole story. Over some thirty years since around 1935 an American couple, Pastor and Mrs. E.D. Willmott, succeeded in converting a few dozen Badagas – again mainly from the Protestant community – to the minority Seventh Day Adventist Church; by the 1970s it had some 200 Badaga members. Then the Naakubetta Bible Fellowship, a conservative Protestant organiza-

tion, emerged in the late 1970s from the evangelism of B.A. Belliraj; but it succumbed to pressures from the parent Church, and the name was changed to Nilgiri Blessing Mission. The members, who were recently baptized Christians, now (2013) number around 1300.

Today some intermarriage happens across these cultural divides,[4] while new orientations are being forged by *all* Badagas towards the larger Indian polity. After national Independence, although a few Badagas continued to become Adventists, the conversion of Hindus to the two major Christian sects came to a halt. There were conversions in the 1960s engineered by a Catholic priest (a Belgian) who was able to provide imported clothing, houses, CARE food packets and even a little land to new converts. But there are no more than a couple of hundred practising Roman Catholic Badagas today, and they have had much intermarriage with non-Badaga Catholics.

In general, the Christian population has continued to increase slowly, if only by the excess of births over deaths. In 2012 the Badaga Christian Association found there were some 4,500 Protestant Christians (*ca* 3 per cent of the Badaga total). While points of disagreement still exist between members of the two main sects (and this pre-eminently in ecclesiastical matters), as between Hindus and Christians in general, these are, it would seem, being obfuscated as other cultural orientations become more relevant to the changing living conditions. There are recent signs, from casual conversation, that the Badagas are adapting their orientations to a newly emerging pattern of social solidarity, one that links all Badagas, whether Christian or Hindu, in the face of competition with other Indians for possible government-bestowed benefits. Some Hindu Badagas, for instance, will now willingly admit that these Christians set them a good example – an allusion to their standards of honesty, hard work, education, and progressive treatment of the womenfolk that are admired in many modern Christians and that have made them a Westernizing model for other Badagas (Ranga 1934: 5-6).

At the end of the century it became apparent to those in the know that the most influential of all Badagas now was a Christian man, namely Dr. William Moses, recently the Bishop of Coimbatore. Belonging to a Gauḍa family that had been converted in 1909, Bishop Moses had been born in Mi:de:ṇu in 1935, studied at Serampore College, and in 1998 was elected Moderator of the Church of South India, thus becoming the nominal leader of some 2.8 million South Indian Christians.

THE ADVENT OF SCHOOLING

Whatever one may think about the missionaries' firmly-held belief that it was their sacred duty to try to convert Badagas to a new faith, there is no escaping the fact that both the French and the Swiss missions had a valuable and permanent impact on village education. Recent demographic literature has repeatedly concluded that there is a definite relationship between increasing levels of education (in particular for girls) and declining fertility. John Caldwell and his associates found in Karnataka, as I have seen amongst Badagas, that 'the cost of educating successive children over a short period' combined with the availability of family planning procedures does lead to a decline in fertility (Caldwell et al. 1988: 161). This progressive relationship has been summarized by Ghosh as follows:

> *Indirect Effects*: (*i*) schooling delays age at marriage and thereby the child-bearing span of female life; (*ii*) education helps acquisition of information on contraceptives and their use; (*iii*) education increases exposure to mass media and printed materials on family planning; (*iv*) education increases aspiration for upward mobility and accumulation of wealth and reduces the desirability of large families; (*v*) education increases employment prospects that compete with child-bearing; (*vi*) education reduces the perceived economic utility of children, thus lowering the demand for them; (*vii*) education facilitates communication between husband and wife that is conducive to lower fertility; (*viii*) education affects fertility by reducing infant and child mortality; and (*ix*) education provides a sense of self-efficacy and rationality that induces the use of contraception as a means of controlling one's life and destiny.
>
> *Direct effects*: Education is supposed to directly affect family size by influencing a broad spectrum of psychological attributes, including freedom from tradition, heightened aspirations, firm views concerning ideal family size, contraceptions, and other modern values. (Ghosh 1990: 24-25)

Because of Badaga access to schools, especially in the Ke:ti area and near the towns, their literacy rates have been much higher than the national rural rates ever since the later nineteenth century when comparative data first became available. Already in the Ke:ti Panchayat area in 1971 the (predominantly) Badaga literacy rate was 74 per cent for the males, and 47 per cent for females. By 2011 the literacy rate for the *whole district* was 85.65 per cent, including its urban population, of course; but we have no figure for the Badaga community, though it could be well above the district average. We know that in 2011 female literacy here was quite high at 79.44 per cent, and average rural literacy (for *all* Nilgiri groups and both sexes) was at a remarkable 81.67 per cent. (This compared with the national average for rural literacy in 2011 of 68.91 per cent, and 73.80 per cent in rural Tamil Nadu state generally.)

The school system in this state has recently provided for five years of elementary school, to be followed by three years of middle school and then three years of high school. The main aim of all diploma-covetous pupils is the Secondary School Leaving Certificate (S.S.L.C.), which can be gained in the final year of high school, and may aid in getting into a college. It is so prestigious a mark of attainment that not a few will own to being 'S.S.L.C. (failed)'; and I even recorded a couple of cases of Ke:ti Valley students who had committed suicide after failing it, and whose ghosts soon returned to haunt their relatives (Hockings 1980b: 164-67; 2012: 387-89).

As to the perceived purpose of education, my data are again in full agreement with the Caldwells and Reddy: 'We find education in rural south India to be favored both as a route to a nonfarming job and as a means of securing literacy and enlightenment. The educated can cope with the modern world and its bureaucrats more easily' (Caldwell et al. 1988: 164). This sentiment, which relates mainly to males, was prognosticated nearly two centuries ago in a resident's comment that, after two schools had been opened in 1821 and 1830, the students already felt they were fitted for something better in life than manual labour (Harkness 1832: 69-70).

Harkness's observation serves to introduce here the exceptional fact that Ke:ti has had an elementary school continuously since a devout benefactor, Judge George J. Casamajor, set one up in the year 1845, with 20 boys and two schoolmasters; and indeed, since 1901, that village had a higher elementary and later still a high school. Within a year of its founding, the first Ke:ti school came under the administration of the Basel Evangelical Mission, and continued so until those missionaries were expelled from India in 1915 (when the Wesleyans took it over). It may be added that by 1961, on the eve of my residence in that village, the Ke:ti Panchayat area had 16 primary schools, one middle school, one high school, and one (none too impressive) public library. Very recently, several private English-medium kindergartens have been established there, and no doubt this has happened in other villages too (Hockings 2012: 179, 279-86).

A brief chronology will serve to exemplify the development of Protestant-inspired education in this particular area during the nineteenth century. This list only identifies some of the milestones in what amounted to a quite remarkable development then for such a small rural area anywhere in India. Indeed, not many small villages in Canada, Australia, New Zealand, South Africa or USA contained any schools by the mid-nineteenth century.

1846 Missionaries running a 'parochial' school at Ke:ti, with 20 boys.
1849 Now a 'vernacular' school, with 77 boys and 6 girls.
1855 From this year on, Ke:ti had 2 schools, one 'parochial' with 10 boys and 4 girls, the other 'vernacular' with 6 boys.
1858 The first Badaga person, Abraham Halea, converted to Christianity. The vernacular school now had 103 boys, but the parochial school had only 7 boys and 3 girls.
1859 A teacher-training class in Ke:ti.
1867 Now 3 schools, as in most years down to 1881.
1870 Two day-schools and two night-schools.
1871 Mission boarding-school and orphanage established, with 5 boys and 3 girls.
1888 Teacher training school with 7 students; total now of 14 schools, with 333 boys and 9 girls altogether.
1890 English-medium school started with 6 boys.
1900 Now 26 schools in the Ke:ti area; also 5 seminaries and 5 training schools. Total pupils under instruction were 95 Christian boys, 30 Christian girls, 555 Hindu boys and 31 Hindu girls, altogether 711 pupils; plus 202 Sunday School students. In addition to these pupils, the Mission had a further 190 pupils in 6 schools in the Kotagiri area, 16 km ENE of Ke:ti.

Several features emerge from this listing. One is that although there were ups and downs in the enrolment figures for specific years in general there was a continuing expansion of the educational network that the Basel Mission was spreading in villages close to Ke:ti. A second point is that female education was never neglected, even though the great majority of Badaga parents then could see no point in sending their daughters to school, and for a while a small monetary inducement had to be offered. Furthermore, for over a century an English-medium education has been available in the village without travelling to a town. The system did not depend particularly on European teachers but, from 1859, undertook the training of local Christians (and not always Badagas) as teachers. Thus by 1900 there were four male and four female missionaries from Europe at Ke:ti; but 42 local Christian catechists and schoolmasters. The parish then contained 401 Protestants, over 10 per cent of whom were therefore employed in education. It seems that most of the schools were quite small, averaging 27 pupils in 1900. And because they were by then dispersed throughout two dozen Badaga hamlets near Ke:ti, they did succeed in bringing basic education, and no doubt plenty of biblical exposure, to the local people. Early in the last century we learn the Badaga schoolboys were 'eager for reading matter of any description' (Stone 1925: 20), and the missionaries of course supplied it.

While the Basel Evangelical Mission, a rather Lutheran organization, was the earliest and always the most dominant evangelizing agency in Badaga history, there was also another Protestant mission that had a further impact on these Ke:ti area villages. Catharine F. Ling, of the Church of England Zenana Mission, is well-known in local history as the person who, during 1904-40, formed the Toda Christian community by single-handedly converting 37 Toda tribal people (Walker 1986: 263–71; Walker, in Hockings 2012: 535-41). But beyond this she and Winifred Stone, an English colleague, did a certain amount of evangelical work in Badaga villages near Ka:ṭe:ri as well. At the same time Kišker̲ (Kishkar),[5] the first Toda Christian convert, was running a night school in or near Ka:ṭe:ri (Rivers 1906: Table 59; Stone 1925: 18-28; Walker, in Hockings 2012: 471-72). As Miss Stone observed, 'The men of this village are mostly attracted by that coveted goal of Indian ambition, Government service . . .' (Stone 1925: 28). Exactly fifty years later a Badaga delegation told the Backward Classes Commission: 'They feel that they are not adequately represented in Government services, in the public sector projects and particularly in the local offices. They attach great importance to Government service' (Backward Classes Commission 1975: 9).

In the face of all this evangelical activity the great majority of the Badaga population remained unconverted, of course, yet they absorbed several important lessons over the years from the agenda of these Mission schools, viz: (1) the value of literacy and numeracy; (2) a knowledge of the Bible stories; (3) some appreciation of the Christian morals and the extent to which they were actually exemplified in the behaviour of the missionary families; (4) an association between being a Christian European and having a perceptibly higher standard of living than any Badaga villagers; (5) some grasp of the European work ethic; (6) a firm awareness that those with schooling could get low-level clerical jobs, or become catechists, overseers on plantations and schoolteachers; and (7) some understanding of how German, Swiss and British family relationships differed from those of Badagas.

The progressive effects of this local education and the desire for modernization among ordinary villagers are clearly reflected in the impressions of one English missionary some 90 years ago – a lady who had worked for many years in the Toda Christian mission:

> . . . the Badagas are a naturally industrious, go-ahead people, often working as rickshaw coolies, builders, road-menders, etc., in order to supplement the scanty income they earn by cultivation of their little fields and the sale of their crops. Many Badaga boys, not content with the education to be had in their own villages, tramp over the hills many miles daily to attend the C.M.S. Higher Elementary or the Municipal High School at Ootacamund, or the Wesleyan Higher Elementary School at Kaity [i.e. the former Basel Mission school at Ke:ti]. They thus pick up a limited knowledge of English and a less limited knowledge of the newspapers, and so learn of the trend of thought in their own country and beyond. (Stone 1925: 25)

No doubt all such developments had started nearly two centuries ago; but they continued throughout the entire twentieth century, bringing to thousands of modern Badagas a non-traditional view of the relations between work, education and family ties, even among those who did not actually attend the Mission schools themselves. I would suggest that the household structure and personal aspirations in this area have been modified in modern times in the direction of Western models which have now been visible in Ke:ti itself for over a century-and-a-half.

Rural education was thus quite a success, for it had had a long history, here thanks chiefly to the efforts of the Basel Mission; and we are told that, fairly recently,

> In a memorandum submitted . . . [to the Backward Classes Commission], it is stated that they [Badagas] have 1,500 graduates, including 50 Engineers, 30 Doctors and 30 Lawyers. For a community of their size this is an impressive achievement. In high schools also their numbers are impressive. A large number of their graduates and under-graduates are employed as teachers in high schools and elementary schools. (Backward Classes Commission 1975: 9)

The implications of these developments are broad and far reaching, and proclaim the emergence here of an urbanizing middle class (which has expanded perceptibly since that 1975 Report). No doubt this emergence has ruffled feathers among some other local groups, who have commonly viewed it as occurring at their own expense:

> In short, the Baḍagas are the true opportunists of the Nilgiris. Their drive, shrewdness, energy, unscrupulousness, opportunism and sheer numerical outflow are misunderstood, resented, and hated by most other tribals, particularly by the Kotas, but also by Kuṟumbas, Iṟulas and Todas. They have evoked the distaste, displeasure, distrust and enmity of the other communities. Clashes were reported and disputes became the topic of the narrative lore of the other groups. (Zvelebil 1982: 62)

Taking a long-term view, the Kota schoolmaster K. Sulli put this matter succinctly: 'When people from Mysore went on just joining the Badagas year by year, just they came to fill up our (inc.) country (lit., they became full in our country) . . . The Kotas, the Todas, the Kurumbas became ruined' (Emeneau 1946: 260-61, lines 43-44, trans.; cf. Mandelbaum, in Hockings 2012: 863-81). But nowadays the Kotas are emulating modern Badagas in many respects (although not in forming a Christian community), as the latter group continue to flourish.

NOTES

1. On the Justice party, see Dirks 2001: 242-43. The great majority of people in this Presidency were not Brahmins and looked upon them as ancient incursors from the north; and yet we know, 'In Madras the civil service and the professions were dominated almost completely by Brahmins. . . .'; Béteille 1969: 35, also 50-52, 164-68, 173-79.
2. Another village had three headmen when its anti-music faction divided into two groups over another matter; these two and the music faction each had a separate headman.
3. These Fathers had all come to India from provincial towns in France: never a Parisian among them! (Béchu 1948: 134-35, 139, 142). The full names were François-Frédéric Deniau (born 24 Feb. 1869 in Le Mans, died 30 Oct. 1909 in Coimbatore); Edmond Jean Baptiste Foubert (born 7 March 1850 at Cambrai, died 22 Dec. 1922 in Montbeton); Jules-Théophile Gudin (born 6 Aug. 1850 at Belley, died 9 April 1916 in Wellington); Jean-Marie-Julien Pottier (born 30 April 1822 in Rennes, died 15 June 1902 in Wellington); Marie-Louis Robin (born 16 Feb.

1865 in Besançon, died 26 July 1909 in Montbeton); Augustin-Antoine Roy (born 21 Jan. 1863 in Poitiers, died 21 Dec. 1937 in Wellington); and Henri-Pierre Joseph-Arthur Tignous (born 29 Jan. 1872 in Toulouse, died during 1930 in Montbeton). The Mission has long maintained a sanatorium at Montbeton, Déptt. Tarn-et-Garonne, in the southwest of France. During the period when these priests retired to that village the population was under 1,000.

4. In the twenty-first century there have even been a few cases of Badagas marrying with Moslems, of either sex, and with Bengali women.
5. He is referred to in a Toda song. Emeneau (1971: 813, Song 210, vs. 6) notes this about him: 'He taught Christian doctrine, as a catechist. He was the first Christian convert . . . , son of three brothers. . . .' It is tantalizing to speculate how this son of three brothers would in all likelihood have been teaching about the Son of a virgin mother to small Badaga audiences which sometimes included the sons of two or even three mothers! That communication would have indeed been intriguing for everyone.

CHAPTER 15

Some Promising Transitions since 1900

NEW FORMS OF TRANSPORTATION

The idea of communication embraces the physical facilities of road and rail transportation, postal and telegraph services, as well as the mass media of radio, film, newspaper, television and the Internet; and also the channels for communication between individuals within a local setting (to be dealt with in the next chapter). Let us review here briefly how the transportation infrastructure has changed over the past century.

Regular improvements in transportation have enabled production and sale of new cash crops, as well as the movement of people. In the nineteenth century all goods had to be carried up or down the long Nilgiri escarpment by coolies, in ox panniers, on horseback, or in bullock-carts.[1] Faced with such restrictions Badagas were scarcely able to export produce to other parts of India in those days (Grigg 1880: 480). Then in 1899 a rack-railway was completed from Coimbatore to Coonoor (a remarkable engineering achievement, one first broached by Ouchterlony in 1851), and by 1908 this had reached to Ootacamund (Hockings 2012: 751). Its construction had involved Badaga contractors and labourers, giving many their first experience of earning regular wages. When the 1914-18 War began there was thus a quick means of exporting vegetables to all parts of India and even beyond, where soldiers were in need of them, and the Badaga farmers benefitted from this.

The first car to be owned by a British resident of Ootacamund was possibly a 1904 Franklin light touring-car;[2] and in that same year twelve local gentlemen founded the Nilgiri Automobile Association. Then in 1905 their first 'motor meet' was held, with six cars in attendance (Eagan 1916: 86). Badagas were at first quite put out by the innovation: 'The car sped along with a warning hum that cleared the road of pedestrians. Frightened of the devil-carriage that ran without horses, any native who might have been on the road, left it and hid in the scrub-jungle till the fearsome machine had passed'; this according to a local novelist, Fanny Penny (1913: 351). So good were the Nilgiri roads by now that annual car races around the district were held for some years, to the undoubted amazement of most villagers. During the 21 years between the two World Wars lorries became common in the district, and roads were further improved to accommodate them (Hockings 2012: 792-95). A few Badagas who became middlemen bought lorries to improve their business. At the same time a bus service began, and in the years since World War II the network of bus routes has become so complex that there is now scarcely any Badaga village without a bus service to one of the towns. Diesel pollution of the local air is no longer an insignificant matter, however: about three hundred routes are travelled (in 2000) within the district, some by several competing companies, and there are a further 40 long-distance services.[3]

No airport has ever been constructed within the district for want of level terrain; Coimbatore has the nearest commercial one, some 88 km. from Ootacamund.

AGRICULTURAL CHANGE OVER THE PAST CENTURY

Until 1863 the Badagas not only cultivated their long-established fields close to the villages but also practiced shifting agriculture in the wooded areas. At that time the government abolished, at least formally, the system of swidden cultivation, which thereby posed a serious threat to those Badaga farmers who had depended on it. According to government experts swidden farming was wasteful of timber resources and led to soil erosion. More significant, though, was an eagerness encouraged among British settlers to cover wide tracts of the district with tea and coffee plantations. In 1863 the British abolished the revenue system current in the Kundena:ḍ area,[4] one that had involved issuing a license for each hoe and each plough without otherwise taxing or delimiting the land a man could cultivate or recording what acreage he was entitled to use. Until these restrictions came into effect many Badaga farmers had made periodic use of lands five to ten times as extensive as their revenue assessments justified.[5] By about 1880 these restrictions, legislated during 1862-64, had become realities in all parts of the Nilgiris.

The rapidly increasing Badaga population was now faced with a depleted acreage of usable farmland, a situation that would worsen through erosion and land sales. For the first time in history their fields, once surveyed and registered in accordance with the Land Settlement rules (completed by 1877), came to have a monetary value – especially as, under the Waste Land Rules, a man's land could be auctioned and thus irretrievably lost if he became too much in arrears with the payment of land revenue. A farmer therefore tried to hold on to as much registered land as he could.[6]

The land legislation did not cause an immediate shortage of land among the Badagas. On the contrary, Grigg noted (1880: 480) that in the 1870s land had been so 'cheap' that the Badagas who did own some or bought more tried to cultivate areas that were too large for their resources, meaning that the labour and capital were spread too thinly across the land to produce adequate returns. The slim yield of soil not properly fertilized and skimpy cultivation of too large a plot impelled the poorer farmers of the late nineteenth or early twentieth centuries to sell land to British planters (see below, p. 270), or to try new occupations so as to earn enough cash to maintain themselves and pay the revenue that their land was assessed for (Shortt & Ouchterlony 1868: 64; Grigg 1880: 325, 471, 480; Ranga 1934: 11-14). Those people who were made landless by restrictions on swidden cultivation in the forest, and also the labour surplus of the rapidly expanding immigrant population, thus had to work in the plantations for wages, which they mostly used to buy grain in the markets. But by 1870 some Badagas were starting to get contracts as construction gangs and labourers on the new acacia and eucalyptus plantations, a few of the women were plucking tea-leaf or coffee-beans and young boys could be seen breaking stones by the roadside.[7]

Early in the twentieth century most Badaga families still owned and cultivated land within 2 km. of their homes. That land was often hilly and always unirrigated. There was relatively little terracing on the hill-slopes (Grigg 1880: 470), and most tilling was still done with ploughs and oxen.[8] The best fields lay in the valley flats, not so much because of the proximity of stream water as because of the rich deposit of topsoil. Badagas had long recognized the differences in soils and terrain, both when choosing where to plant crops and when dividing up the patrimony. Soil distinctions were important to them, but distance from the home was even more significant. Land was therefore categorized by Badagas primarily as home-farm (i.e.

within a half-kilometre), outfield, or forest clearings.[9] The first type got much of the cattle manure and all human refuse; more distant land received little manure and was often left fallow (Grigg 1880: 319-20, quoting from a Revenue Board Report probably of 1863); forest clearings were never manured and might lie fallow for several years. Weeding, like manuring, was for the most part confined to the more valuable crops grown near the home (on agriculture in general, see Hockings 2012: 2-8).

Most of the *cultivable* land had long belonged to Badagas; in the mid-nineteenth century it amounted to 12,750 ha., of which some 6,900 ha. were cultivated every year; but 30 years later 'the occupied area of the plateau has trebled itself . . . mainly due to the extension of cultivation by the Badaga villagers'.[10] At the same time, 'by 1905, eighty per cent of the lands of Ootacamund taluk and forty per cent of Coonoor taluk were declared reserved in over 400 small and large patches under the Madras Forest Act of 1882' (Prabhakar & Gadgil 1995: 162). During the next century nearly all land under subsistence crops (barley, millets and wheat) as well as plateau land growing market vegetables and fruits was farmed by Badagas and Kotas, while a majority of the land for to tea, coffee and cinchona was in British-owned plantations (Muthiah, in Hockings 2012: 709-16). Few reliable figures exist for the total area under crop.[11]

> Major changes in crop emphasis from the late 1800s to the present are best revealed by statistics [relating mainly to] Badaga cultivation. In 1875 there were 15,728 acres of Italian millet, 4,662 acres of little millet, 3,761 acres of barley, 3,430 acres of finger millet, 3,199 acres of wheat, only 754 acres of potatoes, 355 acres of mustard, 169 acres of vegetables, 144 acres of fenugreek, 67 acres of horse gram . . . , and 66 acres of poppies grown on the Nilgiris (Grigg *et al.* 1880: xii). In 1895 Italian millet was still the leading crop, but potato acreage had risen to 2,032 acres. Poppies outlawed by the 1878 Opium Act were no longer grown (Benson 1895: 432-433). Little millet had become the most cultivated cereal in 1905, and finger millet was growing in importance (Francis 1908: 164) . . . In 1914 there were about 4,000 acres with potatoes on the Nilgiris, but by 1920 potato acreage had doubled (Rao and Azariah 1953: 69). Before 1925 finger and little millets became the two important cereal crops, and remained the leading cereals from that time (Wood 1927: 210-223). Potato acreage has continually increased: by 1938 there were 12,000 acres, by 1950 almost 17,000 acres, and in 1960-61 there was a total of 20,600 acres in the main season and 2,400 acres in the lesser (Rao and Azariah 1953: 69; Krishnamurthi 1953: 193) . . . (from Noble 1968: 133-34; 1 ac. = 0.4 ha.)

Some figures might be presented[12] to further illustrate the shift in importance of various crops on the entire plateau from 1905 to 1940 (Table 7). These figures, derived from two official sources (Francis 1908: 164; Madras 1949: 976), show the percentage of the total cultivated area devoted to each crop. It may be noticed that while the figures for each (then undivided) *taluk* in 1905-06 total 100 per cent, those for 1940-41 exceed 100 per cent. This discrepancy reflects one important change in the 35-year period: mixed cropping became a fairly common practice. Thus two crops represented in Table 7 by separate figures would sometimes be growing simultaneously on the same piece of land.

There were very slight changes in the crop pattern for wheat, barley, finger millet and spices. A small area of pulses appeared only in the later figures (though pulses had in fact been grown in the nine-

Table 7: The Nilgiri Plateau: Cropping Change, 1905-40

	*Percentage of total cropped area**			
	Coonoor Taluk (Poranga:ḍ and Me:kuna:ḍ)		*Ootacamund Taluk (Todana:ḍ and Kundena:ḍ)*	
	1905-06	*1940-41*	*1905-06*	*1940-41*
Mainly subsistence crops:				
Wheat	1.7%	2.8%	2.9%	3.3%
Barley	5.1%	2.7%	3.4%	4.2%
Finger millet	1.5%	1.9%	7.1%	4.5%
Slender millet	14.7%	6.3%	4.3%	6.2%
Other grains	13.1%	0.7%	27.8%	1.1%
Pulses	–	1.9%	–	0.5%
Cash crops:				
Vegetables (mainly potato) and fruits	5.2%	18.6%	3.9%	30.3%
	(potato: 4.8%)	–	(potato: 3.2%)	–
Spices, condiments	0.3%	0.7%	0.9%	1.1%
Coffee	44.6%	25.6%	18.1%	15.8%
Tea	7.7%	42.7%	12.8%	32.3%
Cinchona	1.1%	0.8%	10.9%	4.0%
Miscellaneous 'industrial plants'	4.7%	5.9%	7.9%	6.6%

Note: *All percentages are based on acreage.

teenth century). As malaria became less of a problem and treatments other than quinine began to appear in India the importance of cinchona decreased, but that was mainly on the British-run plantations (Philip 2003: 238-273). The miscellaneous 'industrial' plants, mainly eucalyptus, maintained a stable acreage.

These slight fluctuations perhaps tell us little, but there is much more to tell. 'By 1881-1882, 50 per cent of the total area cultivated was under cash crops' (Sutton 2009: 104). The various millets lost much of their significance, even though these had previously been among the staples for Badagas. Their land was planted with potatoes instead – especially after the start of World War I. There were about 1,600 ha. under potato on the plateau in 1914 and, as we have noticed, by 1920 that figure had been doubled (Hanumantha Rao and Azariah 1953: 69), a reflection of wartime demand. In the 35-year period spanned by Table 7 potatoes, along with several minor vegetables, increased their acreage some five- or six-fold. Badagas did not eat much potato; clearly they sacrificed most of the acreage traditionally devoted to staple grains to grow marketable vegetables for cash instead. Whether their diet had improved is not clear. By World War II a mere 3 per cent of the entire Nilgiri population were subsisting primarily on millets; the other 97 per cent depended on purchased rice (Krishnaswami 1947: 464). Coffee was no longer a successful crop in most parts of the plateau because of winter frost, and much of that plantation land was later given over to tea. Together with the development of the first Badaga tea plantations from about 1925 onward, this explains the vast increase in tea acreage over the 35-year period covered in Table 7 (Ranga 1934: 18-22).

For perhaps a century this district had a dual economy: a subsistence economy centred on the villages of Todas, Kotas, Badagas and other local groups; and a capitalist plantation economy responsive to a world market, with its auctions, wholesale prices, mechanisation, and quality standards. Only in the last quarter of the twentieth century did the two economies start to coalesce as farmers of the indigenous groups planted tea cuttings in their fields and began to move toward managing small plantations with better profit margins than the more traditional crops had been yielding.

At first the plantation crops called for more expertise than Badagas could usually muster, and so were mostly confined to European land-holdings; even so, some Badagas were growing tea and a little coffee in the late 1920s (Ranga 1934: 2). But potato was relatively easy to cultivate, especially as a government farm within the district continued to help them with seed, fertilizers and technical advice.[13] During the past eighty years some of the more enterprising Badagas (mainly those able to obtain financial credit) have successfully cultivated tea and coffee on estates both large and small, though this was initially a ruse of theirs to increase the value of their land before selling it to Europeans.[14] Tea has even replaced potato recently.

Chemical fertilizers were first being used sporadically during the early 1920s; before that only cow dung and human refuse had been available (Shortt & Ouchterlony 1868: 44; Grigg 1880: 468; Ranga 1934: 14). These chemicals led to much higher yields in the European vegetable crops and helped confirm the belief that growing food for the market could become a profitable occupation. Improved seeds, notably potato, and insecticides were also adopted by the Badagas (Nambiar 1965: 23), farmers who were 'always willing to test any new method of cultivation, or new crops brought to their notice by the Nilgiri Horticultural Society' (Thurston & Rangachari 1909, vol. 1: 76, quoting from the *Pioneer*, 4 Oct. 1907).

After adoption of fertilizer, insecticide and good seed came the construction of more terraces on some sloping fields. Progress in terracing, however, was much slower than the adoption of other innovations because it demanded a greater capital outlay than many farmers could afford; and most did not possess more than a quarter-hectare of land anyway. Even today some cultivated slopes that badly need terracing because of soil erosion remain unterraced. It is worth noting that in the past several decades the situation has much improved because of the state government's making loans available on relatively easy terms for terrace construction work (Grigg 1880: 470; Ranga 1934: 12-13; Mudaliar 1957: 18; Hockings 1999: 217).

As a result of terracing in many places and minute subdivision elsewhere, fields are usually so small that it has become inefficient, if not impossible, to plough them. For over sixty years therefore the plough and oxen have rarely been seen on the plateau (Ranga 1934: 12-13; Vivekanandam Pillai 1937: 249; Noble 1968: 144-45; see below, pp. 318, 338). Much of the work-load formerly carried by the oxen was taken up by cheap migrant labourers from the plains, mainly from Coimbatore District; men worked for daily wages a little higher than those of women (perhaps Rs. 50 and 40 in 2000). In the twenty-first century, though, the situation has changed dramatically, and is reflected in the surprising fact that the district population, 762,141 in 2001, had *decreased* by 27,000 to 735,071 in 2011: this drop of 3.35 per cent in ten years is unique in Tamil Nadu. Farm labourers and plantation workers have recently been leaving the district in droves for the better-paid jobs now available across the South Indian plains on construction sites; others have simply retired to their home villages in the plains. Over the same period the Badaga population was at a virtual standstill, as my book *Kindreds of the Earth* (1999) had predicted: in 1991 the Indian census counted 134,187 Badagu speakers, while by 2001 this figure had increased by only 327 people, to 134,514. But doubtless hundreds of other Badagas have left for employment opportunities beyond the district boundaries, especially in Bangalore and in various towns of Coimbatore District, and were thus not included in the later figure. Many villages seem almost devoid of younger men nowadays, as houses get locked up and their brightest youngsters have gone off to take up professional jobs across India or are migrating overseas. Farming no longer holds promise of a desirable future.

While profits from potato, tea and coffee acreage have been much higher than from the traditional grain crops the risks are also greater. Not only does one need ready cash for seed or cuttings, fertilizer and labour, but reserve cash too to feed the family should disease ruin the crop during a season. Here the cooperative societies set up under state government guidance have helped Badagas somewhat, although less than might be expected. Short-term loans are available against land securities for all the members of such a society,[15] and long-term loans are obtainable from the Land Mortgage Bank (established locally in 1937; Hockings 2012: 223-24; Heidemann 2006: 235-42).

In earlier times the money lender (a Tamilian Chettiār or Labbai, a northern Mārwāri or Moslem 'Afghan') was an ominous figure in the lives of all too many Badagas; for some he still is. Early in the last century the monthly interest on his loans ranged from 3 per cent to 12.5 per cent of the principal, but though these rates were quite extortionate loans were in general repaid (Thurston & Rangachari 1909, vol. 1: 64; Madras 1928: 55; Ranga 1934: 4). But in the nineteenth century not even these loan facilities were available to the Badagas: usually they could only borrow from wealthy Badagas, preferably someone related to the borrower by marriage but living in a village at some discreet distance from him. No interest would be charged on such loans then (Anonymous 1879: 148).

The first Badaga cooperative society was formed at Kereha:ḍa in 1911, the 'Kerhada Rice Rural Credit Society', named in honour of Mr. S.P. Rice, a former Collector who had initiated interest in the cooperative movement. At that time annual interest rates varied between 24 and 75 per cent of the principal. In 1912 an Act was passed for the establishment of societies with purposes other than credit. By 1918 there were 18 such societies here, and by 1927 the Nilgiris had 54 agricultural credit societies from which the Badagas could obtain loans (Madras 1928: 55-57; Vivekanandam Pillai 1937: 249). By about 1920, however, the Badaga cooperators

> could no longer hope to repay the loan from their earnings and in almost all cases they have had to part with their property for clearing their loans. The malady was aggravated by the imperfect education in co-operation imparted and the want of adequate supervision and control in the beginning. It was then realized that co-operative credit alone was not the remedy and attempts were made to secure for these tribes their necessaries of life at moderate price and save them from the clutches of the unscrupulous shopkeepers. A Purchase and Sale Society was started in 1919, which in 1923 convened itself into the Potato Growers' Purchase and Sale Society and attempted to control the market for potatoes with a view to secure a fair price for the potato crop. In 1924 a Labour Union was organized for their benefit. But all these steps proved of no avail. Want of loyalty on their part led to the collapse of the former in 1925. The latter society is doing no work now. Attempts are now being made to increase their earning capacity by introducing among the Badagas sericulture and improved poultry farming. . . . (Madras 1928: 56)

In 1954 the Reserve Bank of India initiated nation-wide an 'integrated scheme of rural credit' which tied the granting of loans to the marketing of the crop, rather than to the amount of land available as security. The scheme was introduced in the Nilgiri cooperatives.

> The controlled credit scheme works through a linking of the village primary societies, the Nilgiris District Central Cooperative Bank, and the Nilgiris Marketing Society. The village primary societies (and individual members of the Marketing Society) get their seeds and manure from the Marketing Society; the Marketing Society sends the relevant indents and loan applications to the Central Bank for sanction; the members market their harvests (at least enough to cover the loans) through the Marketing Society; the Marketing Society sends the sales proceeds to the Central Bank; the Central Bank deducts the loans and sends the balance to the village primary societies or individual members.

> One difficulty in the scheme is that the maximum amount which any society can lend to an individual member is Rs. 2,000. Even at the inadequate rate of Rs. 500 per acre, members can get through cooperative channels only enough finance for the cultivation of four acres. In the various societies which I visited in the Nilgiris, the officers usually were substantial people with well more than four acres. It was a curious situation to find them put in a position where to meet their current needs, they had to go to private sources. . . . They told me that they got about half of their credit from the society and the other half from the private merchant-moneylenders. Although they sold some of their produce to the marketing society, they usually sold the major portion through the private merchants. They explained that the merchants gave them much more credit than they could get from the society, on condition that they sell their produce through the merchants. They said that the cooperatives were rather inflexible about extending loans, whereas they could count on the merchants to carry them through a bad season or two. When there is a crop failure, they have to go to the private merchant and borrow from him to pay back their loan to the cooperative society. . . . To them this was a kind of "cooperation" and was more important than anything else.
>
> By contrast, when their loans became overdue, the cooperative society cut off their credit. The societies went by rules and regulations which did not benefit the members. They said that from the societies they did not get real cooperation.
>
> These statements did not conflict with what I had been told earlier in the best cooperative agricultural bank in the Nilgiris. There members and office-bearers told me that the rules laid down by Government for the co-operatives were very hard and stringent. They tied the hands of the working officials who would like to do more. Everything was rules and circulars; there was no leeway, no room for initiative. What was crucial was the Government loan, the Government grant, the Government subsidy.
>
> Lest this seem an exaggeration, it may be observed that in Ootacamund there are no less than four Deputy-Registrars of Cooperative Societies; one is General Deputy-Registrar; another is Special Deputy-Registrar to supervise credit and agricultural marketing; a third is in charge of the Cooperative Central Bank; and the fourth runs the Marketing Society. (Thorner 1964: 71-73)

The law by 1970 limited the *monthly* interest on pawned items to a rate varying from 0.75 to 1.5 per cent, depending on the size of the loan. Even so, loans between Badagas might command an interest rate of 1 to 4 per cent per month; while the professional money lenders also secretly charge interest beyond what they are entitled to. Thus on a loan of up to Rs. 20,000, for example (1970 figures), the Mārwāri lender could legally charge only 1.5 per cent per month simple interest. He would give a receipt for that rate but at the same time insist on one year's interest in advance, and compounded, at 2 per cent per month. One should hardly castigate the Mārwāri for his cupidity, or the Badaga for still patronizing him, however, when one learns about the bribes that some local officials have expected in return for granting loans from a cooperative bank.

Yet in the Nilgiris District by 1989 there were three urban cooperative banks, 64 branches of cooperative wholesale stores, as well as 24 thrift and credit societies (and perhaps more today). The cooperative movement has gone a long way towards protecting Badagas from the high interest rates of private moneylenders; the Panchayat Unions and some multi-purpose societies also help farmers by supplying fertilizers, insecticides and modern equipment at cost prices. If these societies operate somewhat more effectively here than in other parts of India, the explanation lies in the fact that the Badaga societies are not in practice *multi-caste* institutions, and the Badagas are relatively well-educated. Societies are run largely by and for the members of this one community, thus avoiding some of the factionalism and favouritism that have commonly pervaded such societies elsewhere in India.

MODERN SYSTEMS OF MARKETING

With the spread of urbanization in the mid-nineteenth century, other markets besides the one at Ootacamund began to cater to the needs of local villagers. Thus regular weekly markets opened at Coonoor, Kotagiri, Wellington, and later in several villages at some distance from any town.[16] The use of these markets by the Badagas is related to two other developments discussed earlier: first, the payment of land revenues and the restriction on use and extension of land caused by the Land Settlement and legislation to stop swidden farming in the forests; and secondly, the consequent movement of numerous Badaga labourers, including women and children, onto the tea and coffee plantations, where they earned a cash wage (Grigg 1880: 34, 471; see above, p. 265).

Greatly increased contact with markets and with Europeans provided the impetus towards full participation in the cash economy, though this transition took a century to complete. For most people the basic requirements of food, goods and services continued to be provided either by their own efforts or by their Toda, Kota and Kur̲umba associates. The itinerant Chetti traders continued to make their monthly visits, though today probably no longer do so anywhere. From 1825 onwards Badaga men could also visit local markets on the plateau for what they had previously bought in Guṇḍulupēṭe and Ka:ramuḍu, but they never sold very much in the markets and thus rarely had spare cash to spend.

In the early days of cash-crop farming few Badagas had enough knowledge or personal contacts to arrange the bulk sale of their produce in a distant market, so they would sell their crops instead to a broker in the Nilgiris; until they learnt that a farmer who could find a market in the plains and negotiate a sale by himself would make bigger profits. An important motivation was the desire to acquire consumer goods that were now becoming available on a scale and in a variety never before known here. Later in the nineteenth century there is evidence of growing affluence that found expression in the shift from thatched to tiled rooves, and from mud-and-wattle to brick construction. '. . . [In] 1871 only 1,914 houses out of the 13,922 in the district were tiled; whereas now [1908] tiles are the rule . . . in Badaga villages' (Francis 1908: 130; cf. Shortt & Ouchterlony 1868: 58; Grigg 1880: 29, 225; 'Geofry' 1881: 132; Pl. 3). For the farming family busy marketing their crops, cash was necessarily the only medium of exchange, and much of their foodstuffs had to be bought in a town bazaar. A great variety of items was also being purchased, the most obvious of which were new clothes: in the 1890s men first began to sport European-style shirts and jackets, and in the 1930s women started to wear coloured *sāris* (BEMS 1897, no. 58: 90; Hockings 1979: *passim*; 2012: 226-33).

We might say that Badaga commitment to the cash economy was complete by about 1930, in which year most of them permanently severed the traditional exchange relationship with Kotas. This from the Badaga point of view was an advantageous move, for it allowed them to buy pottery, rope and metal goods in the bazaar at a lower price than the Kotas commanded, and without delays. While the Kotas had not actually been receiving cash, the traditional dole of grain they were given at each harvest was becoming increasingly valuable to the Badagas because of rising grain prices (Mandelbaum 1955: 240).

For many Badagas with small landholdings the transitional period between the two World Wars was marked by the frustrations of continuing indebtedness. Pieces of their land were sometimes sold to non-Badagas in order to pay off outstanding debts, a previously inconceivable practice; and there were always planters ready to buy. Some men went as far away as the Anaimalai Hills for labouring jobs. Badaga debtors did however work hard to produce profitable cash crops or at least to buy back some of their former lands if they could (Thurston & Rangachari 1909, vol. 1: 64; Ranga 1934: 4).

With the First World War, major changes in marketing practices became apparent. Tea, coffee and cinchona, like potato, presuppose a broad market beyond the Nilgiri Hills, which in turn presupposes adequate transportation. The crucial demand for vegetables to feed the numerous European troops in India, Burma, Malaya and Ceylon stimulated the change in crops documented above (Table 7). Similar conditions arose once more in the Second World War and prompted many more Badagas to try commercial farming. On each occasion cultivators took the risk of exporting potatoes and other vegetables to new and more distant markets, and some made handsome profits (Francis 1908: 167). The risks in this enterprise were real, for men could recall occasions when floods broke the road or rail connections, or the goods reached their destination only after market prices had fallen heavily. The rewards of potato cultivation were however of critical importance in lifting the yoke of indebtedness. During World War II the British administration made a great deal of capital available to Badaga farmers, as part of the Agriculture Department's 'Grow More Food' campaign, and then the independent provincial government continued this programme. This finance, and the profits from selling their highly priced potatoes, did more than any cooperative loan facility to relieve the indebtedness that Badagas had been suffering under for at least half-a-century. One former British resident, on visiting Nanjena:ḍu in 1949, was much impressed with the place and referred to it correctly as 'the largest [village] in this part of the Nilgiris. The intense building activity here was eloquent testimony of the period of prosperity through which these cultivators of potatoes are passing' (Wynter-Blyth 1949: 254).

While tea and coffee yield a higher profit per hectare than potatoes or grains, they are more susceptible to disease than the millets and require greater agricultural skill than all other Nilgiri crops, if they are to attain the standards required by the wholesale purchasing agents. Moreover they need to be produced in large enough quantity to warrant the processing and transportation to Bombay (and after 1940, to Cochin; but recently the auctions have been held in Coonoor). Middlemen, some of them Badagas, were therefore indispensable to the few Badaga tea and coffee growers of the 1920s and 1930s. These middlemen could act as a control on quality and could gather together sufficient produce to make their transaction with an exporter worthwhile. As more and more Badagas became interested in the growing of cash crops, middlemen appeared not only to buy up small quantities of tea, coffee and potato but also to sell the farmers seed, fertilizer and even some insurance.

After Independence profiteering by the middlemen was largely checked by the Nilgiri Cooperative Marketing Society, set up with provincial government aid (Vivekanandam Pillai 1937: 249). Today there are numerous cooperative societies in the Nilgiris which pool the resources of members and also supply cheap fertilizer. Many such societies own local tea-processing factories and warehouses, and are dominated by Badagas. After 1957 heavy loss through potato disease caused a widespread shift to tea or coffee growing,[17] and in the 1970s large acreages were devoted to growing a sturdy new German variety of cabbage which could be trucked off to markets nationwide. Both tea and cabbage were quite successful crops (but see below, p. 339). The availability of help from the Central Cooperative Bank made these unexpected switches in crops possible, for otherwise the initial capital outlay and the small size of most estates would have rendered the new ventures unfeasible. Several cottage industries have also helped diversify the rural economy over the past thirty years or so; in particular beekeeping, (illicit) liquor distilling, milk sales, knitting and embroidery have provided new and regular sources of income for many hundreds of Badaga households.

The early twentieth century saw the rise not only of wealthy Badaga landowners but also of some large-scale labour contractors. A few men profitted by getting the contracts for gangs to dig pits for planting tea-cuttings, pick coffee-beans, cut sections of the new railway, build roads or construct public buildings in the district.[18] The less wealthy Badagas set themselves up as small shopkeepers, tailors or even moneylenders, or found work in a wide variety of urban trades, especially teaching.[19] Whenever possible the more resourceful reinvested their profits in land (Ranga 1934: 10), either tea and coffee estates or farm plots which had formerly belonged to Kotas

(Mandelbaum 1955: 240). Another reinvestment strategy sometimes chosen was in college education for their sons. With the Nilgiri economy fully monetized emphasis was now placed on providing stability for the coming generations.

MODERN EMPLOYMENT

Prior to World War I virtually all Badaga households were cultivating, and the great majority still do today. Here the family has always been the basic unit of production. As much as five months of the year are spent non-productively (Ranga 1934: 9-10), however, but during the other months every member of the household, even a child, would make a contribution to the traditional family economy. Adults work in the fields, helped by boys and girls when necessary (Harkness 1832: 114-15). Men do the heavier work, such as forking soil, ploughing or clearing stones, while women do the lighter work, mainly planting, weeding and harvesting (Ward 1821: lxx, lxxiii; Jagor 1876: 201-02; Anonymous 1879: 149; Ranga 1934: 8; Noble 1968: 143-48). As well as their field-work women are responsible for cooking and for all the housekeeping, including the laundry.[20] Adolescent boys work as cowherds; girls take care of babies whose mothers are out in the fields (Harkness 1832: 113). Children or their grandparents also do the initial preparation of meals before these women return home each day. Those people too old to work in the fields just stay at home minding the children and keeping an eye on what passes within the village (Jagor 1876: 194).

This traditional pattern has been very much modified by school requirements and a trend among the more educated men to work away from the village. At first a few were employed in the towns as peons, clerks, builders and labourers, and throughout the district as primary-school teachers.[21] During the First World War some young men began working in the munitions factory near Wellington (it still employs many Badagas; see below, pp. 319-21). Then, in the 1920s, the first Badagas attended university and then returned to professional jobs in the Nilgiris. Of these professionals the most influential small group have been the parliamentarians – M.Ps and M.L.As – many of them from one extended family whose fortune was initially established by labour contraction (see Diag. 11, p. 205). But more numerous today are the doctors and lawyers. Other Badagas who, although less well-educated, no longer follow a traditional occupation include officials, policemen, contractors, factory workers, bus drivers and teachers. Early in the twenty-first century highly qualified Badaga information technologists may be found not just across India but in California, Canada, Germany, and Britain too, while others have taken up a variety of employment in the Gulf States.

Associated with these changes has been a breakdown of customary labouring methods. There were two kinds of cooperative labour: in one several families (usually from one lineage) would pool their labour to farm an area, and then divide up the produce proportionately; in the other, several families would work for a particular farmer but have no share in his produce; he in turn would help them with their cultivation. For a large landowner this latter system was quite efficient and profitable, although he had to feed those who were working in his fields and was also obliged to give them a big feast on the last day of their field-work (*kambua*), one which enhanced social solidarity. These two techniques of co-operative labour also benefitted the landless, poor people who could thereby share in the harvest of someone else or at least be more regularly fed.

In the early decades of the twentieth century immigrant Kanarese and Tamilians, a few of them the creditors of Badaga farmers, began to buy up former Badaga land and farm it with the help of labourers, both poor Badagas and immigrants. It was probably this trend which led those who worked on Badaga farms to expect payment in cash rather than a share of the harvest or a mutual exchange of labour. Those patterns of cooperation have altogether passed away. The educated would now rather remain unemployed than do work in the neighbour's field, and with the transition to cash-crop farming most feel it is hardly worth helping someone else reap his profit. Things were different when cooperative farming helped to put food into the village's granary baskets.

Among rural Badagas the old order has not been replaced by a class society. We can only identify a professional landowning class, a tenant class and a labouring class in the larger rural society which embraces some other non-Badaga communities as well. The landowners, if Badagas, generally prefer Tamilian or Kanarese tenants, as it is easier to lay down stiff terms for rental and to become stern towards them when such people fail to pay the rent after an unsuccessful season. Badaga tenants have too many methods of pressuring their landlord into overlooking inability to pay the rent on time.

The agricultural labourers have mainly been lowland immigrants, too, especially from Coimbatore District (Cederlöf 1997: 48, 98). It is considered somewhat demeaning by Badagas to take up any such work, particularly under a Badaga proprietor. Social classes are thus not yet to be found within Badaga villages, and these three main social categories in farming are seen by the Badagas as occupational and caste differences (Hockings 2012: 840-48).

CHANGING SOCIAL STRUCTURE

The late twentieth century found an increasing number of young, college-educated Badagas settling in towns with their wives and taking fairly well-paid jobs, sending their children to private schools, enjoying Westernized entertainments, and speaking a lot of English. These people still do observe community endogamy, but in other respects their behaviour suggests that the distinctive identity of the Badaga community is undergoing a basic change. It is no longer uncommon for urban Badagas to address rural Badagas in Tamil, rather than their own language. Some, possibly ashamed of the state government's designation of their people as a 'Backward Class',[22] are managing to merge with the South Indian city society and even deny what they deem an 'uncivilized' parentage. Such people rarely visit their natal villages now. Once marriage with non-Badagas is common and acceptable, as is already true among Christian Badagas, the social palisade around their community will have fallen.

We now examine how the position of the gentry and the roles of the individual have altered with recent changes in the social structure. The central idea here is that social structure can usefully be defined as a system of linked network-clusters and that the status of a villager is determined by his position in these clusters.

The distinction between Badaga gentry[23] and non-gentry is sufficiently precise that all families can be assigned to one category or the other by those who know them. Perhaps 5 per cent of the community is now considered as gentry.

> The term 'gentry' is not widely used in South Asia but it does have utility. . . . The term 'gentry' has had no place in official terminology in South Asia as it has had in China, but an important sector of the village farming population in South Asia more resembles Chinese gentry than European peasantry. I consider the gentry to consist of relatively high-status local

land-owning groups that marry their own kind and form alliances with other high-status families to expand their horizons as they redefine their ties to the land. Gentry families are privileged as mediators with state authorities; and, because of their land holding, education, and urban connections, they are active in commercial networks. (Ludden 1999: 75-76)

Until the mid-nineteenth century the most prestigious family of the Badaga gentry (*manetana*) was the largest family possible; and that position was often achieved through polygynous marriages. In one case during the 1950s, probably a record for Badagas, a wealthy but infertile man had five wives simultaneously. In these families men were often several decades older than their wives; in one case when the patriarch was over 90 the youngest of his three wives was 26 (he stands right behind the Ha:ruva priest in Pl. 7). Polygyny, however, is no longer common, and indeed the changing status of women in this society makes it an unpopular arrangement for most.

During the latter part of the nineteenth century there was a transitional phase when neither the size of the gentry family nor its wealth determined its status: its influence derived mainly from its reputation or strength of character, so we are told. Over the past century all Badaga families, whether gentry or not, had prestige commensurate with their wealth: the unusually affluent family now receives the respect and wields the power of a gentry family even though it is not one.

Generally all the headmen and their key assistants belonged to the gentry; and during the nineteenth century the British appointed the local *maṇega:rs* and *karaṇams* from amongst these people.[24] In the twentieth century, we know, literacy was considered a more important factor than birth for these appointments. In general that century witnessed a broad shift away from ascribed status towards achieved status. It has now become less relevant whether a man was born to the gentry or is a Ha:ruva or Toreya than whether he has acquired college education, a good job, and useful urban connections. However, even though there now are signs of socio-economic classes emerging, as has been evident for quite some time in the great cities of India, rural Badagas do not openly discuss their social life in terms of such distinctions as landed/landless, wealthy/poor or educated/uneducated. We know individuals vary in these qualities, but so far the variation is a matter of degree that has not been schematized in Badaga thinking into a series of neat distinctions.

In the operation of their social system today the Badagas nonetheless recognize a dozen major criteria for social differentiation, which they do conceive as the following dyadic contrasts:

1. Man / woman
2. Adult / child
3. Nilgiri / non-Nilgiri
4. Badaga / non-Badaga
5. Hindu / Christian
6. Gentry / non-gentry
7. Lingayat / non-Lingayat
8. Vegetarian / meat-eater
9. Our phratry / other phratries
10. Agnates / affines (or our clan/other marriageable clans)
11. Our village / other villages
12. Factional divisions.

This classification[25] is one of cross-cutting categories: each person can place himself and everyone he normally interacts with on one side or the other of *each* category. These are at different levels of generality and they have different relevance depending upon the circumstances. An individual's position on each of these contrasts constitutes a role, entailing certain well-recognized expectations of behaviour on appropriate occasions.

How does a social system fragmented by cross-cutting divisions keep from falling apart into small splinter groups? The answer lies with the interaction patterns which are indicative of social cohesion, which mark out the clusters of networks and which counteract the long-standing factional divisions. Four major types of public reciprocity, of which the first is the most widespread, hold together the people separated by these cleavages: (i) public discussions; (ii) the exchange of women between clans in marriage; (iii) joint participation in ceremonial meals; (iv) the exchange of goods and services. All four are types of communication, and to operate as such they must depend on network clusters; in other words, reciprocity can only be maintained on a continuing basis when it activates a persisting social structure. Badagas do not offer their goods, their meals, their daughters or even their conversation in a haphazard way to just *anybody*: the social structure, analysed by Badagas in terms of these dyadic contrasts, determines quite clearly *who* shall receive certain goods and services, *who* shall marry the daughters, and so on. Not only is the pattern of reciprocity dictated by the social structure – by the positioning of network clusters – but it in turn gives coherence to that structure: there is a dialectical process in the integration of this society. If Badagas were to recognize the newly emergent socio-economic classes as a new criterion for social differentiation their communication networks, patterns of reciprocity and system of role allocation would all have to be drastically revised, as perhaps they will be. Now people prefer to think somewhat anachronistically in terms of their old social organization since it provides a reassuring stability to present-day social relations. A strong sense of Badaga identity, long exemplified in the meaning behind the myth of the goddess Hette (Hockings 1989a: 223-28; 2012: 410-14; Heidemann 2006: 169-212), by a continuing regime of Badaga endogamy, and in very recent times by the persistent yet unsuccessful struggle to have the community recognized by the government as a Scheduled Tribe, have played their part in holding the community together.

Although the social system assigns an individual to certain positions from birth, however, he continuously adapts himself to what he perceives of the shifting organization of network clusters. In these adaptations the individual has a certain amount of choice. It is clearly limited by what he considers to be the relevant expectations of his fellows; but cultural norms do not dictate role change so absolutely that a man is unable to exercise his personal preferences. Cultural orientations are used by a Badaga to bolster or direct his motivations in the pursuit of the valued ends of his life. Thus while he is busily making a living, gaining respect and maintaining status he apparently goes through a continuing process of re-evaluating these activities in the light of changing conditions and new information. Re-evaluation takes the dual form of private thought or even of meditation sometimes, and of informal public discussions about his clique, their friends, and their various attitudes to life. So important is this re-evaluation process that many men can be seen devoting a major part of their waking time to it. The womenfolk are no doubt equally concerned with re-evaluation through conversations, but they do have to work physically at the same time (Harkness 1832: 114; Metz 1864: 98-99; Benbow 1930: 3-5; Vivekanandam Pillai 1937: 247; Subrahmanyam 1962: 5-6; see Pl. 10).

In such discussions the Badagas experience the need to make manifest from time to time the norms by which their behaviour is guided. This process not only makes the norms explicit but reinforces their validity in most cases too. At the same time ambiguous or anachronistic norms are subject to scrutiny and then modification or total rejection. In view of this re-evaluation process, it is no longer enough to know that a modern Badaga is a male of a certain age, from a certain village and phratry or of one particular category in their social system in order to predict how he will conduct himself in any given situation. We also need to understand the more transient social formations and networks that he is associated with, the social functions of these formations and networks, and also the manner in which their members are recruited. As I have observed on numerous occasions, the play of elementary logic, of conflicting orientations, personalities and proverbs, the relevance of everything said to everyone within earshot, are all factors that can promote fascinating and valuable conversation among Badagas. Slowly yet dynamically their culture is changing, not simply through external programmes devised for local modernization, but consciously, indeed conscientiously, through this tedious and time-consuming procedure. Faced with the requirement to vote for different parliamentary candidates, confronted with propaganda on the value of family planning or with another current topic, individuals will discuss the issues, try to reach a consensus, and then very often act accordingly.

Those cleavages in the social system across which conversation is not permissible are barriers to the free flow of communication, and on either side of these barriers variant orientations develop. If one is to understand cultural change one should pay some attention to this mechanism, for it is illuminating. The crucial factor here is the re-evaluation process, for conversations contributing to it take place separately for the different phratries and factions and for males and females. Children furthermore are intellectually equipped for only a very peripheral part in adult discussion. Over the passing years some rather different adaptations to living conditions therefore tend to have been worked out by each phratry or faction, by men and women, by the successive generations. This accounts for the most obvious subcultural variations within the community; and because the children naturally grow into adults and replace the older generation in most roles, an on-going process of changing cultural adaptations is going on, even though the model for thinking about social relations has remained remarkably stable for several generations.

The Badaga community has sometimes been called a caste, but many are eager to have its members recognized by the government as a tribe now; and they are more strongly aware of their identity as Badagas, one of the many groups for which the modern Tamil Nadu government shows particular concern and beneficence by treating as a 'Backward Class'.[26] Thus the chances of some material betterment through wider employment opportunities which prompted a handful of Badagas even a century-and-a-half ago to change their attitudes sufficiently to become Christians now prompt people to alter other orientations – not allied to religious values but rather to a secular government, its available benefits, and its new ranking of employment and educational priorities. Such a change in orientation holds out the chance of upward mobility, but in that process conversion to Christianity has become an anachronistic mechanism.

NOTES

1. Ward 1821, lxv; see above, p. 181. Until 1878 the mails were carried by teams of runners; Grigg 1880: 408. For fuller details on transportation to the early markets and mails, see Hockings 2012: 562-68, 720, 792-94.
2. A four-cylinder air-cooled car made around 1904 by H.H. Franklin in Syracuse, New York; Hockings 2012: 795, fig. 282.
3. The district is unusually well endowed in this respect, for it is only the size of Warwickshire or Luxemburg and slightly smaller than Rhode Island State. From Ootacamund most of the major cities of south India can also be reached: Chennai (Madras), Madurai, Salem, Kanyakumari, Pāḻani, Pondichery (Puducherry), Mysore, Bangalore, Palghat, Kozhikode (Calicut), Coimbatore, etc.; Selvaraj 1998. On pollution, consult Krishnan, in Hockings 2012: 290-93.
4. Transferred back to Coimbatore District from Malabar in 1860; Grigg 1880: 309, 322-23; Macleane 1893: 216; Thurston & Rangachari 1909, vol. 1: 78-79.
5. Grigg 1880: 316, 321. For fuller details on this agricultural legislation, cf. ibid.: 314-27. On the shortcomings of their agriculture, see Shortt and Ouchterlony 1868: 31-36; Grigg 1880: 480; 'Geofry' 1881: 132-35.
6. Grigg 1880: 325. The Settlement of land-holdings took place in 1864-1884; ibid.: 321-23; Sutton 2009: 73-84.
7. BEMS 1858, no. 18: 93; 1860, no. 20: 59; McPherson 1870: 15, 18, 21; Grigg 1880: 34, 219-20; Sutton 2009: 129. Tea-pickers were usually lowland labourers, for Badaga women were then afraid of being near any jungle even when in gangs. It is beyond the purview of this book to discuss either forest management or labour relations on the British-owned plantations; but a critical analysis of these matters is given by Philip 2003: 71-131, and Sutton 2009: 114-59.

8. A few ploughs were still in use recently near the Si:gu:ru Pass; other villages preserve old ploughs to venerate at an annual ceremony; but in general ploughs went out of use seventy years ago; Ranga 1934: 8.
9. Francis 1908: 165-66; Ranga 1934: 11-14. The lands are called respectively *ha:ḷi hola, ka:ḍu hola* and *so:le hola*; Hockings and Pilot-Raichoor 1992: 159, 561, 588, 617.
10. Grigg 1880: 13, citing Ouchterlony 1848: 14; Shortt & Ouchterlony 1868: 14. Ouchterlony calculated 'existing' agricultural land at 9,620 ha.; Sutton 2009: 56. It may be illuminating to cite an example of just one administrative 'village' – Ke:ti Village – which reflects how much of the plateau land was formerly owned by Badagas. The available figures come from the 1881 land settlement records – 33 years later than Ouchterlony's data – and demonstrate how 3,235 ha. of this particular 'village' (actually it is a grouping of nearly two dozen small hamlets; see Pl. 1) were distributed in the last years before the widespread adoption there of a cash economy:

Badaga farming lands	2,083 ha.
Badaga grazing ground	204 ha.
Toda grazing lands	51 ha.
Village sites (mainly Badaga)	90 ha.
Government forest areas	123 ha.
Anglo-Indian orphanage and school	307 ha.
Plantations (mainly British-owned)	175 ha.
Government cinchona plantation	2 ha.
Available for sale	200 ha.

(*Source*: Benson 1881: 188-89)

From these data it is clear that this area, by no means an atypical one, was farmed largely by Badagas. (The 200 ha. 'for sale' is somewhat misleading, since it was mostly in steep rocky places ill-suited to any cultivation.) Cinchona was always grown for quinine production by the government, never by private farmers; Philip 2003: 238-73; Muthiah, in Hockings 2012: 207-08.
11. Grigg 1880: 321 mentions that there were 29,912 acres (12,105 ha.) of farming land on the plateau in 1862-63, but considers this 'a fictitious number'. Fifteen years earlier John Ouchterlony had estimated that the Badagas alone were using 12,750 ha.; Grigg 1880: 13.
12. Land utilization figures for this entire district, 1905-60, in Nambiar (1965), do not isolate the position of Badaga agriculture.
13. Ranga 1934: 68. As early as 1877 the Government Horticulturist in Ootacamund, A. Jamieson, had circulated 'a simple treatise on potatoe [*sic*] cultivation for the guidance of the Badagas', had arranged for the distribution of seed potatoes, and had promised to visit the Badaga gar-

den plots (*South of India Observer* 11 (no. 88, 10 Nov.), 1877: 5). By 1908, Francis (p. 167) could state: 'Potatoes are much exported to Ceylon, the Straits [Malaya] and Burma. . . .' It was in 1908 that the commercially valuable railway that connected Ootacamund with the plains was at last completed (it had first been proposed by Ouchterlony in 1851; Ouchterlony 1858: 8, line 5296).

14. Ranga 1934: 14-15, 18-22. 'In fact many planters advance money to Badagas to enable them to dig pits and plant tea . . . with the intention of being able to purchase that land'; ibid.: 15.
15. Merchants also granted credit for purchase of daily needs – at much inflated prices; Ranga 1934: 73-74; Vivekanandam Pillai 1937: 249. Such traders are an excellent example of Simmel's 'resident stranger', whose presence catalyses a peasant economy by affording credit; Simmel 1923: 509-12. It is worth noting that post office savings banks had existed in India since 1882.
16. De:vaso:le, Kolekombe, Se:la:se, Gu:ḍalu:ru, Manju:ru, Ki:e Kotagiri, Neḍuguve, and Naḍuvaṭṭa; Baikie 1857: 38, 88; Grigg 1880: 471.
17. Nambiar 1965: 23. The first time this problem beset Badaga farmers was in 1880; BEMS 1880, no. 41: 37; Grigg 1880: 134.
18. Ranga 1934: 7-9. Badaga contractors had been involved in such work since the mid-nineteenth century; McPherson 1870: 21.
19. Natesa Sastri 1892: 753; Francis 1908: 129; Thurston & Rangachari 1909, vol. 1: 63; Ranga 1934: 8; Vivekanandam Pillai 1937: 248. The jobs included barbers, blacksmiths, brickmakers, builders, carpenters, clerks, domestic servants, forest guards, gardeners, painters, printers, rickshaw-pullers, stone-breakers, tailors, teachers, water-carriers, even coolies, washermen and scavengers. Aside from gardening, none was a traditional occupation.
20. Jagor 1876: 201-02; unlike most Hindus, the Badagas do not employ washermen, except perhaps in very recent times, and in towns. On the annual round of labour, see above, p. 98.
21. These were mainly Christians.
22. The designation is not recent; Francis 1908: 265. On the Backward Classes generally, see Béteille 1969: 87-145. Recently the Nilgiri Hill Tribe Badaga Welfare Association was formed to promote government action in classifying Badagas as a Scheduled Tribe, which would bring material advantages for the community.
23. *Manetana*, literally 'house-stage' or 'house-level'; Hockings & Pilot-Raichoor 1992: 453; cf. Kannaḍa *manĕtana*, translated as 'household,' 'race, family' by Kittel 1894: 1207, the connotation being a family of worthy people.
24. Grigg 1880: 366. These men were village magistrates and clerks; see above, p. 48, n. 8, and pp. 195-96.
25. These social distinctions have declined to some degree over a century

of history. They are, however, crystallized in various proverbs, as well as being universally recognized normative concepts. One proverb, for example, says: 'Although it is hot water, it will douse fire' (Hockings 1988: 343, no. 665). It refers to group loyalties: though we might have a friendship with a man of another lineage, village, faction, phratry or community, we will take the side of our own group against his when the need arises. Other proverbs relate to particular social distinctions. E.g. between one village and another:

'Even if he is headman of his own village, he is not superior to the son of the lowest widow in the last house outside the village' (Hockings 1988: 445, no. 908).

'Without [some] cunning, don't go to Jakkata; if poor, don't go to Ke:ti' (Hockings 1988: 297, no. 548b).

E.g. between phratries:

'If a crow makes a dropping [on you, it's a] bad sign; if a Ha:ruva shouts [at you, it's a] bad sign' (Hockings 1988: 230, no. 365a).

E.g. between affines and agnates:

'If brothers curse each other, [one can still] build his house on his brother's threshold; if in-laws quarrel, [one should] leave and run away' (Hockings 1988: 347, no. 675b).

'Although she is our sister, is her husband ours?' (Hockings 1988: 89, no. 9a).

26. See note 22.

CHAPTER 16

Communication and Society during the Twentieth Century

BAJAN AND KRISHNA WORSHIP

These styles of Hindu worship are innovations for the Badagas who, as we know, are Shaivites (Krishna and Rāma are both Vaishnavite deities, on the other hand; Karl 1945: 5). The performance of *bajan* (*bajane*, group hymns) began amongst them some sixty years ago, and so popular has it become that many villages have one or more sets of *bajan* instruments and hold a weekly performance of the sacred songs, which are hymns mainly in praise of Lord Krishna. They are played on the instruments of Tamilnad, not of the Nilgiris, and the words are Tamil, not Baḍagu. Many villages have recently built a *bajan* house specifically for these devotional evenings; it is owned by the village in common and is viewed as a kind of temple. Inside are lithographic prints of Krishna and other gods and perhaps an image to which *pu:ja* is performed during the course of the devotions. Once a year donations are solicited from every household in a village for support of its *bajan* singing group. Not every villager is interested in this form of worship, but its popularity has clearly been on the increase, especially among those youths who have regarded it as a modern, urbane form of Hindu worship. The rising interest in *bhajan* has been noted elsewhere in south India during the past half-century (Singer 1959: 148-49).

TAMILIAN AND KANARESE CELEBRATIONS

During the late nineteenth and the entire twentieth century the Badagas were always a minority of the Nilgiri population (735,071 in 2011); in 2001 they made up only 17.6 per cent of the district total. Heavy immigration into the hills, along with greatly improved communications with the lowlands to the north and east, especially the frequent, cheap bus services (pp. 247, 285), explain in part the proliferation of alien religious practices among the Badagas during the past century. And among Wainad Gauḍas there has been a comparable influence from Malabar, an effect of heavy immigration of labourers from that direction since the early years of Independence.

Over the past fifty years a variety of memorial ceremonies has been instituted for the anniversaries of individual deaths; previously there had no been no such commemoration (Hockings 2001: 61). A few corpses, or their ashes, have been buried at places beyond the village burial grounds, and stones have been raised to mark such spots, or even memorial statues erected. Here the closer relatives may perform an annual *pu:ja*; or they may do *pu:ja* at home before a photograph of the deceased. Some families invite more distant relatives to the ceremony; others do not, but may distribute food to the indigent. Some hold the ceremony in the daytime, others at night. Some will go straight to work after the *pu:ja*, others would never work on that solemn day. In short, the scale and the form of a modern memorial ceremony will vary from family to family, yet the general pattern often reflects Tamilian Hindu influence.

As well as these new mortuary ceremonies, several annual festivals have been adopted from neighbouring plains people with varying degrees of enthusiasm and support: over the past sixty to eighty years Di:pavaḷi, Ka:rttige and Ma:rgaḻi have all been adopted from Tamilnad into many villages (just as the Ma:ri festival was a century ago); and Dasara, long the biggest public celebration in Mysore city, has also been adopted – all of them in quite attenuated form.[1]

Di:pavaḷi, the day on which the mythical Rāma was crowned after his return from Sri Lanka, is given little importance. A minority of Badagas wear new dresses for the occasion, but otherwise do not have so much as a *pu:ja* in honour of Rāma or Krishna.

Ka:rttige extends over three days in November or December, but only the first day, dedicated to Shiva, assumes any importance. All the houses display lights throughout the night, and the priest does a *pu:ja* at the village temple, attended by most villagers. On the third day, dedicated to Vishṇu, very few lights remain burning.

Dasara is also celebrated here, on a small scale compared with the major Badaga festivals at sowing- and harvest-time. It is universally supposed to last for ten days at the end of September, but only on the evening of the ninth do Badagas hold any celebration, and this a simple *pu:ja* to images or prints of gods that are kept in the houses. On that occasion some Badagas also do *pu:ja* to bring blessings on agricultural implements and even schoolbooks and motorcycles.

After Ka:rttige comes the month of Ma:rgaḻi (Dec.-Jan.); it is the most inauspicious month of the Dravidian calendar. Some Badagas have now adopted the Tamilian practice of doing a protective daily *pu:ja* throughout the month. Early each morning a group of men will go along every village street singing *bajan* songs about Shiva and Vishṇu. Before this daily tour the women clean the houses, put auspicious markings on the ground outside the doorways and leave their doors open with a lamp burning inside until the *bajan* group has passed by. The many villages that have adopted this ritual conclude the unlucky month with a big communal feast.

In short, we find that there is some local variation in the form taken by the borrowed memorial ceremonies and festivals. They are not celebrated by all Badagas, and those who do so generally show less enthusiasm for them than for native Badaga festivals. Furthermore, Badagas are much less enthusiastic about them than are all the Tamilian and Kanarese people now living in the Nilgiris.

CHANGING PATTERNS OF MARRIAGE AND RESIDENCE

Since 1890 quite small minorities in nearly all of the phratries have contracted marriages beyond the boundaries of their community. A few Oḍeyas, Kaṇakkas and Adigaris have, as we have seen (p. 248), arranged marriages with Lingayat girls from Mysore, most usually from Mysore city itself. Some Be:ḍas and Kumba:ras have sought brides from the Bēḍa and Kumbāra castes of the plains, too. With the improved transportation and literacy throughout south India, such marriage links have become feasible; moreover, the Lingayat cases reflect a move towards closer ties with the land of orthodox Lingayatism to the north.

Since 1950 there have also been occasional marriages between a Gauḍa man and a Badaga Christian girl, always provided that the girl's ancestry traced back to a clan other than the man's. Badaga Christian women have also become preferred brides for Toda Christian men (Walker 1986: 273). These unions, which earlier would have been unthinkable, or at least have resulted in excommunication of the Christian partner, now do occur among the more progressive, especially those who have had a college education.

These shifting patterns of alliance have altered the phratry system but little, although changing criteria in marriage arrangements have had a profound impact. The appearance of dowry-like transactions in a society which previously expected only a type of bridewealth is the most portentous of a whole complex of changing criteria. Before the wedding the boy's family always pays the *hoṇṇu* to the girl's family; *hoṇṇu* thus has the appearance of a bride-price, but this is not a good English translation of the term. It is money to be spent on the gold ornaments that bedeck the bride when she leaves her home to join her husband and without which the marriage should not be performed. By meeting the expense of the ornaments, the groom's family ensures that the ceremony will proceed. If a divorce should later occur the wife must return the ornaments or their cost, together with any other gifts of clothing or jewellery that her husband might have made (Harkness 1832: 116-17; Metz 1864: 86-87; Thurston & Rangachari 1909, vol. 1: 105-06; Tignous 1911: 119). With rising gold prices the *hoṇṇu* has also increased steadily. Early in the nineteenth century it was generally '15 to 20 rupees' (Ward 1821: lxxi); but later, 'on an average between twenty and twenty-five rupees' (Harkness 1832: 42); by 1867 it was Rs. 80;[2] early in the twentieth century it was about Rs. 100;[3] in the 1930s and 1940s it was more often Rs. 150 (Ranga 1934: 3); twenty years later yet it was usually about Rs. 200 (Moses 1964: 4); while nowadays it will go very much higher than this, especially in view of the continuing devaluation of the rupee (Rs. 54 = U.S. $1 in 2013).

Though *hoṇṇu* is still usually paid, a gift from the girl's family has become a common feature in many recent marriages. Some older men, especially those with marriageable daughters, attribute the expectation of such a present to the avarice of modern youth, but the broader reason for the development is that eligible young men show much greater variability both in their family's wealth and in their own potential to earn than was true in earlier generations. Previously the most affluent and prestigeful families were the landed gentry, and gentry youths would normally marry only the daughters of the gentry. Today a wealthy Badaga, whether of the gentry or not, may sometimes be willing to offer hundreds of thousands of rupees if his daughter can marry into another affluent family. Such a gift is not a dowry, for it is not agreed to as a condition of marriage and is not handed over with any ceremony. It is, however, deemed appropriate when a boy's family has benefitted him with the prestigeful expense of a university education, which promises secure support and some enhanced status for the wife. Several thousand Badaga men had (by 2000) earned college degrees, as had quite a few hundred girls; the numbers are greater still in the present century. The preponderant choice of groom is thus between a secondary-educated or a tertiary-educated man, and one method of ensuring the girl's marriage with a college graduate is the payment of what one elder described as a 'bribe'. While not an old Badaga custom, it has now become quite fashionable.[4]

The usual preference has been for marriage with a bilateral cross-cousin (see pp. 113-14), a girl whom a youth often finds in the same village into which his sister has married. This is still the normal choice: either he marries his sister's husband's sister (a cross-cousin) or else a related neighbour of that husband. The recent intrusion of a demand for a substantial present into this reciprocal exchange between two clans and two villages can be an unpleasant shift away from custom: two families, lineages or villages which have exchanged several daughters in marriage have established an alliance that proclaims their social equality (Hockings 1977: *passim*). If one side now seeks a financial settlement it could rupture this stability, since such a gift will suggest social *inequality* between the contracting parties. Offering a financial inducement for a progressive, educated groom is like purchasing security for one's daughter.

No longer are the wealthiest families members of the gentry. The latter have recently been supplanted by *parvenus* with the ability to wield more influence and political power. These *nouveaux riches*, contractors, businessmen, dealers in illicit liquor,[5] and plantation owners, have wherever possible reinvested their earnings in tea or coffee estates, or private bus lines. Occasionally too this new-found capital has been invested in Badaga-owned businesses in the Nilgiri towns or in Coimbatore City. But another popular type of investment has long been to send sons to college, which can bring prestige to any family in quite a short space of time. Those who obtain a degree in law, medicine or today information technology are assured a particularly high social position in the Nilgiris, where they prefer to practice, but those who manage only a B.A. or B.Sc. find it brings some prestige although rarely a well-paying job. Commonly, the upwardly mobile families have wanted their sons to get a bachelor's degree and then settle down in their home villages and farm their land – which is by no means always a popular choice with modern sons, however. As we have seen (p. 271), many are deserting their natal villages for more attractive opportunities beyond the district.

Among those wealthy enough to expect or to pay a substantial gift at marriage, fulfilment of their traditional roles in the society can become a problem-laden, anachronistic burden. Such men can command annual incomes a hundred times greater than the average for other men from their home village. As a consequence of this newly apparent inequality the wealthy are constantly being plagued by importunate villagers and distant relations, perhaps too by Kota and Toda friends, who try to activate traditional bonds of kinship or friendship so as to grasp their share in the power and influence of the *nouveaux riches*. It is therefore not surprising that the wealthiest Badagas have tended to leave their natal villages altogether and then build themselves more comfortable homes in a town or in the middle of their tea estates. As the wealth of these families grows and as the possibility of their upward mobility, as modern Indian families rather than Badaga villagers, becomes a reality, attitudes towards the traditional society and its marriage regulations change. It seems that no longer are the requirements of their old culture so demanding or so relevant, since these people are now oriented towards a larger, urbane south Indian society whose aims and ideals are for them enshrined in the morality and the cultural paraphernalia of modern romantic Indian films.

MIGRATION

The Badagas nonetheless have a very stable society: its population has not become subject to major geographic movements in recent decades, aside from a little outward expansion of the most highly trained professionals. It has felt the impact, on the other hand, of the heavy, government-sponsored immigration of Tamilians who came from Sri Lanka, who were 'dumped' in large numbers in the Nilgiris District during the late twentieth century, and who in some localities have caused social problems by squatting on the land of Badagas (Haldorai 1993; Heidemann, in Hockings 2012: 858-59).

In a previous study (Hockings 1999: 229-30), I have identified five kinds of migration pattern found among Badagas themselves:

1. In-migration of brides, which is balanced against out-migration of other brides, since these are virilocal and mostly exogamous villages;
2. Young men going off to the cities for study, then to take up urban professions;
3. Families moving to land available elsewhere in the Nilgiris: this may be a family-owned plantation somewhere nearby, or it may be farmland that chances to be available in the wife's natal village. In other words, the general rule of virilocal residence is sometimes converted to uxorilocal residence, especially when the wife does not have any brothers to inherit her father's land;
4. Some families moving elsewhere in India, or even overseas, because of urban employment opportunities or professional job transfers;
5. Widows often and divorcees nearly always return to their father's or brother's home. Some bring children with them too.

Study-migration (2, above) may only take a young person away for a few years, but the other patterns of migration listed here are likely to be fairly permanent, with (4) and (5) now common. Not indicated here, because it is not a long-term migration, is the frequent visiting of their natal home by married daughters. 'The female population of a village is never constant in size and never composed of the same individuals for more than a few days at a time' (Jacobson 1977: 266). Some widows have returned to their natal homes; some girls have left the Nilgiris District altogether in marriage, however, while others are temporarily in other parts of India for a more advanced education.

Emigration beyond the Nilgiris had not been an important factor until very recently. One small milestone was the establishment of the Chennai Badagas Association in Madras in 1968. A measure of how much out-migration had occurred in the past for reasons of both employment and higher education is also given in the figures from the national census of India half-a-century ago. This cites the number of Badaga speakers throughout India in 1961 as 85,463, and of Badaga speakers in the Nilgiris District as 84,823. The difference is thus only 640, or 0.7 per cent. These 640 people were mostly living elsewhere in Madras state, primarily college students or the permanent inhabitants of a small and ancient Badaga settlement in the Biligiri Rangan Hills of neighbouring Periyar district, to the east. Only 55 males and 37 females were to be found elsewhere, and then only in Kerala or Mysore states. That small number still represented a significant increase from the emigrants of twenty years before: in

1941 only 270 Badagas lived elsewhere, and nearly all of them in the nearby Biligiri Rangan hamlets, the Ha:sanu:ru Badagas (see above, pp. 130-31, and Hockings 2012: 135-36). Those people were at that time only 0.48 per cent of the Badaga total, and cannot be viewed as migrants anyway.

By 2011 there were perhaps 2,000 Badagas living overseas. In that year the International Badaga Association had 1,500 members (most of them admittedly living in India) but they included hundreds in the United States and in a dozen other countries, with the Persian Gulf states claiming several dozens. Since these persons are primarily Internet-users today (http://www.badaga.org,) and most of those settled in the United States have brought their families along, one may guess that the American Badagas now number a thousand or so, and are there to stay. One prime use for Internet sites is to locate suitable Badaga brides or grooms for these professionals. It is not uncommon for such settlers to invite their parents to come for long visits to California or the New York area; their baby-sitting abilities can prove invaluable. The small numbers in several other countries are in many cases graduate students.

NETWORKS OF COMMUNICATION

The Impact of Towns

The availability of a profusion of buses has helped the Badagas in more matters than marketing and migration over the past few decades. Villagers are now able to go to town frequently – typically once or twice a week – and their children can attend high school or even college without losing much contact with the home. (Ootacamund today has two colleges and Coonoor another, all three affiliated with Madras University; there are also a College of Pharmacy and a Government Polytechnic in Ootacamund, and the Defence Services Staff College at Wellington; Gopalakrishnan 1995: 1106-15; Hockings & Mulley, in Hockings 2012: 285-86.) Literacy and newspapers in Tamil have spread, too, in part because of the easy transportation system (Hockings 2012: 642-44). The literacy rate has of late been seemingly higher on the rural Nilgiri Plateau than in Madras City: back in 1963, I calculated that 70 per cent of adult Badaga males and 52 per cent of females were literate; while in 1961, according to the census of that year, 70 per cent of Madras city males and 48 per cent of females were literate.[6] Even the oldest of Badagas are people who are often quite familiar with daily news stories, weather forecasts, and national political events (Hockings 1999: 243-45).

The cheap railway and bus services have made visits to the great pilgrimage centres of south India possible for thousands: the famous Hindu temples at Cape Comorin, Madurai, Pāḻani, Tirupati and Tanjavūr now receive Badagas almost daily, as does the Pattesvara temple in Coimbatore (Perūr). Nor must we overlook the business trip; for increasingly farmers as well as traders find it worth visiting cities when they have a harvest to sell or bulk supplies to purchase.

The modern cities and great pilgrimage centres can have two different types of psychological effect: a city shows the Badaga visitor profusions of consumer goods, among them new household devices, radios, watches, bicycles, computers, cellphones, cameras and television sets, as well as interesting foods, cloths and ornaments; the pilgrimage centre, on the other hand, stresses ties with the mythical past of south India, with the gods represented in the Hindu temples, with priestly authority and with the grand history of those temples themselves. It is an important distinction: the man who goes to a distant temple may come home with his attention focussed on the past and on separation of the self from worldly matters, whereas the man coming from a business trip may be full of a desire to buy some item he has seen, or try out a new skill, or save money so that his child might attend college in the city.[7] The distinction between the conservative and the modernizing effects of travel is to a certain extent paralleled in the personal choice between mythical and modern film themes or between religious and secular magazines. Not all their contact with the cities necessarily introduces people to modern ways of life; and not all of those who patronize radio, films or periodicals are drinking at a source of non-traditional knowledge, for although the media may be modern the villager discriminates in what he will derive from them.

As awareness of news is a crucial aspect of modernization psychology, half-a-century back I tried to discover the news-gathering habits of men and women in two sample villages in the centre of the plateau; and although this was in 1963, 20 years before television came to the villages, they already had several other distinct sources of news available, namely from newspapers, radio, friends, relatives at home, or a local official.

Film-going Habits

Film-going is one highly popular activity that does not require literacy, and hence is potentially open to all, especially the poor. In the eyes of many Badagas one of the greatest benefits of the bus system has been that it has permitted frequent trips to cinemas in the towns. In the later twentieth century most families saw films often, and what was seen had a great impact on them. For those with the necessary equipment, DVDs can also be watched at home nowadays.

Some of the most popular films are dramatizations of Indian history or of epic stories which reinforce traditional ideas about Hinduism and the nature of the cosmos. But equally popular are the films about modern life, about social problems like divorce, urban crime, widow remarriage, 'love' marriages and intercaste marriage; dramas which are presented against a background of affluence that is unfamiliar yet fascinating to the villager. These modern themes extol city life, non-traditional marriage practices and luxury goods such as cameras, watches, television sets, mechanical toys or sports cars. The impact of these films over the past half-century is clear: younger Badagas yearn for cellphones, motorcycles, computers and all the other paraphernalia that they have come to associate with a modern urban life.

Radio

Among the most commonly desired gadgets in the later twentieth century were transistor radios, which were appreciated as a source of light music. For decades now every village has had at least one set, either owned privately or provided by the government; local tea-shops also have radios. All-India Radio presents much government information, especially talks directed towards improvement of farming and village cooperatives. These broadcasts – given in the Tamil language – are not very much listened to, because the vast majority of village radios are constantly tuned to light music coming from commercial radio. In a sample of 420 Badaga men and women in 1963, 17 per cent said they never listened, 16 per cent only heard music, 38 per cent heard news as well as music, 14 per cent listened specifically for news broadcasts, while only 2 per cent mentioned informative talks as being of interest to them.[8] I found then that the higher the incidence of regular listening, the higher the popularity of news broadcasts, two variables that were correlated no doubt with the length of time that a village had been electrified. Since 2000 All-India Radio has maintained a 1602 kHz transmitter in Ootacamund.

Newspapers

Another matter on which that same village sample was questioned concerned reading habits. Here there was a big sex gap, the women reading much more seldom, whether because of inability, lack of interest, or lack of spare time.

My survey on the use of the media in 1963 showed that radio was much less effective as a source of news than the regional press. It was also found that the farther away from towns respondents lived, the less information they got from friends and the more from newspapers; only for items of local news were friends everywhere more effective than newspapers as channels of communication. When a Tamil newspaper reaches a village it commonly circulates and gets read aloud to a much larger number of people than one copy could reach in a town. The wide circulation of papers and the presence of well-educated men even in out-of-the-way villages helps explain the unusually high levels of knowledge about the world beyond the Nilgiris that Badagas have long commanded.

Television

As in much of Asia today, television has revolutionized knowledge of the outside world among Badaga villagers. Sets have been found in more well-to-do houses in some villages for over 30 years now, and their communicative effectiveness has only been limited by the numbers who could view each set. The loft (*aṭḷu*) in many of the traditional homes has been converted into a TV-viewing room.

At the time of writing this second edition of the present book, there are thousands of urbanized, well-educated Badagas who can make use of e-mail, fax, Skype, and the Internet. Quite a few dozens of them today are information technology specialists who work not in the Nilgiris but in places like Silicon Valley, California – which has some 20 well-to-do Badaga families in 2013 – and elsewhere too in the Western world.

Intra-village Networks

Beside the traditional marriage and exchange networks which supplied Badagas with their basic needs, there have always been social networks through which important information has passed by word of mouth. These have been modified and amplified in the past century and have become linked to some extent with the mass media (on local networks, see Hockings 1977: *passim*).

In Hulla:ḍa, a typical, central village of the Gauḍa phratry, there have been four types of network: intra-village, inter-village, inter-tribal and a newer type, village-and-town. Each of these categories can be subdivided along the following lines.

There were in 1963 several different adult male *loci* for decision-making and opinion formation in that village. The most important of them were usually these:

i. the traditional council, and especially the village headman;
ii. the festival committee;
iii. elders of the four indigenous lineages and of a fifth composite group of more recently settled families;
iv. three middle-aged, influential men;
v. the local Swatantra Party organizer;
vi. the well-educated young people.

Two or three of these groupings may operate together in popularizing an idea or solving a problem that faces many in the village. In a class by themselves are the women's work-groups, small cliques of village wives who habitually work together in the fields and elsewhere, exchanging gossip and favours in the process. These female networks link up with the male ones through the wives of influential men (cf. Pl. 9). In a general way, it will be seen that the women's knowledge of and interaction with the outside world is rather less than men's; yet women definitely have sufficient information at their disposal to make up their own minds about the important issues of modernization, and the men would seem not to be highly influential over them, since the opinions and preferences of the two sexes are often quite divergent. After *ca* 1975 elderly women in this particular village began to counsel the younger ones about the need for birth control (Hockings 1999: 187-93). By the end of the twentieth century a few of the women in this particular place were urban-based professionals, including one medical doctor.

The sequence of contacts that have to be made if someone in the village is to influence or be influenced by people in the above list constitutes an intra-village network.

Inter-village Networks

Two kinds of network fall under this heading, one linking agnates, the second affines. The first are ritual and juridical networks, linking up with distantly related men in other villages of the commune. This commune was first settled, they claim, by a man who founded the maximal lineage to which nearly all of the inhabitants belong. Hulla:ḍa people mostly belong to one of the three major lineages, this one established some two centuries ago by Konga Hettappa, one of the commune founder's three sons. Within Hulla:ḍa and the closest nearby village, Ke:ti, the lineage is further divided into four minimal lineages, each descended from one of Konga Hettappa's four sons. The more important festivals are celebrated in common by all 25 villages in the Ke:ti commune, using ritual personnel from any one of them. Serious problems are discussed by all the village headmen at the commune council. The Hulla:ḍa villagers can establish contact with the wealthiest and most influential men in their commune by activating these two networks, either through a village headman or through a friend who has helped in the rituals.

Secondly, the marriage and visiting networks link Hulla:ḍa with villages beyond this commune. Marriages account for a network of social contacts with nearly two dozen other villages, and these networks are frequently activated by informal visits and by attendance at the festivals, weddings and funerals of affines. Small loans may be sought along these networks (Hockings 1982: *passim*; 1999: *passim*).

Inter-tribal Networks

A long time ago the Badagas of Hulla:ḍa village were linked, for certain economic and ritual purposes, with particular Kota, Toda, Kuṟumba or Chetti men. For the most part these associations have fallen into abeyance, and are no longer relevant in daily life, but until about 1930 they did follow the pattern detailed in Chapters 7-9.

Village-and-Town Networks

These more modern networks may be classified roughly as either formal or informal. The formal ties are those that use the recognized channels of local government. Information about personal or legal problems may sometimes be obtained from the *panchayat* office in the next village. A clerk in that office, which is an organ of the state government, will either supply information himself or direct the enquirer to a government office in town (where he will quite possibly be sent to yet other offices!).

The informal ties between town and village make use of Badaga friends and relatives who work, study or live in the towns, or connect with non-Badagas living in the towns who know where to get information or how to solve a problem. Informal networks are often used by villagers when the formal ones fail to resolve a difficulty: this is probably true of most communication systems (Frank 1958-59: *passim*).

THE POSITION OF BADAGAS IN NILGIRI SOCIETY TODAY

The customary interdependence that pertained between the Badagas and other groups is so complex and yet so loose that it changed to varying extents in different parts of the plateau during the past century. Some Badagas are much more dependent than others on the cash economy and usually try to avoid the burden of old obligations. The potentialities of a labour market, nearness of bus routes to town shops, aboriginal residence patterns, and the relative proximity of tribal settlements have all been important in determining the extent to which the Badagas of each village have dropped their traditional ties with the indigenous tribes.

Thus, to cite one example, Badagas of the Kundena:ḍ region have tended to be more conservative in outlook than other Badagas: in that area they have never adopted the worship of the goddess Ma:ri which entered the Nilgiris in the nineteenth century; furthermore, some may still invite a Kota band to play at their ceremonies and in other ways keep up their ties with the nearby Kota village. Elsewhere on the hills nearly all Badagas eschew contact with Kotas, as they now consider it demeaning. A modern Badaga who wants to be regarded as an orthodox Shaivite would not wish to attend any funeral where Kotas play dance-music beside the corpse: not only have the (formerly) carrion-eating Kotas (Breeks 1873: 42; Grigg 1880: 205, 479; Mandelbaum 1960: 274) become 'Untouchables' in the modern terminology (a term first used in 1908), but Hindu orthodoxy frowns upon the idea of dancing at a funeral. The new orientation – for someone who is now more a Hindu citizen and less a Nilgiri peasant – seems appropriate to any Badaga who finds himself competing for jobs or for official favours with people from all over south India, or who perhaps will vote for some Hindu chauvinist politician from the BJP. The relatively conservative Badagas of Kundena:ḍ, on the other hand, are among the wealthiest villagers in the district, as nearly all of their land is now given over to flourishing tea or coffee plantations.[9] This source of profit and employment is apparently secure enough that these people have not felt themselves in serious competition for positions with men from elsewhere: their confidence in the future has allowed them to continue at least some ceremonial links with the local Kotas. Virtually no tools are now being made by those Kotas, however, since the great quantity of specialized metal items, including machinery, needed on a plantation can only be sought in town stores; and furthermore these particular Kotas are preoccupied with their own tea estates. Both Kotas and Badagas here activate their traditional relationship only so far as economic expediency permits: where the required tool is too complicated for a blacksmith to make, where the market has the same item at a lower price, or where one's labour can better be spent on plantation tasks than on some customary obligation, the traditional links have fallen into abeyance (Mandelbaum 1955: 240).

Similar adaptations to the expanding cash economy may be seen in other aspects of the traditional inter-community relations. Few if any Todas, to mention just one other example, now take the trouble to make their annual rounds of Badaga villages in search of their customary dues: the Todas feel this smacks of beggary, while many Badagas would find reasons for not giving anything. Badagas for their part never request the Todas to come and take their gifts, and only rarely may seek out a Toda friend when a special requirement can be obtained only from him.

In a survey made in 1963 I found that 33 per cent of Badaga respondents no longer had any contact with or firm attitude towards the Todas, Kotas or Kuṟumbas; and the younger they were the more distant they felt from these tribes. Nevertheless many more respondents in all age groups disliked the Kuṟumbas than disliked Todas or Kotas: the old fear of witchcraft was lingering on. In the middle age group of that sample (35 to 54 years) there was a significant correlation[10] between dislike of Kuṟumbas and a feeling that the world in general is a dangerous and evil place – an interesting confirmation of my earlier assertion that witchcraft accusations against Kuṟumbas long ago were manifestations of more general feelings of insecurity and stress (see above, pp. 232-34).

Over the past 40 years or so modernization has proceeded apace, and much has changed. The widespread access to colour television, the adoption of family planning, the increasing age of women at first marriage, more motorized transportation, and the appearance of educated Badagas of both sexes in an ever-widening range of occupations, have been some of the most dramatic developments. But as urbanized Badagas become more and more involved in their jobs and their nuclear families, adherence to distinctively Badaga community values may have lessened for these people. For, as Clifford Geertz once said of irrigated rice cultivation in Java,

> The absence of pressures toward interfamiliar co-operation exerted by the technical requirements of wet-rice growing, as well as lessened effectiveness of the traditional forms of village government in the face of the complexities of urban living, severely weaken the social supports of the syncretic village pattern. When each man makes his living – as chauffeur, trader, clerk, or laborer – more or less independently of how his neighbors make theirs, his sense of the importance of the neighborhood community naturally diminishes. A more differentiated class system, more bureaucratic and impersonal forms of government, greater heterogeneity of social background, all tend to lead to the same result: the de-emphasis of strictly geographical ties in favor of diffusely ideological ones. (Geertz 1959: 40)

The Badagas are not involved in rice cultivation, but their 'strictly geographical ties' are nevertheless beginning to lose some of their force, for much the same reasons as they have in Java.

However, during the latter years of the 1980s Badagas began to agitate for a different categorization of their community by the state government. Up till then they had been treated by that government as an Other Backward Class (OBC). In censuses early in the twentieth century British officials had identified them by the term 'primitive tribe' (e.g. Yeatts 1932: 306). Then during the 1980s they were briefly labelled 'Adivasi' and 'Scheduled Tribe'. By 1989 the state government termed them a 'Backward Class'. Thus on May 16 of that year there was a massive but peaceful demonstration of Badaga men and women along the streets of Ootacamund, headed by a portrait of the goddess Hette, a display sponsored by the Federation of Badaga Associations. The demonstrators petitioned the Collector to request that the Central authorities reclassify Badagas as a Scheduled Tribe, thus giving them access to a number of special benefits, including reserved seats in university and reserved government jobs (Radhakrishnan 1989). Although some supportive messages were indeed conveyed to them from various high officials in New Delhi, after several years the request was rejected.

Still, a widespread aspiration for community betterment remains, and shows no signs of abating. An American archaeologist noted:

> the way one analyzes the archaeological past has implications for the present. . . . Indigenousness in the Nilgiris is a claim to power and influence. Each of the groups inhabiting the Nilgiris at the time of the arrival of the British made and continue to make claims to their long-term (often aboriginal) occupation of the hills and to their past relative statuses. Claims about the past, about when and under what circumstances each indigenous group found itself in the Nilgiris, and claims about one's dominant or dependent status characterize relationships between the native Nilgiri populations and between those communities and the state. There is an inherent assumption that present ethnic identities match prehistoric ones rather than being products of historical interaction. Each group is understood as being unchanging, possessing an essential character. Therefore, claims about the past are ways one discovers one's essential form. For example, some Toda claimed the Kotas were their servants in the prehistoric past, while there are Kota claims of once having had significant authority over the entire Nilgiri Mountains. . . . These countervailing claims were and are not without consequences. The British colonial administration took the Toda claims seriously, which had negative implications for the Kota. Indeed, the assumed long-term isolation of some of these communities from the centers of Indian civilization piqued the interest of the British who afforded them . . . limited privileges. . . . Thus, claims about the past gave advantage and disadvantage to groups in the present. Even the present affirmative action policies of the Indian government for scheduled tribes and disadvantaged castes provide incentives to local peoples to identify themselves deep in an aboriginal past. Affirmative action programs offer jobs, education, and other economic benefits to such "tribal communities". Thus, the past is not a neutral subject for the Nilgiri communities but an arena of potential struggle for economic benefits. (Zagarell 1999: 190-91)

In general Badagas feel little compunction today to maintain a traditional association with the other local tribes that is clearly not an economically feasible one. Among the indigenous peoples they are taking the lead in finding and internalizing new orientations, which help them secure a place in the national economy and society at the expense of their traditional position in Nilgiri society. While Kotas, Kuṟumbas and even some Todas now are adopting the Badagas as their model (for example, in modern housing styles; Noble 1997: *passim*; Noble, in Hockings 2012: 55-58), the Badagas are following urban Tamilians and Christians in valuing the products of modern technology, seeking monetary profit, good education and a Westernizing life-style, all of which they think to be appropriate in a modern, urban context.

NOTES

1. Benbow 1930: 39, 42. Other Tamilian festivals now celebrated by some Badagas are Pongal, Ma:ri Habba (but not yet in Kundena:ḍu), Ranga-na:tan car festival, and the birthdays of various gods; Stokes 1882: 173.
2. BEMS 1867, no. 28: 70. It did range as high as Rs. 150 or 200; cf. Metz 1864: 99, and Grigg 1880: 222.
3. But 'varying from Rs 10 to Rs 200 . . .'; Natesa Sastri 1892: 763; cf. Tignous 1911: 119, and Vivekanandam Pillai 1937: 250.
4. Dowry may once have been a Badaga custom; Harkness 1832: 41-42; Metz 1864: 87. Even in the later twentieth century Badagas were supposed to give their daughters upon marriage a present (*aḍo:li*) of at least one milking buffalo, one cow and one trained ploughing ox. If she is later divorced the gift is returned to her father.
5. The official claims (Madras 1965: 23) that 'The vigilant working of the Prohibition department has made [liquor] Prohibition a success in this district' are farcical and were belied by prosecution statistics. It merely provided a further concern for a burgeoning bureaucracy and another cottage industry for the landless. Most villages had at least one still in full-time production during the latter half of the twentieth century. Illicit distillation, transportation, sale or possession of liquor were common offenses in that period, yet they made a number of men very wealthy; Hockings 1980b: 31-34; 2012: 82-83.
6. India 1962: 133. Moses 1964: 33, found 73 per cent of Badaga males and 50 per cent of females literate ($N = 200$). My sample in 1963 was 420 persons.
7. There are a few who combine the business trip with a pilgrimage, but this is not usual.

8. This purposive sample was drawn from 656 interviews in the district.
9. The rise of Kunda people from dire poverty to extreme wealth during the course of the twentieth century is the subject of a closely-observed novel by the acclaimed Tamil writer Rajam Krishnan (1925-2012), *When the kurinji blooms* (in Tamil, 1963; English translation, 2002). It examines the lives of three generations living in two Kunda villages, thus encompassing in fiction a convincing account of the predominant cultural changes that Badagas were undergoing during that century, from traditional farming activities to the tensions and rewards of modern life.
10. $C^2 = 5.18$, $P < 0.03$. This middle-aged group had grown up during the slump which spanned the 1930s and which is reflected in the low food-grain prices of those years; see Madras 1965: 37.

CHAPTER 17

The Pace of Modernization Quickens

THE STATE OF THE MODERN NILGIRI ECONOMY

This district, although not highly commercialized except in the plantation sector, has for long been quite progressive both educationally and economically, as compared with many other parts of India that lie beyond the great cities. This situation has been true since late in the nineteenth century, and has been documented in Chapters 10 and 14. In 1993 the Economic Intelligence Service,[1] which accords a relative index value of development of 100 to India as a whole, gave an index of 135 to Tamil Nadu state and of 173 to the Nilgiris district. These indices were inversely correlated with the annual growth in population, which that Service then put at 2.14 per cent for all of India, 1.40 per cent for Tamil Nadu, and 1.13 per cent for the Nilgiris. Population density for the district was almost exactly the national figure (which of course is much conditioned by all the urban agglomerations): 278 per sq. km. in the Nilgiris, 273 in the Indian Republic, but 429 in Tamil Nadu state as a whole.

Other unusual statistical features of the Nilgiris stand out in that report of the Economic Intelligence Service. In a total area of 2,549 sq. km. it was estimated in 1993 that 56 per cent of the district was nominally forested, while another 24 per cent was the net sown area. This was a stark contrast with other districts in the same state, which showed very different proportions indeed: 16 per cent forested and 44 per cent sown for Tamil Nadu state as a whole. Deforestation was certainly occurring on the Nilgiri Hills, but perhaps at a slower pace than in other districts. It needs to decrease even more, as we have known for more than a century, to counter the effects of soil loss and climate change.

The Nilgiris district population in that same year, 1993, was estimated as 353,430 urban plus 356,780 rural people; an even split, but a somewhat artificial distinction perhaps, for many of the village clusters had only recently been incorporated within newly created *urban* boundaries, in addition to the five 'older' towns of Coonoor, Gudalur, Kotagiri, Ootacamund and Wellington. The Badagas, by contrast, were 24,294 urban but 109,893 rural in 1991. By 2011 the rural literacy rate of this district was 81.67 per cent, compared with an all-India figure of 68.91 per cent, while female literacy continued to be unusually high (79.44 per cent district-wise).

The major economic activity nowadays is plantation agriculture, although tourism is also an important part of the economy. Thus 69 per cent of the total cropped area in 1993 was devoted to tea, 15 per cent to coffee, 6 per cent to potatoes, and 4 per cent (in the Wainad, not in Badaga territory) to irrigated rice. Ginger and cardamom were the only other crops to (slightly) exceed 1 per cent of the cropped acreage. Given the dominance of high-value plantation crops, it is not surprising to find that in 1993 the value of the output per hectare of the major Nilgiri crops was put at Rs. 21,288, as compared with only Rs. 6,622 for Tamil Nadu State, and Rs. 3,576 for India as a whole: this value for the Nilgiris was therefore six times the national average. (Figures for the value of output per capita are proportionately very similar: Rs. 1,862 in the Nilgiris District in 1993.) Annual per capita food grain production has consequently been very low: just 6 kg. per person in the Nilgiris, as compared with 124 kg. in Tamil Nadu and 173 kg. in India generally (to quote 1993 figures again; the exchange rate was then Rs. 31.38 = US $1).

Another marker of the advanced state of the regional economy in which the Badagas participate is the comparatively great extent of the road network (Hockings 2012: 792-95). In 1993 the Nilgiris had 162 km. of road per 100 sq. km. of land surface, as compared with 128 km. for Tamil Nadu State and 60 km. for India as a whole. Bank credit per hectare for agriculture was also far higher in this district than in the state or in the nation: in 1993 it was estimated at Rs. 6,409 in the Nilgiris, Rs. 2,985 in Tamil Nadu state, but Rs. 1,046 for all of India.

No doubt these summary economic statements mask much of the diversity found even within such a small district. Commercial cultivation of minor crops there includes banana, tapioca, sugar cane, garlic, sweet potato, ginger, turmeric, finger millet, pepper, cardamom and castor. Besides tapioca, the main grain produced here is rice; but few of these are Badaga products (Hockings 1999: 214).[2]

The recent figures for food grain production illustrate a phenomenon that is widespread in developing countries. As more and more people move into better paid, non-food-producing employment, or they produce only such export crops as tea or pepper, a majority of the district's population is put in the position of having to buy its grain from elsewhere. But that 'elsewhere' in our case is the poorer, more backward rural plains of southern India that are devoted solely to rice production. In the Nilgiris there have recently been only 12.5 kg. of locally grown grain per person *per annum*; and as the population swells in other rice-growing areas during the new century, those producers are likely to have less rice available for export to the cities and to the Nilgiris district, unless biotechnology can come to their rescue by dramatically increasing yield. This is a possibility.

Nonetheless, some needed help has come to the district economy from the Planning Commission in New Delhi. Over the past quarter-century development of the Nilgiris district has quickened in part through a special central government scheme, the Hill Area Development Programme (Venugopal, in Hockings 2012: 414-15), which has injected funds into a number of local development projects. The National Committee on the Development of Backward Areas recommended in 1981 that:

> A broad-based strategy of action has to be evolved with a view to substantially improving the economic conditions of the inhabitants of hill areas. The backwardness of hill areas is not always due to lack of natural resources but largely due to continued neglect and lack of concerted action to develop their potential. The economic programmes for hill areas have to be formulated and executed in a coordinated fashion. The fragmentary approach in the past has adversely affected progress in these critical areas in various ways. It has confused priorities. It has impeded proper coordination and synchronisation of inter-related programmes. The programme for hill areas should be an integrated development programme for building up of infrastructure and supplying a package of inputs and other services almost simultaneously. Each component of the programme has to be inter-related and coordinated with the other components with the ultimate aim of maximising production and benefiting the hill people economically. (Quoted by '*Hillwatch*' 1988)

For the Nilgiris this approach had to address the radically different factors of an ecologically sensitive hilly environment and a need to develop more work for the burgeoning local population. No doubt the Programme has brought a fair amount of financial assistance to most local departments of the state's government, including roads, tribal welfare, sericulture, cooperative tea factories, horticulture, the growth of small or village industries, dairy development, health and medical services, fisheries, animal husbandry, tourism, cinchona, veterinary education and research, minor irrigation projects, Ootacamund's water supply, pollution control of the Ooty Lake, and eco-development by the Home Guards ('*Hillwatch*' 1988). No doubt, too, these are all worthwhile areas to spend money in, yet the results have been rather disappointing, since the resources were spread too thinly and there was no integrated approach to address the varied social and ecological problems in this district.

These problems have been apparent since about 1970: they have included continued heavy immigration of unskilled Tamilians, many of them from the Scheduled Castes and many others from Sri Lanka, who hoped to find labouring jobs; also a 'burgeoning floating population of tourists'. The change in urban population over 40 years has been large. Thus in 1971 Coonoor had a total population of 38,007, 16.1 per cent of whom were from Scheduled Castes (S.C.); Kotagiri then had 18,909 people, including 15.2 per cent S.C; while Ootacamund had 63,310 people, including 19.3 per cent S.C. Forty years later the urbanizing cluster at the centre of the district – i.e. Ootacamund (now with about 100,000 inhabitants), Wellington, Coonoor, and six adjoining Badaga communes – included 32 per cent of the district's S.C. total population, which was 238,014, and which by chance was itself 32 per cent of the district's total population. That these hill towns plus Kotagiri became a kind of Mecca for the work-hungry Scheduled Castes is indicated by the pronounced increase over 40 years, both in total and as a proportion of the urban population. In the rural areas there were a further 85,485 S.C. people, who made up 35.92 per cent of the district's S.C. total. And because of the general population growth, there followed unchecked encroachment on land, much of it steep enough to be prone to erosion; also overcrowded housing with makeshift 'hutments'; the destruction and pollution of water sources and woodland; inadequate public sanitation; lack of fuel and fodder supplies; and constant pollution of the urban air by diesel fumes. In the summer of 1987 and later several Badaga villages had to be supplied with their drinking water from a truck because many streams were drying up – and not because of weather so much as field irrigation. Several droughts have also had their impact on agriculture, plantations and the production of hydro-electric power (*'Hillwatch'* 1988: *passim*). Clean water is becoming a sought-after resource, even though we get two monsoons here.

AGRICULTURE AND TEA PLANTING

One can illustrate the scope of modern agricultural change by looking at Nanjena:ḍu, a large Badaga village in Me:kuna:ḍ; because for this place it is possible to state the acreage of specific crops both in 1881 and in 1955 (Table 8). During that long period the cultivated area here only increased by 1 per cent, making the data from these two years quite comparable. What is remarkable is the big shifts, mainly from subsistence to cash crops, that three-quarters of a century saw: tea quadrupled its acreage; Italian millet, formerly a staple grain, disappeared altogether in favour of little millet (and, more

Table 8: Crops Cultivated in Nanjena:ḍu Village, 1881 and 1955

Crops cultivated	*1881*	*1955*
Grains		
Italian millet (*Setaria italica*)	607.00 ha.	–
Barley (*Hordeum sativum*)	8.90 ha.	1.21 ha.
Finger millet (*Eleusine coracana*)	–	1.62 ha.
Little millet (*Panicum sumatrense*)	–	125.45 ha.
Wheat (*Triticum dicoccum*)	–	2.02 ha.
Vegetables		
Garlic	–	0.40 ha.
Coriander	–	1.01 ha.
Legumes	–	3.44 ha.
Miscellaneous vegetables	32.37 ha.	2.43 ha.
Commercial crops		
Tea	52.62 ha.	208.36 ha.
Potato	–	437.37 ha.
Cinchona	101.20 ha.	–
Eucalyptus	–	28.33 ha.
TOTAL	802.09 ha.	811.64 ha.

Source: Weigt 1970: 339; 1 hectare (ha) = 2.471 acres (ac.)

importantly for every family, purchased rice); cinchona was being grown here no more because the market for it had disappeared, now that other cures than quinine were available for malaria; and potato had become a major cash commodity. During 1955-2013 millets and even potato were slowly decreasing in area.

A former Nilgiri resident, on a post-war visit to Nanjena:ḍu, commented on 'the period of prosperity through which these cultivators of potatoes are passing. In them skill in agriculture is combined to a truly remarkable degree with an acute money sense' (Wynter-Blyth 1949: 254). Since 1955 the main trends have been a decline in little millet and potato, but a continuing increase in the area under tea.

Nanjena:ḍu has also been the scene of an agricultural drama that has had nationwide ramifications:

> Most of the village land here is owned by a community of commercially oriented farmers . . . who have been cultivating potato and tea. Just outside the village is a hamlet of scheduled caste labourers who were working on Badaga fields. In 1990 several among them occupied the village grazing lands, in part encouraged because the then District Collector was actively assigning land to lower-caste families. The Badagas rose as one and ensured that they were evicted, and the District Collector transferred. Similar skirmishes have been reported from many other parts of the country as well. (Gadgil & Guha 1995: 66)

Several more Badaga villages witnessed similar scenes. As for the other post-Independence agricultural trends these are also illustrated in Ke:ti, where in 1962 the Badagas were growing barley, cabbage, garlic, beans (*Phaseolus vulgaris*) and potato as their main summer crops, but with small acreages of amaranth, beetroot, carrot, coriander, mustard, peas, pumpkin, tea and some other beans (*Vicia faba* and *Dolichos lablab*); and the winter crop in early 1963 included, in addition to most of those items included in Table 8, some maize, onions, tomatoes, turnips and wheat. By the 1990s, not all of these crops were to be found anywhere there, because of a general switch to tea cultivation wherever possible.

> Endowed with elevation, climate, soil and a generally well-distributed 100–120 cm of rain, making fluctuations in crop less apparent, the Nilgiris has some of the highest yielding tea estates in the world . . . [S]ignificantly, the Nilgiris has the largest number of small holdings besides a hundred factories to produce 35 million kg of tea a year from the yields of these holdings. (Muthiah 1993: 27)

Since the 1970s, the Crop Diversification Scheme has been trying to encourage local farmers to switch over from potato, which had become unprofitable because of parasites, to a cash crop of tea. The immediate problem in making this switch however was a monetary one, since any farmer now planting his land with tea cuttings would not see any harvest for the first three years. Clearly, he needed to be tided over with the guarantee of an interim income, provided by the government. Similarly, all tea needs pruning once every five years. At that time all remaining leaf will be sold for low-grade tea and the branches used for firewood. But then there is no further yield for a year, and so the state government also compensates the grower for this shortfall at a rate (1994 figures) of Rs. 6,000 per hectare (U.S. $200 then). Otherwise, the normal plucking rounds are done by the small growers 22–25 times a year,[3] though leaf is never plucked between December and March.

This would appear to be an adequate and fair-minded intervention by government into what is, after all, a private capitalistic venture. The problems for small growers in the Nilgiris, some 90 per cent of whom are Badagas, have come however with recent fluctuations of the world tea market and the unwillingness of the Indian Tea Board to set maximum and minimum prices for leaf (which it was empowered to do in 1952). In April 2000 therefore there came a procession estimated at 150,000 of tea-cultivating protestors marching through Ootacamund, along with hunger-strikes and other peaceful demonstrations. By May of 2000 petitions were being given to officials, and then the district was quickly brought to a standstill. There were large public demonstrations of Badaga men and women, many thousands blocking the main roads in Kotagiri, Eḷḷena:yi and elsewhere, along with marching through the streets of Ootacamund, some of the men 'half naked', while certain people threw rocks at shop-fronts and set fire to buses; all to support their demand that the government set a minimum price of Rs. 15 for green leaf, so as to protect their own investment in small tea plantations. Altogether 550 Badagas were arrested; and, for the first time in history, there were mass arrests of women too who had indeed been courting arrest, although they were quickly released by the cowed authorities. In essence, Badaga tea-growers were demanding government protection of their industry, in the face of a customs duty of a mere 7.5 per cent levied on the tea imported from Sri Lanka, which helped to depress the price of Nilgiri tea (Radhakrishnan 2000). In 1999 the green leaf from Badaga growers was still getting Rs. 13 per kg., yet by May 2001 this price had dropped to Rs. 5 (even Rs. 4 in May 2003), and at a time when inflation had brought the rupee to its lowest value (it was Rs. 54 = U.S. $1 by 2013). The government's immediate response to these demonstrations was to reduce the sales tax on all made tea from 8 to 4 per cent, increase the import duty on tea (primarily Sri Lankan) from 15 to 35 per cent, and pay the small growers a subsidy of Rs. 5 per kg. of made tea (Haldorai 2000).

This low return had become a serious problem for all the growers during the 1990s. A green-leaf buyer in a village near Ke:ti was getting leaf from about 100 acres of land in 1994, all owned by Badagas. He estimated that a good field would yield some 4,000 kg. per acre per year – but after application of 700 kg. of urea or ammonia-based fertilizer, costing Rs. 1,750 then. The other essential costs of cultivating 1 acre (0.4 ha.) of tea in the central Ke:ti area were (in 1993 figures) Rs. 1,000 for weeding and maintenance, Rs. 4,000 or more for plucking, and Rs. 1,500 for fencing and care-taking. This suggests the cost of producing 1 kg. of green leaf was a little more than Rs. 2, while it was barely getting Rs. 3 in the auctions. But this presumes a full production of 4,000 kg. on each acre: in point of fact drought, frost or other local disasters can greatly reduce the production. If it is raining, the pluckers who have been hired for the day still have to be paid. In 1993 that meant giving Rs. 16 (or Rs. 22 by 1994), plus Re. 1 for a coffee, to each woman. On a normal day she would pluck about 20 kg. of leaf. If just one 15-day plucking round is missed, the crop becomes almost useless; and this might happen if there is a shortage of female pluckers, for men will not do the job.

One might expect the small farmer, faced with such crippling difficulties, to think about reverting to more traditional crops, *but he cannot do so*. In converting his land into a tea plantation he covered the slopes in a tight network of ditches and banks: only a massive mechanized terracing and uprooting of tea bushes could ever make the land again look the way it did – and in the process the topsoil would be lost! In short, conversion to tea is an irreversible process. No one, and certainly not the state government, is willing to meet the heavy expenses and risks that would be involved with trying to go back to unprofitable vegetable farming on the same piece of land. Thus in becoming capitalistic planters these farmers have unwittingly become enslaved by market forces.

LAND-HOLDING

Within the Nilgiris District from the middle of the nineteenth century that characteristic 'instrument of imperialistic exploitation' the Euro-pean planter was making his presence increasingly felt alongside the resident peasant farmers. If not born in India, his place of origin was usually somewhere in the British Isles; yet he was rather independent of the British administration, living remotely on his land almost like a third force distant from the rule of British-Indian law, on the one hand, and the vast millions at whom it was directed, on the other. An early observer, Edward Money, saw nineteenth-century planters as 'retired or cashiered Army or Navy officers, medical men, engineers, veterinary surgeons, steamer captains, chemists, shop-keepers of all kinds, stable-keepers, used-up policemen, clerks and goodness knows who besides' (quoted in Muthiah 1993: 133). Many of them were Irish or Scots. They were frankly in the district to make money, and scarcely for any other reason; whereas some at least of the missionaries and the local British administrators were there because of their presumed *mission civilisatrice*.

The planting industry had its root in a British Crown resolution of 1824 to facilitate the passage of land into European hands for coffee cultivation. The Wynaad Coffee Plantation, established by Parry and Co. in 1841, was one of the first in India, and 'the earliest instance of the entry of organized metropolitan capital into the plantations of South India' (Raman 1991: 244). By the 1860s the practice of commercial tea plantation also was established; and indeed, when there came a big decline in coffee cultivation in the Nilgiri region in the 1870s as a result of the 'deadly leaf-blight in the mid-1870s and a glut of cheap coffee from Brazil', this 'precipitated a progressive and steady rise in the cultivation of tea' (idem). Thus,

> In almost all the tea-growing regions in South India forest land which was officially labelled as 'waste land', was made available to the European planters free of [tax] assessment for five years, on the condition that at least one-fourth of the land would be planted within the first three years. Large-scale forest plunder was [thus] virtually legalized consequent on this stipulation . . . In places like Wynad and Nilgiris, many of the Europeans were freeholders . . . In addition to land at throw away prices, huge sums were spent by the state authorities to build up planting infrastructure such as the construction of 'planters' roads', the maintenance of hospitals, setting up of plantation crops experimental stations [such as at Kallar] and so on . . .

> By the turn of the century, the then dominant proprietary concerns were largely replaced by large corporate firms many of which were incorporated overseas. . . . So the tea plantations in South India, either corporate or individually owned, largely belonged to Europeans. . . . There was no fall in the area under tea even during the Depression. The area continued to increase throughout the first half of the twentieth century with a marginal fall in the mid-forties. . . . It is important to note that production was 'solely' for the external market. (Abbreviated from Raman 1991: 244-46)

Purely economic considerations coloured relations between this European plantocracy and the local peoples. The former bought up 'surplus' lands from the latter groups at what were then thought of as low but fair market prices (though it would later come to look more like land-grabbing): thus '. . . the tribes of Nilgiris like the Badagas were dispossessed through the direct 'purchase' of their land by European planters' (ibid.: 246). From the 1870s until the present day plantations have also offered poorly but regularly paid labouring jobs to landless Badagas and members of other groups: 'The workers were paid low wages and provided with practically no facilities . . . [T]he workers were paid a wage rate of 3 to 4 annas for men and 2 to 3 annas for women which again remained stagnant for more than a decade from 1881 onwards' (ibid.: 248).[4]

Nor did things improve much in the early twentieth century, for '. . . the pre-Depression wages . . . were 7 and 5 annas for men and women respectively. . . . Money wages remained stagnant for about fourteen years (1930-44) . . . at 5 annas for men and 3 to 4 annas for women. These were precisely the wage rates of the depression years' (ibid.: 255-56).

But aside from these two economic exceptions, of either selling their land or having to work as plantation labourers, the Badagas never engaged much with the planting industry until, from the 1920s onwards, some small Badaga tea farmers emerged to swell its ranks. By 1956, a decade after Independence and after all those Britons who had decided not to stay on in India had sold up their estates and left, quite a large number of Badagas had capitalized on this much-changed situation; for I counted within the plateau area of the district a total then of 112 planters with Badaga names, making up 42 per cent of the over-all total.[5] (Thirty-eight other plantations in the same area were owned at that time by companies without a named proprietor.) In contrast, the Wainad area then had no Badaga estate proprietors.

The twentieth century quite understandably saw a marked decline in available land per capita, as Table 9 illustrates. 'As population has grown, average farm size has fallen to a point where many farming families do not need the labor of young children' (Caldwell et al. 1988: 184). This is the case in the Nilgiris today. It was possible to make a precise comparison of one administrative 'village', Śo:lu:ru, at two points some 80 years apart. Although a few other communities live there as labourers, this 'village' (actually a commune) may be considered typical of Badaga settlements, and has hardly changed its official boundaries since the Land Settlement of 1884.[6] Table 9 shows the typical, much-diminished amount of mean land-holding in this particular Badaga commune.

Table 9: Comparison of Data for Śo:lu:ru (Sholur) Village, in 1884 and 1962

Economic feature	*1884*	*1962*
Total 'village' area	9,113 ha.	9,111 ha.
Registered patta lands	913 ha. (all Badaga-owned)	1,619 ha. (nearly all Badaga)
Number of *pattas* (deeds)	49 single registrations; 63 joint ones (i.e. 112 total)	372 total
Population (1881, 1961)	1,772 (all communities)	8,518 (all communities)
Total houses	384	930
Mean household size	4.61 persons	9.15 persons
Estimate of cropped area	749 ha. (in 1880–81)	607 ha.
Average cultivated area	0.42 ha. per capita	0.07 ha. per capita (in 1961)

Sources: Based on McIver & Stokes 1883; Benson 1884; Arputhanathan 1953: 43; and Subrahmanyam 1962: 3-4.

From Table 9 evidence of several important shifts emerges:

i. In eighty years the population increased fivefold;
ii. In eighty years the size of households doubled, from an average of 4.61 to an average of 9.15;[7]
iii. In eighty years the number of registered land-holdings (i.e. *pattas*) has more than tripled;
iv. In eighty years the area of *patta* land doubled through the release of government-held reserves (but was not all cropped);
v. Fragmentation of holdings has thus been taking place;

vi. The estimate of the total cultivated area in 1962 was a little below that for 1880-81;

vii. Average cultivated area thus dropped from 0.42 ha. per capita in 1881 to 0.07 ha. per capita around 1961; in other words, only one-sixth as much cropped land is being used for each person as was the case in 1881.

As we see, in modern times the size of land-holdings per capita has been steadily declining, so that it comes as no surprise to find this paralleled by a declining fertility of the soil. Most land-holdings of a family are quite small. In 1963, after questioning a sample of Badagas in Hulla:ḍa and O:rana:yi, I found that the median holding was about 2 acres (less than 1 ha.). The smallness of the average farmer's plot, along with the repeated failure of potato crops over the past several decades, have certainly been two of the more important factors prompting Badagas to look for prolonged education for their boys and girls, with a view to their getting future employment in government, banks, schools, businesses, or other urban contexts.

LOCAL INDUSTRIALIZATION

The village economies have never been industrialized, in part because Badagas had no traditional crafts, and local farming does not lend itself to mechanization in the way that it had to in vast tracts of Australia, the USA, Canada, the Ukraine, Russia and Argentina which were feeding the newly expanding countries of the West in the nineteenth century. There will be no great expansion of machinery sales or repair shops in an area of small land-holdings like the Nilgiris. Even tea, the main local plantation crop, which is nowadays harvested by machine on flat land in Japan, will continue for long to be plucked using human labour on the Nilgiri Hills (just as it is in China, Sri Lanka and Assam). It makes no economic sense to bring in costly machinery here when labour remains so readily and cheaply available, and wholesale tea prices so depressed. But one *can* use cheap cooly (i.e. non-Badaga) labour, without necessarily involving one's wife and sons in the tedious field-work of a small tea plantation. It is only in the last several years of the present century that construction work on the plains has begun attracting labour away from the Nilgiri plantations – a source of much concern for all the local planters today.

Given the present shortage of arable land and the depressed state of farming and of tea prices, it is not surprising that a small minority of Badagas in the more central villages have found jobs as labourers, clerks or managers in a few local factories. The most important of these has been the old Government Cordite Factory, at Aravanga:ḍu, a Central Government munitions enterprise opened in 1901, and the first place in India to generate hydroelectric power.

Further industrialization only occurred long after Independence. The basic aims of India's Third Five-Year Plan were to sustain economic growth at over 5 per cent a year; to develop a self-generating economy, with self-sufficiency in food grains; to expand industrial capacity until, after a decade, India might in the early 1970s be largely independent of foreign aid for further industrial development; to make maximum use of manpower and open new areas for employment; and finally to move towards greater equality of income and opportunity for every social group in the country.

It did not altogether work out that way, of course. Foreign aid has continued to pour into the country for decades as an important part of the national budget; and as Scarlett Epstein has shown (1973), the rural rich have been getting richer as the poor get poorer. The Green Revolution did help to increase the production of grains, and there has been broad industrial development, however. Overall, this was intended as a programme by which the nation might 'pull itself up by the bootstraps'. For the Nilgiris, in particular, the Plan meant the initiation of a raw film factory, the extension of rural cooperative organizations, and above all else the continued construction of a large Canadian-sponsored hydroelectric system. Between 1924 and 1989 six power-houses were built here (Hockings 2012: 436-37).

Close to the Cordite Factory at Aravanga:ḍu is a smaller factory, the Needle Industries. Founded in 1950, it has employed women in the main and – like that other factory – was built on the site of a nineteenth-century brewery that probably gave employment to a few Badagas even then (Francis 1908: 290, 312; Gopalakrishnan 1995: 527, 531). So both of these factory sites have been in operation for a very long time, and are nothing new to the local Badagas.

In 1967 a large new factory making raw film was opened just outside Ootacamund: this was Hindustan Photo Films (or HPF, incorporated in 1960), another Central Government undertaking that now employs about 4,000, including several hundred Badagas. In contrast to the tea factories, this one obviously has to use modern equipment and procedures to make photo-sensitive materials and survive. It tends to employ college graduates, who seem to relish the chance of having a government clerical or manufacturing job that is within the boundaries of their own district (Gopalakrishnan 1995: 529-31). With Eastman Kodak filing for bankruptcy in 2012 and a worldwide switch from film cameras to digital cameras being now far advanced one has to wonder how secure the future of HPF will be, however.

Another factory that makes seed and other agricultural products, namely Rallis India Ltd., was set up in 1971 not far from Śo:lu:ru, and employs 330 people. In the past few years the Ponds Company, producing cosmetics, opened a small factory to process mushrooms, close to the Needle Industries (Gopalakrishnan 1995: 532-33). And in addition there are dozens of cooperative tea factories which also offer some labouring positions. It must be noted, however, that these places are still essentially drying and packing sheds equipped with machinery owing its design to the late nineteenth century. Compared with these above-mentioned undertakings, factory work in the local tea industry has mainly been a tedious labouring experience with unchanging work habits and types of equipment.

Among these factories, the Cordite Factory has been the longest employer of the greatest number of local villagers: it has now been helping some households for four generations, by adding the regular income of one or two men to the uncertainties of the farm revenues.

That there has not been more industrialization here is probably a blessing in disguise for, as two ecologists have pointed out, the impact on the environment is usually grievous: '(a) Indian industry is highly inefficient; (b) industry has no commitment to sustainable resource use or the maintenance of a clean environment; (c) employment in industry has grown very tardily. These are the hallmarks of India's high cost – low quality economy' (Gadgil & Guha 1995: 31).

GROWTH OF THE BADAGA POPULATION

It is quite remarkable that, although the national census began in 1871, there are actually reliable earlier enumerations of the Badagas and other local people, done by interested British officials, from the years 1812, 1821, 1825, 1844, 1847 (this census under-enumerated), 1856 and 1866. It means that the time-depth of the census documentation in the Nilgiris is among the longest in the non-Western world (Japan, China and Jamaica being the record-holders in this respect).

As Appendix 2 shows quite dramatically, the Badaga population has been increasing steadily since 2,207 people were enumerated in a preliminary yet revealing census made by Keys in 1812, on the very eve of their first European contact. But by the end of the twentieth century growth was at a standstill: the census total of 134,187 Badagas in 1991 had only increased to 134,514 by 2001.

Badaga was enumerated as a separate language category in every census from 1871 to 1971; language is an excellent marker of ethnic identity, and thus of their total. In the 1971 census, though, we read that 'Badaga is considered to be a dialect of Kannada in the Kannada, Badaga and Kodagu Sub-group of the Dravidian family.' This flies in the face of our lengthy dictionary of their language (Hockings & Pilot-Raichoor 1992); but, dialect or not, a total of 104,392 Badaga speakers was still published for 1971. But then in 1981 the Badagas simply disappeared from census view: evidently they were added into the national total of Kannaḍa speakers. These latter, recent immigrants from Karnataka, form quite a small minority in the Nilgiris District, and yet their total suddenly jumped to 157,672 in the 1981 census because of this administrative decision.

We certainly believed in our *Dictionary* that we were documenting a distinct language, rather than a dialect of Kannaḍa; and the eminent Dravidian linguist, M.B. Emeneau, made the situation quite clear, too. He wrote: 'Badaga is obviously closely related to Kannada. . . . However, . . . it is possible to identify several features in which it agrees with the languages of the Nilgiri subgroup (Kota and Toda) rather than with Kannada' (1989: 135).

The annual rate of growth of Badagas from 1951 to 1961 averaged 2.7 per cent, and that from 1961 to 1971 was 1.8 per cent. Since there was no obvious down-turn in health, it is clear that this decrease was an effect of the partial adoption of birth control practices. Since these continued to be more widely adopted during the 1970s in many villages, it is reasonable to assume an annual growth rate of 1.5 per cent after 1971. Then in 1975 came a report of the Backward Classes Commission citing an official figure of 125,821 Badagas for that year. But this figure is questionable: it was probably not based on an enumeration, but rather an extension from an earlier figure based on an assumed rate of increase.

There is little doubt that up to 1975 the community had been steadily increasing (Appendices 1 and 2). Yet my demographic study of four central villages over one generation, 1963-90, presented compelling data to indicate that as Badaga women gained more control over their own fertility since their adoption of family planning methods there from approximately 1975, the size of the family declined to a point where, in some villages, scarcely two children per couple altogether were being born, on the average, by the 1980s, and the Badaga population has thus been levelling off since then (Hockings 1999: 171-93).[8] So if we rely on the 2001 census figure of 134,514 Badagas, then we can assume that birth control is being so effectively pursued nowadays that there is virtually no population increase.

In that 1999 study I have espoused an economic theory of population decline which is generally called the cost-benefit approach. Its central assumption is that Third-World parents recognize that they get some utility from their children (as a kind of consumer goods, as producers, and as old-age insurance); but also that they will incur costs for their children. A principle thus emerges which balances the benefits, which generally decrease with any economic improvement, against the costs, which regularly increase. This principle in general qualifies the desired number of children.

John Caldwell found, on the basis of his research in West Africa, that while the traditional family was large and wealth tended to flow from the more junior to the senior generations, after a demographic transition and radical readjustment in values, modern families became much smaller and wealth tended to flow from parents to their children, especially to fund their education. Namboodiri systematized these ideas about wealth flow in a series of hypotheses (1986):

(1) it is only if the family becomes nucleated that fertility will decline;
(2) industrialization is not a necessary precondition for fertility decline;
(3) fertility decline starts with the reversal of direction of the inter-generational wealth flow, which in all traditional peasant societies has been from the younger to the older generation.

All three features have been found true of recent Badaga household life, as hallowed attitudes about the family have altered. Certainly, many sons were called for when there was high infant mortality, and everyone worked on their land; but no longer.[9]

The frequent observation that young men educated in a city college will require sophisticated wives is motivation enough to keep teenaged girls in school, with the hope of ultimately linking them to financially-sound spouses; but it has the unplanned effect of reducing the total number of fertile years of these young women. Some of them now miss the opportunity to marry altogether: thus one elderly Gauḍa couple, for example, were living with their children as a joint-stem family in 1990 that included two unmarried daughters aged 43 and 39, as well as a married son aged 37 and his dependents (Hockings 1999: 220). In earlier times such a household would have been almost unthinkable.

A change in values about household organization and size is not just a response to the changing economic conditions but an acknowledgement that the quality of life today is different. So, following from the discussion of schooling in Chapter 14, we should ponder whether the example of the German, Swiss, British and Westernized Indian missionary and schoolteacher families living in the Ke:ti Valley area, Kotagiri or elsewhere in the nineteenth century had already suggested an alternative approach to child-raising for local Badagas; it was certainly a very visible model. I suspect that these people became a significant reference group and avenue for modernization, though without prompting mass conversions; for barely 3 per cent of Badagas are Christian today.

THE MODERNIZATION PROCESS

By labelling the Nilgiri indigenes 'hill-tribes', British officialdom was also marginalizing these people from the Imperial endeavour in the later nineteenth century (Francis 1908: 138). This is especially ironic when one considers that the summer residence of the Governor of Madras Presidency, here at Government House, became the temporary headquarters of the regional government for 4-5 months of each year from 1870 on (Hockings 2012: 396-98). The hill-tribes were recognized as living by different rules and, in the Toda case, received considerable encouragement to do so. Those people who might count in India's future, it was thought, were the 'Bengalee baboos', men who would become the clerks and middle-level administrators of Her Majesty's Indian Empire; the 'martial races', preeminently the high-status Rajputs and Sikhs; the Anglo-Indians, reliable patriots who could operate the machinery; and the Parsis, ever trustworthy middlemen, bankers and traders – it was *these* people for whom the policies had been primarily fashioned, the people in whose hands India's future was ultimately seen to rest (long after the lesson of the Mutiny). Several English-medium universities were opened in big cities and medical schools started, with a view to making these categories of reliable people yet more valuable contributors to the building of the Indian Empire. The education of small hill-tribes, by contrast, could safely be left in the hands of German and other missionaries who (until 1914) could do no harm. So far as the Nilgiri region was viewed, it included no indigenous native princes, no local Brahmins, no indigenous bankers, few valuable raw materials. Plantation crops were the one attractive prospect and were to be expanded from 1893 onwards, with the guidance of the United Planters' Association of Southern India), then largely a British fraternity (Muthiah, in Hockings 2012: 961-66; Philip 2003: 107-31).

The marginalization of the small Nilgiris district is quite ironic when we reflect that since Independence it has been producing two of the four most prominent foreign currency-earners in the Indian economy, tea and textile yarn from polyfibres produced from the eucalyptus plantations (the other two big national exports are fish and leather, and only in the present century has computer software become a major export; Gadgil and Guha 1995: 27). Perhaps the Nilgiris district is too far away from any big city to play a serious role in modern influence-peddling politics. The fact that years of agitation to change the Badaga community's status from a Backward Class to a Scheduled Tribe have yet to bear fruit hardly bespeaks a strong national power-base here.

Religious Changes

The historical impact of the Europeans who were connected with the Basel Mission, and of other British residents, shopkeepers, planters and local officials, is relevant to an important debate within demography: has it been possible in Third World countries for fertility to decline without Westernization occurring more or less simultaneously? Freedman (1979) has developed such an argument. From what has been presented here, however, it should be quite clear that in villages near the towns and mission stations the visibility of European family models and of Christian values has been consistently present for more than two full lifetimes, despite minimal industrialization or conversion at such places. One could hardly argue that, even though present, these alien lifestyles had no impact whatever on Badagas, when it is evident that quite a few hundred Badagas who were attracted to a Church *did* adopt the ideal of a nuclear household and even a European style of men's dress and of *décor* in their houses. Whatever the original motives of the missionaries might have been, in retrospect it would seem clear that they offered models for modernization in their schools, in their public behaviour, and in their own European family relationships and home settings.

The process of modernization has brought about some changes in Badaga religion, aside from the conversions. Hindu temples may nowadays have electric lighting, for example, although electrical cable is strictly a polluting material as it is covered with rubber, which the most conservative of villagers would consider to be 'like leather'. Polluting anthropologists and other strangers, among them government dignitaries, are now conducted inside most of the temples, sometimes with a certain fanfare. Another change has come with the new value placed on time: ceremonies that used to last for three days are now finished in one, those that ran for a week now last for only three days; and in general there is a short-cutting of the inessential elements of ritual. No longer is every ritual item in a ceremony or festival performed properly. Some ceremonies show signs of dying out, so irrelevant have they become. The annual festival for Be:ḍa Sa:mi (the Lord of the Hunt) now rarely occurs, and only at a few villages. The aid of this god was sought to protect the villagers and their fields from tigers, pigs, bears, porcupines or other destructive wild animals (Metz 1864: 67-68; Francis 1908: 339-40; Emeneau 1971: 5, 42, 564, 744); but nowadays, with the increase in the non-Badaga rural population, illegal hunting and even poisoning of carnivora, and the great extension in the area of tea estates, predatory tigers or other large animals have become so rare on the plateau that there is little practical need to propitiate Be:ḍa Sa:mi.

In tandem with the shortening of inessential ritual, such as in funerals, which do not last longer than a day any more (Hockings 2001: 65), there has come a reduction in fears about pollution. The anthropologist who, fifty years ago, could hardly set foot across Badaga thresholds, is now as welcome in many village homes as any other non-Badaga of some repute. Furthermore all too many Badagas have over those same fifty years suffered the indignity of being jailed, usually for offences against Prohibition regulations. Who can know what they might have eaten or whom they had touched while in the Coimbatore Jail? Yet when these men return home, they rarely have to undergo the traditional rituals that would remove the impurities caused by any distant travel. No one would now be outcasted, either, for having eaten with a non-Badaga somewhere, or taken a trip to Delhi: it happens all the time.

One thing that we do not find in this corner of India is any definite religious opposition to human sterilization, education for girls, divorce, widow remarriage, or adult marriage for young women, as is still commonly encountered elsewhere in both Hindu and Muslim societies. The Badaga Shaivism, never having been a scriptural religion for them, is not a rigorously prescriptive one either. Funerals today are often curtailed or reorganized for the convenience of some family members. More than one villager attending a funeral confided to me that he had no real conviction there was any life after death. I would conjecture that such lightly held religious views have made it easier for the Badagas to modernize. The fact that they have so rapidly reduced their fertility is related to this: women, who in other peasant societies have tended to be poorly educated and conservative, here showed me as early as 1963 that even when little educated they were much more likely to turn to scientific medicine for resolving health problems than were their menfolk; and barely a decade later they turned to sterilization and contraception too.

Lingayats, over the past century at least, have taken up the worship of gods other than Shiva. The non-Lingayat Badagas have also adopted new gods, mostly Sanskritic deities related to Shiva, such as his sons Gaṇapati and Subramaṇia, and also the popular Aiyappan. An interesting parochialization of the great Hindu tradition is to be seen in the temple established at Tu:raṭṭi for a stone brought there from Benares (Varaṇasi); or the silver image of Subramaṇia brought to a Ka:ṭe:ri temple from Benares; or the 'footprint of Rāma', one *avatar* of Vishṇu, found on a rock at Manjakombe.

Viewing all of these strands of modernization, Heidemann (1997: 64) saw signs of a cultural revitalization in the 1970s and 1980s. The catalyst for this was the heavy influx of Tamil-speaking workers from Sri Lanka, many of them squatters on traditional Badaga lands (Heidemann, in Hockings 2012: 858-59; see above, p. 294); combined perhaps with the lacklustre performance of the German scientific experts (of the Indo-German Nilgiris Development Project) in halting the devastating potato blight of the 1960s (Neunhäuser, in Hockings 2012: 440-42). Science and internationalism were then unable to answer the needs of many. So 'Badagas sought refuge in their unity, strengthened their traditions by joining clubs, created new symbols of their old world, composed various hymns to their mother-goddess Hette, employed city professionals to produce music-cassettes in their villages, and celebrated the Festival of Hette with more fervour than before' (Heidemann 1997: 64, trans.). Traditionalists still abound, and their concerted effort over more than two decades (still unsuccessful in 2013) to have the Badaga people classified by government as a Scheduled Tribe, at least to get access to benefits, must be seen as a measure of their political influence.

Westernization, Urbanization and Industrialization

In discussing modernization, I have viewed it as a general process of cultural and economic change that can encompass three more specific processes, viz: Westernization, Urbanization or Industrialization. Some humanists might add Christianization as a fourth process. At any given time each can be occurring by itself or in association with the other two. Modernization could be seen as a communication process in which traditional peasant populations acquire and use more education and information about the nation state in which they live. As a result their orientations towards the outside world change, and their attitudes towards urban culture raise new possibilities in their minds. Modern sports and twenty-first-century forms of entertainment, especially television, cinema, film music, and the Internet, have become very attractive. Films and Internet materials not only offer a mental escape, but suggest new fashions in dressing, travel, being employed, housing, behaving, and relating to the opposite sex.

A result of this exposure is urbanization, a change in values that favours the employment, shopping, social life and general ambience associated with cities. Its practical effect has been a move to the towns by many of the most educated, most progressive, most employable and competent young and middle-aged people. The relative wealth of this new elite or 'new middle class', if I may so designate it, has been invested in houses in town, equipment for those houses, private English-medium schooling for the children, computers, cars or motorcycles, and modern styles of clothing and furniture. This change is certainly an irreversible process; not to say that everyone who wants to get modernized must move into a town, but they will adopt many of the urban-centred values just referred to, even if still living in a village home out of preference or necessity. Villages like Eḍapiḷḷu, which are very close to a town, now contain many such urbanized households, in up-dated double-storey houses.

The modernization of these people has been different from that of the Western world, and indeed of other parts of India, for it has not been dependent on industrialization so much as on the commercialization of agriculture and plantations, combined with widespread opportunities for schooling. Only a small minority of Badagas have been working in factories. Clearly modernization means more than just getting a steady job in industry. It is participation in the modern mass media of the nation – seeing films frequently, reading newspapers and magazines, listening to radio or watching television. It is attaining a sufficient level of education to obtain 'white collar' urban (and preferably government) employment and, in the case of young women, to attract a well-employed groom. And, as was mentioned, it is shopping in town and visiting, even studying, in modern cities.

These aspects of modernization turn the eyes of the youth away from farm-work, which is easily seen today as being dirty, tedious, unrewarding and low-status. By 1970 tea began to appear a better prospect than traditional agriculture, if a family owned some land, and it could then produce green leaf using the labour of cheaply hired pluckers rather than the family members. Whether tea or vegetables are now grown, the demonstrably shrinking land-holdings do not require the numbers of family workers that they employed in previous generations. This fact, when combined with the continuing shortage of good urban jobs, the high costs of bringing up children today, and the decreased need to produce extra sons to replace those who might die in childhood, goes a long way towards explaining the reduced fertility over the past generation or two among the Badagas. All of these factors were certainly understood even half a century ago by the Badaga womenfolk, whether educated or not.

The long-available school education, much English and Tamil literacy, and recent participatory use of several mass media, have combined to propel the Badaga community towards modernization. While men have tended to have more education, more urban contacts, and greater multilingualism – as is true throughout much of Asia – it is the somewhat schooled category of Badaga women who by 1963 could already see India's future lying in industrialization; who have opted for modern medical practices and who, by agreeing to their sterilization after one or two children, have over the past several decades begun to take control of their fertility and so play a more central role in the future of their families and community. Any development worker or public health official who still thinks that in a patrilineal society it is the men who will always be 'in control' of attitudes and developments should take note of this finding.

The effects of this recent change have been widespread in Badaga society. The child-woman ratio has dropped appreciably, and with lower fertility and lower infant mortality the toll on women's health has lessened while their life expectancy increased. A switch from potatoes and other farm crops to tea has also had a similar effect, by much reducing the number of days that Badaga women would be labouring in their fields. With fewer children in the family, a college education has become more accessible to teenagers, especially since several undergraduate colleges were opened in the Nilgiris over the past fifty years (Hockings and Mulley, in Hockings 2012: 285-86). The employment, lifestyle, health and longevity prospects of the younger generation thus look brighter than they ever did before.

The Demographic Transition

In summarizing these developments, we can see in Diag. 12 the start of a demographic transition among the Badagas.

> It is probably true that declining mortality has to a considerable extent allowed fertility decline and to a lesser extent the rise in the age at female marriage, but in neither case has it been the cause. The truth seems to be that a range of demographic changes occurred at much the same time neither because of close interrelation nor because of coincidence, but because they are all products of massive social and economic changes during the last half-century. (Caldwell et al. 1988: 255)

HISTORY AND ECOLOGY

With all the changes I outlined above, the natural resources of the land have suffered, and continue to do so. For, 'though environmen-

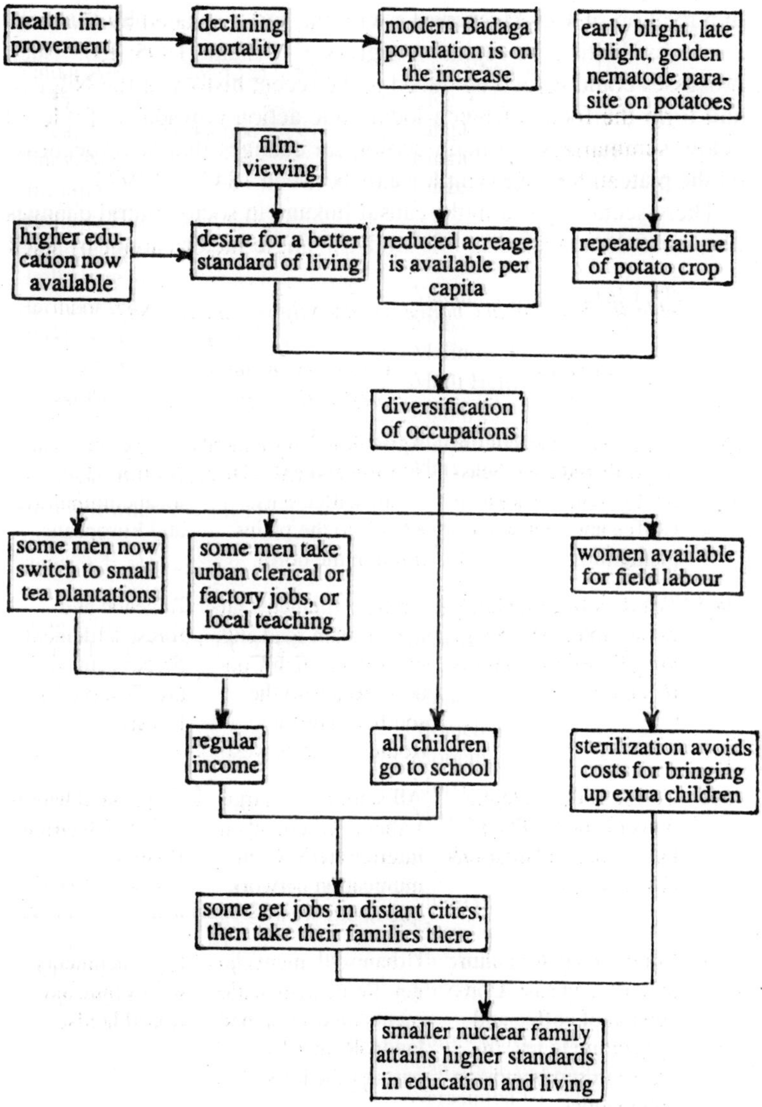

Diagram 12: Factors Leading to a Demographic Transition

tal history offers some of the most original and challenging history now being written, it inevitably tells the same dismal tale: of land taken, exploited, exhausted; of traditional cultures said to have lived in a relation of sacred reverence with the soil displaced by the reckless individualist, the capitalist aggressor' (Schama 1995: 13).[10] Such processes could indeed be traced in the recent history of the Nilgiris, and form the focus of much local civic action nowadays. Table 10 below summarizes the main ecological changes that have occurred on the plateau for four sample years between 1847 and 1990.

There seems to be a multi-causal linkage in sociocultural changes like those documented in this study: a single factor cannot by itself

Table 10: Ecological Changes on the Nilgiri Plateau, 1847-1990

Year	*Land use*	*Communications and settlements*	*Legal categories*
1847	Subsistence agriculture in north and east. Seasonal grazing in west. Coffee and fuel-wood plantations.	Agricultural settlements in north and east. Three urban settlements. Routes to the plains through the north.	Land controlled controlled by local communities and Europeans.
1905	Tea & coffee plantations in the south (18.75 sq. km.) Forest plantations (6 sq. km).	Urban settlements larger. A main road and railway through Coonoor. Roads to the southern portions. Routes towards west.	Revenue and forest settlement 55 per cent of area reserved as forests.
1950	Coffee and tea plantations in south (47 sq. km.). Forest plantations (18 sq. km.).	All settlements larger. Labour settlements in interior areas. Communication network into south-west.	Forest land leased to T.N. Electricity Board.
1990	Commercial agriculture in north and east. Conversion of coffee and agriculture to tea. Increase in scrublands on outer slopes.	Urban settlements larger. Permanent settlements on encroached lands. Routes to all parts of the hills.	Encroachments on revenue and leased lands.

Source: Based on Prabhakar & Gadgil 1995: 165, Table 1.

cause a new situation, but several discernible factors, including unpredictable ecological changes, combine to cause variant patterns of a new situation. This process may be stated in another way. When a community shifts from subsistence cultivation to rational participation (i.e. maximization of gains) in a cash economy, certain changes follow in their culture and social organization; changes which are conditioned by a combination of local ecological factors, outside governmental activity, a changing labour market, the availability of certain goods, services and entrepreneurial personnel, adequate flow of information, and the play of chance events (historical accidents). Because the combination of all these conditions varies from region to region, the manner of the economic transition will also vary. We should thus not expect a replication of the successive phases of the Badagas' development elsewhere in India, even though such people as the neighbouring Coorgs may suggest a superficial parallel (Srinivas 1952: *passim*; Muthanna 1953: *passim*).

The Badagas' transition to a cash economy depended in part on very favourable ecological conditions. Their land and the Nilgiri climate were well suited to the new crops, and for some decades in the nineteenth century it was even possible to extend the area of cultivation. A protectionist government fixed grain prices, provided roads and encouraged railway construction, and even supplied Badagas with technical information and improved seeds. No external pressure was placed upon them to make the transition; yet some of the more affluent farmers living near towns took the chance with initial crops of marketable vegetables or grain to sell to the local breweries. Their decision found some reward and incentive in the profits from the market; and with the advent of the railway and the First World War this expanded dramatically. Once some success in the market had brought these profits into their community, reinvestment and spending took a variety of forms. The Badaga economy became increasingly differentiated, there was much variation in wealth from one family to another, class differentiation based on affluence began to emerge, and most families sought to maximize their gains, even at the expense of their time-honoured relations with the neighbouring tribes.

Though the details of their history are unique, there are certain regularities that tie the Badaga case in with others; in particular, the modern stress on education, the desire for non-essential consumer goods, reinvestment of profits in land (Epstein 1962: 326-28), the role of mass media in popularizing urban tastes (Rao 1966), reduction of the birth rate (Hockings 1999: 171-93), the replacement of traditional cooperative associations by market relations and the new cooperative societies, and the periodic restructuring of their society through factional disputes.

NOTES

1. Most of the statistics early in this chapter were drawn from the report, *Economic Intelligence Service – Profiles of Districts – November 1993* (Bombay: Centre for Monitoring Indian Economy).
2. Bauxite is an important mineral product (32,485 tonnes in 1993), not mentioned in this volume because it has no particular significance for the Badagas, although it is quarried in the area; Hockings 2012: 123.
3. The United Planters' Association of Southern India (based in Coonoor) now recommends 38-45 times, but that will require more fertilizer and some careful plucking.
4. Another source recorded the monthly wages in 1877 as being Rs. 4.5 for women, and Rs. 6.5-7 for men; an anna was Re. $^{1}/16$.
5. This number includes proprietors but not managers; UPASI 1956.
6. It is 19 km. by road from Ootacamund, and embraces the Badaga commune of So:lu:ru. The small amount of land deceptively classified in the surveys as 'available for sale' was in fact so steep and rocky that even today it has scarcely any economic use, unless perhaps for common grazing. For an analysis of the disputes over land between Śo:lu:ru people, British settlers and the government, see Sutton 2009: 64-68.
7. That Śo:lu:ru was not atypical in this respect is suggested by the fact that in 1867 the average number of persons per Badaga household for the entire district was 4.36. This reflects the rarity of extended families even then; Shortt & Ouchterlony 1868: 61.
8. In recent years several sites on the Internet have given wildly exaggerated figures for the Badaga total population. Thus in 2011 one could read that they numbered 145,000 (in 1991), 245,400 (now?), 350,000, and even 400,000! There is no evidence for such numbers: by my calculations, we are looking at roughly 18 per cent of a district population of 735,000 (in the 2011 census).
9. One Indian study concluded ominously that in order to achieve a 95 per cent probability of having one son survive to adulthood, a couple would need to produce six children; May & Heer 1968.
10. On environmental history, see too Gadgil & Guha 1995: *passim*. For documentation of the processes Schama refers to, see Sutton 2009: *passim*.

CHAPTER 18

A Summary and Conclusions

To the extent that the data permit, we have seen how the Badagas migrated to the Nilgiris in small bands from a few villages of southern Mysore between the sixteenth and eighteenth centuries, the main flow of refugees coming during 1565-1617. Some came out of fear of the invading Moslems, some because of famine, and a few were brought to the plateau by the chieftains of Ummattūr. While the Lingayats mostly originated in the more southerly villages of Saragūr and Angala, the majority of the population came from villages in one tiny area of about 20 by 30 km., lying immediately to the east of the temple town of Nanjangud. Once on the Nilgiris they cleared forested land, scattered their small hamlets across the rolling hills, and continued to pursue a mixed farming economy, one augmented by some hunting and swidden cultivation. Those things which were needed but they did not themselves produce were either obtained from the neighbouring Todas, Kotas, Kuṟumbas, Iṟulas or Chettis or might be bought in several market towns near the foot of the hills, usually by bartering home-grown millets.

Up to the late eighteenth century coinage, although in wide use across India, was hardly in circulation on the Nilgiri plateau; usually it would change hands only during family ceremonies. The levying of tribute under Haidar Ali and Tipu Sultan, and the continuing demand for land revenue at the old government outpost of Daṇṇayaka Ko:ṭe, put some pressure on Badaga farmers to sell more in the nearby markets in order to get enough coinage to pay their assessments. At about this time, if not before, some differentiation based on wealth was becoming apparent within the community: certain men who were descended from the villages' founders became more affluent and were treated as gentry, although at the other extreme there were people so poverty-stricken that sometimes they even had to contract their children into servitude with well-to-do families.

Though the British had acquired the Nilgiri Hills by the Treaty of Seringapatam in 1799, they were slow to appreciate their prize. It was only after twenty years, and several minor explorations, that a British official, John Sullivan (Pl. 16), the Collector of Coimbatore, held serious thoughts of settling on the plateau. No doubt he was prompted by his own romantic inclinations after hearing the reports of other weekend explorers and making a brief tour of the healthy hills for himself; but he was also invited to come there by Badagas, as they wanted someone to survey their lands and let them know if they were being assessed for too much revenue.[1] The train of events which the energetic John Sullivan initiated brought towns, markets, highways, public buildings, cash and governmental administration almost overnight to a people who had previously existed without the benefit of any such facilities in their mountainous home.

As soon as Sullivan had taken up residence in what later became Kotagiri he began experimenting with several European crops, also giving seeds to some interested Badagas. Even after his arrival, while the very new township of Ootacamund was becoming established, British officials continued for a decade to collect the land revenue down in the plains. They had adopted a policy of fixing grain prices, which gave some encouragement to those Badagas who sold their grain surplus in the lowland towns; and this indirectly fostered the practice of storing credit gained there by selling the food grains for coinage. After 1823 several main roads were appearing and a market was established at the new town of Ootacamund. Thereafter the Badaga economy slowly became monetized, with Ootacamund as the centre for their trade. By 1840 Badagas were making many of their bazaar purchases with coinage.

The first total of the Badaga population (in 1812) was only 2,207, but by 1821 – perhaps a better census than that in Keys' survey – it had reached 3,778. The British population increased rapidly too, offering people who lived near the towns a chance to labour for a cash wage or to grow European vegetables for the small market that was unexpectedly on their doorstep. While their tradition of intensive farming in nearby fields was well suited to the new crops, and the Nilgiri climate by chance blessed their endeavours, learning to compete in a labour market was another matter: it was only because some feared that the alien government might otherwise increase the land tax, out of revenge, that some Badagas came to be persuaded to work for Europeans.

The early British influences on Badaga culture were, as we have seen, the introduction of a local market, of a cash economy and a demand for labour and vegetables. But this was enough to trigger a rise in the fortunes of the community and also to prompt a remarkable increase in the size of the Badaga population, as the censuses make clear. Another significant British innovation was education. Within just a year of Sullivan's arrival a school had been opened in De:na:ḍu; yet it was only after 1856 that Badagas perceived some value in schooling. That value lay in the novel acquisition of Tamil literacy, which was slowly becoming seen as the one sure passport to such coveted official positions as village accountant (*karaṇam*).

During the 1860s and 1870s legislation brought montane shifting cultivation to an end, and with it cutting timber from the jungle, and paying a light tool tax on un-demarcated land-holdings. No longer was there land available for everyone to clear and farm, since the government now owned the forests, and those who could not pay the land tax became tenant smallholders, landless labourers or plantation workers. These successive blows to common farming practice, following hard upon the first Christian conversion in 1858, fostered a half-century of mistrust of Europeans that the numerous epidemics, droughts, conversions, temple rebuildings, and surveys of land-holdings did nothing to dispel. Over that same period land erosion became a serious problem too, the fields were poorly manured and rarely terraced, much Badaga land was sold to the planters, and their indebtedness became widespread. Only villages near the towns gained a measure of prosperity. Jakkatala, a prime case, sold much of its land to the government for Wellington Barracks,[2] then profitted further from contracts for gangs of labourers to build the barracks and other public structures. By the turn of the twentieth century a few families had become really wealthy as contractors, mostly in building the railway from the plains to Ootacamund.

By the beginning of the twentieth century the Badaga population had climbed to 34,000 (having increased more than tenfold over the preceding century), and the density of the rural labour force in the Nilgiris had also increased appreciably through continued immigration. Alongside this growth, Grigg (1880: 321) had observed, '. . . each year has the area of cultivation and permanent occupation been extending with the growth in numbers of the hill-tribes [i.e. of Badagas], the increase of wealth among them, and the great extension of plantations.'[3]

Although tea, coffee and potato had been grown in the district for over half-a-century before, it was only with the onset of the First World War and the recent completion of the Nilgiri railway that Badagas shifted the emphasis in their farming from millets to potato and in the 1920s to tea as well. This made many of them into cash-crop farmers, since they did not eat much potato and consequently had to buy their food grains in the bazaar. The initial interest in the cultivation of tea had been merely a ruse to increase the value of their land before selling it to European planters.

By now the Badaga Christians were viewed as a separate caste, and the old antagonism over Christian conversion had given place to a new realism that accepted the British, tolerated their religion, and sought to collaborate with them in the realms of commerce and administration. The occasional massacres of Kuṟumba people in former times had also come to a complete halt.

Land fragmentation and indebtedness continued as heart-rending problems for the twentieth-century farmer, but new techniques of commercial cultivation did raise the per capita income appreciably for many. Chemical fertilizers and insecticides were now coming into use, along with good seed and reputable tea cuttings. Money lenders, middlemen and truckers all appeared on the scene to answer local commercial needs. Many of the hillsides were now being terraced to allow efficient farming (Pl. 14), while the emergence of cooperative societies from 1911 helped with this procedure, as well as with the more general problem of rural credit.

These new directions in the farm economy were fully in evidence by 1930, when most Badaga villages broke off their time-honoured exchange relationship with the Kotas, Todas and Kuṟumbas and began doing without their services, instead seeking in town markets the artefacts that those tribesmen had previously made. The ostensible reasons for this critical break are several. The Badagas usually mention the increasing cost of having a Kota band at their ceremonies; while Kotas speak of an insulting article in a national newspaper of 1928, *The Hindu*, which was implying that the Kotas were descended from ancient unions of Todas with Badagas.[4] A glance at the population figures in Appendix 2, however, makes it clear that the overriding reason for the break must have been the disproportionately large number of Badagas. By 1931 there were 42,500 of them, too many to be adequately supplied in the customary way by just a few hundred Todas and Kotas.

The Second World War brought a further surge in the demand for potatoes to feed the many thousands of European troops stationed throughout South and Southeast Asia; at the same time government financing helped growers, with the result that this new capital and the high prices potatoes were fetching greatly alleviated the former indebtedness of Badagas. Yet in the decade after 1957 the potato production fell sharply with a series of disease-ridden crops and tea, first planted by Badagas some four decades before, now became a popular cash-crop too. By 1970, with fungus and certain parasites still affecting the potatoes, a sturdy marketable cabbage had, under German sponsorship, also become an important crop.

Colonialism – a term we can use to describe the British presence on the Nilgiris – had rapidly promoted a separation that was not only social (even racial, according to the prevalent European view of things), but was also economic. For already, by about 1840, it would be fair to say that the Nilgiris had dual economies, one purely subsistence (among Badagas and other indigenous peoples) and the other capitalistic (for the first coffee plantations were then appearing). The legacy of colonialism is still a dominant factor in the Nilgiri economy: one small region with two economic systems, and two technologies. For in truth, Indian Independence did almost nothing to break down the distinction between subsistence technology that was geared to providing indigenous people with the goods, foods and services that they were habituated to, and the capitalistic plantation and factory technology that could only exist because of the requirements of the outside world, namely the markets beyond the Nilgiris.

> The modern period is marked by a massive growth in communication networks; the growth of non-agricultural labour settlements; the large-scale conversion of reserve forest areas into forest plantations; and the degradation of the Nilgiri slopes into scrub vegetation. (Prabhakar & Gadgil 1995: 163)

Modern Badagas nevertheless do enjoy quite a high standard of living, occupy comfortable tiled houses, send their children off to college, make frequent visits to various south Indian cities, make use of English, see numerous films, and utilize the newest mechanical devices, especially television, the phone and the Internet. The minority who now live in the Nilgiri towns, among them hundreds of Christians, have taken on a variety of newer urban jobs and are found in most of the professions. Few were actively involved in the Independence movement, fewer are under the influence of M.K. Gandhi's philosophy, and fewer still understand or care about Marxism; for here the Communist vote has been negligible, and the idea of revolutionary communism unappealing. For the Badagas change means securing profit in a capitalist economy, adopting a Westernized style of individual responsibility, and thus shifting away from ascribed social status towards that which is achieved.

This transformation has come about while physical communications have been improving markedly. Nearly all of the villages are linked with the towns by regular bus services. For an entire century there has been a railway link to the cities of the plains. Many of the middlemen who offer fertilizer or buy potatoes have their own lorries; large-scale tea planters have cars or jeeps. Radios are widely accessible now that the villages are electrified; yet radio is mainly a channel for light music and is not as important as the 'social' films and television programmes in introducing modern, primarily urban, values and wants to the Badagas. Newspapers have a broad circulation even in the villages and are much more effective than radios in transmitting news. Colour television has been seen in many of the villages for the past quarter-century. Today, therefore, every Badaga village has easy access to information about the world beyond the Nilgiris, by seeing films, reading the papers, watching TV, or by talking with friends and relatives who work in the towns.

This ready availability of information has helped the Badagas to become ever more involved in national and state politics, with a particular view to bettering the lot of their people and controlling the size of their families. Yet while they are now more politically active, as a government anthropologist pointed out,

> The Badagas tread on thin ice – while they have 'prospered' in Tamilnadu and have greatly benefitted by the absence of the higher caste[s] in the region, they are very much against the Tamil settlers in the Nilgiris, the latter being a potential threat to their interests. Their culture and language [are] distinct from [those] of the Tamils and hence they fight against the Tamilization of the Nilgiris [exemplified in the recent but unpopular conversion of Ootacamund to Udhagamandalam – P.H.]. Here lies the basic contradiction. The average Badaga is conscious of . . . what objectively determines an individual's status and hence makes serious efforts to accumulate property and 'modernize' but at the same time he is forced to realize the contextual and culture-based situation which gives rise to 'communal'

politics. The interplay of these opposing forces is in the best interests of those who have been able to amass some wealth for themselves. When participating in the wider arena such people tend to take radical postures and do not seem to give any weightage to traditional practices but back in their home regions they become champions of the traditional inter- and intra-group relationship. (Misra 1985: 335-36)

The history of the Badaga people follows a pattern that has been observed elsewhere, as for example in the American West (Meinig 1972: 163; Norton 1984: 73). In Stage I people are selected from a source region and become transplanted by particular circumstances into a new area. They never represent a cross-section of the parent society. Experimental adaptation of imported cultural traits to that new environment follows. In Stage II, a cohesive new society is formed from the amalgam of immigrants, as they adjust to the isolation of the place and its environmental features. This new regional culture has a high potential for cultural lag and divergence from the earlier forms. In Stage III, a strong impact of the national culture begins to be felt because of expanding nation-wide communication patterns, marketing networks and administrative control of the facilities, all of which diffuse through some 'central place', in this case Ootacamund, to the outlying settlements. Only those cultures that have a tenacious pattern of religious, linguistic, artistic and other features can persist in a distinct form. Stage IV, which evidently is beginning to materialize in the Nilgiris, marks the dissolution of a historic regional culture as all its areas become fully exposed to the national cultural traditions. It is during this stage that a new consciousness emerges of local cultural and environmental values.

In 1867, the year when a third school was opened for Badaga children and solid brick temples were appearing in some of their villages, Karl Marx wrote in the opening pages of *Das Kapital* (vol. I, 1867): 'The country that is more developed industrially only shows, to the less developed, the image of its own future'. And the Badagas were already on the road to that new future.

NOTES

1. A survey was actually made in 1820; see above, p. 285, n. 6, and Hockings 1989c: 334-42.
2. Most people of Jakkata were very reluctant to sell so much land, though, and the negotiations went on for several years; Sutton 2009: 35-40.

3. So also the Sanitary Commissioner, Dr. Cornish: 'I have no doubt the native population is increasing, and that the position of the Badaga has materially improved. I notice especially the facts that they are now tiling their houses, that their women and children earn money on the tea and coffee estate, and that they buy rágí [millet] and grain from the low country, and get a better market for their straw and cattle. They wear jewels of gold and silver, saved from their earnings'; quoted by Grigg 1880: 34. This contrasts with the situation that pertained at the beginning of the British occupation of the hills when the Badagas were so few in proportion to the land available that there was no need for crop rotation, since fields could be left fallow for years at a time; Mackworth 1823: 124-26.
4. Emeneau 1946: 265, n. 12, however, gives the date of this contentious article as April 28, 1930. Ranga (1934: 4) reports that around the year 1930, 'In addition to this heavy expenditure upon funerals, more than three hundred Badagas cease work for more than two days and live at the expense of the relatives of the deceased or the people of the village. The expenses of a funeral incurred by all the Badagas in a hamlet come to more than Rs. 600. To add to this, their European employers lose their confidence in the ability of these people for regular service since they cease work without giving any notice whatever . . .'; similarly Metz 1864: 89-90.

APPENDIX 1

Population of the Main Nilgiri Communities

Indigenous Groups

Badagas (including Christians)	134,514 (2001 census)
Kotas	2,072 (2001 census)
Toda (including Christians)	1,001 (2001 census)
Paniyas (including Christians)	6,210 (1981 census)
Iṟulas and Kasavas	7,045 (1981 census)
Kuṟumbas	4,354 (1981 census)
Kattu-Nayakas	1,245 (1981 census)
Ūrāḷis	203 (1981 census)
Others	*ca* 600,000
District total	764,826 (2001 census)

APPENDIX 2

Badaga population growth, compared with that of Todas and Kotas, 1812-2001

Census	*Badaga*	*Kota*	*Toda*
1812	2,207	130	179
1821	3,778	317	222
1825	5,147	*ca* 336	326
1847 *	6,569	307	337
1856	13,352	484	316
1866	17,778	802	704
1871	19,476	1,112	693
1881	24,398	1,067	689
1891	29,613	1,201	739
1901	34,178	1,267	807
1911	38,180	1,163	748
1921	40,329	1,204	640
1931	43,075	1,123	597
1941	56,047	952	630
1951	67,251	1,200	879
1961	85,463	956	765
1971	104,392	1,269	930
1975	(?) 125,821	*ca* 1,348	1,102
1980	*ca* 127,142	1,446	*ca* 1,167
1985 (est.)	*ca* 132,000	*ca* 1,544	1,232
1988	?	?	1,027
1991	134,187	?	?
2000	?	?	1,195
2001	134,514	2,072	1,001

* The 1847 census was under-enumerated: cf. Marshall 1873: 102, and Grigg 1880: 30.

APPENDIX 3

THE BADAGA *NA:ḌS*, COMMUNES AND VILLAGES

Biligiri Rangan Hills/ Me:l ˊsi:me

Aṭṭapa:ḍi *
Oḍamaṇḍe
Osaṭṭi/Hosaṭṭi/Hosahaṭṭi
O:ḍemandu
Ko:ṭḷa:ḍa/Ko:ṭe ha:ḍa
De:vanatta
Puṇaju:ru
Maṇuhaṭṭi
Ma:vaḷḷa
Ma:vuhaṭṭi
Me:l Ma:vaḷḷa
Si:gaṭṭi

Kunde/Kundena:ḍu si:me

Eḍeka:ḍu commune:

Arekaḍavu = Eḍeka:ḍu =
Taleyaṭṭi/Talehaṭṭi & Naḍuhaṭṭi
Kunjano:re
Kuṇḍana:ḷi
Naḍuhaṭṭi
Mukkimale
Su:ṇḍaṭṭi/Su:ṇḍehaṭṭi

----

*Note: * The order given is that of the Dravidian alphabet*

Kiṇṇakore commune:

Ummatapaḍige Me:lu:r
Osaṭṭi/Hosaṭṭi/Hosahaṭṭi
Kiṇṇakore (has *akka bakka*)
Bikkaṭṭi
Hiriyasi:ge

Ki:ekunda commune:

Arekaṇḍi = Manju:ru
Osaṭṭi/Hosaṭṭi/Hosahaṭṭi
Kaṇḍibikke
Kariamale
Ki:ekunda (has *akka bakka*)
Tu:ne:ri
Ba:ko:re
Bikkaṭṭi
Manju:ru
Maṭṭakaṇḍi
Maṇikal
Mullagu:r

Muḷḷimale commune:

Naḍuhaṭṭi
Muḷḷimale

Me:lkunda commune:

Aṭṭumaṇṇu

Keccigaṭṭi
Kerepa:ḍu
Me:lkunda (has *akka bakka*)

Todagana:ḍu si:me/ Todana:ḍu si:me

Ebbuna:ḍu commune:

Ebbuna:ḍu (has *akka bakka*)
Osaṭṭi/Hosaṭṭi/Hosahaṭṭi = Me:laṭṭi
Kambaṭṭi
Ka:ḷemora
= Morakuṭṭi/Morakoṭṭuhaṭṭi
Kengamuḍi

Kagguci/Kaggusi commune:

Ajju:r
Kagguci/Kaggusi
(has *akka bakka*)
Kaḍehaṭṭi
Kaligaṇaṭṭi/Kalingaṇaṭṭi/Kalingam arahaṭṭi
Ta:terebennu
Di:naṭṭi
Naḍuvo:re
Banahaṭṭi
Bikkemarahaṭṭi/Bikkemorahaṭṭi
Billikambe Ki:yaṭṭi
Billikambe Me:laṭṭi
Maṇuhaṭṭi
Soḍalivo:re
Honnatale

Kaḍana:ḍu commune:

Aṇikore
A:ḍaṭṭi/Ha:ḍaṭṭi = Ka:ḍaṭṭi/
Ka:ḍuhaṭṭi = Ha:laṭṭi
Iḍuhaṭṭi
Ulupaṭṭi
U:morahaṭṭi/Hu:morahaṭṭi
Oḍehaṭṭi
Osaṭṭi/Hosaṭṭi/Hosahaṭṭi =
Tumanaṭṭi Hosaṭṭi
Kaḍana:ḍu (has *akka bakka*)
Kappacci
Kambaṭṭi = Me:l Kambaṭṭi
Karimora
Ka:vitore = Ka:viḷo:re
Kiy Oḍeyaraṭṭi
Kundeçappe/Kundesappe
Kendore
Koṇḍaṭṭi = Jakkaḷo:re
Kodamuḍi
Kodamuḍi Ki:yu:r
Tumana:ḍa
Tumanaṭṭi
Tu:ne:ri
Da:vaṇi
Diṭṭuhaṭṭi
Naḍuhaṭṭi
Bakka:raṭṭi
Baṭṭakore
Baralaṭṭi
Billikambe
Be:ragal/Be:ragalaṭṭi/Be:regallu
Mainele
Maḍitore
Marekallu
Ma:vukallu
Me:l Oḍeyaraṭṭi
Me:l Ha:ḍaṭṭi
Moraṭṭuva
Mo:rikallu
Su:ṇḍaṭṭi/Su:ṇḍehaṭṭi
Ha:laṭṭaṇe

Ku:kal commune:

Uyilaṭṭi = Huliyaṭṭi
Eḍeyu:ru
Kambaṭṭi
Kambaṭṭikambe
Ku:katore
Ku:kal/Kukallu (has *akka bakka*)
Ku:rumuḍi

De:gili/De:hili
Si:gemorahaṭṭi
Si:gola

Cinna Kunnu:r commune:

Ba:ramaṇṇu
Bendaṭṭi
Kengal
Kokkutale
Koṇagaṭṭi
Ko:eka:ḷu
Cinna Kunnu:r/Pu:sekunnu:r (has *akka bakka*)
Mottakambe

Tu:ḍegu:r commune:

Attikallu
Arehaṭṭi
Asugenetore
Ekko:ṇi (has *akka bakka*)
Kaḍeso:le
Kallaṭṭi
Ka:ḍaṭṭi = Ka:vaḍaṭṭi = Ki:e Kavaraṭṭi
Ka:repiḷḷu
Kempola
Taṭṭene:ri
Banjimora/Bannimara
Bikkaṭṭi
Malligo:re
Ma:sikal/Ma:sikallu
Me:l Kavaraṭṭi
Me:l Malligo:re
Ha:vare
Hullaṭṭi

Torehaṭṭi commune:

U:rumale
Osaṭṭi/Hosaṭṭi/Hosahaṭṭi
Ka:rekallu
Ta:maravare = Nellimandu
Toreyaṭṭi/Torehaṭṭi

Nanjena:ḍu commune:

Avare
Kappatore
Ki:e Ka:vaṭṭi/Ki:e Ka:ve
Kurutuguḷi
Nanjena:ḍu
Baiga:ḍa
Bingicakallu/Bincikal
Me:l Ka:vaṭṭi/Me:l Ka:ve

So:lu:ru commune:

Arehaṭṭi
A:ka:su = Talemale
U:rhaṭṭi = So:lu:ru (has *akka bakka*)
Osaṭṭi/Hosaṭṭi/Hosahaṭṭi
Ko:ṭaṭṭi/Ko:ṭehaṭṭi
Taṭṭene:ri
Bikkekanḍi
Be:ko:ḍu

Porangana:ḍu/Poranga:ḍu

Note: the villages that are named in this section of Appendix 3 are all shown on Map 4, p. 71.

Kengare commune:

Kengare (has *akka bakka*)
Ne:rimorahaṭṭi
Mandalukambe/Mandaluhaṭṭi
Ha:laṭṭi
Hulivare

Ko:ḍamu:le commune:

Aremaṇehaṭṭi
Ko:ḍamu:le
Osaṭṭi/Hosaṭṭi/Hosahaṭṭi = Hu:ruṇekambe
Ko:ḍamu:le (has *akka bakka*)
Ha:lakare/Ha:lake:ru

Jakkata/Jakkato: commune:

Osaṭṭi/Hosaṭṭi/Hosahaṭṭi
O:danaṭṭi
Ka:rakore
Ki:e Bikkaṭṭi/Cinna Bikkaṭṭi
Jakkata/Jakkato: (has *akka bakka*)
Be:raṭṭi
Manjitala/Manjida
Malligo:re
Me:l Bikkaṭṭi
Honnemuḍi

Jakkana:ri/Jakka:re commune:

Aruve:ṇu
Aruve:ṇu/Haruve:ṇu Ke:ti Ke:ri
Aruve:ṇu/Haruve:ṇu Naḍuhaṭṭi
Arebeṭṭu = Beṭṭaṭṭi
Kacceriha:ḍa = Kalla:ḍa
Kesala:ḍa
Jakkana:ri (has *akka bakka*)
Tumbu:ru
Dabbakambe
Diṇṇiyu:r
De:pa:nu
Bengaḷa:ḍa
Muḍiakambe
Se:lavare/Se:lo:re
Ha:lamane

Doḍḍamanehaṭṭi commune:

Imbimorahaṭṭi/Imbiyamorahaṭṭi
Imbimora Hosaṭṭi = Osaṭṭi/Hosaṭṭi/Hosahaṭṭi = Himbara Hosaṭṭi = Hu:mora Hosahaṭṭi
Kaguḷa
Kekkaṭṭi = Doḍḍamanehaṭṭi = Bikkaṭṭi = Bikkemarahaṭṭi/Bikkemorahaṭṭi
De:na:ḍu Osake:ri/Hosake:ri
De:na:ḍu Toreyake:ri
Tumbimale/Dumbimale
Paḍumuḍi
Honnaṭṭi

Ta:ndana:ḍu commune:

Aṇehaṭṭi
Arekambe
Arehaṭṭi
Oḍḍe:ṇu Ki:yaṭṭi
Oḍḍe:ṇu Me:laṭṭi
Kaḍako:ḍu = Sibbikallukambe
Kaḍekambaṭṭi = Kambaṭṭi
Kanne:ri
Kanne:rimukku
Ka:viḷo:re
Kiḷinjumandu
Ki:e Kappaṭṭi
Ki:y Aṇehaṭṭi
Kunnihaṭṭi/Kunnihiṭṭe
Keccigaṭṭi
Ke:rubeṭṭa
Ko:ṭena:yi
Guṇḍa:ḍa
Jakkakambe
Jakkaḷoḍe
Ta:ndana:ḍu (has *akka bakka*)
Ta:ḷo:re
Dimbaṭṭi
Naṭṭakallu
Naḍu Kappaṭṭi
Na:ragere
Puḍiyangi = Puḍihangu
Baṭṭakore
Bendaṭṭi
Be:ṭla:ḍa
Be:rage:ṇi
Maruḷakambe
Mi:nikambe
Me:l Kappaṭṭi
Morahoḍḍe
Sa:maladiṭṭu
Sippigehaṭṭi/Sippihaṭṭi
Su:ṇḍaṭṭi/Su:ṇḍehaṭṭi

Se:lakore
Ha:yu:ru
Hullattaṭṭi
Horaso:le

Tu:ne:ri commune:

Amba:le/Amma:le
Iḍukore
Uyilaṭṭi
Oḍeyaraṭṭi
Kaḍugaṭṭi/Kaḍugatore
Ku:njo:le/Ku:nuso:le
Tu:ne:ri
De:na:ḍu Ki:yaṭṭi
De:na:ḍu Naḍuhaṭṭi
De:na:ḍu Me:laṭṭi = Bendaṭṭi
Beḷḷa:ḍa/Huṭṭu:r Beḷḷa:ḍa
Muttarabi:ge
Me:laṭṭi/Me:lu:r
Suḷḷigu:ḍu
Su:ṇḍaṭṭi/Su:ṇḍehaṭṭi
Haṭṭiya:ḍa
Ha:lu:ru = Haduveyu:ru = Havvu:ru
Hiṭṭegallu Ki:yaṭṭi
Hiṭṭegallu Me:laṭṭi

Niruguve/Neḍuguve commune:

Osaṭṭi/Hosaṭṭi/Hosahaṭṭi
Kurukutti
Koṭṭunaṭṭi/Koṭṭuna:yi
Niruguve/Neḍuguve (has *akka bakka*)
Pi:ṇaṭṭi

Pedduva commune:

Aḍḍavaḷe/Aḍḍave
Arekore
Iutore
Irupukallu
Eḍapiḷḷu
Osaṭṭi/Hosaṭṭi/Hosahaṭṭi = Pi:naṭṭi
Kaiga:ra Naḍuhaṭṭi
Kauvaṭṭi/Kauve/Kave/Kavaṭṭi
Kaṭṭebeṭṭu
Kaḍeguḍi
Kalna:yi
Kallaṭṭi
Ke:ḍuha:ḍa/Ke:ruha:ḍa
Ke:rbennu
Ga:tigaṭṭi/Ga:tiguḷi/Ga:tige
Togalaṭṭi
Tottamokke
Naḍu Kauvaṭṭi = Naḍuhaṭṭi (has *akka bakka*)
Panni:ruhaṭṭi/Panne:ruhaṭṭi
Pudumandu
Pedduva (has *akka bakka*)
Bayengi
Beṭṭaṭṭi
Bebbe:ṇu
Ma:niha:ḍa
Mokkaṭṭi
Ha:lke:ru
Honno:re

Bandime commune:

Bandime (has *akka bakka*)

Ba:muḍi commune:

Ba:muḍi (has *akka bakka*)

Mi:de:ṇu commune:

Kappaṭṭitore
Ke:rukambe
Koṇa:kore
Baṭṭakore/Iḷa:ḍa/Iḷuha:ḍa
Mi:de:ṇu
Happaṭṭi

Sakkata/Sakkatore/Sakkato: commune:

Sakkata/Sakkatore/Sakkato:

Hubbatale commune:

Karimorahaṭṭi
Cinna Hubbatale = Hubbatale Me:laṭṭi
Hubbatale Ki:yaṭṭi (has *akka bakka*)

Me:kuna:ḍu/ Me:kuna:ḍu si:me

Adigaraṭṭi commune:

Aṇehaṭṭi
Adigaraṭṭi (has *akka bakka*)
Arehaṭṭi
Muṭṭina:ḍu

Ittalar commune:

Ittalar = Etelarekaṇḍi
Oṭṭimara Hosaṭṭi
Osaṭṭi/Hosaṭṭi/Hosahaṭṭi
O:ṇikaṇḍi
Tu:ḍale

Ka:ṭaru/Ka:ṭe:ri/Ka:ṭe:ru commune:

Eḍehaṭṭi
Ka:ṭaru/Ka:ṭe:ri/Ka:ṭe:ru (has *akka bakka*)
Tu:raṭṭi
Naḍuhaṭṭi

Ke:ti commune:

Accanakal
Accanakal Ki:yaṭṭi = Kaḍehaṭṭi
Accanakal Me:laṭṭi = Talehaṭṭi
Aṇehaṭṭi
Arehaṭṭi = Poro:raṭṭi
Ellena:yi = Ba:vaṭṭi
Oḍeyaraṭṭi = Ki:y Oḍeyaraṭṭi = Kolekombe
Oḍeyaraṭṭi = Me:l Oḍeyaraṭṭi
Osaṭṭi/Hosaṭṭi/Hosahaṭṭi
Kammandu
Kekkaṭṭi
Kenguṇḍu/Kenguṇḍe
Kera:ḍakambe
Kereha:ḍa
Ke:ti (has *akka bakka*)
Ke:titore/Ke:tore
Ke:rkaṇḍi
Kodangaṭṭi
Ti:ḍehaṭṭi
Toreyaṭṭi/Torehaṭṭi
Daḍahaṭṭi
De:na:yi
Manepaṭṭu
Mokkaṭṭi
So:reguṇḍu
Ha:la:ḍa
Hulla:ḍa

Tanga:ḍu commune:

Arehaṭṭi
Oḍḍe:ru
O:ranayi/Tanga:ḍu O:ranayi
Kanne:ri
Ga:ikaṇḍi/Ga:ndikaṇḍi
Tanga:ḍu (has *akka bakka*)
Tanga:ḍu Arehaṭṭi
Mandaṇe
Ha:lakore

Tambaṭṭi/Ta:mbaṭṭi commune:

Tambaṭṭi/Ta:mbaṭṭi (has *akka bakka*)

Tudu:ru (abandoned commune):

Eriguiha:ḍa
Kagge:ri
Kaṇuvaṭṭi
Kiḷinja:ḍa
Kuriyamale

Kembu:tuke:ru
Koṇamotta
Kolekombe
Ko:ṭekallu
Go:ṇuhaṭṭi/Go:ṇe:ru
Ta:yimale
Ti:ḍere
Tudu:ru (had *akka bakka*)
Tu:ha:ḍa
Danahaṭṭi
Ni:raḷḷakambe
Ni:rbambehaṭṭi
Nellihaṇe
Pillu:r
Banahaṭṭi
Baralaṇe
Billimale
Be:ko:ḍu
Mallikore
Ma:riammakaṇḍi
Muṭṭina:ḍu
Se:lemorahaṭṭi
Se:leha:su
So:leyaṭṭu
Haṇemaṇṇu/Haṇeyamaṇṇu
Hattare
Hanimaṇṇu
Halasaṇe
Ha:yu:ru
Ha:la:ḍa
Huguo:ru/Huguo:re

Ba:kola commune:

De:na:ḍu
Ba:kola
Benga:ḷamaṭṭa/Benga:lu
Mainele
Maccikaṇḍi/Ma:sikaṇḍi
Manjakombe
Maṇuhaṭṭi
Mi:ke:ru
Muduhola

Me:lu:ru commune:

Angaḍihaṭṭi
Aṭṭubailu
Arehaṭṭi
A:regacci = Toreyaruhaṭṭi
U:marakaṇḍi/Hu:morakaṇḍi =
Himbarakaṇḍi = Humbarakaṇḍi
U:morahaṭṭi/Hu:morahaṭṭi
U:rdiṭṭu
Oḍḍe:ruhaṭṭi = Ki:e Ko:ḍe:ru
Karikalbeḷ
Kallakore
Ka:so:le
Kunnakambe
Ko:ka:la:ḍa
Ko:tibennu
Goḍalaṭṭi
Toreyaṭṭi/Torehaṭṭi
Naiyaṭṭi
Nundua
Pudugaṭṭi
Po:rti
Bikko:lu
Bembaṭṭi
Beḷḷa:ḍa
Be:gamandu
Be:lito:
Me:lu:r/Me:lu:ru (has *akka bakka*)
Me:lu:r Hosaṭṭi (has *akka bakka*)
Me:l Ko:ḍe:ru
Happuko:ḍu
Haḷḷa:ḍi
Ha:laṭṭaṇe
Ha:laṭṭi

So:gatore commune:

O:rana:yi/Ho:rana:yi
Cakkaḷaṭṭi/Sakkaḷaṭṭi
Doḍḍaṇṇi
Ne:rikambe
Sa:lemu:r
So:gaṭṭi/So:gatore

Hulikal commune (most of the hamlets have been abandoned):

Kaḍeko:ḍu
Kenduva
Ko:ṭaṭṭi/Ko:ṭehaṭṭi
Ko:ḍaṭṭi
Ta:veka:ḍu
Pannamaḍe
Pannave:ṇu
Banahaṭṭi
Beṭṭaṭṭi
Bendaṭṭi
Hulikal (has *akka bakka*)

Wainad Gauḍas

Ko:lepaḷḷi commune:

Osaṭṭi/Hosaṭṭi/Hosahaṭṭi
Ka:ḍaṭṭi
Ka:yilaṭṭi
Kunnihaṭṭi
Korangupaḍi
Kolehaṭṭi
Ko:lepaḷḷi
Naḍuhaṭṭi
Naḷḷihaṭṭi
Mukkuhaṭṭi
Muḷḷihaṭṭi

Śo:la:ḍe commune:

Perumpaḷḷi
Ma:rakare
Śo:la:ḍe

Other village clusters:

Nandaṭṭi
Pandalu:ru
Pa:ḍantora
Baḍagahaṭṭi
Be:kikare
Ma:sukoḷḷi
Va:sukolli

(Total of 468 hamlets, with 41 communes)

APPENDIX 4

The Orthography of the Badaga Language

Baḍagu was essentially an unwritten language until the publication of my book, *Counsel from the Ancients: A Study of Badaga Proverbs, Prayers, Omens and Curses* (1988). Locally, however, many have used the Tamil script for daily writing of this language, and for well over a century, although that script is much less able to accommodate the sounds of the Badaga language than the Kannaḍa script would be; but the Nilgiris District does lie within Tamil Nadu. (The missionaries in the nineteenth century sometimes wrote this language in the Kannaḍa script which, though rather more precise phonetically, did not catch on locally.)

The orthography used in this and other modern writings on the Badagas, including especially *A Badaga-English Dictionary* (Hockings and Pilot-Raichoor 1994) and my *Counsel from the Ancients*, uses a modified Roman script because it is easy to type; viz:

(1) there are five vowels, i e a o u, and each also has a long form by the addition of a colon,
thus i: e: a: o: u:

(2) there are fifteen consonants,
p b v m
t d l n r
ś/c j y
k g
h

(3) in addition, there are four retroflexed consonants, printed thus:
ṭ ḍ ḷ/(l) ṇ

Full details of the phonology and grammar of this language have been presented by Christiane Pilot-Raichoor in *Counsel from the Ancients*, 51-84.

References *

Ainslie, Whitelaw, 'Observations on atmospheric influence, chiefly in reference to the climate and diseases of eastern regions, in five parts. Part I. *Journal of the Royal Asiatic Society of Bengal*, 2 (1835): 13-42 (1834).

Anonymous, 'Some Indian hill tribes,' [by S.W.H.]. *Dublin University Magazine*, 93 (n.s. 3): 143-52 (1879).

— [Note on the Nilgiri mission.] *Evangelisches Missions-Magazin*, 31: 122 (1887).

— 'Success and persecution on the Nilgiris.' *Harvest Field* (ser. 3), 5: 546-51 (1894).

— *Periplus of the Erythræan Sea / Periplus Maris Erythriæ* (of *ca* 70 CE): see Schoff 1974.

Arokiaswami, M., 'The Ummattūr chieftancy.' *Quarterly Journal of the Mythic Society*, Culture and Heritage Number: 156-62 (1956).

Arputhanathan, J.I., *1951 census handbook: the Nilgiris District*. Madras: Government Press (1953).

Baber, Thomas Hervey, 'Journal of a route to the Neelghurries from Calicut.' *Asiatic Journal* (new ser.), 3: 310-16 (1830).

Backward Classes Commission, 'Badagas.' In their *Report of the Backward Classes Commission Tamil Nadu*, 1: 7-9. Madras: Government of Tamil Nadu, mimeograph (1975).

Bacon, Thomas, 'Neilgherries.' In his *The Oriental annual; containing a series of tales, legends, & historical romances* . . . 7: 201-10. London: Charles Tilt (1840).

Baikie, Robert, *The Neilgherries: including an account of their topography, climate, soil and production; and of the effects of the climate on the European constitution*, 2nd edn. Calcutta: I. Thomas (1857).

Balfour, Edward Green, *The cyclopaedia of India and of eastern and southern Asia, commercial, industrial and scientific; products of the mineral, vegetable, and animal kingdoms, useful arts and manufactures*. 3rd edn., 2 vols. London: Bernard Quaritch (1884-85).

---

*

The full bibliographic details for the Nilgiris can be found in my (1996) book, *Bibliographie générale sur les Monts Nilgiri de l'Inde du sud 1603-1996 / A Comprehensive Bibliography for the Nilgiri Hills of Southern India, 1603-1996 / Eine umfassende Bibliographie der Nilgiri-Berge Südindiens*. Bordeaux: Université Michel de Montaigne [Espaces Tropicales 14].

Basel German Evangelical Missionary Society, *Report of the Basel German Evangelical Missionary Society . . . Report of the Basel German Evangelical Mission in south-western India*. Mangalore. [Annual, 1846-1913; here referred to as BEMS; also available in German]

Basel Mission, Presbytery minutes of the Basel Mission, Ketti 1887-1905. Ms (in the possession of Paul Hockings) (1905).

Béchu, Léon-Auguste, *History of the Coimbatore Mission (South India)*. Bangalore: Bangalore Press (1948).

Beidelman, Thomas O., *A comparative analysis of the Jajmani system*. Locust Valley: Augustin (Association for Asian Studies Monograph, no. 8; 1959).

Belli Gowder, M.K., A historical research on the hill tribes of the Nilgiris. Accanakal; ms (1923-41).

— [Note on Badaga origins.] *South of India Observer* (13 Feb. 1926).

— Origin of the Badagas. Accanakal, ms (1938-41).

BEMS See Basel German Evangelical Missionary Society.

Benbow, Jessie K., The Badagas—Beliefs and customs. Bangalore: United Theological College; ms (1930).

Benson, Ralph Sillery, *Descriptive memoir . . . [and] survey and settlement register of the village of Kethi in the Merkunad division of the Nilgiri District*. Ootacamund: Revenue Settlement Office (1881).

— *Descriptive memoir . . . [and] survey and settlement register of the village of Sholur in the Toda-nad division of the Nilgiri District*. Ootacamund: Revenue Settlement Office (1884).

— *A statistical atlas of the Madras presidency; compiled from existing records . . .* Madras: Department of Land Records and Agriculture (1895).

Bertrand, Joseph, *La Mission du Maduré d'après des documents inédits*, vol. 2. Paris: Poussielgue-Rusand (1848).

Béteille, André, *Castes: Old and new; Essays in social structure and social stratification*. Bombay: Asia Publishing House (1969).

Birch, DeBurgh, 'Topographical report on the Neilgherries.' *Madras Journal of Literature and Science*, 8: 86-127 (1838).

Bird-David, Nurit, 'The Nilgiri tribal systems: A view from below.' In Hockings 1997b: 5-22 (1997).

Blasco, François, 'Montagnes du sud de l'Inde: Forêts, savanes, écologie'. *Institut français de Pondichéry, Travaux de la section scientifique et technique*, 10, fasc. 1 (1971).

Blavatsky, H.P. (Helena Petrovna Blavatskaia), *Au pays des montagnes bleues*. Paris: Éditions du Monde moderne (1926).

— *The people of the Blue Mountains*. Wheaton: Theosophical Press (1930).

Breeks, James Wilkinson, *An account of the primitive tribes and monuments of the Nīlagiris*. (Posthumous: Maria Breeks, ed.) London: India Museum (1873).

Buchanan, Francis (afterwards, Buchanan-Hamilton), *A journey from Mad-*

ras through the countries of Mysore, Canara, and Malabar, performed under the orders of the most noble the Marquis Wellesley, Governor General of India, for the express purpose of investigating the state of agriculture, arts, and commerce; the religion, manners, and customs; the history natural and civil, and antiquities, in the dominions of the Rajah of Mysore, and the countries acquired by the honourable East India Company, in the late and former wars, from Tippoo Sultaun, vol. 2. London: W. Bulmer and Co. (1807).

Bühler, Johann Michael, 'Ueber das Volk und die Sprache der Badaga im Dekkanischen Indien.' *Zeitschrift der Deutschen Morgenländischen Gesellschaft*, 3: 108-18 (1849).

Burrow, Thomas, and Murray Barnson Emeneau, *A Dravidian etymological dictionary*, 2nd edn. Oxford: Clarendon Press (1984).

Burton, Richard Francis, *Goa, and the Blue Mountains; or, six months of sick leave.* With introduction by Dane Kennedy. Berkeley, Los Angeles, Oxford: University of California Press (1851 [1991]).

Butterworth, Alan, *The southlands of Siva: Some reminiscences of life in Southern India.* London: John Lane, the Bodley Head Ltd. (1923).

Calcutta Monthly Journal, *Calcutta Monthly Journal*, [News item about a Kuṟumba massacre] (1836).

Caldwell, John C., Palli Hanumantha Reddy, and Patricia Caldwell, *The causes of demographic change: Experimental research in South India.* Madison: University of Wisconsin Press (1988).

Cederlöf, Gunnel, *Bonds lost: Subordination, conflict and mobilisation in rural South India c. 1900-1970.* New Delhi: Manohar (1997).

Centre for Monitoring Indian Economy, *Economic Intelligence Service – Profiles of Districts – November 1993.* Bombay: Centre for Monitoring Indian Economy (1993)

Coleridge, Henry James, *The life and letters of St. Francis Xavier*, vol. 1. London: Burns and Oates (1872).

Congreve, Harry, 'The antiquities of the Neilgherry Hills, including an inquiry into the descent of the Thautawars or Todars.' *Madras Journal of Literature and Science*, 14 (i): 77-146 (1847).

Das, Gopi Nath, 'The funerary monuments of the Nilgiris.' *Bulletin of the Deccan College Research Institute*, 18: ix-x and 140-58 (1957).

Davidar, Ephraim Reginald Chandrasekhar, *Cheetal walk: Living in the wilderness.* Delhi: Oxford University Press (1997).

Deschamps, Hubert, & Jean Poirier, 'Histoire et ethnologie.' In *Ethnologie générale.* Jean Poirier, ed., pp. 1433-64. Paris: Gallimard; Encyclopédie de la Pléiade (1968).

Dharmalingam, Ari, 'Voters in Nilgiris: Apathy towards elections.' *Hindu*, 85 (16 Feb. 1962).

Dirks, Nicholas B., *Castes of mind: Colonialism and the making of modern India.* Princeton: Princeton University Press (2001).

Dubois, Jean-Antoine, *Hindu manners, customs and ceremonies.* Trans. by Henry K. Beauchamp. Oxford: Clarendon Press (1817 [1906]).

— See also Pope, George U.

Dulles, John Welsh, *Life in India; or, Madras, the Neilgherries, and Calcutta. Written for the American Sunday School Union.* Philadelphia: American Sunday-School Union (1855).

Dutt, Romesh Chandra, *Economic history of British India under early British rule.* London: Kegan Paul, Trench, Trübner & Co. (1908).

Eagan, John Samuel Chiswell, *The Nilgiri guide and directory, a handbook of general information upon the Nilgiris for visitors and residents*, 2nd edn. Madras: S.P.C.K. Press (1916).

Elmore, Wilber Theodore, Dravidian gods in modern Hinduism; a study of the local and village deities of southern India. *University Studies* [Lincoln, Neb.] 15 (1) (1915).

Emeneau, Murray Barnson, 'Toda marriage regulations and taboos.' *American Anthropologist,* 39: 103-12 (1937).

— 'Toda culture thirty-five years after: an acculturation study.' *Annals of the Bhandarkar Oriental Research Institute*, 19: 101-21 (1938).

— 'The Christian Todas'. *Proceedings of the American Philosophical Society*, 81: 93-106 (1939).

— 'Kota texts. Part four'. *University of California Publications in Linguistics*, 111: 191-335 (1946).

— *Toda songs.* Oxford: Clarendon Press (1971).

— *Toda grammar and texts.* Philadelphia: American Philosophical Society; (Memoirs of the American Philosophical Society, 155; 1984).

— 'The languages of the Nilgiris.' In Hockings 1989b: 133-43 (1989).

Eppler, Paul, *Geschichte der Basler Mission 1815-1899.* Basel: Verlag der Missionsbuchhandlung (1900).

Epstein, T. Scarlett, *Economic development and social change in South India.* Bombay: Oxford University Press (1962).

— *South India: Yesterday, today and tomorrow; Mysore villages revisited.* London and Basingstoke: Macmillan (1973).

Fenicio, Jacome, 'Two Portuguese Mss. on the mission of Todamala'. In *A collection of annual reports relative to the state of the Portuguese Jesuit Missions in the East Indies; of various dates, from 1601 to 1659.* British Museum Additional Ms. 9853, ff. 464-65, Ms. 25-26 vol.; and ff. 477-82, Ms. 40 vol. Trans. by A. de Alberti in Rivers 1906: 719-30 [whence my pagination] (1603 [1906]).

Firth, Raymond William, *Elements of social organization.* London: Watts & Co. (1951).

Francis, Walter, ed., *Madras District Gazetteers. The Nilgiris*, vol. 1. Madras: Superintendent, Government Press (1908).

Frank, André Gunder, 'Goal ambiguity and conflicting standards: An approach to the study of organization'. *Human Organization,* 17: 4, 8-13

(1958-59).

Freedman, Ronald, 'Theories of fertility decline: A reappraisal.' *Social Forces*, 58 (1): 1-17 (1979).

Fuchs, Stephen, *Rebellious prophets: A study of messianic movements in Indian religions*. London: Asia Publishing House (1965).

Fürer-Haimendorf, Christoph von, 'Hereditary friendship and inter-tribal sex relations between Todas and Mudugas'. *Man*, 54: 24, 28-29 (1954).

Funnell, Don, and Romila Parish, *Mountain environments and communities*. London and New York: Routledge (2001).

Gadgil, Madhav, and Ramachandra Guha, *Ecology and equity: The use and abuse of nature in contemporary India*. London and New York: Routledge (1995).

Gamble, James Sykes, and Cecil E.C. Fischer, *Flora of the Presidency of Madras*. Calcutta: Botanical Survey of India; 3 vols. (1915-36 [1956]).

Gaymard, Félix-Adolphe, *Les Badagas, tribus des Montagnes Bleues de l'Hindoustan*. Coonoor: New Albion Press (1924).

Geertz, Clifford, 'The Javanese village.' In *Local, ethnic and national loyalties in village Indonesia* (G.W. Skinner, ed.); 34-41. New Haven: Yale University Cultural Report Series, Southeast Asia Series (1959).

'Geofry', *Ooty and her sisters, or our hill stations in South India, with sketches of hill tribes, their customs, caste, religion, &c., also, tea, coffee and cinchona cultivation, &c., and appendix of routes; distances and fares*. Madras: Higginbotham and Co. (1881).

Ghosh, Bahnisikha, *The Indian population problem: A household economics approach*. New Delhi: Sage Publications (1990).

Gillin, John, *The ways of men: An introduction to anthropology*. New York: Appleton-Century-Crofts Inc. (1948).

Gole, Susan, *A series of early printed maps of India in facsimile*. Delhi: Jayaprints (1984).

Gopalakrishnan, M., ed., *Gazetteers of India: Tamil Nadu State, The Nilgiris District*. Madras: Government of Tamil Nadu, Commissioner of Archives & Historical Research (1995).

Gover, Charles Edward, *The folk-songs of southern India*. Madras: Higginbotham and Co. (1871).

Grigg, Henry Bidewell, ed., *A manual of the Nīlagiri District in the Madras Presidency*. Compiled and edited by H.B. Grigg. Madras: E. Keys, Government Press (1880).

Gurukkal, Rajan, *Social formations of early south India*. New Delhi: Oxford University Press, 2010.

Haldorai, R., 'Lankan influx worries Badagas.' *Indian Express* (Coimbatore edition), 61 (10 Oct. 1993).

— 'Tea growers call off agitation'. *Indian Express* (Coimbatore edition), 68 (27 May 2000).

Hanumantha Rao, K., and M.D. Azariah, 'Potato on the Nilgiris'. In *Horticultural and economic plants of the Nilgiris* (S. Krishnamurthi, ed.); 67-79. Coimbatore: Coimbatore Co-operative Printing Works Ltd. (1953).

Harkness, Henry, *A description of a singular aboriginal race inhabiting the summit of the Neilgherry Hills, or Blue Mountains of Coimbatoor in the southern peninsula of India*. London: Smith, Elder. and Co. (1832).

Harvest Field, *The harvest field: A missionary magazine*. Bangalore (1880-1924).

Hayavadana Rao, Conjeeveram, 'Political history'. In Francis 1908: 90-122 (1908).

— *Mysore gazetteer compiled for government*. Bangalore: Government Press (1930).

— *History of Mysore (1399-1799 A.D.)*. Vol. 1. Bangalore: Superintendent at the Government Press (1943).

Heidemann, Frank Michael, 'Politik und Religion in der Nilgiri-Gesellschaft Südindiens: Status, Macht und duale Souveränität der Badaga'. Berlin: Freie Universität; Habilitationsschrift, Philosophie und Sozialwissenschaften II (1997).

— *Akka Bakka: Religion, Politik und duale Souveränität der Badaga in den Nilgiri Süd-Indiens*. Berlin: Lit Verlag (2006).

'Hillwatch', 'Development or destruction?' *Indian Express* (Madurai edn.), 56 (24 Sept. 1988).

Hockings, Paul E., Communication and cultural change in an emergent region of south India. Mimeo. Stanford: Stanford University (1965a).

— Cultural change among the Badagas, a community of southern India. Berkeley: University of California, Ph.D. dissertation in Anthropology (1965b).

— 'On giving salt to buffaloes: Ritual as communication'. *Ethnology*, 7: 411-26 (1968).

— 'Paikara: An iron-age burial in south India'. *Asian Perspectives*, 18: 26-50 (1976).

— 'Communication networks'. In *Dimensions of social change in India*, (M.N. Srinivas et al., eds.); 475-86. New Delhi: Allied (1977).

— 'Badaga apparel: Protection and symbol'. In *The Fabrics of culture: the anthropology of clothing and adornment*. (Justine M. Cordwell & Ronald A. Schwarz, eds.); 143-74. The Hague: Mouton Publishers (1979).

— *Ancient Hindu refugees: Badaga social history 1550-1975*. The Hague: Mouton Publishers; New Delhi: Vikas Publishing House (1st edn. of the present book; 1980a).

— *Sex and disease in a mountain community*. New Delhi: Vikas Publishing House; Columbia, Mo: South Asian Books (1980b).

— 'Badaga kinship rules in their socio-economic context'. *Anthropos, 77:* 851-74 (1982).

— *Counsel from the ancients, a study of Badaga proverbs, prayers, omens and curses*. Berlin and New York: Mouton de Gruyter (1988).

— 'The Badagas.' In Hockings 1989b: 206-31 (1989a).

— *Blue Mountains: The ethnography and biogeography of a South Indian region*. (Paul Hockings, ed.), New Delhi and New York: Oxford University Press (1989b).

— 'British society in the Company, Crown and Congress eras.' In Hockings 1989b: 334-59 (1989c).

— 'The cultural ecology of the Nilgiris District.' In Hockings 1989b: 360-76 (1989d).

— 'Ethnic identity in a complex society: The Badaga case.' *Bulletin of the National Museum of Ethnology* (Osaka), 18: 347-64 (1993).

— *Bibliographie générale sur les Monts Nilgiri de l'Inde du sud 1603-1996 / A Comprehensive Bibliography for the Nilgiri Hills of Southern India, 1603-1996 / Eine umfassende Bibliographie der Nilgiri-Berge Südindiens*. Bordeaux: Université Michel de Montaigne; [Espaces Tropicales 14] (1996).

— 'Badaga Epic Poetry.' In Hockings 1997b: 293-315 (1997a).

— *Blue Mountains revisited: Cultural studies on the Nilgiri Hills*. (Paul Hockings, ed.). New Delhi and New York: Oxford University Press (1997b).

— *Kindreds of the earth: Badaga household structure and demography*. New Delhi and Thousand Oaks, Cal.: Sage (1999).

— *Mortuary ritual of the Badagas of Southern India*. (*Fieldiana, Anthropology*, new series, 32.) Chicago: Field Museum of Natural History (2001).

— *Encyclopaedia of the Nilgiri Hills*. (Paul Hockings, ed.). 2 vols. New Delhi: Manohar (2012). (The articles cited from this book are by E.R. C. Davidar, Homi Eduljee, Frank Fletcher, Franciscan Missionaries of Mary, Frank Michael Heidemann, Paul Hockings, Siddharth Krishnan, Marie-Claude Mahias, David G. Mandelbaum, Philip K. Mulley, S. Muthiah, Peter Neunhäuser, William Noble, Jean-Philippe Puyravaud, Soňa Řezničkova, Ahmed Sait, Dharmalingam Venugopal, Anthony R. Walker, Allen Zagarell and Kamil V. Zvelebil.)

Hockings, Paul Edward, and Christiane Pilot-Raichoor, *A Badaga-English Dictionary*. Berlin and New York: Mouton de Gruyter (1992).

Hodgson, Brian Houghton, 'Aborigines of the Nilgiris, with remarks on their affinities'. *Journal of the Royal Asiatic Society of Bengal*, 25: 31-38, 498-522 (1856).

Hough, James, *Letters on the climate, inhabitants, productions, &c. &c. of the Neilgherries, or Blue Mountains of Coimbatoor, South India*. London: John Hatchard & Son (1829).

Illustrated Catholic Missions, *Illustrated Catholic missions: An illustrated monthly record in connection with the Society for the Propagation of the Faith*. London, New York (1886).

India, Government of, *Census of India, Paper No. I of 1962, 1961 Census, Final Population Totals*. Delhi: Government of India Press (1962).

Jacobson, Doranne, 'Flexibility in Central Indian kinship and residence.' In *The new wind: Changing identities in South Asia,* (Kenneth David, ed.); 263-83. The Hague and Paris: Mouton Publishers (1977).

Jagor, Andreas Feodor, 'Die Badagas im Nilgiri-Gebirge'. *Verhandlungen der Berliner Gesellschaft für Anthropologie, Ethnologie and Urgeschichte,* 1876: 190-204 (1876).

— *Aus Fedor* [*sic*] *Jagors Nachlass mit Unterstützung der Jagor-Stiftung herausgegeben von der Berliner Gesellschaft für Anthropologie, Ethnologie und Urgeschichte unter Leitung von Albert Grünwedel. I. Band. Südindische Volksstämme*. Berlin: Dietrich Reimer (1914).

Jervis, Humphrey, *Narrative of a journey to the Falls of the Cavery; with an historical and descriptive account of the Neilgherry Hills. – With plates*. London: Smith, Elder and Co. (1834).

Jogi Gowder, B.K., et al., The origin of the Badiga Brahmins of Nilgiris, and the temple of "Mahalinga" at Melur village in Merkunaad division in the district of Nilgiris. Ootacamund (no date).

Kapp, Dieter B., and Paul E. Hockings, 'The Ku̱rumba tribes.' In Hockings 1989b: 232-48 (1989).

Karandikar, S.V., *Hindu Exogamy*. Bombay: D.B. Taraporevala (1929).

Kariabettan, N., 'Kallaṭṭi ko:ṭṭai' [Kallaṭṭi fortress]. *Malai Na:ṭu Kural* (Ketti), Sept.: 14 (1958a).

— 'Ni:la malai va:cikaḷ' [The inhabitants of the Nilgiri Hills]. *Malai Na:ṭu Kural* (Ketti), July: 2-4 (1958b).

Karl, William Victor, The religion of the Badagas. Serampore: B.D. thesis (1945).

Keys, William, 'A topographical description of the Neelaghery Mountains. From a letter by William Keys, Assistant Revenue Surveyor, to W. Garrows, Collector of Coimbatore.' In Grigg 1880: xlviii-li [whence my pagination] (1812).

King, William Ross, *The aboriginal tribes of the Nilgiri Hills*. London: Longmans, Green, and Co. (1870).

Kipling, Rudyard, *Second Jungle Book*. Garden City: Doubleday (1895).

Kittel, Georg Ferdinand, *A Kannaḍa-English dictionary*. Mangalore: Basel Mission Press (1894).

Krishnamurthi, Sundaram, ed., *Horticultural and economic plants of the Nilgiris*. Coimbatore: Coimbatore Co-operative Printing Works Ltd. (1953).

Krishnaswami, S.Y., *Rural problems in Madras: Monograph*. Madras: Superintendent, Government Press (1947).

Krishnan, Rajam, *Kurinjit tē̱n*. Madras: M.L.J. Press, 1963. (Reprinted at Madras : Pāri Putakap Pa̱ṉnai; 1977)

— *When the kurinji blooms*. Uma Narayanan and Prema Seetharam, trans.

New Delhi: Orient Longman (trans. of Krishnan 1963; 2002).

Lawley, Annie Allen Cunard, & Fanny Emily Farr Penny, *Southern India.* London: A. & C. Black (1914).

Leschenault de la Tour, Jean Baptiste Louis Claude Théodore, 'Relation abregée d'un voyage aux Indes orientales'. *Mémoires du Museum d'histoire naturelle,* 9: 245-74 (1822).

Lévi-Strauss, Claude, *Les structures élémentaires de la parenté,* 2nd edn. Paris, The Hague: Mouton & Co. (1968).

Ling, Catharine Frances, 'Mission work on the Nilgiris'. *Harvest Field* (ser. 3), 111: 74-77 (1892).

Lowie, Robert Harry, *Social organization.* New York: Rinehart & Co., Inc. (1948).

Ludden, David, *An agrarian history of South Asia.* Cambridge: Cambridge University Press (The New Cambridge History of India, IV.4; 1999).

Lütze, Christoph Wilhelm, 'Auf den blauen Bergen. Einige Beobachtungen über den Einfluss der Missionsschulen'. *Evangelische Heidenbote,* 1887: 13-14 (1887).

— 'Verfolgung auf den Blauen Bergen'. *Evangelische Heidenbote,* 1894: 19-23 (1894).

— 'Keti.' *Jahresberichte der evangelischen Missionsgesellschaft zu Basel,* 1899: 45-50 (1899).

McIver, Lewis, and Gabriel Stokes, *Imperial census of 1881. Operations and results in the Presidency of Madras,* 5 vols. Madras: E. Keys, Government Press (1883).

Mackworth, Digby, *Diary of a tour through southern India, Egypt, and Palestine in the years 1821 and 1822. By a Field-Officer of Cavalry.* London: J. Hatchard and Son (1823).

Macleane, Charles Donald, *Manual of the administration of the Madras Presidency, in illustration of the records of government and the yearly administration reports. In three volumes,* Vol III. Madras: Superintendent, Government Press (1893).

MacNamara, Thomas F., 'Some ceremonies of South Indian hill tribes.' *Irish Ecclesiastical Record* (ser. 4) 31: 141-55 (1912).

Macpherson, Evans, 'Letter to John Sullivan Esq. Dated June 12, 1820'. In Grigg 1880: lv-lx [whence my pagination] (1820).

McPherson, James, *The Neilgherry tea planter.* Madras: Higginbotham & Co. (1870).

Madras, Government of, *Statistical appendix for the Nilgiri District (The Nilgiris, Vol. II).* Madras: Superintendent, Government Press (1928).

— *A statistical atlas of the Madras Province revised and brought up to date to the end of Fasli 1350 (1940-41).* Madras: Superintendent, Government Press (1949).

— *Village officers' and ryots' manual.* Madras: Government Press (1958).

— *A statistical atlas of the Nilgiris District.* Madras: Government Press

(1965).

Maffei, Giovanni Pietro, *Ioan. Petri Maffeii, Bergomatis, è Societate Iesv, Historiarvm indicarvm libri XVI. Selectarvm, item, ex India epistolarum, eodem interprete, libri IV. Accessit Ignatii Loiolae vita. Omnia ab auctore recognita, & nunc primum in Germania excusa. Item, in singula opera copiosus index.* Rome: Coloniae Agrippinae, in officina Birckmannica, sumptibus Arnoldi Mylij (1589).

Malinowski, Bronislaw C., 'Anthropology'. *Encyclopaedia Britannica*, 13th edn., 1st supp. vol.: 132 (1926).

Mandelbaum, David Goodman 'The world and the world view of the Kota'. In *Village India* (McKim Marriott, ed.); 223-54, Chicago: University of Chicago Press (1955).

— 'Social trends and personal pressures'. In *Anthropology of Folk Religion* (Charles M. Leslie, ed.); 221-55. New York: Vintage Books (1960).

— *Society in India*, 2 vols. Berkeley, Los Angeles and London: University of California Press; Bombay: Popular Prakashan (1970).

Markham, Clements Robert, *Travels in Peru and India while superintending the collection of Chinchona plants and seeds in South America, and their introduction into India*. London: John Murray (1862).

Marshall, William Elliot, *A phrenologist amongst the Todas or the study of a primitive tribe in South India: History, character, customs, religion, infanticide, polyandry, language*. London: Longmans, Green and Co. (1873).

Marx, Karl. *Das Kapital*. Vol. I. Hamburg: Meissner (1867).

May, David A., and David M. Heer, 'Son survivorship motivation and family size in India: A computer simulation.' *Population Studies, a Journal of Demography*, 22: 199-210 (1968).

Medical Board Office, Madras, *Report, on the medical topography and statistics of the Neilgherry Hills. Compiled from the records of the Medical Board Office. Published by order of Government*. Madras: R.W. Thorpe, Vepery Mission Press (1844).

Meinig, D.W., 'American wests: Preface to a geographical introduction.' *Annals of the Association of American Geographers*, 62: 159-85 (1972).

Metz, Johann Friedrich, 'Missionswanderung auf den Bergen'. *Evangelische Heidenbote*, 1863: 132-34 (1863).

— *The tribes inhabiting the Neilgherry Hills: Their social customs and religious rites*, 2nd edn. Mangalore: Basel Mission Press (1864).

— 'IV. Von den Nilagiri's.' *Jahresberichte der evangelischen Missionsgesellschaft zu Basel*, 1865: 83-87 (1865).

— 'Aus der Badaga-Gemeinde'. *Evangelische Heidenbote*, 1866: 142-45 (1866a).

— 'Von den Nilagiri's'. *Evangelische Heidenbote*, 1866: 119-20 (1866b).

— 'IV. Von den Nilagiri's. Wachsthum der Badaga-Gemeinde.' *Jahresberichte der evangelischen Missionsgesellschaft zu Basel*, 1867: 95-97

(1867).

'Miles, Arthur' (pseud. of Gervée Baronti, afterwards Breckenridge), *Le culte de Çiva*, 2nd edn. Paris: Payot (1951).

Miller, E. Joan W., 'The naming of the land in the Arkansas Ozarks: A study in cultural processes'. *Annals of the Association of American Geographers*, 59: 240-51 (1969).

Misra, Promode Kumar, 'Tribal mobilisation in Southern India.' In *Tribal Movements in India*. (Kumar Suresh Singh, ed.); 2: 325-37. New Delhi: Manohar (1985).

Mörike, Carl Eberhart Gottlieb, 'Mission of the Basel Society on the Neilgherries'. In *Proceedings of the South India Missionary Conference, held at Ootacamund, April 19th-May 5th, 1858* (Miron Winslow, James Sewell, Alexander Burrowes Campbell, and Peter S. Royston, eds.); 94-96. Madras: Society for Promoting Christian Knowledge (1858).

Morris, Brian, 'Hill Pandaram.' In *Encyclopedia of world cultures, Volume 3 South Asia* (Paul Hockings, ed.; David Levinson, gen. ed.); 98-101. Boston: G.K. Hall. (1992).

Moses, William, 'Tribal awakening in the Nilgiri Hills: The church's responsibility.' Serampore: B.D. thesis (1964).

Mudaliar, N. Murugesa, 'Change comes to the Ketty Valley.' *Indian Farming*, 6 (10): 17-18 (1957).

Mullens, Joseph, 'Mission in the Nilgiri Hills.' In his *Missions in South India visited and described by Joseph Mullens*; 59-62. London: W.H. Dalton (1854).

Murdock, George P., *Social structure*. New York: Macmillan Co. (1949).

Murray-Aynsley, Harriet G.M., *Our tour in Southern India*. London: F.V. White and Co. (1883).

Muthanna, I.M., *A tiny model state of South India*. Mysore: Usha Press (1953).

Muthiah, S., *A planting century: The first hundred years of the United Planters' Association of Southern India 1893-1993*. New Delhi, etc.: Affiliated East-West Press Private Ltd. (1993).

Muzzy, C.F., 'Account of the Neilgherry hill tribes.' *Christian Instructor and Missionary Record*, 2: 358-66 (1844).

Naik, Iqbal Abdul Razak (Mrs. N.K. Wagle), 'The culture of the Nilgiri Hills with its catalogue collection at the British Museum.' London: London University; Ph.D. dissertation in Archaeology (1966).

Nambiar, P.K., *Census of India 1961, vol. IX, Madras, Part X-x, District Census Handbook, Nilgiris, vols. I and II*. Madras: Huxley Press (1965).

Nambiar, P.K., and T.B. Bharathi, *Census of India, 1961, vol. IX, Madras. Part VI, Village Survey Monographs, 23. Nellithorai*. Delhi: Manager of Publications (1965).

Namboodiri, N. Krishnan, 'Social development and population change — A reappraisal of selected theories.' In *Fertility and mortality: Theory, methodology and empirical issues* (K. Mahadevan, ed.). Pp. 37-54. New Delhi: Sage (1986).

Nanjundayya, Hebbalalu Velpanur, and L. Krishna Anantha Krishna Iyer, *The Mysore tribes and castes*. Mysore: The Mysore University; 4 vols. (1931-35).

Natesa Sastri, Sangendi Mahalinga, 'The Baḍagas of the Nīlagiri District'. *Madras Christian College Magazine*, 9: 753-64, 830-43 (1892).

Nayak, H.M., ed., *Epigraphia Carnatica. Mysore District (Gundlupete, Nanjanagudu and Heggadadevanakote Taluks)*. Vol. 3. Mysore: Institute of Kannada Studies, University of Mysore (1978).

Nicholson, Frederick Augustus, *Coimbatore*. Madras: Superintendent, Government Press (1898).

Noble, William Allister, 'The shifting balance of grasslands, shola forests, and planted trees on the upper Nilgiris, southern India'. *Indian Forester*, 93: 691-93 (1967).

— 'Cultural contrasts and similarities among five ethnic groups in the Nilgiri District, Madras State, India 1800-1963'. Baton Rouge: Louisiana State University; Ph.D. dissertation in Geography and Anthropology (1968).

— 'Nilgiri Dolmens (South India)'. *Anthropos*, 71: 90-128 (1976).

— 'Nilgiri prehistoric remains.' In Hockings 1997b: 102-32 (1997).

— 'Toda huts and houses: Traditional and modern.' In Hockings 1997b: 192-230 (1997).

Norton, William, *Historical analysis in geography*. London and New York: Longman (1984).

O'Malley, Lewis Sydney Steward (ed.), *Modern India and the West: a study of the interaction of their civilizations*. London: Oxford University Press (1941).

Orans, Martin, *The Santal: A tribe in search of a great tradition*. Detroit: Wayne State University Press (1965).

Ouchterlony, John, 'Geographical and statistical memoir of a survey of the Neilgherry Mountains, under the superintendence of Captain J. Ouchterlony. 1847'. *Madras Journal of Literature and Science*, 15: 1-138 [1849; reprinted in Shortt and Ouchterlony, 1868, whence my pagination] (1848)

— [Minutes of evidence given during Ouchterlony's examination by the Select Committee on Colonization and Settlement (India), on 10 and 15 June 1858.] In *Third Report from the Select Committee on Colonization and Settlement (India), with the minutes of evidence* (Parliamentary papers, 415); 1-48. London: House of Commons (1858).

Penny, Fanny E. F., *Love in the hills*. London: Chatto & Windus (1913).

Périé, Edmond, 'Mission de Coimbatore. Résumé historique de l'évangélisation des Badagas et bénédiction d'église à Ketti (Nilgiris)'. *Bulletin de la Société des Missions-étrangères de Paris*, 12: 96-103, 159-67

(1933).

Pharoah and Co., 'Neilgherries (The sanitarium of Southern India.)' In their *A gazetteer of Southern India, with the Tenasserim Provinces and Singapore* . . . ; 467-88. Madras: Pharoah and Co. (1855).

Philip, Kavita, *Civilising natures: Race, resources and modernity in colonial South India*. Hyderabad: Orient Longman (2003).

Phythian-Adams, Edward Gwynne Phythian, *The Madras Regiment 1758-1958*. Wellington: The Defence Services Staff College Press (1958).

Pope, George Uglow, ed. [3rd edn. of Dubois 1906] . . . *with notes, corrections and additions by Rev. G.U. Pope. Translated from the French manuscript*. Madras: Higginbotham and Co. (1879).

Prabhakar, R., and Madhav Gadgil, 'Maps as markers of ecological change: A case study of the Nilgiri Hills of Southern India.' In *Nature, culture, imperialism: Essays on the environmental history of South Asia*. (David Arnold and Ramachandra Guha, eds.); 152-84. New Delhi and New York: Oxford University Press (1995).

Price, John Frederick, *Ootacamund: A history. Compiled for the Government of Madras*. Madras: Superintendent, Government Press (1908).

Radhakrishnan, D., 'De-witched, village still haunted.' *Hindu*, 110 (April 22, 1987).

— 'Badagas demand ST status.' *Indian Express* (Coimbatore edition) 57 (17 May 1989).

— 'Tea growers' agitation turns violent.' *Hindu*, 123 (16 May 2000).

Raman, K. Ravi, 'Labour under imperial hegemony: The case of tea plantations in South India, 1914-46.' In *The South Indian economy: Agrarian change, industrial structure and state policy c. 1914-1947*. (Sabyasachi Bhattacharya, Sumit Guha, Raman Mahadevan, Sakti Padhi, D. Rajasekhar, and G.N. Rao, eds.); 243-67. Delhi: Oxford University Press; Trivandrum: Centre for Development Studies (1991).

Ranga, Nagayya Gogineni, *The tribes of the Nilgiris (their social and economic conditions)*. Bezwada: Vani Press (Andhra Economic Series, no. 5; 1934) .

Ranganātan, A.K., (pseud. 'Hilpaks' or 'Hill Fox'), *Ni:lakiri carittiram*. (Mundram pākam). [History of the Nilgiris (Third part); in Tamil]. Ootacamund: Saint Regina Press (1960).

Rao, K. Hanumantha, & M.D. Azariah, 'Potato on the Nilgiris.' In Krishnamurthi 1953: 67-79 (1953).

Rao, Y.V. Lakshmana, *Communication and development: A study of two Indian villages*. Minneapolis: University of Minnesota Press (1966).

Rea, Alexander, *G.O., No. 665, 28th July 1910. Epigraphy*. Madras: Government of Madras, Public Department (1910).

Réclus, Élie, *Primitive folk: Studies in comparative ethnology*. New York: Scribner & Welford; London: Walter Scott (1891).

Rhiem, Hanna, 'Die Badagas'. *Allgemeine Missions-Zeitschrift*, 27: 497-509 (1900).

Rice, Benjamin Lewis, *Epigraphia Carnatica, vol. III: Inscriptions in the Mysore District (Part I); published for Government.* Bangalore: Government Central Press (1894).

— *Mysore, a gazetteer compiled for Government*, rev. edn., 2 vols. London: Archibald Constable & Co. (1897).

Richards, Frederick J., 'Badaga and Toda months', *Man*, 20: no. 13, pp. 23-25 (1920).

— 'Note on the cultural geography of the Wynad.' *Indian Antiquary*, 61: 170-74 (1932).

'Rifle', 'The hill tribes of the Neilgherries', *Indian Antiquary*, 2: 32 (1872 [1873]).

Rivers, William Halse Rivers, *The Todas*. London: Macmillan and Co. (1906).

Roychoudhuri, A.K., 'Consanguineous marriages in Tamil Nadu.' *Journal of the Indian Anthropological Society*, 15: 167-74 (1980).

Sanderson, George P., *Thirteen years among the wild beasts of India: Their haunts and habits from personal observation. . . .* London: Wm. H. Allen & Co. (1878).

Sandford, J.R., 'Notes on the recent opening of some pre-historic graves in the Coimbatore District, Madras Presidency.' *Journal of the Anthropological Society of Bombay* 3: 461-71 (1894).

Sarada Raju, A., *Economic conditions in the Madras Presidency 1800-1850*. Madras: University of Madras (1941).

'Satchit, T.M.', ed. (pseud. of T.M. Satchidanandam Pillai), *Who's who in Madras, 1940*. Cochin: The Pearl Press (1940).

Sawday, George W., 'A visit to Kaity'. *Harvest Field*, 5: 8-15 (1884).

Schad, Friedrich, 'Arbeit unter den Badaga'. *Jahresberichte der evangelischen Missionsgesellschaft zu Basel*, 1908: 132-36 (1908).

Schama, Simon, *Landscape and Memory*. New York: Alfred A. Knopf (1995).

Schlatter, Wilhelm, *Geschichte der Basler Mission 1815-1915. Mit besonderer Berücksichtigung der ungedruckten Quellen . . . II. Band: Die Geschichte der Basler Mission in Indien und China. Mit 2 Karten.* Basel: Verlag der Basler Missionsbuchhandlung (1916).

Schoff, Wilfred H. (ed.), *The Periplus of the Erythæan Sea. Travel and Trade in the Indian Ocean by a Merchant of the First Century*, 2nd edn. New Delhi: Oriental Books Reprint Corp. (1974).

Schurhammer, Georg, *The mission work of the Jesuits in Muthedath (alias: Arthunkal) and Porakad in the 16th and 17th centuries*. Alleppey: Santa Cruz Press (1957).

Schusky, Ernest Lester, *Manual for kinship analysis*. New York: Holt, Rinehart and Winston (1965).

Selvaraj, K.M., *Creative publications' Nilgiri 2000 A to Z Nilgiri business directory*. Ootacamund: Shiva Sakthi Printers (1998).

Sewell, Robert, *Lists of the antiquarian remains in the Presidency of Madras. Archaeological Survey of Southern India reports*. Old Series, vol. 1. Madras: Government Press (1882).

Shaposhnikova, Liudmila Vasil'evna, *Taīna plemeni Golubykh gor*. Moscow: Akademia Nauk S.S.S.R. (1969).

Shortt, John, and John Ouchterlony, *An account of the tribes on the Neilgherries, by J. Shortt . . . and a geographical and statistical memoir of the Neilgherry Mountains, by the late Colonel Ouchterlony*. Madras: Higginbotham & Co. (1868).

Simmel, Georg, *Soziologie, Untersuchungen über die Formen der Vergesellschaftung*, 3rd edn. Munich & Leipzig: Duncker & Humbolt (1923).

Singer, Milton Borah, 'The great tradition in a metropolitan center'. In his *Traditional India: Structure and change*. Monograph of the American Folklore Society, Bibliographical and Special Series, 10: 141-182 (1959).

Société des Missions-étrangères, *Bulletin de la Société des Missions-étrangères de Paris*. Hong Kong: Société des Missions-étrangères (1922+)

South of India Observer, 'The Nilgiri Gold Reefs.' *South of India Observer*, 14 (22, May 29): 6 (1880).

Srinivas, Mysore Narasimhachar, *Marriage and family in Mysore*. Bombay: New Book Co. (1942).

— *Religion and society among the Coorgs of South India*. Oxford: Clarendon Press (1952).

— *Caste: A trend report and bibliography*. New York: Johnson Reprint Corp. (1965)

'Stocqueler, J.H.' (pseud. of Joachim Heyward Siddons), 'Madras'. In his *The hand-book of India, a guide to the stranger and traveller, and a companion to the resident . . .*, 2nd edn.; 567-90. London: Wm. H. Allen & Co. (1845).

Stokes, William, 'Mission work amongst the Badagas and other hill tribes on the Nilgiris'. *Harvest Field*, 3: 169-70 (1882).

— 'Ein dunkles Bild des Heidenthums'. *Evangelische Heidenbote*, 1883: 6-7, 11-12 (1883a).

— 'Mission work on the Nilgiri Hills'. In *Report of the second decennial missionary conference held at Calcutta, 1882-1883* (John Murray Mitchell & George Henry Rouse, eds.), 283-93. Calcutta: J.W. Thomas, Baptist Mission Press (1883b).

Stone, Winifred M., *Ups and downs on the Nilgiris*. London: Church of England Zenana Missionary Society (1925).

Stuart, Harold Arthur, *Census of India, 1891, vol. XIII, Madras. The report on the census*. Madras: Superintendent, Government Press (1893).

— *Report on the administration of the police of the Madras Presidency,*

1900. Madras: Superintendent, Government Press (1901).

Subrahmanyam, C.V., Socio economic survey, with special reference to the assessment of the effects of plan projects and savings patterns. Ootacamund: Government Arts College; mimeo (1962).

Sullivan, John, 'To the editor of the Government Gazette.' Copy of an anonymous letter dated 30 Jan., reprinted in Grigg 1880: lii-lv [whence my pagination] (1819).

Sutton, Deborah, *Other landscapes: Colonialism and the predicament of authority in nineteenth-century South India*. Copenhagen: Nordic Institute of Asian Studies (2009; reprinted, 2012, at Hyderabad: Orient BlackSwan).

Tanna, Kaku J., *Plantations in the Nilgiris – a synoptic history*. Wellington: C.D. Dhody & Sons (1970).

Taylor, Philip Meadows, *Tippoo Sultaun: A tale of the Mysore War*. London: Richard Bentley; 3 vols. (1840).

Thorner, Daniel, *Agricultural cooperatives in India: A field report*. Bombay: Asia Publishing House (1964).

Thurston, Edgar, *Ethnographic notes in Southern India*. Madras: Government Press (1906).

— *Omens and superstitions of Southern India*. London, Leipzig: T. Fisher Unwin (1912).

Thurston, Edgar, and Kadamki Rangachari, *Castes and tribes of Southern India*. Madras: Superintendent, Government Press; 7 vols. (1909).

Tignous, Henri Pierre Joseph Arthur, 'In the Nilgherries'. *Illustrated Catholic Missions*, 26: 99-102, 116-19, 154-57 (1911).

UPASI, *Planting directory of Southern India. Compiled by the secretary, UPASI*. Coonoor: The United Planters' Association of Southern India (1956).

Van der Geest, Sjaak, 'Missionaries.' In *Encyclopedia of Cultural Anthropology* (David Levinson and Melvin Ember, eds.); 3: 797-801. New York: Henry Holt and Company (1996).

Verghese, Isaac, 'The Kota: Their dreaded life of Kurumba sorcery.' *Bulletin of the Cultural Research Institute (West Bengal)*, 5: 98-106 (1966).

Vivekanandam Pillai, T.H., 'The Badagas'. *Journal of the Madras Geographical Association*, 12: 246-50 (1937).

Wainwright, Frederick Threlfall, *Archaeology and place-names and history: An essay on problems of co-ordination*. London: Routledge & Kegan Paul (1962).

Walhouse, Moreton John, 'Archaeological notes. No. XIX. – "Passing through fire".' *Indian Antiquary*, 7: 126-29 (1878).

Walker, Anthony Rupert, *The Toda of South India: A new look*. Delhi: Hindustan Publishing Corporation (1986).

— 'The western romance with the Toda.' In Hockings 1997b: 106-35 (1997).

— 'Early seventeenth century Christian missions to the Toda of the Nilgiri Hills (1969/93).' In his *Between tradition and modernity, and other essays on the Toda of South India*; 89-114. Delhi: B.R. Publishing Corporation (1998).

Wallace, Anthony Francis Clarke, 'Revitalization movements'. *American Anthropologist*, 58: 264-87 (1956).

— *Religion: an anthropological view*. New York: Random House (1966).

Ward, Benjamin Swain, 'Geographical and statistical memoir of a survey of the Neelgherry Mountains in the province of Coimbatore made in 1821 under the superintendence of Captain B.S. Ward, Deputy Surveyor-General'. In Grigg 1880: lx-lxxviii [whence my pagination] (1821).

Watt, George, 'Coffea arabica'. In his *A dictionary of the economic products of India*, 2: 460-91. London: W.H. Allen & Co.; Calcutta: Superintendent of Government Printing, India (1889).

— 'Tea'. In his *A dictionary of the economic products of India*. Vol. 6 (pt. 3): 417-79. London: W.H. Allen & Co.; Calcutta: Superintendent of Government Printing, India (1893).

Weber, Max, *From Max Weber: Essays in sociology*. Trans. by Hans H. Garth and C. Wright Mills. New York: Oxford University Press (1946).

— *The theory of social and economic organization*. Trans. by A.M. Henderson and Talcott Parsons. New York: Oxford University Press (1947).

Webster, Noah, *Webster's new collegiate dictionary*. Springfield, Mass.: G. & C. Merriam Company (1967).

Weigt, Ernst, 'Beobachtungen in den Nilgiris mit besonderer Berücksichtigung den Dörfer Nanjanad und Srimadurai'. *Tübinger geographische Studien*, 34: 325-43 (1970).

White, Gilbert, *The Natural History of Selborne*. London: T. Bensley, for B. White and Son (1789).

Wieland, Gottlob, 'Aus der Nachthütte in Woderu'. *Evangelische Heidenbote*, 1900: 85-86 (1900).

Wilks, Mark, *Historical sketches of the South of India, in an attempt to trace the history of Mysoor; from the origin of the Hindoo government of that state, to the extinction of the Mohammedan Dynasty in 1799. Founded chiefly of Indian authorities collected by the author while officiating for several years as political agent at the court of Mysoor, 1810*. Edited with notes by M. Hammick. Mysore: Government Branch Press; 2 vols. (1930).

Winslow, Miron, *A Comprehensive Tamil and English Dictionary*. Madras: P.R. Hunt (1862). Numerous modern reprints from Wiesbaden: Franz Steiner, and New Delhi: Asian Educational Services (1977-2001).

Wiser, William H., *The Hindu jajmani system: A socio-economic system inter-relating members of a Hindu village community in service*. Lucknow: Lucknow Publishing House (1936).

Wood, Ravenshaw Cecil, *A notebook of agricultural facts and figures.* Madras: Government Press (1927).

Wynter-Blyth, Mark Alexander, 'The Nilgiris revisited.' *Journal of the Bombay Natural History Society*, 48: 246-60 (1949).

Yeatts, William Walter Murray, *Census of India 1931. Volume XIV. Madras. Part II. Imperial and provincial tables. Calcutta: Government of India Central Publication Branch (1932).*

Young, Donald Smith, 'An account of the general and medical topography of the Neelgerries.' *Transactions of the Medical and Physical Society of Calcutta*, 4: 36-78 (1827 [1829]).

Yule, Henry, and Arthur Coke Burnell, *Hobson-Jobson. A glossary of colloquial Anglo-Indian words and phrases, and of kindred terms, etymological, historical, geographical and discursive.* London: John Murray (1903).

Zagarell, Allen, 'State and community in the Nilgiri Mountains'. *Michigan Academician*, 26: 183-204 (1994).

— 'Hierarchy and heterarchy: The unity of opposites.' In *Heterarchy and the analysis of complex societies* (Carole L. Crumley, Robert M. Ehrenreich, and Janet E. Levy, eds.); 87-100. Arlington, Va.: American Anthropological Association (Archeological Papers of the American Anthropological Association, 6; 1995).

— 'The megalithic graves of the Nilgiri Hills and the Moyar Ditch'. In Hockings 1997b: 23-73 (1997).

— 'Tradition, Community, and Nilgiri Rock Art.' In *Material Symbols: Culture and Economy in Prehistory* (John E. Robb, ed.); 188-204. Carbondale: Center for Archaeological Investigations, Southern Illinois University (Occasional paper, 26; 1999).

Zvelebil, Kamil Veith, *The Irula (Ḗṟla) language. Part II.* Wiesbaden: Otto Harrassowitz (1979).

— 'Problems of identification and classification of some Nilagiri tribes: Iṟulas-Urāḷis, Kāṭṭu Nāyakas/Jēnu Kuṟumbas, Sōlegas.' *Anthropos*, 76: 467-528. Reprinted, 2001, in his *Nilgiri Areal Studies* (Jaroslav Vacek and Jan Dvořak, eds.); 39-107. Prague: Charles University, the Karolinum Press. (1981).

— *The Irula (Ḗṟla) language. Part III. Irula lore, texts and translations.* Wiesbaden: Otto Harrassowitz (1982).

— 'Economic and Social Relations of the Nilgiri Tribes.' In his *Nilgiri Areal Studies*, (Jaroslav Vacek and Jan Dvořak, eds.); 137-53. Prague: Charles University, the Karolinum Press. (Originally published in 1955 as 'Hospodářské a společenské vztahy Nīlagirských Kmenů.' *Československá Ethnografie*, 3: 236-48.) (2001)

General Index *

Note: * Phonetic spellings have been used except where other spellings are already well established in English. Diacritical marks follow the usual conventions of Dravidian phonology, except that a colon after a Badagu vowel makes it long.

Name Index

Place-name Index *

* Place-names are written phonetically except where other spellings are already well established in English. Nilgiri names are rendered according to their Badaga pronunciation. Diacritical marks follow the usual conventions of Dravidian phonology, except that a colon after a vowel makes it long.

Plates

Note: Photograph sources are given on pp. xiii-xiv.

Plate 1 *Top*: Wenlock Downs in the 1930s. *Bottom*: Ke:ti *u:ru* (commune), *ca* 1948

Plate 2 *Top*: The ruined ramparts and battlements of Daṇṇayaka Ko:ṭe.
Bottom: The Madhavaraya Temple (a Vaishnavite one) at Daṇṇayaka Ko:ṭe; Rangasāmi Peak is towering in the background; both photos, 2012.

Plate 3 *Top*: Drawing of medieval carvings on an orthostat near Me:lu:ru.
Bottom: Ekko:ṇi, the head village of Tu:ḍegu:r commune, in 2013.

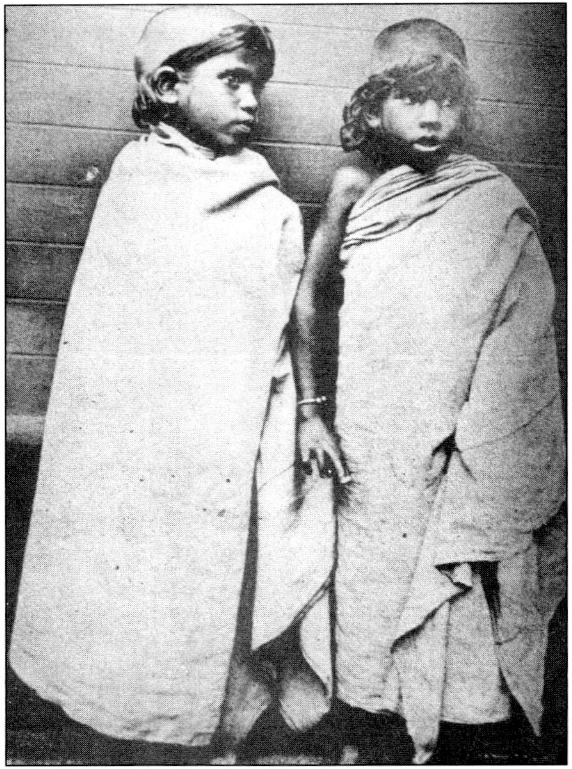

Plate 4 *Left*: A Toda couple, both wearing the embroidered shawl (*pu·txuṭi*), 1963.
Right: Two Badaga girls, *ca* 1900, with their heads shaved.

Plate 5 *Top*: The original Maha:linga temple at Me:lu:ru.
Bottom: The rebuilt stone temple of Maha:linga, *ca* 1900.

Plate 6 *Top*: Elders gathered beside the *akka bakka* in Ke:ti, 1963.
Bottom: A row of houses with work-space in front, Ka:ṭe:ri.

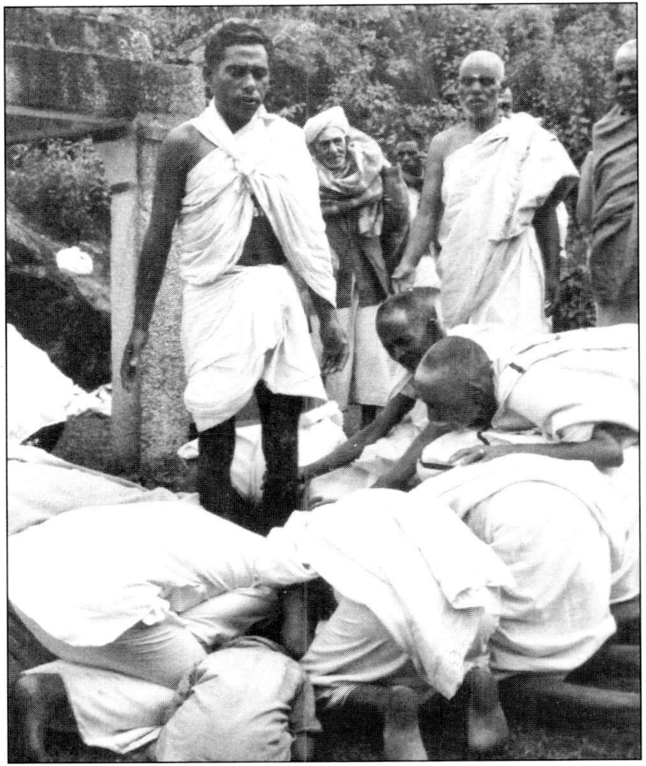

Plate 7 *Left*: A Ha:ruva priest being venerated during an annual ceremony in Ke:ti, 1963. *Right*: A *guru* coming from Mysore, being venerated as a *linga* while he stands on a fresh Kaṇakka grave; Ka:ṭe:ri, 1970.

Plate 8 Firewalking at Jakkane:ri, 1963.

Plate 9 *Left*: The divisional headman (*pa:ṛpatti*), here dancing at a funeral in Orana:yi, 1963. *Right*: Pada Raja Gowda, the paramount chief of the Badagas (1956-76), and also headman of Tu:ṇe:ri; his gold earrings were of a traditional design; 1972.

Plate 10 *Top*: Cattle threshing grain in Orana:yi; the men are hired labourers. *Bottom*: Women's group preparing food beside a house in Ki:ekunda village; all wear *sāris* in place of their traditional dress.

Plate 11 The memorial ceremony (*manevale*) at Kaḍana:ḍu in 1905.

Plate 12 The seven-tiered catafalque (*guḍikat*) erected at the memorial ceremony (*manevale*) in Kaḍana:ḍu, March 1905.

Plate 13 *Left*: Women with offerings at a funeral. *Right*: Men's dancing dress, only seen now at a few funerals.

Plate 14 *Left*: Terraced fields growing potatoes and eucalyptus trees below Orana:yi, 1963.
Right: Widower with a ceremonial knife at his wife's funeral; Hulla:ḍa, 1963.

Plate 15 *Top*: A band of Kota musicians. *Bottom:* Chetti merchants resting their bullocks on the Coonoor Ghat road; both photos, *ca* 1900.

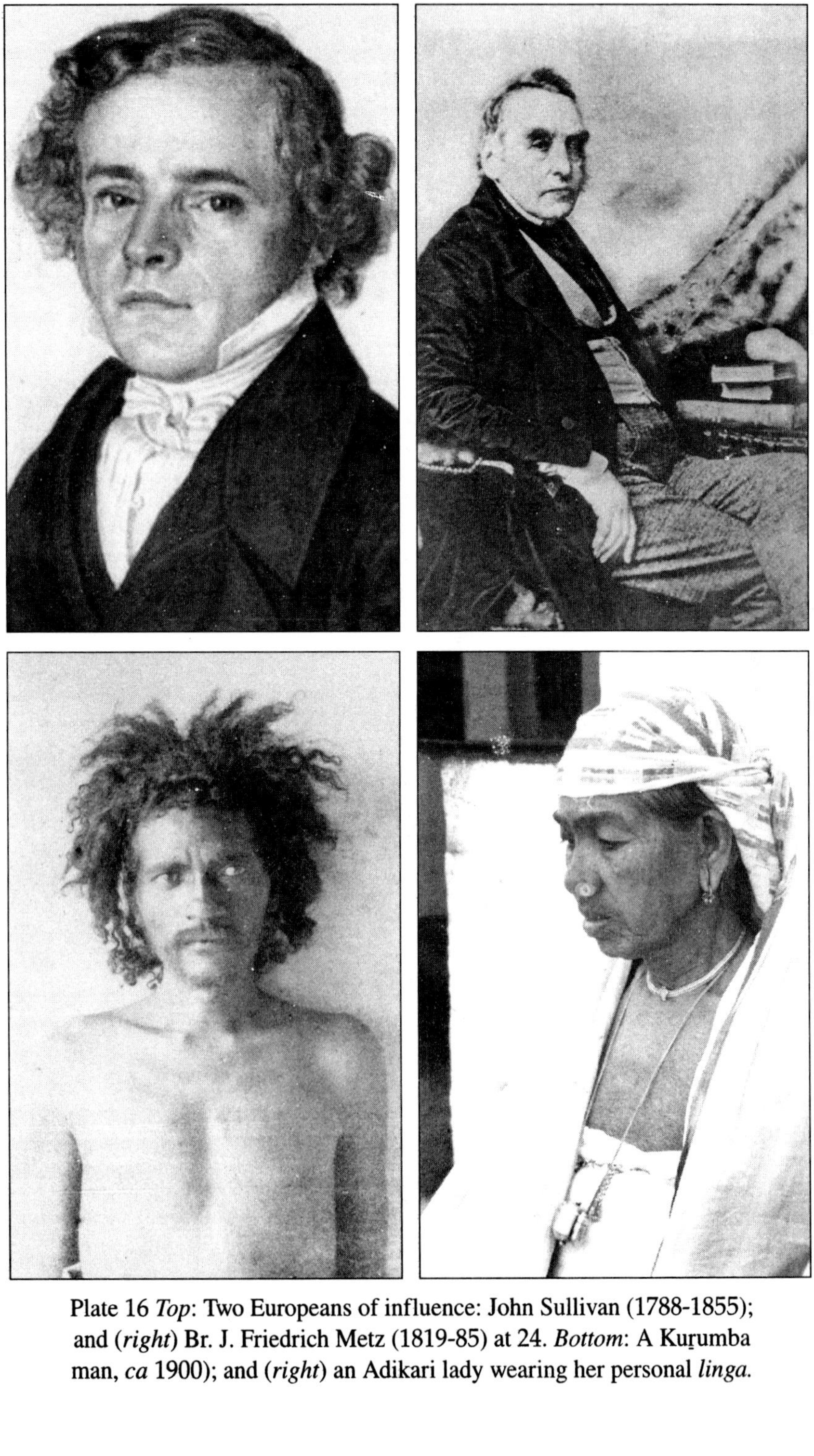

Plate 16 *Top*: Two Europeans of influence: John Sullivan (1788-1855); and (*right*) Br. J. Friedrich Metz (1819-85) at 24. *Bottom*: A Kuṟumba man, *ca* 1900); and (*right*) an Adikari lady wearing her personal *linga*.